THE USBORNE ILLUSTRATED ENCYCLOPEDIA

THE NATURAL WORLD

SCHOLASTIC INC.
New York Toronto London Auckland Sydney

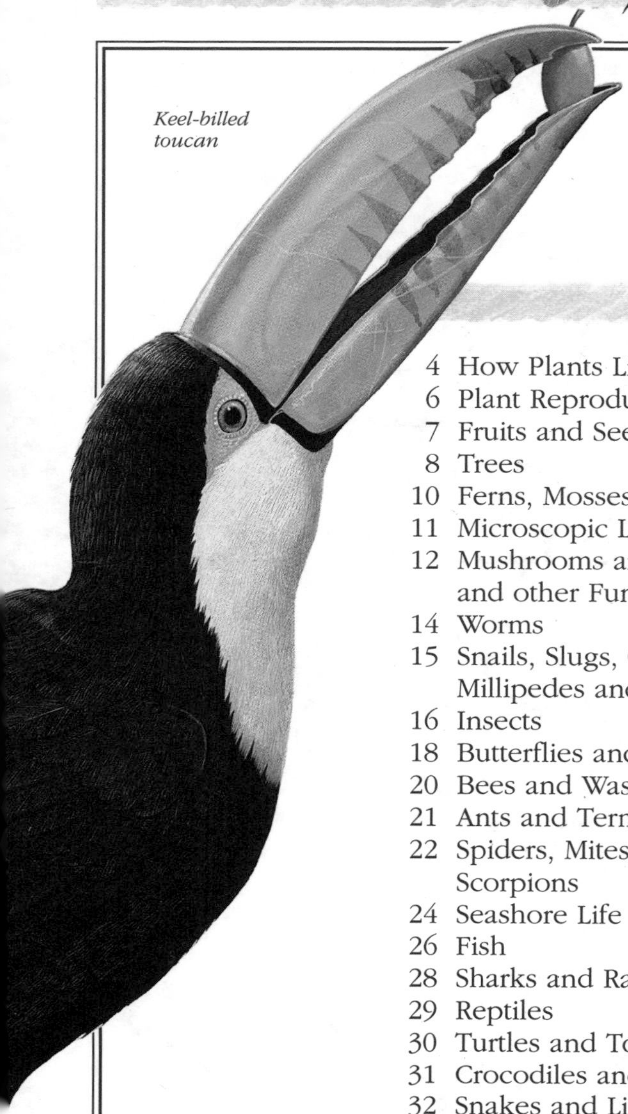

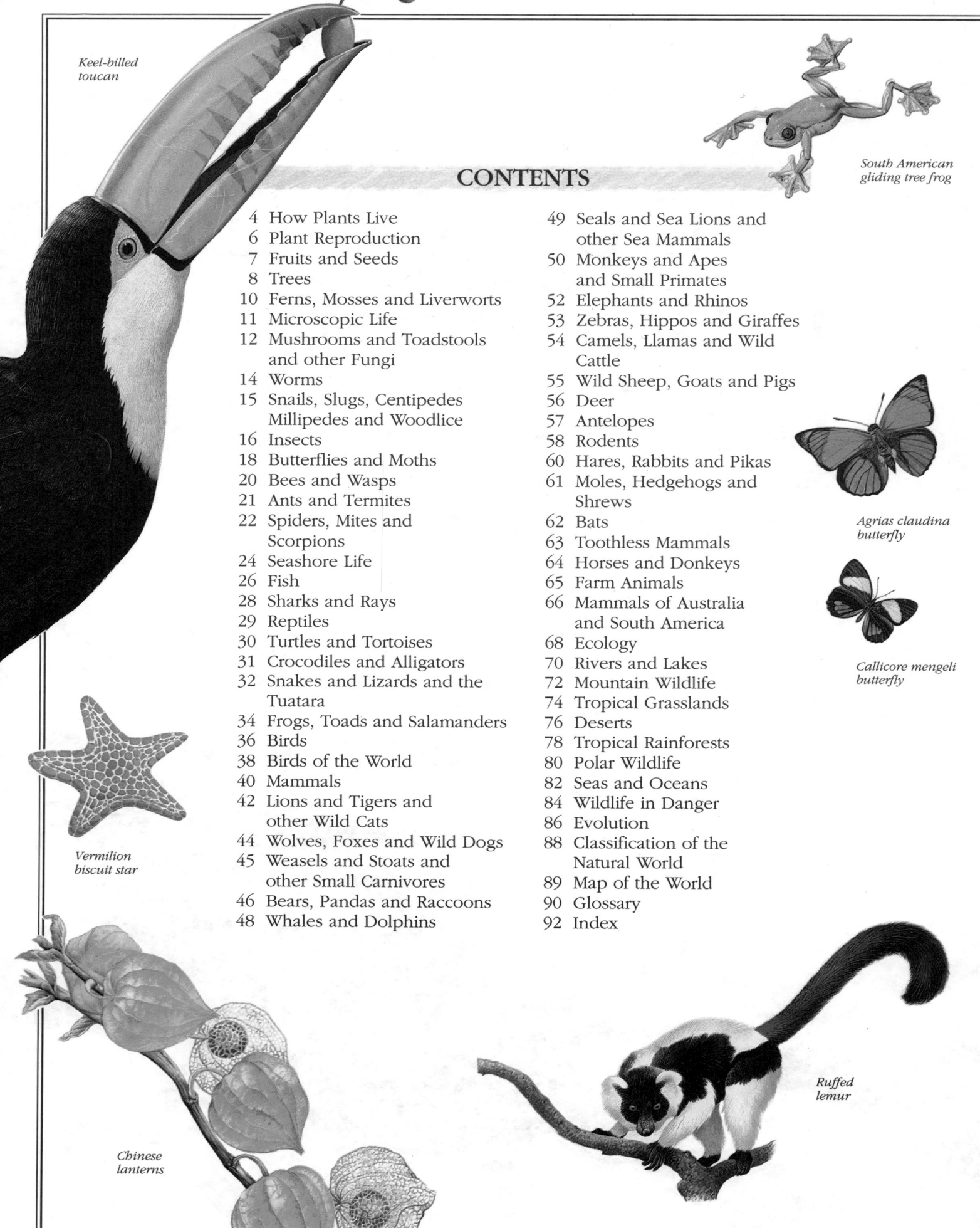

Keel-billed toucan

South American gliding tree frog

CONTENTS

Agrias claudina butterfly

Callicore mengeli butterfly

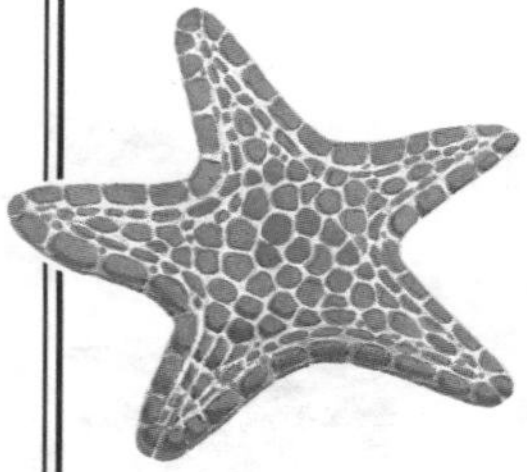

Vermilion biscuit star

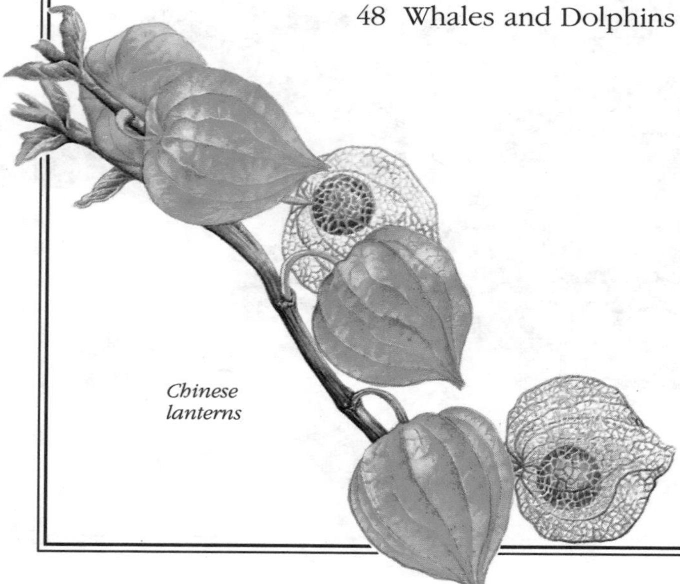

Chinese lanterns

Ruffed lemur

Buff-tailed bumblebee

Hyacinth macaw

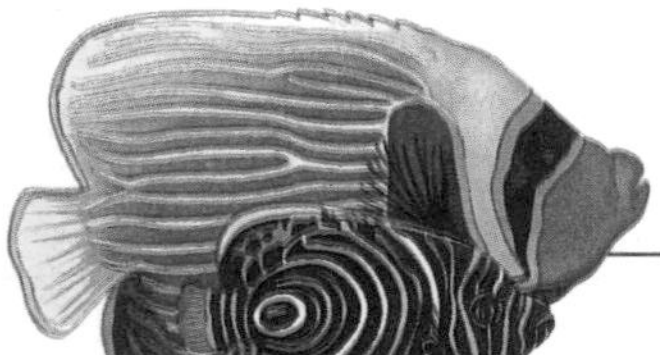

Emperor angelfish

INTRODUCTION

This book is packed with fascinating information about the plants and animals of our world, and the environments in which they live. To find out about a type of plant or animal, look in the list of contents on the opposite page. If you are not sure which group it belongs to, look up its name in the index.

If there are any scientific words you do not understand, you can look them up in the glossary on pages 90-91. Some words have an asterisk* after them. This means you can find out more about them on the page listed in the footnotes at the bottom of the page you are reading.

Many pages have an activity or project for you to do, or advice on how to watch wildlife. These activities will help you observe the natural world and see for yourself how some of the plants and animals live. Remember, if you need an animal for a project, treat it very gently and return it to the place where you found it as soon as possible.

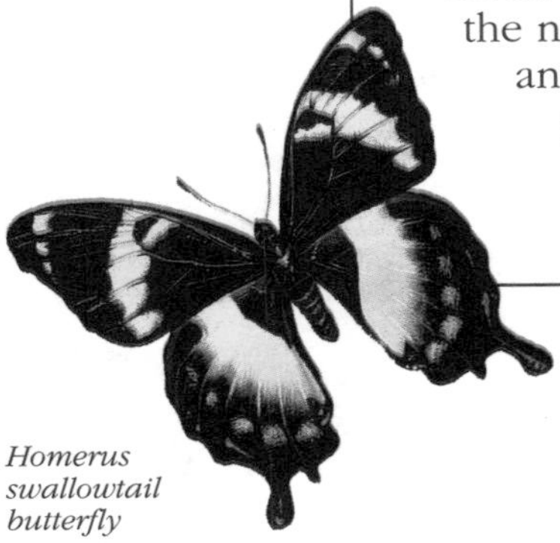

Homerus swallowtail butterfly

Milk snake

Editor: Lisa Watts
Designers: Melissa Alaverdy and Julia Rheam
Series Designer: Amanda Barlow
Science Consultant: David Duthie
Project Editor: Felicity Brooks

With thanks to
Ruth King, Robin Farrow, Cathy Lowe, Mike Unwin
and Margaret and John Rostron

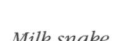

Forester moth

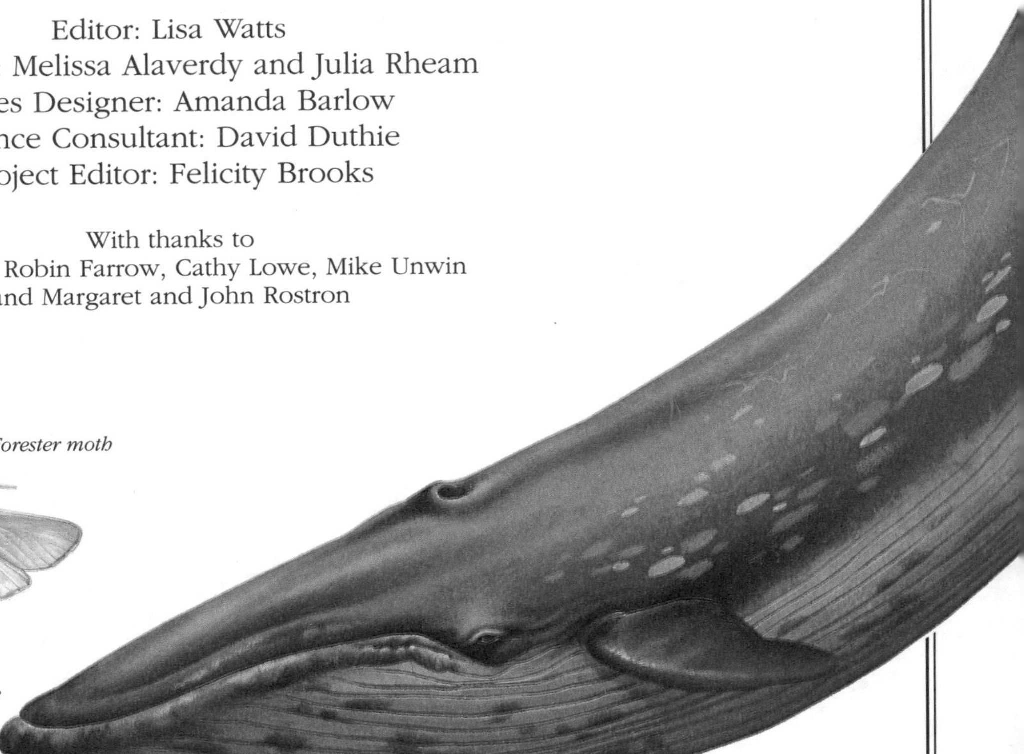

Blue whale

The twisting stems of lianas carry water to their leaves high up in the rainforest treetops.

HOW PLANTS LIVE

Without plants there would be no life on Earth. Plants grow by making their own food from basic substances found in the soil and air by a process called photosynthesis. Animals cannot make food, so they have to eat plants (or other animals that have eaten plants) to survive.

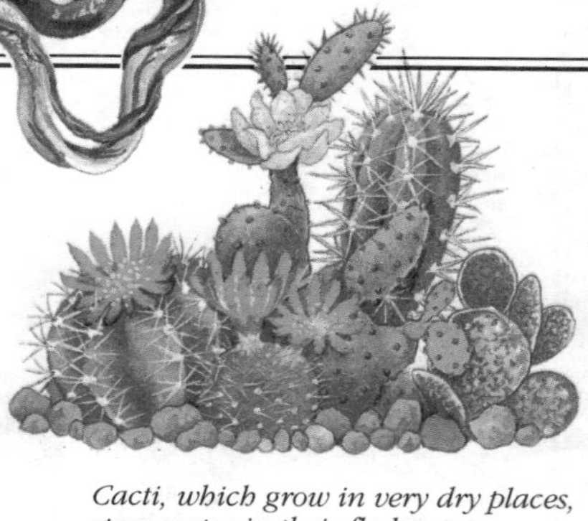

Cacti, which grow in very dry places, store water in their fleshy stems.

LEAVES

Leaves are a plant's food factories. In the cells of the leaves there are tiny bodies called chloroplasts where the food is made by photosynthesis (see right). The chloroplasts contain a green substance, called chlorophyll, that makes the leaves look green.

Magnified view of a leaf cut in half to show the cells inside.

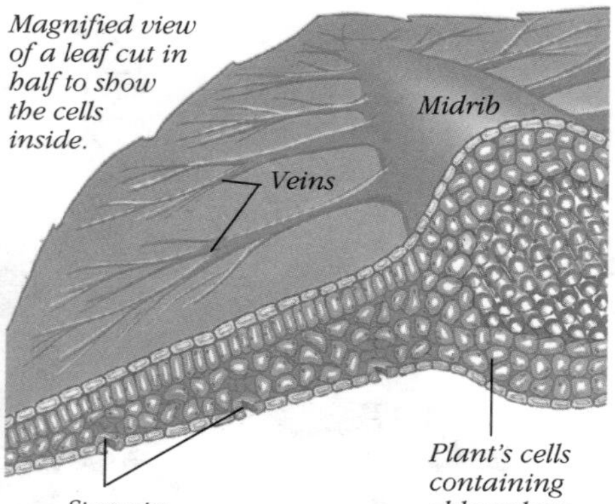
Midrib
Veins
Stomata
Plant's cells containing chloroplasts

For photosynthesis, the leaves need water and carbon dioxide gas from the air. Water is carried from the stem to the leaves through the midrib and veins. Holes in the leaf surface, called stomata, allow water to evaporate and air to pass in and out.

There are many different shapes of leaves. Looking carefully at the shape of a plant's leaves, and the way they are arranged on the stem, can help you to identify a plant.

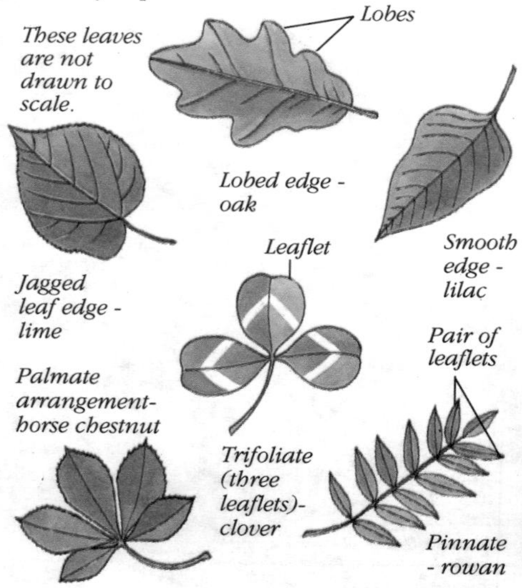
These leaves are not drawn to scale.
Lobes
Lobed edge - oak
Smooth edge - lilac
Jagged leaf edge - lime
Leaflet
Pair of leaflets
Palmate arrangement- horse chestnut
Trifoliate (three leaflets)- clover
Pinnate - rowan

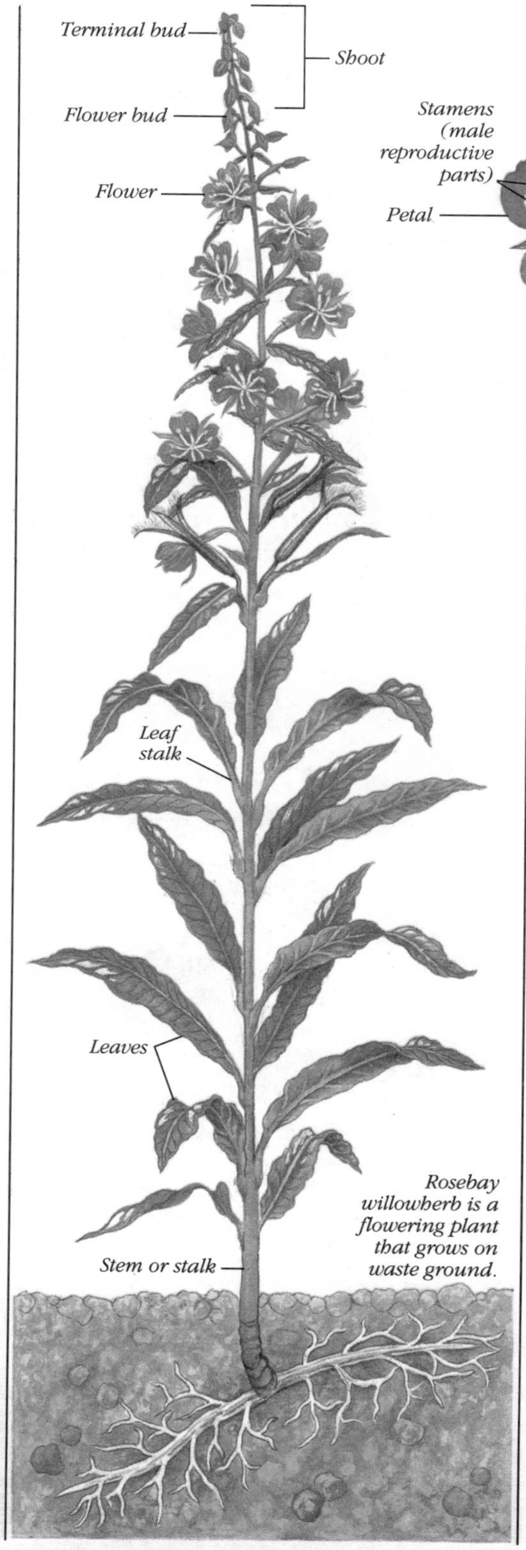
Terminal bud
Shoot
Flower bud
Flower
Leaf stalk
Leaves
Stem or stalk

Rosebay willowherb is a flowering plant that grows on waste ground.

FLOWERS

A plant's flowers contain its reproductive organs, the parts with which it will make seeds from which new plants will grow. The reproductive organs are surrounded by petals and leaf-like sepals to protect them. The petals are often bright and scented to attract insects, birds and other animals, which play an important role in plant reproduction*.

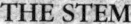

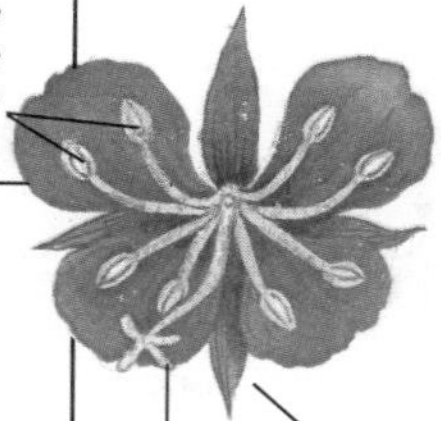
Stamens (male reproductive parts)
Petal
Sepal
Tip of carpel (female part)

THE STEM

The stem supports the leaves and carries water from the roots. It contains bundles of tubes called vascular tissue. There are two kinds of tubes: xylem for carrying water, and phloem for carrying dissolved food substances. The plant grows from the terminal bud at the tip of each stem.

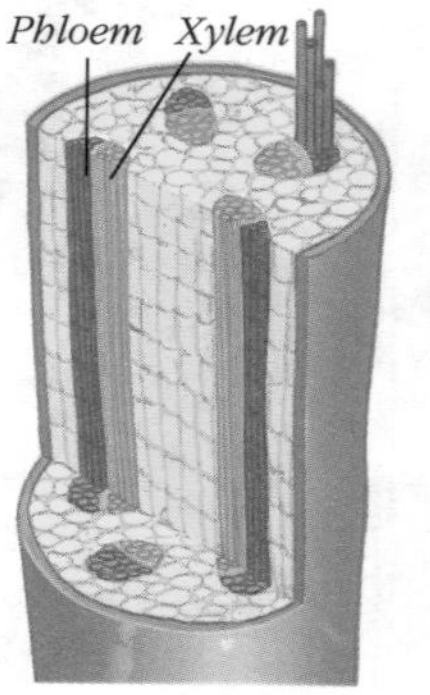
Phloem
Xylem

Magnified view of stem cut to show tubes inside

ROOTS

Roots anchor a plant in the ground and suck up water and dissolved mineral salts from the soil. Like the stem, roots are made of vascular tissue. They are covered with tiny hairs through which water enters the roots. Some plants, such as carrots, radishes and turnips have one large tap root, where the plant stores food, surrounded by smaller secondary roots. Others have many fine, fibrous roots.

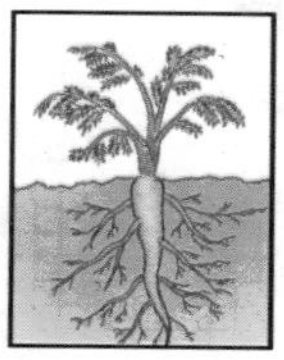

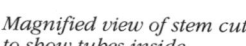

Tap root (carrot)

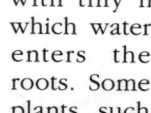

Fibrous roots

* Plant Reproduction, 6

PHOTOSYNTHESIS

Photosynthesis is the process by which green plants make food in their leaves. During photosynthesis, water and carbon dioxide are converted into glucose and oxygen. The glucose is the plant's food.

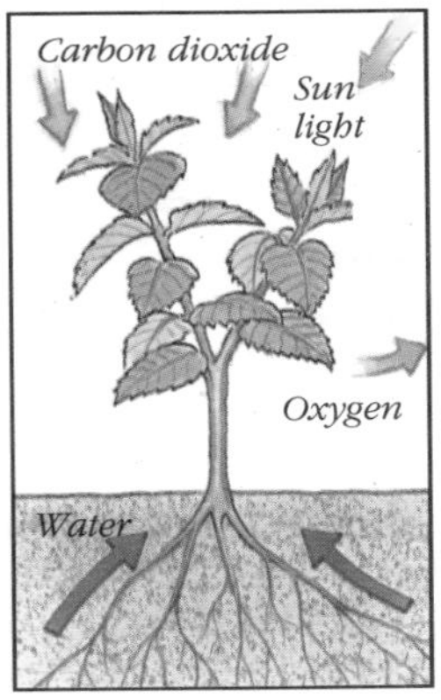

Carbon dioxide
Sun light
Oxygen
Water

Plants do not need all the oxygen gas that they make during photosynthesis and some of it goes back into the air.

Photosynthesis is powered by energy from the Sun. Chlorophyll, which is the green substance in the plant's leaves, absorbs energy from sunlight and converts it into a form of chemical energy that can be used during photosynthesis.

WHY PLANTS NEED WATER

Plants need water for photosynthesis, and also to replace water lost by transpiration (see below). Without enough water, the plant's cells become limp and the plant wilts. Plants take their water from the soil, and the water also contains the mineral salts that the plants need for their growth.

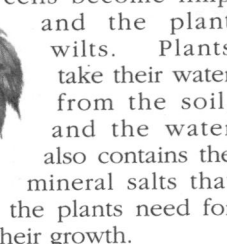

TRANSPIRATION AND OSMOSIS

Transpiration is the evaporation of water from a plant's leaves. As water evaporates, more water is sucked up from the roots to replace it. This is called the transpiration stream. The water passes through the plant by osmosis.

Osmosis is the passage of water from a weaker solution to a stronger solution. The water in a plant's cells is a weak solution of mineral salts. When water in the cells in the leaves evaporates, the solution in the leaf cells becomes stronger, so water passes into them from cells nearby. This sets up a chain reaction through all the cells of the plant.

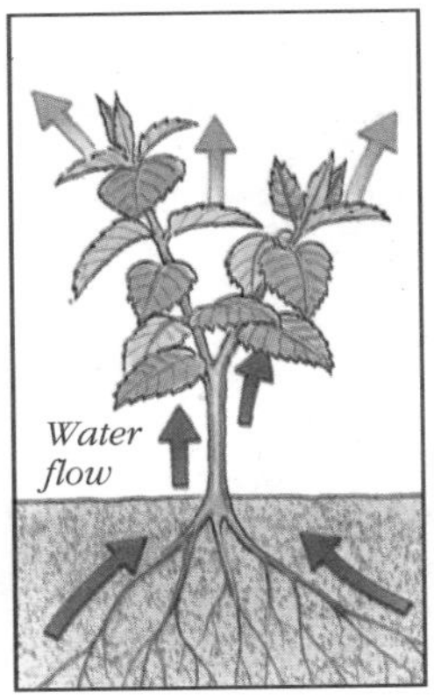

Water flow

PLANT SENSITIVITY

Plants are sensitive to, and react to, certain forms of stimulus, such as light. The way plants react by turning or growing to (or away from) a stimulus, is called tropism.

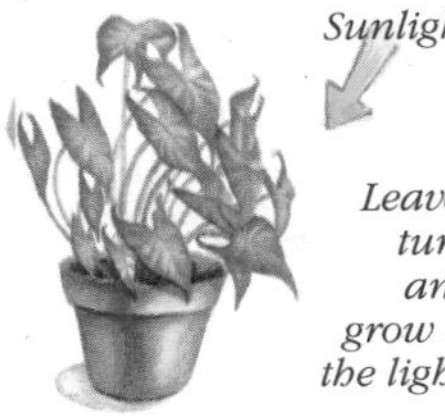

Sunlight

Leaves turn and grow to the light.

For example, if you place a plant on a sunny windowsill, after a few days most of the leaves will have turned toward the light. This reaction is called phototropism. Hydrotropism is the way roots grow toward water and geotropism is the way they react to the pull of gravity by growing down.

PARASITIC PLANTS

A few plants do not make their own food. They live on other plants and take food from them. They are called parasites and they may eventually kill the plants they are living on.

Mistletoe has green leaves so it can make its own food, but it also sucks food and water from the trees on which it lives.

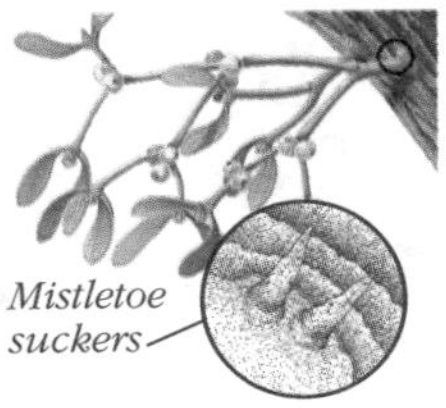

Mistletoe suckers

The rafflesia plant is a parasite that grows on the roots of lianas in rainforests. It has huge, foul-smelling flowers.

CARNIVOROUS PLANTS

Some plants that grow in poor soils, or dark forests, absorb extra food by eating insects and other small animals. They are called carnivorous (meat-eating) plants.

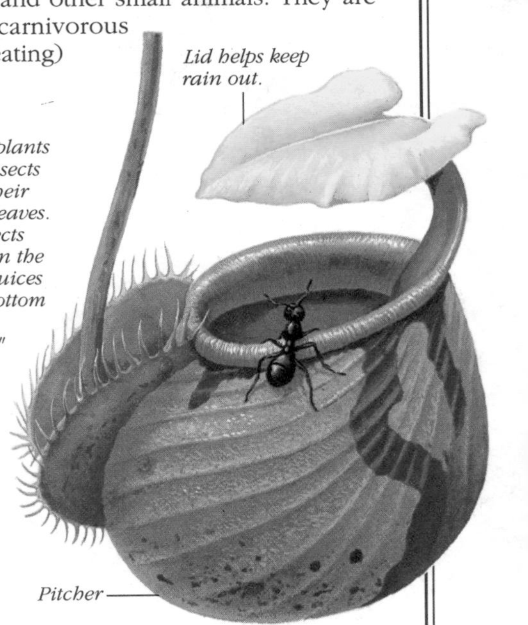

Lid helps keep rain out.
Pitcher

Pitcher plants catch insects inside their hollow leaves. The insects drown in the plant's juices at the bottom of the "pitcher"

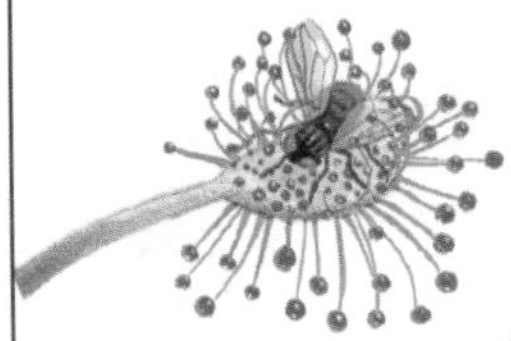

Sundew plants have sticky tentacles on their leaves. The touch of an insect stimulates the tentacles to curl over and trap the insect.

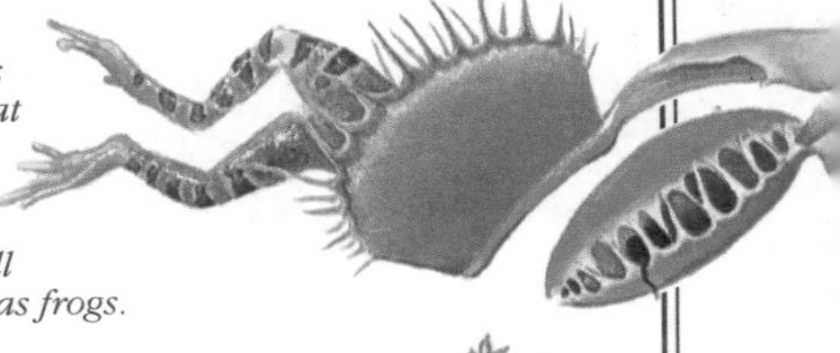

Venus fly traps have leaves that snap shut like jaws. They trap insects and even small animals such as frogs.

SEE FOR YOURSELF

1. To test a plant's sensitivity, you can grow some dried kidney beans in a jar as shown below. Keep moist, and after about a week the beans will have sprouted shoots and roots.

Place beans between paper towel and jar.

2. Turn the jar on its side. After a day, the shoots will have turned to grow up again because of phototropism - the plant's reaction to light. The roots bend down because of geotropism - the plant's reaction to gravity, and hydrotropism - its reaction to water.

3. To see how a plant sucks water up to its leaves, put a stick of celery in some water stained blue with ink or food dye. Leave the jar and celery near a window for a few hours, then examine the celery.

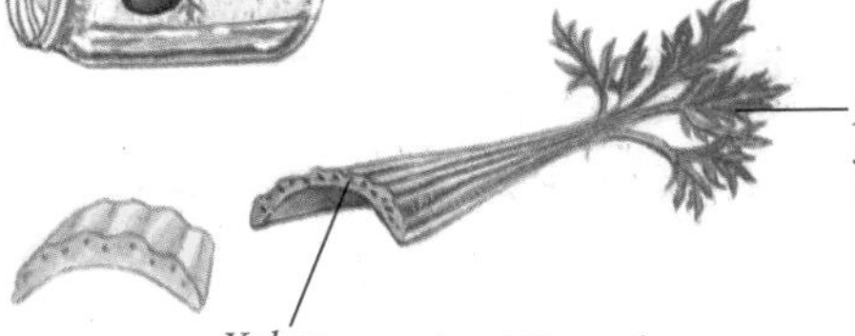

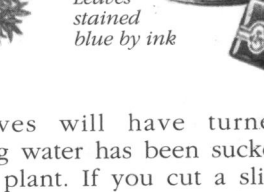

Leaves stained blue by ink
Xylem tubes stained blue

4. The leaves will have turned blue, showing water has been sucked right up the plant. If you cut a slice from the base of the stem you will see the xylem (water-carrying tubes) stained blue.

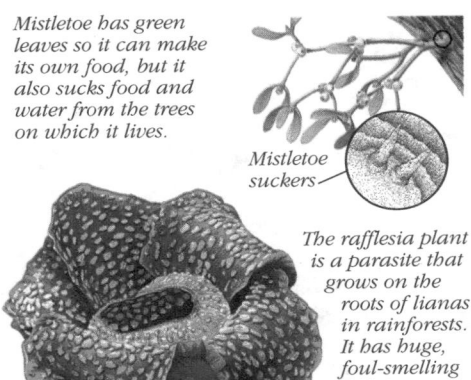

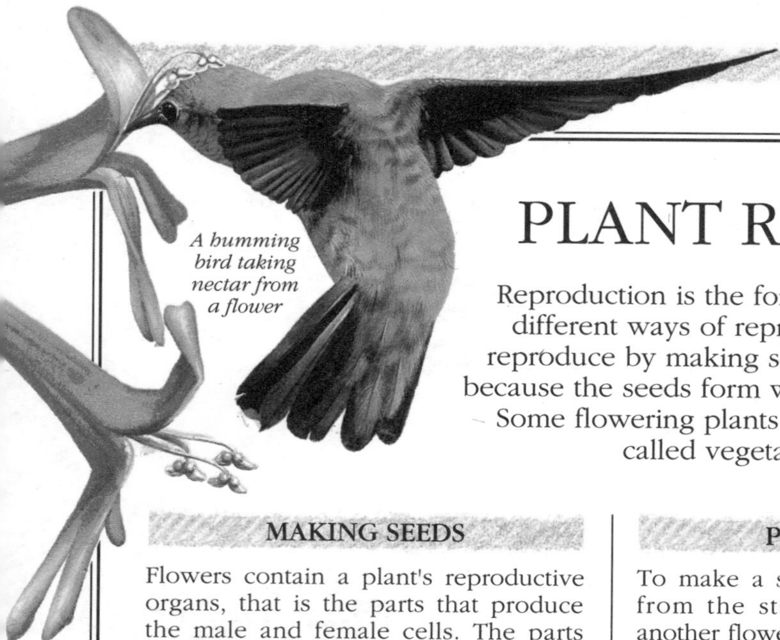

A humming bird taking nectar from a flower

PLANT REPRODUCTION

Dog rose

Reproduction is the formation of new life. Plants have several different ways of reproducing themselves. Flowering plants reproduce by making seeds. This is called sexual reproduction, because the seeds form when a male and female cell join together. Some flowering plants also have other forms of reproduction, called vegetative or asexual reproduction.

MAKING SEEDS

Flowers contain a plant's reproductive organs, that is the parts that produce the male and female cells. The parts that produce the male cells are called stamens and the parts that contain the female cells are called the carpels.

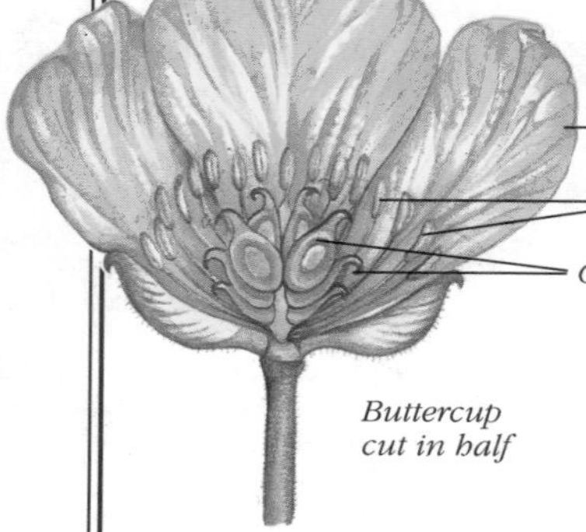
Petal
Stamens
Carpels

Buttercup cut in half

Carpels
Ovary

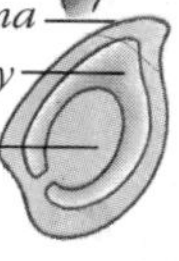
Stigma
Ovary
Ovule

Enlarged carpel cut in half

Some plants have one carpel in each flower. Others, such as buttercups, have many. Inside each of the carpels there is an ovary containing one or more ovules, the female cells. Each carpel has a sticky top, which is called the stigma.

Stamens produce thousands of tiny grains called pollen, and each of the grains contains a male cell. The stalks of the stamens are called filaments and the tips are called anthers. The anthers contain the pollen sacs where the pollen is made. When the pollen is ready, the pollen sacs split open.

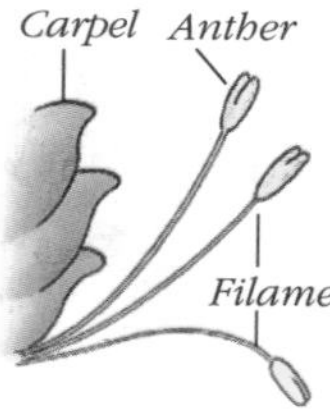
Carpel
Anther
Filaments

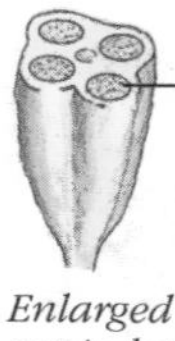
Pollen sac

Enlarged anther cut in half

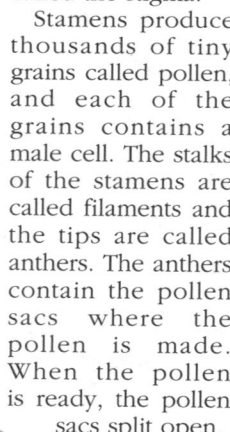

Poppy flowers have only one carpel containing many ovules. Poppy pollen is black.

POLLINATION

To make a seed, pollen has to travel from the stamens to the stigma of another flower of the same type. This is called pollination. The pollen may be carried from flower to flower by insects, bats or birds, or by the wind.

Insects visit flowers to collect nectar, a sugary liquid produced at the base of the petals. When they land on a flower, pollen sticks to them. On visiting another flower, the pollen rubs off on the stigma, the tip of the carpel.

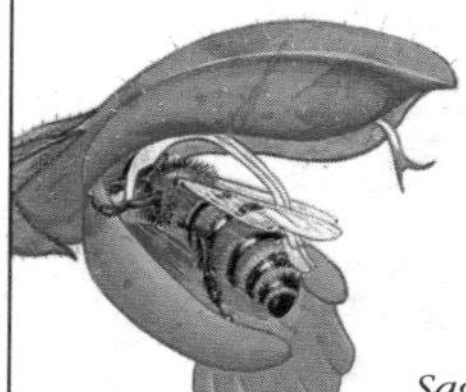

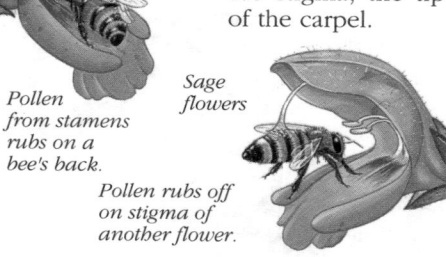

Pollen from stamens rubs on a bee's back.

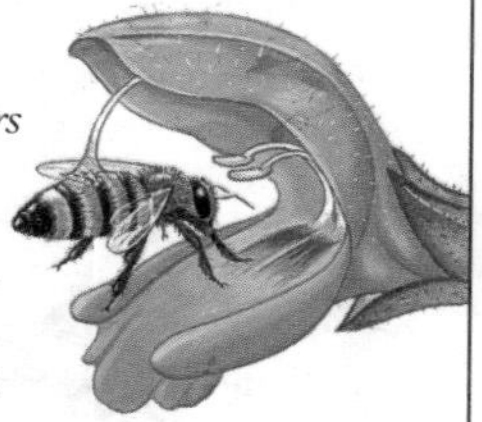

Sage flowers

Pollen rubs off on stigma of another flower.

Flowers pollinated by insects usually have bright petals and produce a scent to attract the insects. The petals often have patterns, called honey guides, that direct insects to the nectar.

Azalea produces a strong scent.

Buddleia attracts butterflies.

Honey guide on pansy

Flowers that are pollinated by the wind, for example the flowers of the eucalyptus tree, have very small petals and do not produce a scent or nectar. Their pollen is fine and smooth and the stamens hang outside the flowers so the pollen is blown away easily.

Stamens

Eucalyptus flowers

FERTILIZATION

When a grain of pollen lands on a stigma, it grows a tube down through the carpel to the ovules so the male and female cells can join. This is called fertilization and the joined cells are called a zygote.

After fertilization, the ovary grows to become a fruit and the seeds form. The plant no longer needs its other flower parts and they wither and die.

Each seed contains an embryo that will develop into a new plant, and food, called endosperm, to provide energy for the new plant to grow.

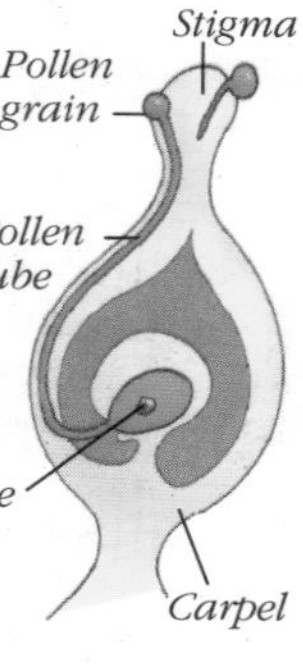
Stigma
Pollen grain
Pollen tube
Ovule
Carpel

VEGETATIVE REPRODUCTION

Some flowering plants produce new plants without making seeds. This is called vegetative or asexual reproduction because it does not involve a male and female cell joining. These plants have special stems or roots that can make shoots that grow into new plants. There are several different kinds of stems and roots.

Daffodil bulb

A bulb is a short underground stem with fleshy leaves.

Crocus corm

A corm is the swollen base of a stem.

Strawberry plant

A runner is a stem that grows along the ground.

A rhizome is an underground stem with scaly leaves.

Mint rhizome

A tuber is a swollen underground stem or root.

Potato tuber

The fruits of the rose are called rose hips.

FRUITS AND SEEDS

Fruits of the Chinese lantern plant

Flowering plants reproduce themselves by producing seeds, and the seeds are protected by fruit. Some fruits have thick, fleshy layers that are good to eat, but others are merely dry cases that hold the seeds. Each seed contains an embryo that, when conditions are right, will grow into a new plant.

FRUIT

When the seeds form inside a flower, parts of the flower develop to become the fruit. There are many different types and shapes of fruit. Some foods that we call vegetables, for example tomatoes, are in fact fruits.

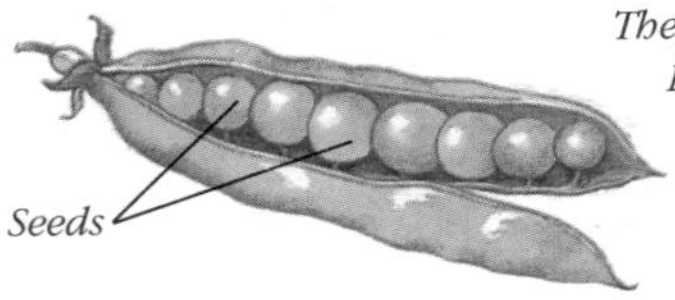
Seeds

The fruit of the pea plant is called a legume or pod. The peas are the seeds.

Orange seed

Oranges and blackcurrants are fleshy fruits that contain seeds.

Blackcurrants

The fruit of the wheat plant is called grain. Each stalk carries many grains.

Walnut

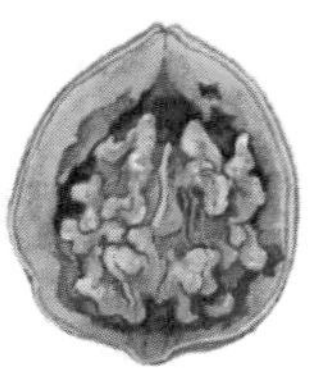

Nuts are dry fruits with hard shells. Each nut contains one seed.

An achene is a small, dry fruit with only one seed. Ash achenes grow in bunches.

Apple seed

Pomes are fruits with thick flesh surrounding a core containing seeds. An apple is a pome. Pomes are called false fruits because they develop from the base of the flower as well as the carpel.

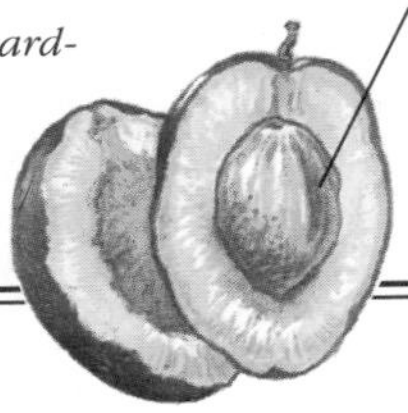
Plum seed

A fleshy fruit with a hard-cased seed is called a drupe. Plums and peaches are drupes.

SEED DISPERSAL

Plants have developed various ways of scattering their seeds so they do not compete with the parent plant for space, light and water. This is called seed dispersal. Seeds may be dispersed by animals, by wind or water, or by explosion when the fruits split open.

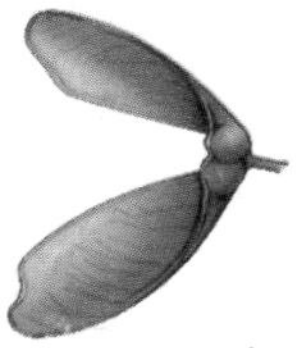

Winged maple seeds

Seeds dispersed by the wind are very light and have hairs or papery wings to help the wind carry them. Seeds dispersed by explosion develop in pods. When the pods dry out, they split open, scattering the seeds away from the parent plant.

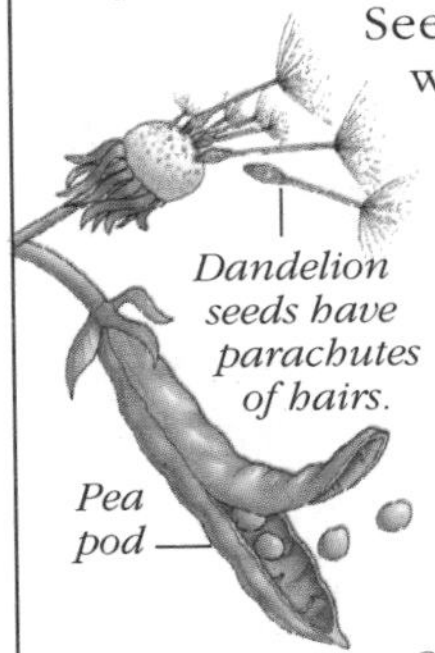
Pea pod

Dandelion seeds have parachutes of hairs.

Seeds that are dispersed by water, such as coconuts, have waterproof shells. Coconuts are the seeds of coconut palm trees. They float in rivers or the sea until they are washed up on a shore.

Fleshy fruits, such as berries, are eaten by birds and animals and the seeds are deposited in their droppings. Seeds with hooks, such as burdock, cling to animals' fur, and nuts and grain may be carried away and buried.

Strawberry

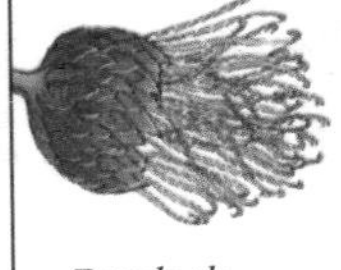

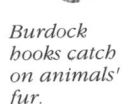

Burdock hooks catch on animals' fur.

Acorn

Acorns are buried by squirrels and some may grow into trees.

GERMINATION

When conditions are right, a seed will begin to grow into a new plant. This is called germination. To germinate, it needs warmth and water. The seed case splits open and the first shoot and root, called the plumule and radicle, grow. The first two leaves are called cotyledons. They are often a different shape from the later leaves.

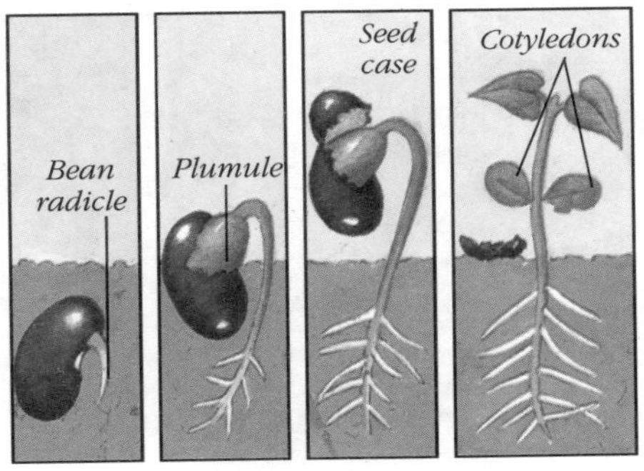
Bean radicle
Plumule
Seed case
Cotyledons

SEE FOR YOURSELF

You can probably find lots of seeds in the kitchen at home. Rice, lentils and dried beans are all seeds.

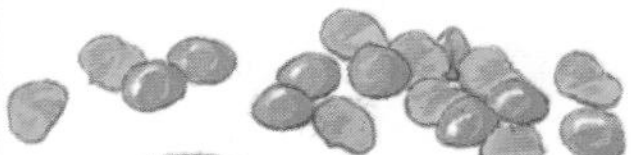

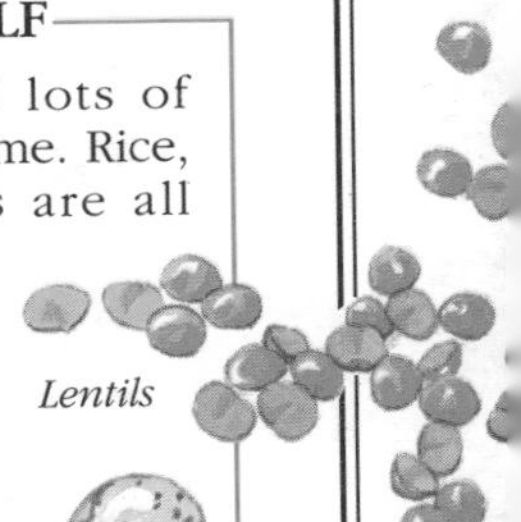

Lentils

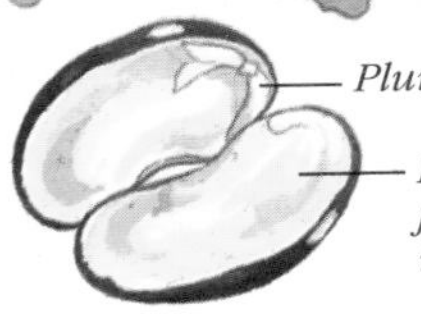
Plumule
Endosperm - food store for new plant

Kidney bean split open

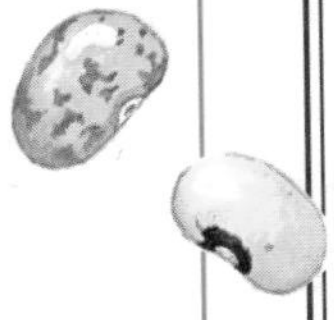

Soak some beans or lentils in water overnight, then split them open. You can see the plumule and food store for the new plant. To grow seeds (but not rice), place them on a piece of paper towel in a saucer, and water them to keep them moist. Each day, rinse the seeds in a sieve and put them back. After a few days, they will have sprouted. If you like, you can plant them in small pots.

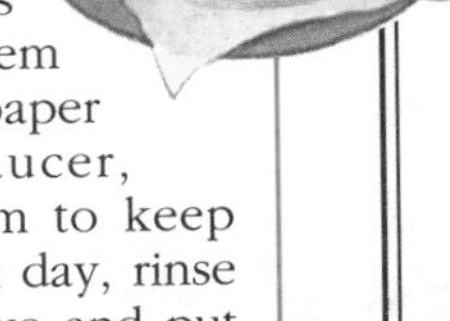

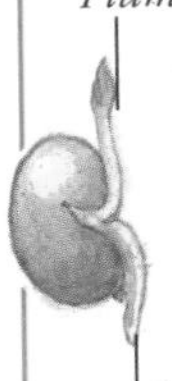
Plumule
Radicle

Coconut palm tree

In autumn, or the dry season, most broadleaved trees produce seeds and lose their leaves.

TREES

Trees are the largest plants and they also live the longest. Some live for several hundred years and the oldest tree in the world (a bristlecone pine tree in the USA) is said to be 4,900 years old. Trees play an important role in nature. They help maintain the balance of gases in the atmosphere, their roots hold the soil in place, and they suck up water from the ground and release it back into the air from their leaves.

BROADLEAVED TREES

Broadleaved trees, such as oaks and chestnuts, have soft, flat leaves. Their seeds are enclosed in fruits, which may be hard like acorns, or soft like cherries. When it is very cold or dry, most broadleaved trees are deciduous, that is, they lose their leaves (see opposite).

Acorn - fruit of the oak tree

Sweet chestnut leaf

Sweet chestnut

Chestnuts in seed cases

English oak leaf

Holly leaf - holly is an evergreen broadleaved tree.

Apple blossom

To make seeds, broadleaved trees produce flowers. When pollen from one flower joins with, or fertilizes, the ovules in another flower, the seeds begin to form (see Plant Reproduction*). Some trees have flowers that produce both pollen and ovules, for example, fruit-tree blossom. Others have separate flowers for pollen (male flowers) and ovules (female flowers).

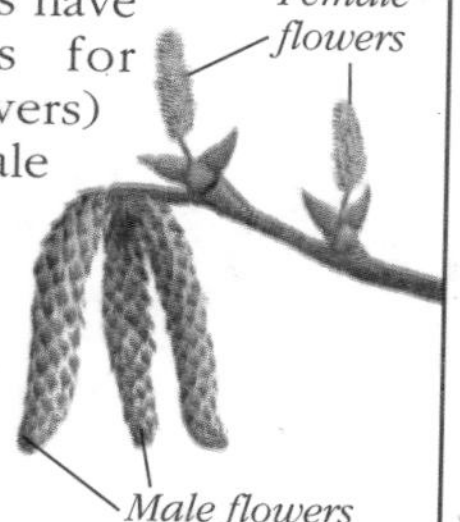
Female flowers
Male flowers are called catkins.
Silver birch flowers

CONIFEROUS TREES

Coniferous trees, such as fir trees, have waxy, needle- or scale-like leaves and their seeds are protected by cones. They grow in cooler parts of the world and most are evergreen, that is, they do not lose all their leaves at the same time (see opposite).

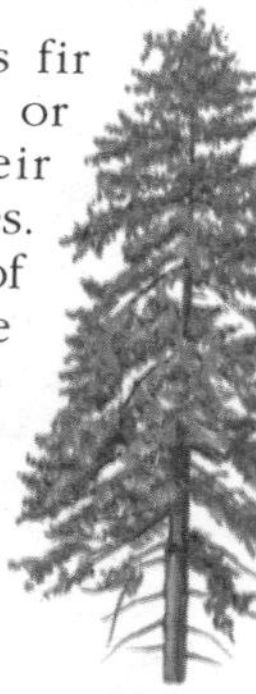
Douglas fir

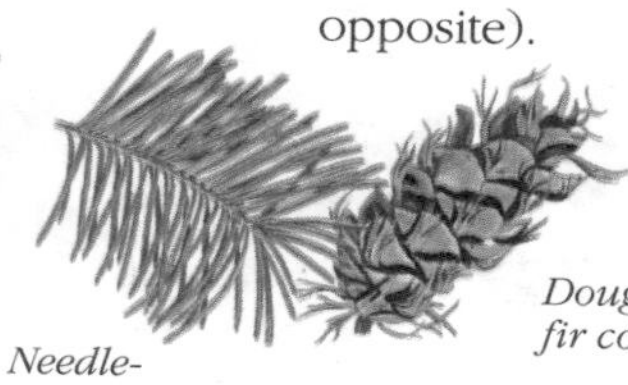
Needle-like leaves of the Douglas fir

Douglas fir cone

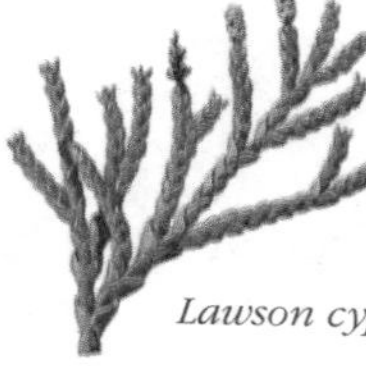
Scaly leaves

Lawson cypress

Corsican pine needles

Blue Atlas cedar

In spring, conifers produce soft, male and female flowers. The male flowers produce pollen and the female flowers have ovules (see Plant Reproduction*).

When pollen blows onto and fertilizes the ovules in the female flowers, the seeds begin to form. The scales of the female flowers close and become woody to form a cone to protect the seeds. It takes a year or more for the cones to become ripe.

Female flower
Male flower
Norway spruce

Female flower
Male flower
Unripe cone from previous year
Scots pine

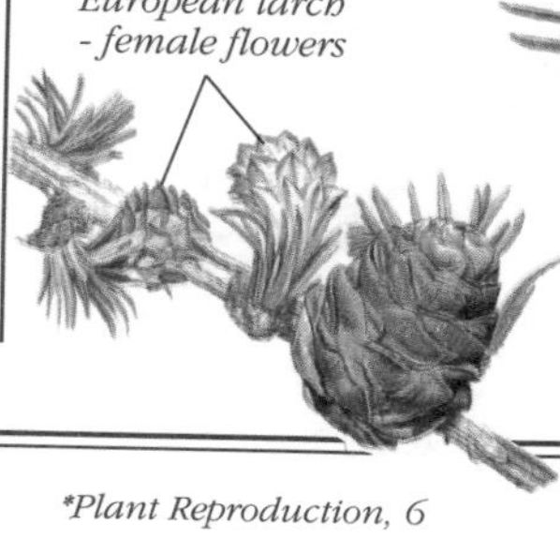
European larch - female flowers

PALM TREES

Palm trees have large leaves with no branches. The leaves grow straight out of the tops of the trunks, which are made of fibrous strands supported by a substance called lignin. Their seeds are protected by fruits, for example, bananas, dates and coconuts. Palm trees grow mainly in tropical areas.

Canary palm

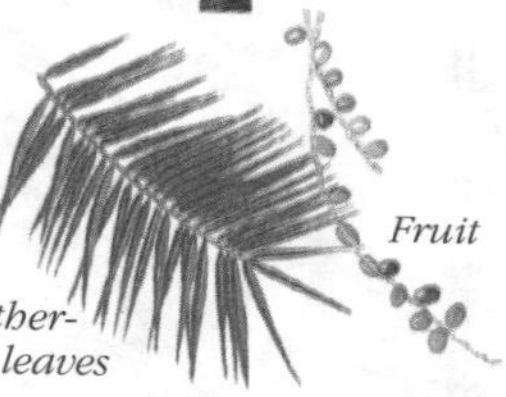
Fruit
Feather-like leaves

LEAVES

A tree makes all its food in its leaves. The leaves contain tiny bodies, called chloroplasts, where the food is made from water and carbon dioxide gas by the process of photosynthesis*. The chloroplasts contain a green substance, chlorophyll, that absorbs the sunlight that powers the process of photosynthesis.

A network of tiny veins carries water to the cells. On the underside of the leaf there are minute holes, called stomata, that open and close to let gases in and out.

Magnified view of veins
White poplar leaf

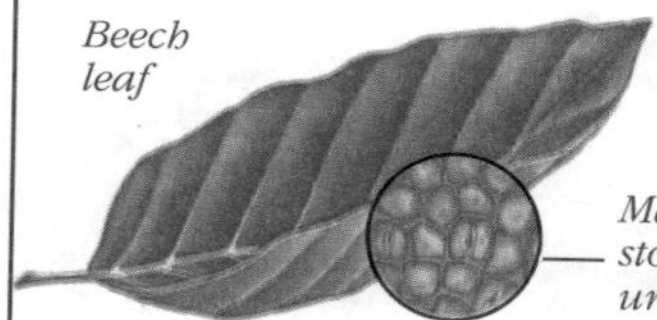
Magnified view of stomata on underside of leaf
Beech leaf

In the daytime, leaves take in carbon dioxide from the air and use it for photosynthesis. They give off oxygen, a waste product of photosynthesis. In this way, trees help provide the oxygen that animals and people need to breathe.

*Plant Reproduction, 6

*Photosynthesis, 5

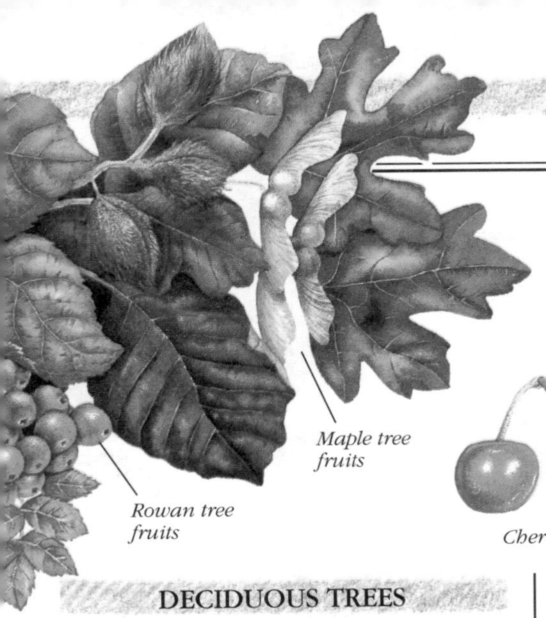
Maple tree fruits
Rowan tree fruits

TREE FRUITS AND SEEDS

Trees reproduce themselves by making seeds and the seeds are protected by fruits. The fruit may be a papery wing, a fleshy fruit such as a peach or date, or a cone. The fruits help the seeds to be spread away from the trees so they have room to grow. Some are blown away by the wind. Others may be carried away by animals, birds or people.

Cherry seed

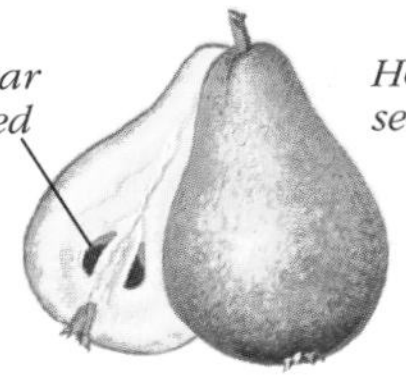
Pear seed

Hornbeam seed
The fruit is a dry wing.

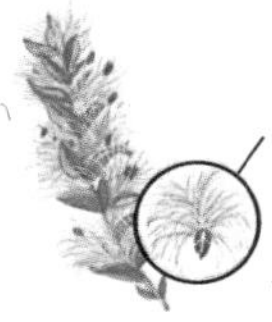
Seed with feathery top
Willow

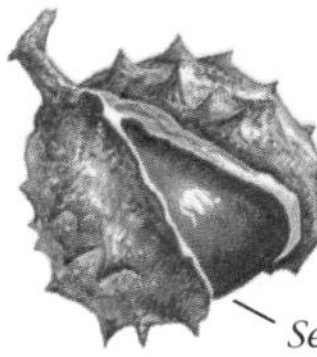
Horse chestnut fruit case
Seed

DECIDUOUS TREES

Deciduous trees lose all their leaves in the winter or dry season. This protects the trees so they do not lose water from their leaves when it is too dry or cold to take up water from their roots.

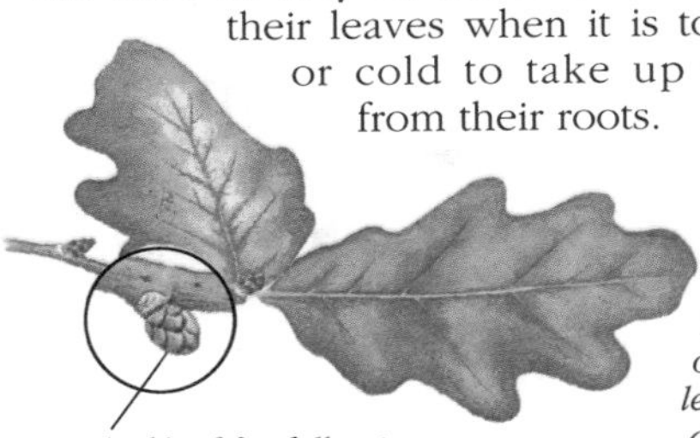
English oak tree leaves in autumn
Bud of leaf for following year

In the autumn, or dry season, the green chlorophyll in the leaves breaks down and they turn orange and brown. A corky layer grows across the leaf stalks and the leaves fall off.

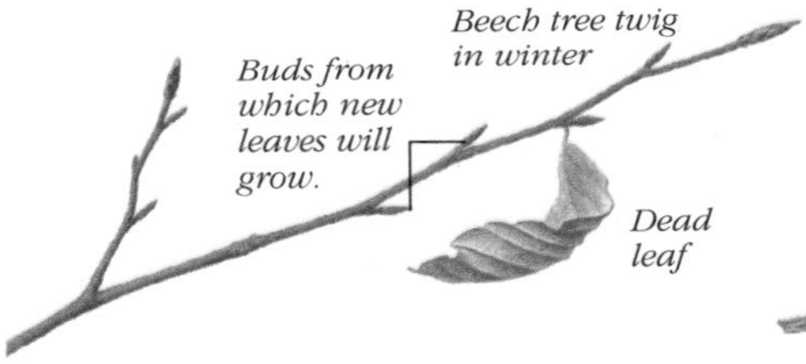
Beech tree twig in winter
Buds from which new leaves will grow.
Dead leaf

EVERGREEN TREES

Evergreen trees lose their leaves, but not all at the same time. Each leaf lasts for two or three years. The leaves have a waxy coating that stops them from losing too much water. Most conifers and palm trees are evergreen, and in hot places that have no cold or dry season, so are broadleaved trees.

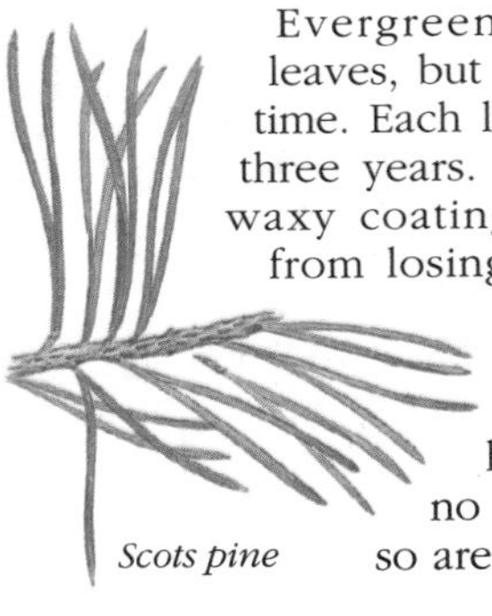
Scots pine

SEE FOR YOURSELF

In early spring, you can force buds to open by bringing them indoors. Some good ones to try are horse chestnut, birch, willow and forsythia. Put the twigs in water in a warm place.

CONES

The seeds of coniferous trees are usually protected by cones. When the seeds are ripe, the scales of the cones open on a dry day to release the seeds.

Seed
Scots pine cone

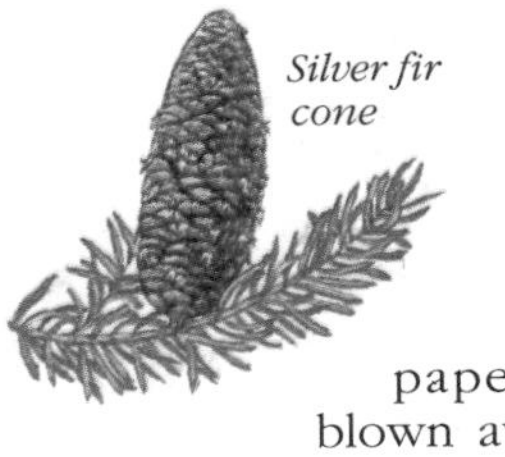
Silver fir cone

Some cones have papery seeds that are blown away. Heavier seeds fall to the ground and may be carried away by animals or birds.

European larch cone

Lodgepole pine cone

Yew

Different types of coniferous tree have different shaped cones and yews have cup-shaped "berries" instead of cones. Birds eat the berries and the seeds are deposited in their droppings.

TREE ROOTS

Roots anchor the tree in the ground. The central tap root goes straight down and the large side roots have feeding roots branching off them. The feeding roots are covered with tiny hairs that absorb water and mineral salts from the soil.

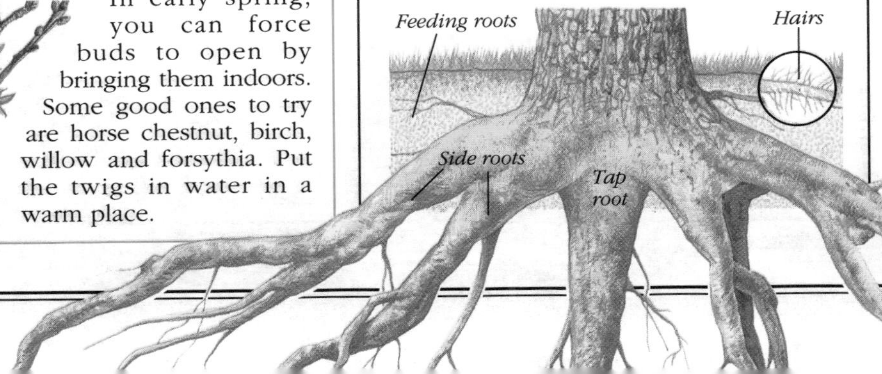
Feeding roots
Hairs
Side roots
Tap root

TREE TRUNKS

A tree trunk is a thick, woody stem that supports the tree and carries water and food to and from the leaves.

The wood is made up of tubes. The tubes in the middle of the trunk are called heartwood. They are very strong and help support the tree. The rest of the wood is called sapwood because the tubes carry sap (water and mineral salts) up the tree. A layer of tubes just under the bark carries food from the leaves to other parts of the tree.

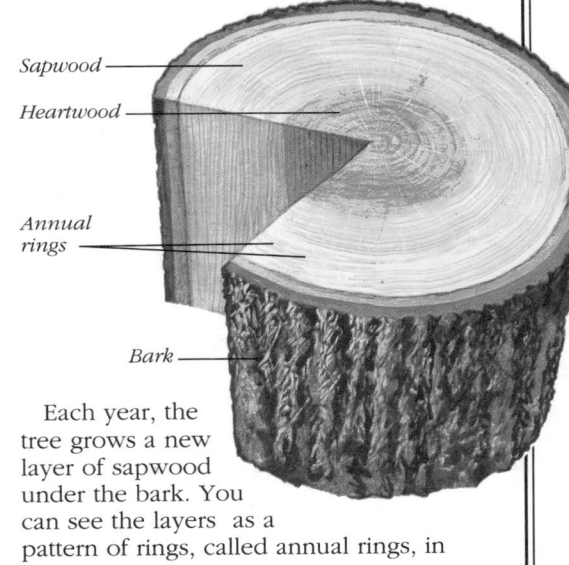

Sapwood
Heartwood
Annual rings
Bark

Each year, the tree grows a new layer of sapwood under the bark. You can see the layers as a pattern of rings, called annual rings, in a tree stump.

The bark stops the tree from drying out and protects it from disease. Bark cannot grow or stretch, so it splits or peels as the trunk gets wider, and new bark grows underneath.

Silver birch bark
English oak bark
Scots pine bark
Beech bark

FERNS, MOSSES AND LIVERWORTS

Ferns and mosses grow thickly in the damp conditions of tropical rainforests. Here, they are growing on the branch of a tree.

Ferns, mosses and liverworts are simple plants that grow in damp places. They grow in woods, on moorlands and by streams, and also in hot, damp, tropical rainforests. These plants are the descendants of some of the first land plants that lived 400 million years ago. They do not produce flowers or seeds and reproduce by a method that developed before flowering plants evolved.

Fronds

Hart's tongue fern

REPRODUCTION

To reproduce themselves, these plants pass through two stages. In the case of ferns and liverworts, these stages are on separate plants. Mosses produce the two stages on the same plant.

In the first stage, the plant is called the gametophyte and it produces male and female cells called gametes.

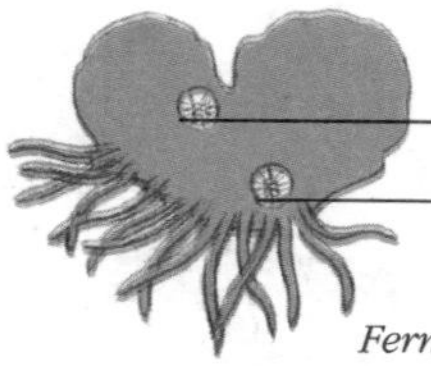
Female cells
Male cells

Fern gametophyte

Moss gametophyte

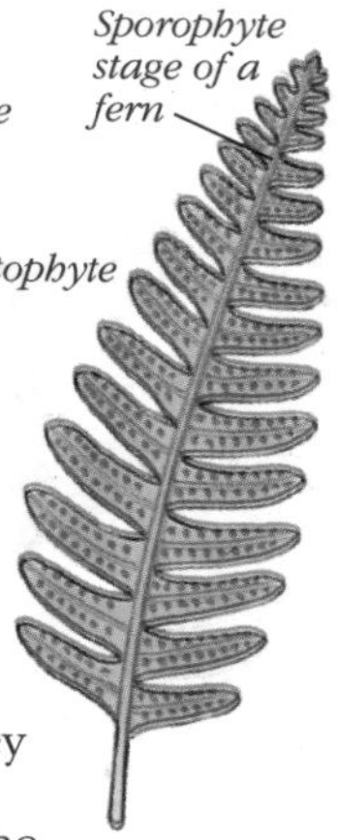

Sporophyte stage of a fern

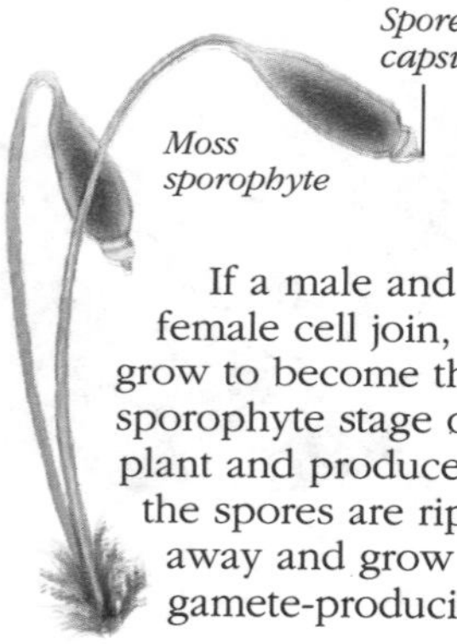
Spore capsule

Moss sporophyte

If a male and female cell join, they grow to become the sporophyte stage of the plant and produce spores. When the spores are ripe, they blow away and grow into new, gamete-producing plants.

CLUB MOSSES AND HORSETAILS

Club mosses and horsetails are related to ferns. They are the survivors of ancient plants that grew as tall as trees about 350 million years ago.

Today, horsetails grow about 10-20cm (4-8in) tall, although one tropical species grows up to 8m (26ft) tall. Club mosses grow along the ground.

Horsetail

Stag's horn club moss

Yellow "horns" hold the spores on this club moss.

FERNS

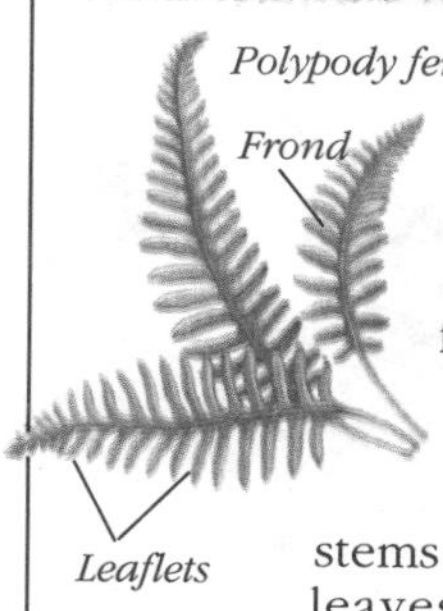
Frond
Leaflets

Polypody fern

Ferns grow in damp, shady places all over the world. In tropical areas, a type of fern called a tree fern, grows about 25m (80ft) tall.

Most ferns grow from underground stems called rhizomes. The leaves are called fronds and they may be solid or made up of many small leaflets.

Ferns spread by sending up new shoots from their underground stems, and also by producing spores. The spores develop on the underside of the fern's leaves and are usually covered by small flaps of leaf.

These pictures show different types of ferns.

Bracken

Hard fern

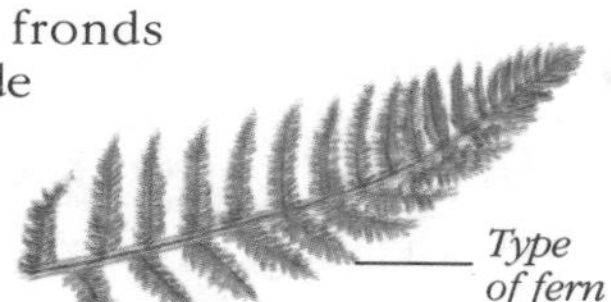

Type of fern called a male fern

Wall rue fern

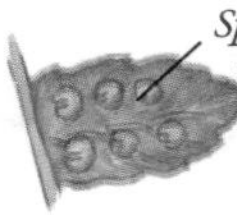

Spore sacs on underside of fern leaflet

MOSSES

Mosses grow on the ground and on walls, rocks and tree trunks. They have stems with simple leaves, and root-like growths called rhizoids. Some mosses form dense springy cushions and others have stems that creep along the ground.

Mosses reproduce with spores that develop in tiny capsules on stalks. The spores grow into new moss plants. These plants then produce male and female cells that fuse and then grow to form a new spore capsule.

Silver cord moss

Sphagnum moss spore capsule

LIVERWORTS

Liverworts are very primitive plants that grow in damp places on the surface of the soil or rocks. They have no proper leaves or roots. The body of the plant is called the thallus and it is anchored to the ground by simple growths.

Liverworts increase by growing branches that eventually separate from the main plant, and also by producing spores.

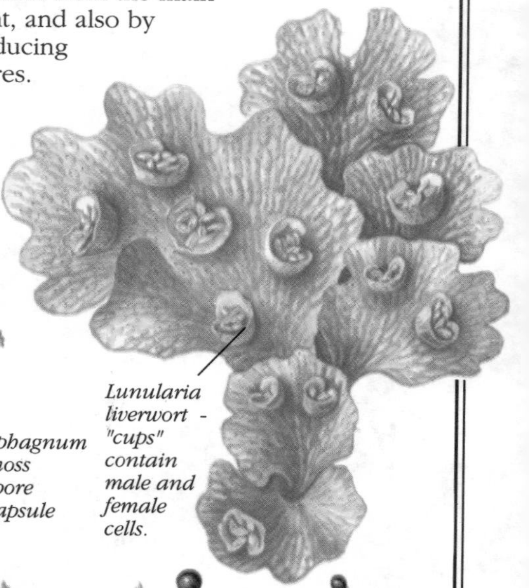

Lunularia liverwort - "cups" contain male and female cells.

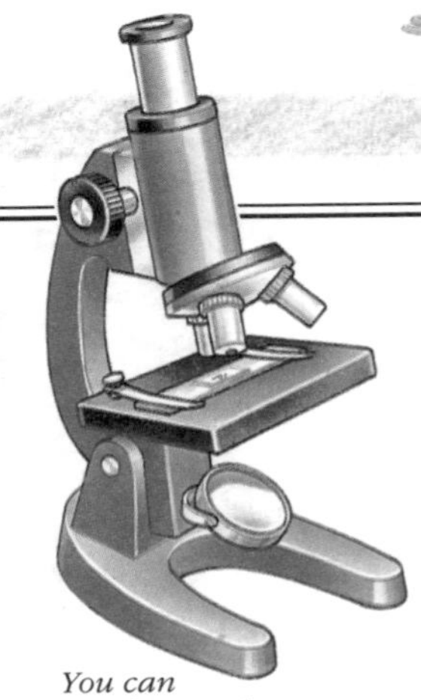

You can see algae and protozoa with a microscope.

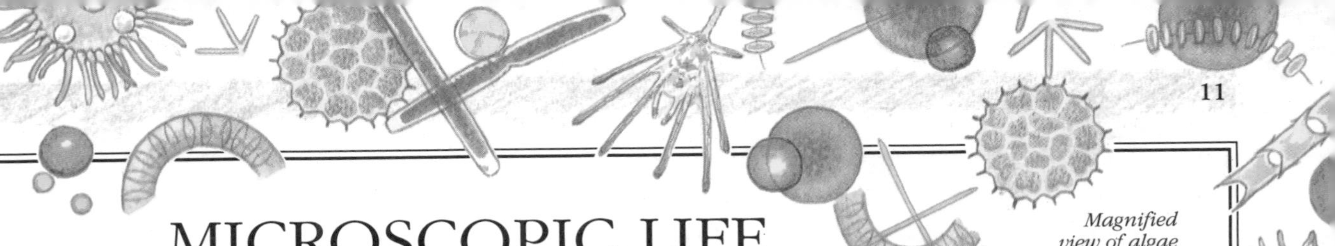

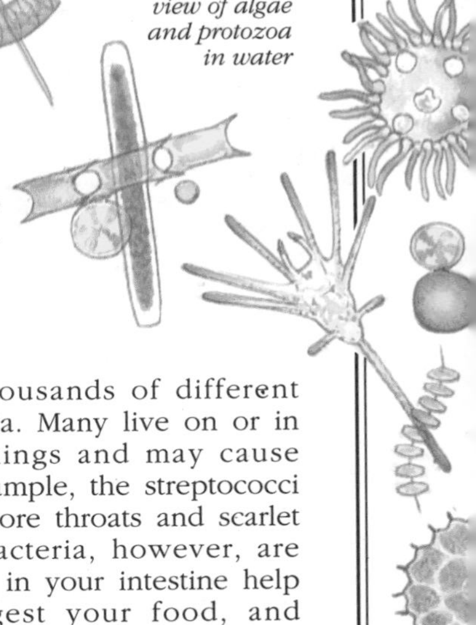

Magnified view of algae and protozoa in water

MICROSCOPIC LIFE

All around us, in the air, soil and water, there are thousands of minute organisms. Most of them are very simple and are related to the earliest forms of life that developed over 3,000 million years ago. As well as plant-like organisms, which belong to a group called algae, and animals, which belong to a group called protozoa, there are bacteria and viruses. Bacteria are neither plant nor animal, and viruses, scientists believe, are on the borderline between living and non-living things.

ALGAE

Algae are simple, plant-like organisms that grow in water. There are many different kinds. Some are made of only one cell and are too small to be seen with the naked eye. Other types of algae, for example, seaweeds*, are made up of many cells. Most of the single-celled algae grow in the sea and are part of the plankton* on which many different sea creatures feed.

Seawater algae seen through a microscope

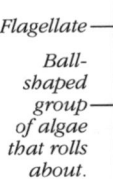

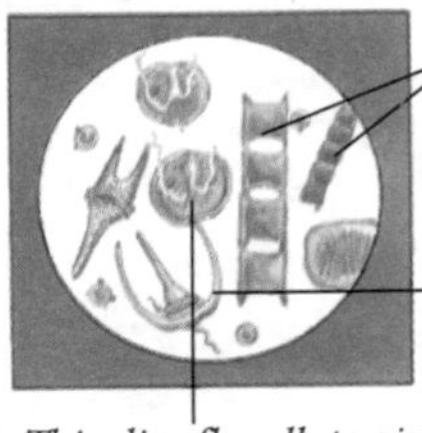
Diatoms - yellow-green algae with outer cases of a hard substance called silica
Dinoflagellate - alga with two whip-like hairs
This dinoflagellate gives off light and can make the sea seem lit up.

Algae have no roots or leaves. They absorb all the substances they need from the water. They contain the green substance, chlorophyll, so they can make their own food by the process of photosynthesis*. As well as chlorophyll, some algae contain red and brown substances that help them absorb sunlight underwater.

Freshwater algae seen through a microscope

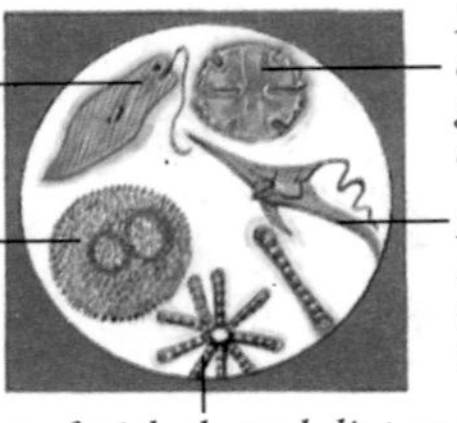
Flagellate
Ball-shaped group of algae that rolls about.
Desmids are bright green algae.
Flagellate alga with whip-like hair

Group of stick-shaped diatoms

Some of the single-celled algae can move. They have whip-like hairs, called flagellae, that wave backward and forward and move the algae toward sunlight.

Large groups of microscopic algae living together are called colonies. They can be seen with the naked eye as green slime on underwater rocks.

PROTOZOA

There are over 30,000 different kinds of protozoa, which means first animals. They are all very simple, single-celled creatures that live in water and feed on algae and other protozoa, and are in turn eaten by fish.

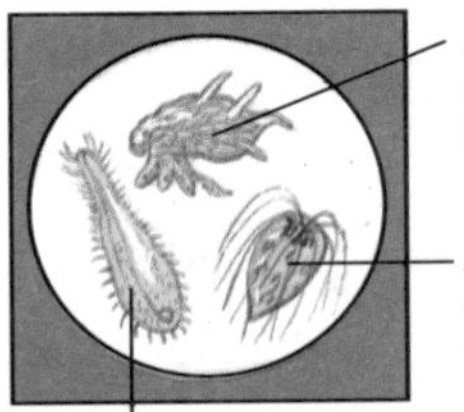
Shelled amoeba - an amoeba (see below) with a hard shell
Flagellate protozoa covered with long, whip-like hairs
Ciliate protozoa have tiny hairs, called cilia, that they use to move along.

AMOEBAS

Amoebas are a kind of protozoan. They live in water and also in the bodies of animals where they can cause many different illnesses.

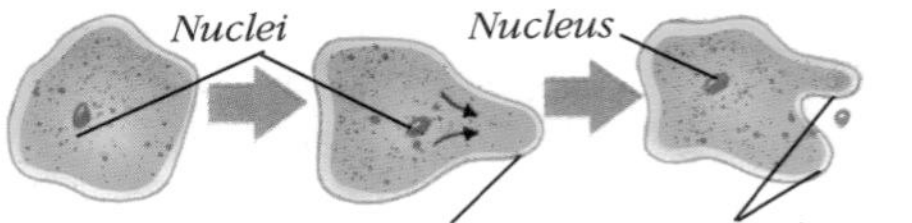
Nuclei
Nucleus
Pseudopodium
Two pseudopodia

Amoebas can move about by changing shape. Part of the cell pushes forward to form a "foot" called a pseudopodium and the rest of the cell flows into the foot. By putting out two pseudopodia, they can surround food particles. The food is held in a food vacuole inside the cell while it is broken down and digested. Amoebas reproduce by dividing in two, a process that is called simple fission.

BACTERIA

Bacteria are very tiny organisms made up of just one unit that is simpler and very different from a plant or animal cell.

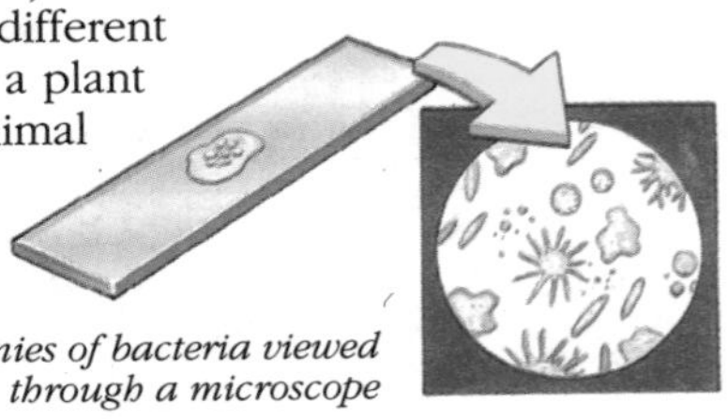

Colonies of bacteria viewed through a microscope

There are thousands of different kinds of bacteria. Many live on or in other living things and may cause disease. For example, the streptococci bacteria cause sore throats and scarlet fever. Other bacteria, however, are useful. Bacteria in your intestine help you digest your food, and cheese and yogurt are formed by the action of bacteria.

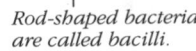

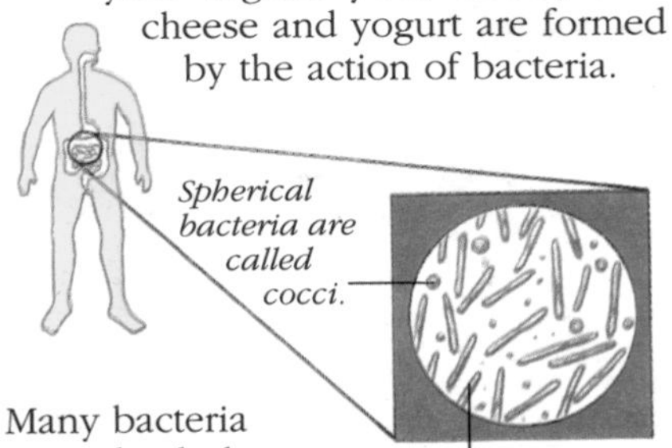
Spherical bacteria are called cocci.
Rod-shaped bacteria are called bacilli.

Many bacteria live on dead plants and animals and cause them to decay. In this way, bacteria help recycle the basic substances of which living matter is made.

VIRUSES

Viruses are the smallest living things yet discovered. Although they have some of the characteristics of living things, for example, they can reproduce to increase their number, some scientists think they are just complicated chemical substances.

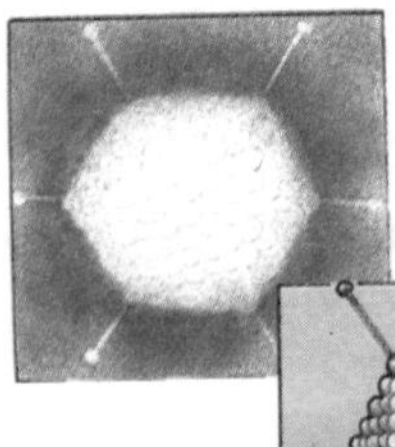

A throat infection virus viewed under a powerful electron microscope

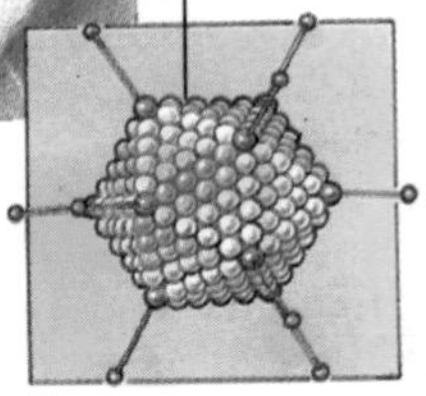

Models of viruses help scientists investigate them.

Viruses cannot exist on their own. They invade the cells of living things and "force" these cells to make more viruses like themselves. They cause many different diseases, ranging from colds and measles to AIDS.

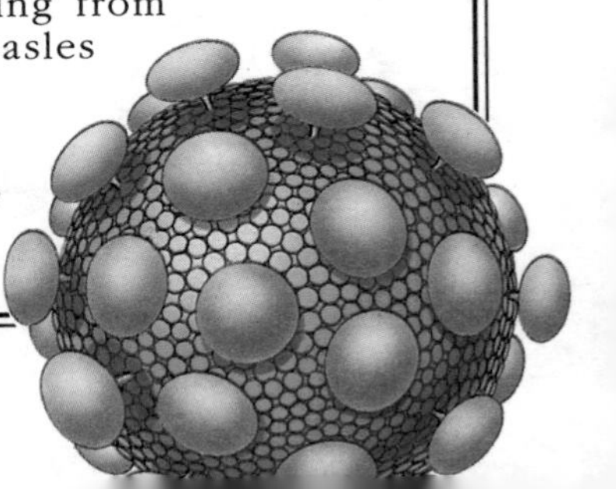

A model of the AIDS virus

*Seaweeds, 25; Plankton, 82; Photosynthesis, 5

Fly agaric is poisonous. It grows under birch and pine trees.

MUSHROOMS, TOADSTOOLS
AND OTHER FUNGI

Mushrooms, toadstools and the yeast that is used to make bread are all different kinds of fungi. Although some fungi grow in the ground, they are not plants because they cannot make their own food. Fungi play a very important role in nature. They break down dead plant and animal matter so the basic chemicals of which the plants and animals were made can be used again.

Amethyst deceiver grows in woodlands and smells slightly of garlic.

HOW FUNGI GROW

The main part of a fungus is a mass of threads, called hyphae, that grow on plant or animal matter. A few fungi, for example yeast, are single, cell-like units that do not have threads.

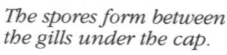

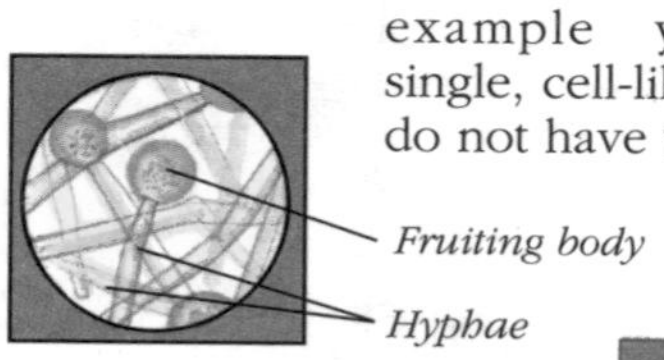
Fruiting body
Hyphae

Magnified view of fungus on bread

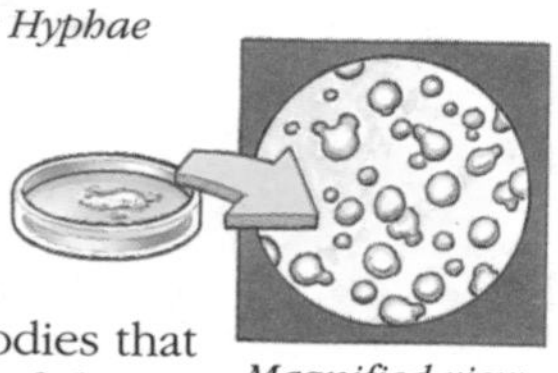

Magnified view of yeast cells

To reproduce itself, the fungus grows fruiting bodies that contain millions of dust-like spores. Mushrooms and toadstools are fruiting bodies. Other fungi produce fruiting bodies that can only be seen with a microscope.

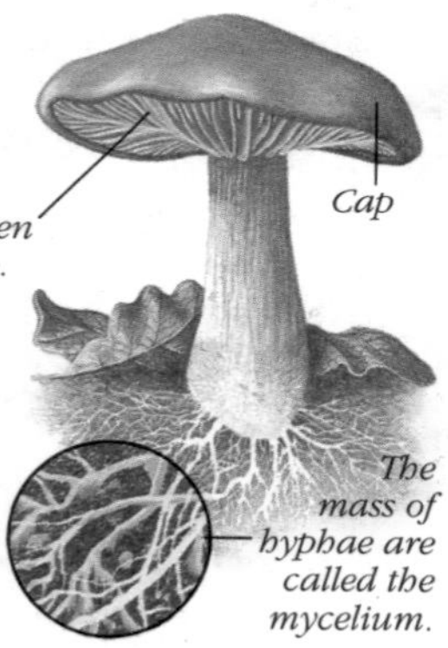
Wood blewit
Cap
The spores form between the gills under the cap.
The mass of hyphae are called the mycelium.

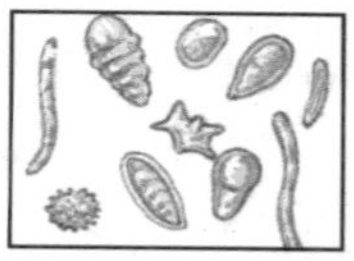

Different shaped fungal spores

Fungus spores are everywhere - in the air and in the soil. When they land on a suitable substance, and there is water and warmth, new threads of fungus will start to grow.

Fungi grow and feed on plant or animal matter. They release chemicals that make the plant or animal matter decompose (break down into the simpler substances of which it is made). The fungus absorbs some of the substances but others are released back into the soil from where they can be taken up again by living plants.

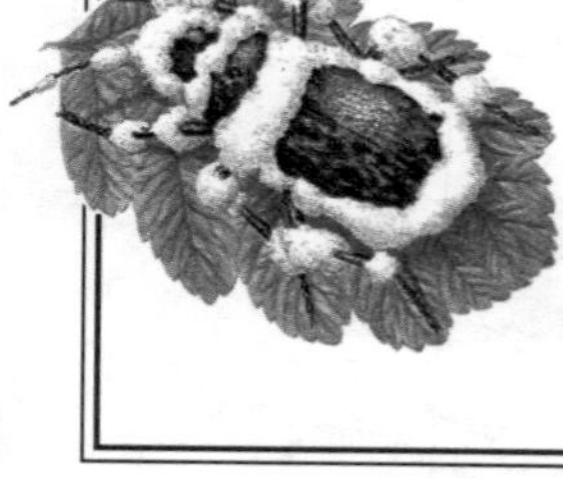

Beetle covered with fungus that is feeding on its body

USEFUL FUNGI

Fungi that feed on dead plants or animals are called saprotrophs. Saprotrophs are normally useful as they help to break down dead matter. Some fungi, for example, fly agaric, grow on living plants without harming them and the fungus and plant may even benefit each other. These fungi are called symbiotic fungi. Many orchids (a type of flower) grow with fungi and the nutrients released by the fungi help the orchids to grow.

HARMFUL FUNGI

Fungi that feed on living matter are called parasites. They harm or even kill the plant or animal they live on. Mildew is a harmful fungus that destroys crops, and Dutch elm disease is caused by a fungus that blocks the circulation of water in elm trees. On people, athlete's foot is caused by a fungus that lives on warm, moist skin.

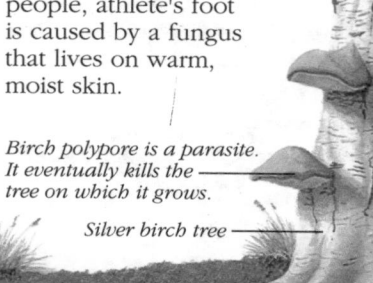

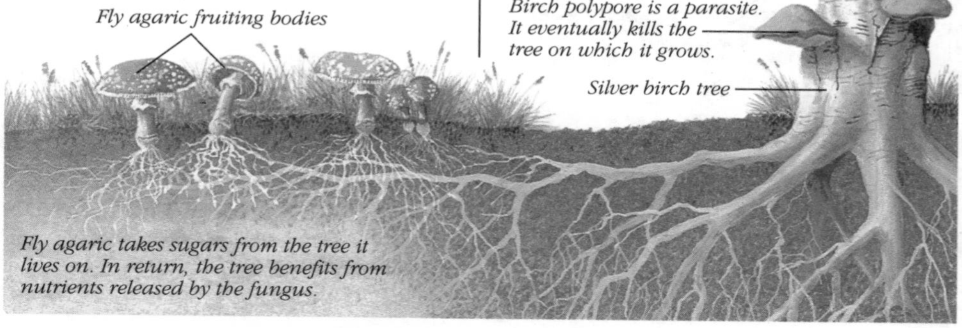
Fly agaric fruiting bodies
Birch polypore is a parasite. It eventually kills the tree on which it grows.
Silver birch tree

Fly agaric takes sugars from the tree it lives on. In return, the tree benefits from nutrients released by the fungus.

YEAST

Yeast is a useful fungus that lives on the sugars found in fruit. When yeast breaks down sugar, it makes alcohol and the gas carbon dioxide.

Yeast has been used for thousands of years to make alcohol and bread. When added to dough, the bubbles of carbon dioxide make the bread rise.

Wine
Beer
Bread

PENICILLIN

The medicine, penicillin, is made from a fungus called *Penicillium* that grows on fruit. *Penicillium* gives off chemicals that kill bacteria, and these chemicals can be used to fight diseases caused by bacteria. Other types of *Penicillium* are used to make cheeses, such as the French cheese called Camembert.

SEE FOR YOURSELF

To see how the air is full of fungus spores, and in what conditions they grow, leave a slice of fresh bread on a table for a few minutes to expose it to the air. Then cut it into four pieces. Put three of the pieces into plastic bags labelled B, C and D and seal them.

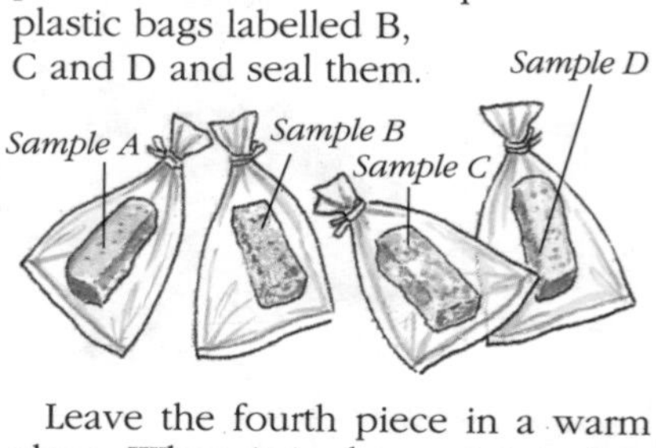
Sample A
Sample B
Sample C
Sample D

Leave the fourth piece in a warm place. When it is dry, put it in bag A. Put A and B in a warm room, C in a fridge and D in a freezer. After a week, examine the bread without opening the bags, then throw the bags away. The very dry (A) and very cold (D) bags have the least amount of fungus, because fungi need warmth and moisture to grow.

MUSHROOMS AND TOADSTOOLS

Mushrooms and toadstools are the fruiting bodies of different kinds of fungi. The fruiting bodies usually form in autumn, but the fungi are in the soil all through the year. They grow in damp fields and dark woods as, unlike green plants, they do not need sunlight.

In the pictures on this page, the fungi are arranged in groups according to the shape of their fruiting bodies.

Many toadstools, and some mushrooms, are extremely poisonous. Never pick them without expert advice.

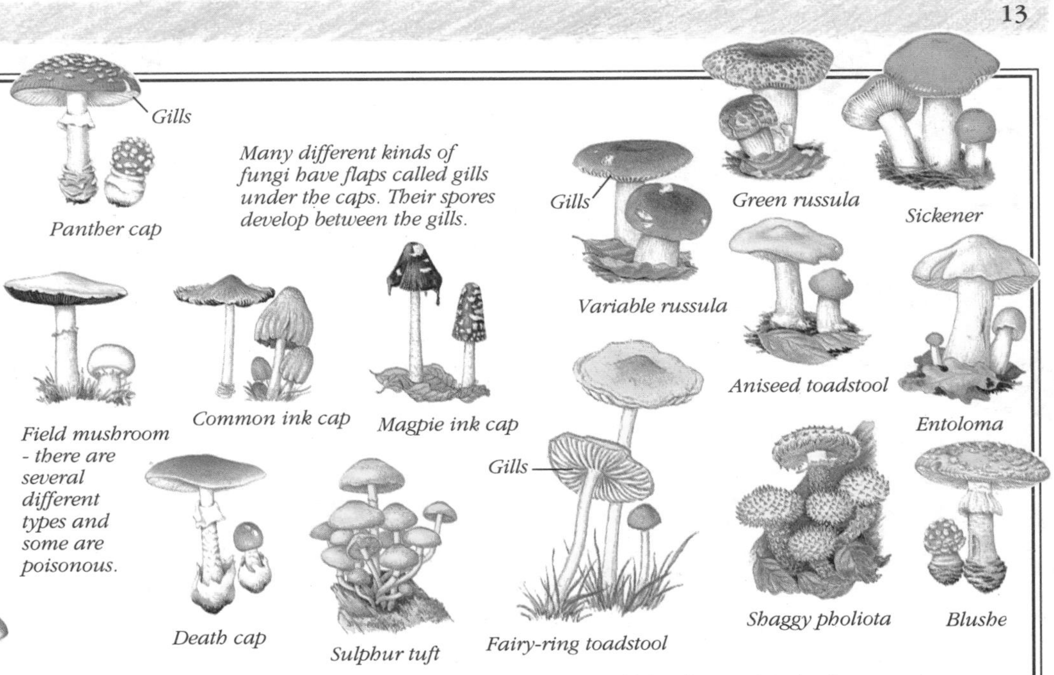
Gills
Panther cap
Many different kinds of fungi have flaps called gills under the caps. Their spores develop between the gills.
Gills
Variable russula
Green russula
Sickener
Aniseed toadstool
Entoloma
Field mushroom - there are several different types and some are poisonous.
Common ink cap
Magpie ink cap
Gills
Death cap
Sulphur tuft
Fairy-ring toadstool
Shaggy pholiota
Blushe

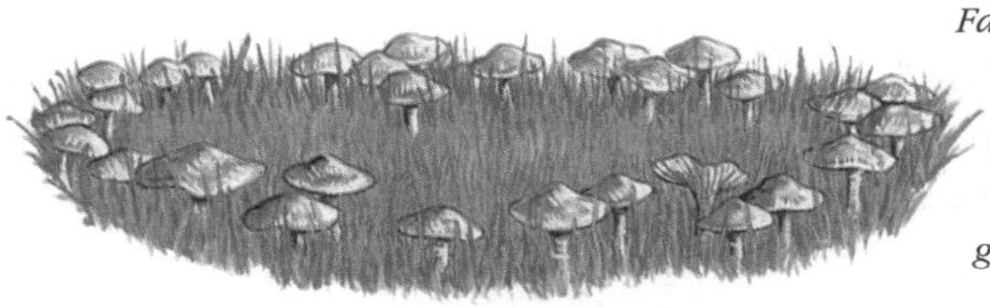

Fairy ring toadstools often grow in rings and where the fungus grows, there is a ring of rich green grass. The threads of the fungus growing in the soil break down dead matter and release minerals that make the grass grow better.

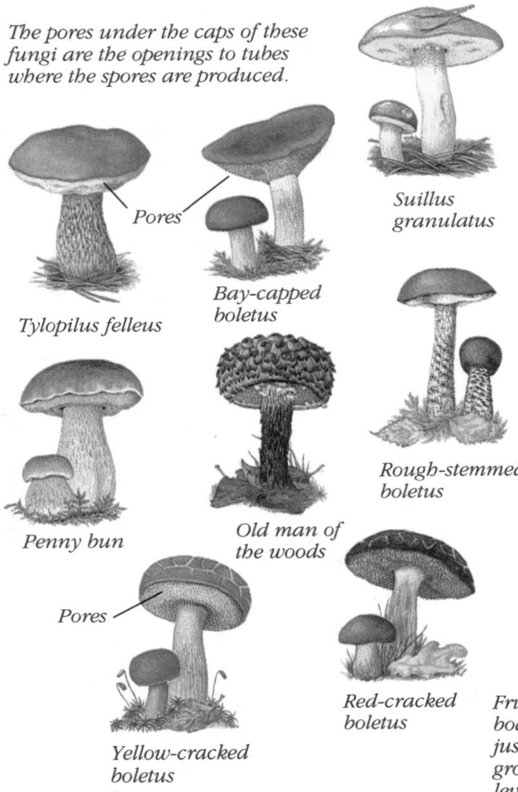
The pores under the caps of these fungi are the openings to tubes where the spores are produced.
Suillus granulatus
Pores
Tylopilus felleus
Bay-capped boletus
Penny bun
Old man of the woods
Rough-stemmed boletus
Pores
Yellow-cracked boletus
Red-cracked boletus

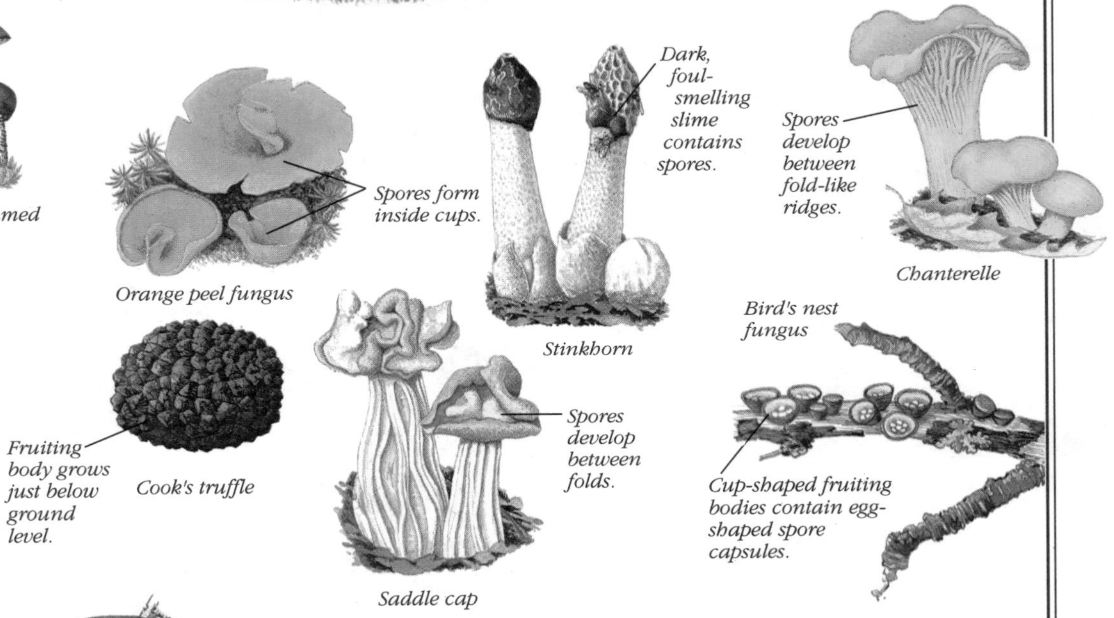
Spores form inside cups.
Orange peel fungus
Fruiting body grows just below ground level.
Cook's truffle
Dark, foul-smelling slime contains spores.
Stinkhorn
Spores develop between folds.
Saddle cap
Spores develop between fold-like ridges.
Chanterelle
Bird's nest fungus
Cup-shaped fruiting bodies contain egg-shaped spore capsules.

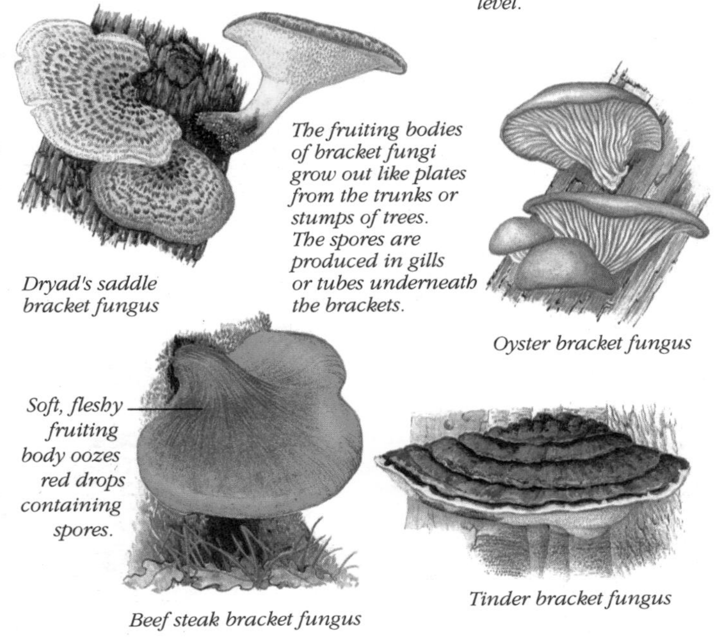
Dryad's saddle bracket fungus
The fruiting bodies of bracket fungi grow out like plates from the trunks or stumps of trees. The spores are produced in gills or tubes underneath the brackets.
Oyster bracket fungus
Soft, fleshy fruiting body oozes red drops containing spores.
Tinder bracket fungus
Beef steak bracket fungus

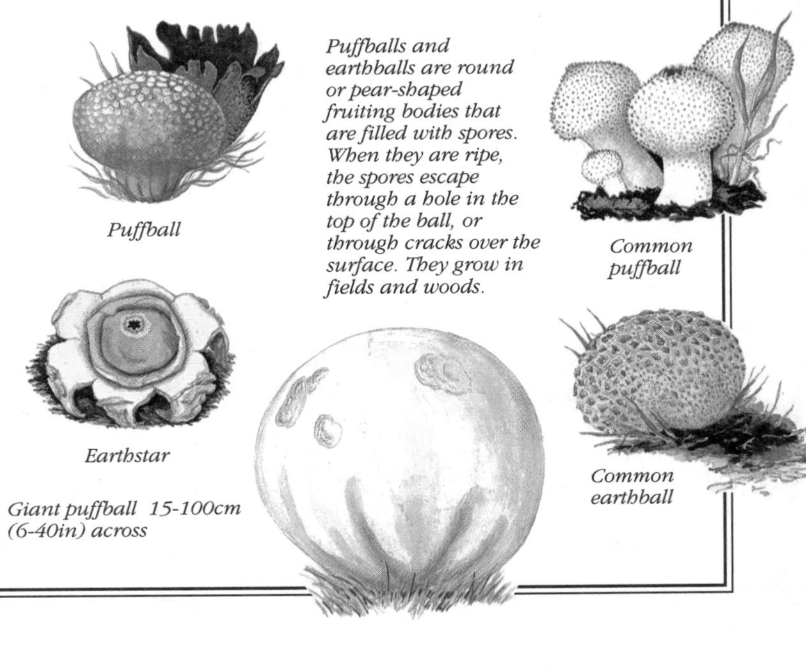
Puffball
Puffballs and earthballs are round or pear-shaped fruiting bodies that are filled with spores. When they are ripe, the spores escape through a hole in the top of the ball, or through cracks over the surface. They grow in fields and woods.
Common puffball
Earthstar
Giant puffball 15-100cm (6-40in) across
Common earthball

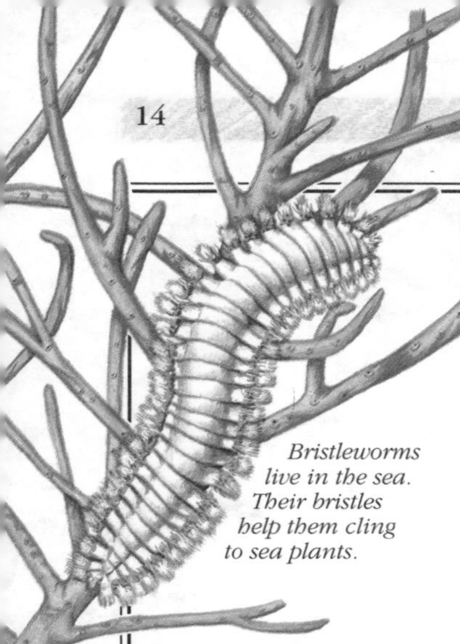

Bristleworms live in the sea. Their bristles help them cling to sea plants.

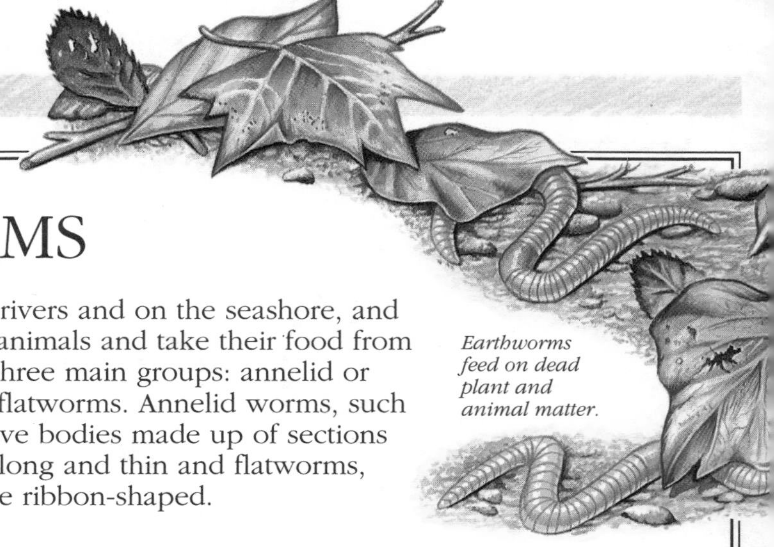

Earthworms feed on dead plant and animal matter.

WORMS

Worms live in the soil, in ponds and rivers and on the seashore, and many are parasites: they live in other animals and take their food from them. Worms can be divided into three main groups: annelid or segmented worms, roundworms and flatworms. Annelid worms, such as earthworms and bristleworms, have bodies made up of sections called segments; roundworms are long and thin and flatworms, such as tapeworms, are ribbon-shaped.

EARTHWORMS

Earthworms live in soil all over the world and some Australian earthworms can grow over 3m (nearly 10ft) long. The body of an earthworm is made up of segments and it has bristles that help it to grip the soil as it moves through its tunnels.

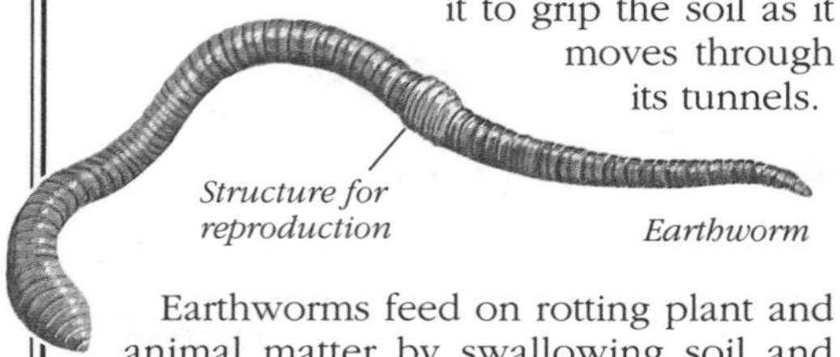

Structure for reproduction

Earthworm

Earthworms feed on rotting plant and animal matter by swallowing soil and digesting the dead plants and animals. The waste soil that comes out of their bodies contains minerals. In this way, earthworms help recycle the substances that plants need to grow.

An earthworm's burrow may reach 2m (6.5ft) below the surface. Worms drag dead leaves into their tunnels and store them in their burrows. This helps to return minerals to the lower levels of the soil. The tunnels also allow air and water to reach the roots of plants.

LEECHES

Leeches are segmented worms. Some live by sucking blood from animals or people and others are predators. Horse leeches swallow small worms, snails insects and tadpoles.

In the past, doctors used the medicinal leech to suck blood from sick people in the belief that taking away "bad blood" would make them better.

Leeches swim with waving movements.

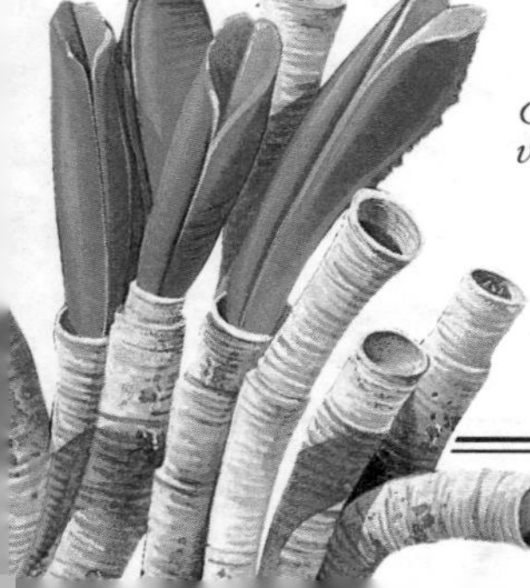

Giant tube worms live in the very deepest parts of the oceans over 10,000m (33,000ft) below sea level. They belong to another group of worms called beard worms and they feed on bacteria.

BRISTLEWORMS

There are thousands of different species of bristleworms, including ragworms, lugworms, keel worms and the sea mouse. Bristleworms are annelid worms. They all live in the sea or sand and have bristles along their sides that help them move over sea plants and the sand. They mainly eat plants and dead sea animals.

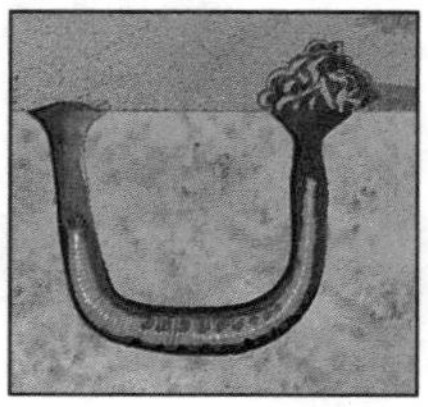

Lugworms live in U-shaped burrows in the sand. They swallow sand and feed on dead plant and animal matter. The waste sand that comes out of their bodies is left as squiggly casts.

Ragworms burrow in the sand and feed on small creatures which they grip with their jaws. The bristles along their sides make them look like pieces of torn rag.

Bristles help worms grip the sand.

The sea mouse is a bristleworm. It is covered with short hairs and is about 10cm (4in) long.

Keel worms live in chalky tubes on rocks or shells. They collect food with tentacles that poke out f their tubes.

ROUNDWORMS

There are over 10,000 different species of roundworms. They have pointed ends and no segments and many are so small they cannot be seen without a microscope. Many cause diseases in plants and animals. Hookworms are believed to be the cause of illness in over a quarter of the world's population.

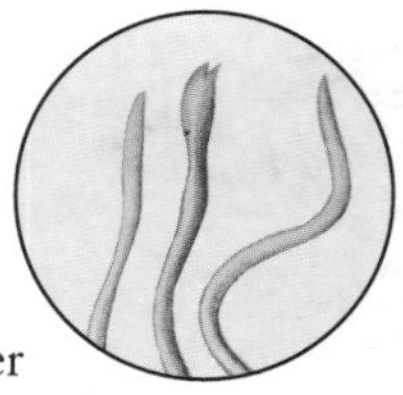

Pinworms - a species of roundworm

TAPEWORMS

Tapeworms live in the intestines of small mammals and sometimes people. They are made up of many segments and can grow over 2m (6ft) long. The segments are all identical and if any break off, they can grow to become new worms.

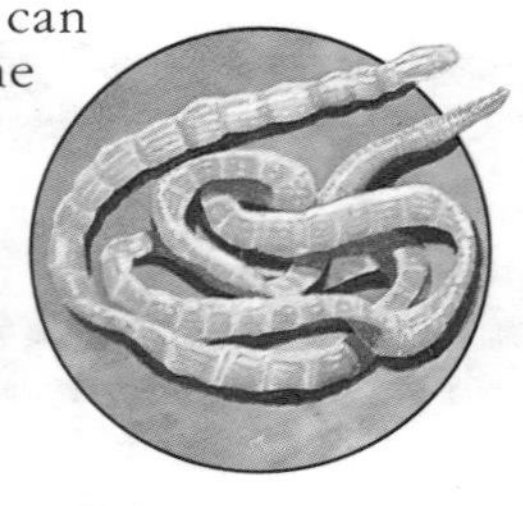

The head of the tapeworm embeds itself in the wall of its host's intestines. It absorbs food all along its body.

A tapeworm produces eggs that pass out of the animal it is living in and are eaten by a second animal. The eggs hatch into larvae that burrow into the animal's flesh, where they stay until the animal happens to be eaten. Then the larvae grow into new tapeworms in the intestines of the new host.

FLUKES

Flukes are a kind of parasitic flatworm. Like tapeworms, they need two hosts to complete their life cycle. They live in the livers of sheep. Their eggs pass out of the sheep and the larvae grow in small water creatures such as pond snails.

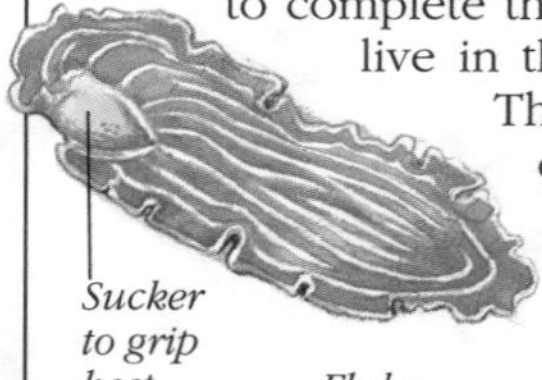

Sucker to grip host

Fluke

SEE FOR YOURSELF

To see how earthworms mix up soil, put layers of sand and soil in a large, transparent container. Add a few worms and some leaves. Then tie some paper around the container to keep out the light.

After a few days, examine the container to see how the worms have mixed up all the layers. Then very carefully put the worms back where you found them.

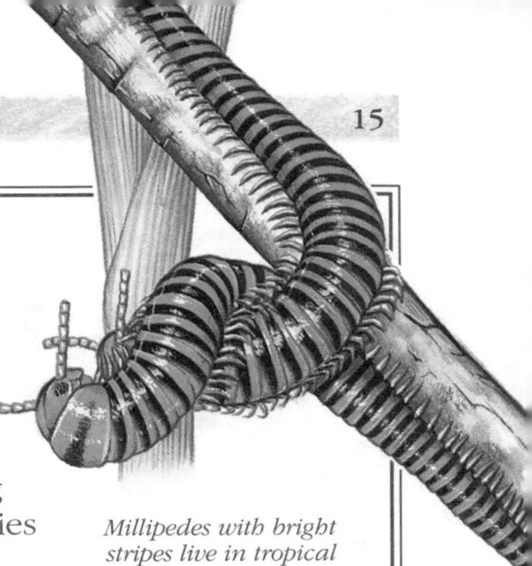

Above: pointed snail; above right: great grey slug

Banded snail

Millipedes with bright stripes live in tropical rainforests. These ones are mating.

SNAILS AND SLUGS

CENTIPEDES, MILLIPEDES AND WOODLICE

Snails and slugs belong to a group of animals called gastropods*, which means "belly-feet". Centipedes, millipedes and woodlice belong to a group called arthropods*, which means "jointed-feet", and their bodies are made up of many segments. They all live in damp places so their bodies do not dry out, and some slugs and snails live in water.

SNAILS

Snails live in damp places, among plants, under stones or in the soil. Like shellfish, they are molluscs* and they belong to a group of molluscs called gastropods.

Plug of mucus

In very dry weather, snails pull their bodies inside their shells. Their slimy mucus hardens to form a plug.

During the day, garden snails cluster together in damp, shady places. They come out to feed at night and then return to their resting places, following their trails of mucus. They feed on plants, scraping off the surface of the leaves with their rough tongues.

Snails lay round white eggs and bury them in holes in the ground.

Snails are hermaphrodite, which means that each snail has both male and female sex organs. After mating, they lay eggs which hatch about four weeks later. The baby snails have thin shells that get bigger as the snails grow.

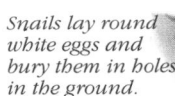

The shell of the African giant snail is about 20cm (8in) long. Giant snails eat plants, fruits and dead animals. Beside this giant snail there is a baby giant snail.

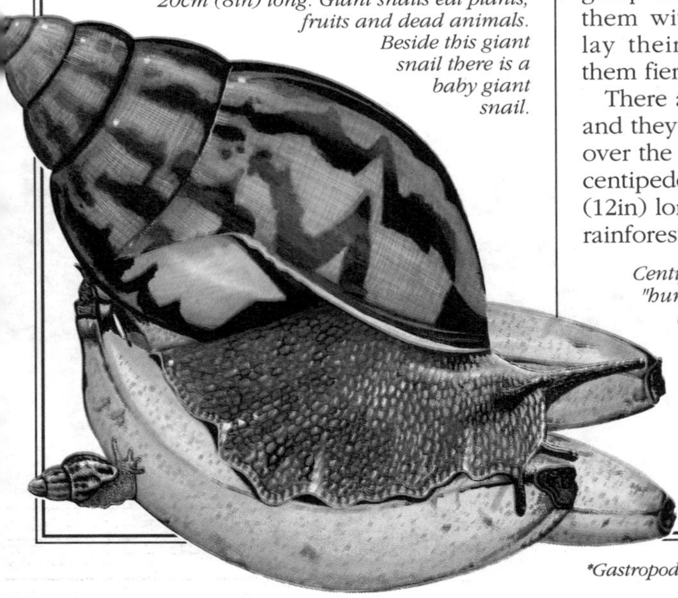

SLUGS

Slugs are snails that have no shells. There are land slugs and sea slugs, which are called nudibranchs. Land slugs feed on plant matter and sea slugs are carnivores.

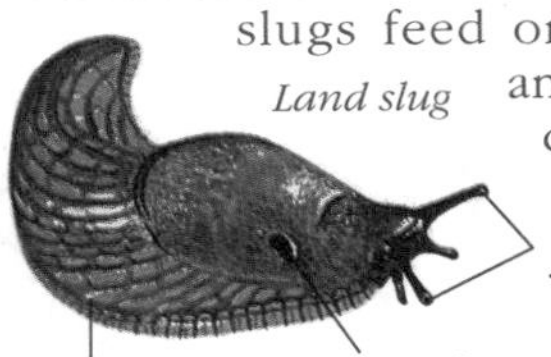
Land slug
Tentacles for feeling and smelling
Muscular foot
Breathing hole

In cold or very dry weather, land slugs burrow deep in the soil. They come out at night when it is damp or rainy and move along by stretching and contracting their muscular foot. They also make a trail of slime that helps them slide along. The slime has an unpleasant taste and this helps to protect them from predators.

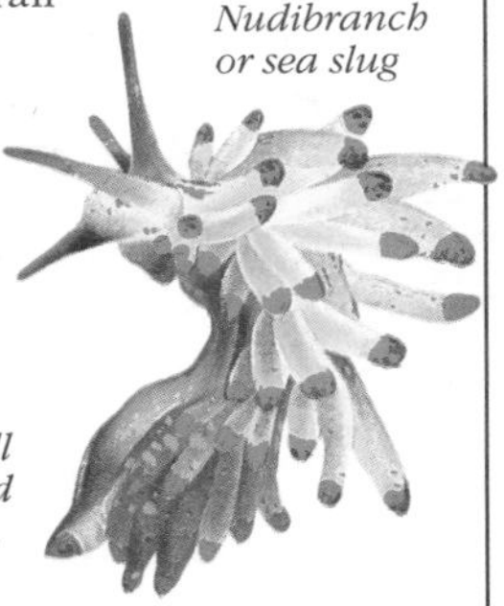
Nudibranch or sea slug

Sea slugs live in seas all over the world and feed on small sea creatures. Their bright patterns warn that they are poisonous.

CENTIPEDES

Centipedes are fast hunters. They come out at night and feed on animals such as slugs, woodlice and earwigs. They grasp them with their fangs and kill them with poison. Female centipedes lay their eggs in the soil and guard them fiercely against predators.

There are 2,800 species of centipedes and they are found all over the world. Giant centipedes over 30cm (12in) long live in rainforests.

Antennae
Giant centipede

Centipede means "hundred legs" but most species have only 30.

MILLIPEDES

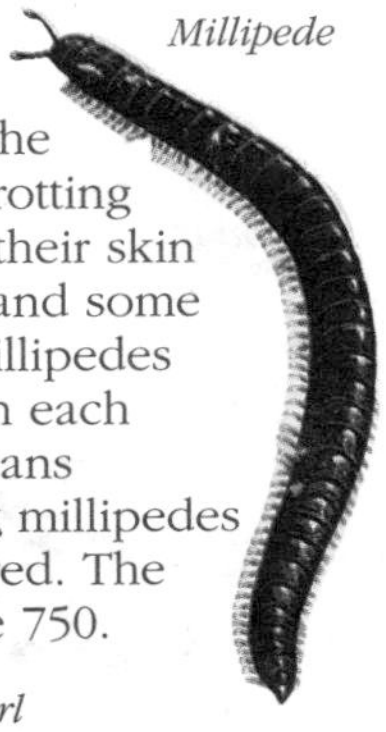
Millipede

There are about 8,000 different species of millipedes. They live in the soil and feed mainly on rotting plants. The segments of their skin overlap to protect them and some can curl up into balls. Millipedes have two pairs of legs on each segment. Their name means "thousand legs" but most millipedes have only about a hundred. The longest have 750.

Millipedes curl into tight balls when they are disturbed.

Pill millipedes (right) look like woodlice but have more legs.

WOODLICE

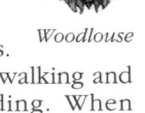

Woodlice belong to a group of arthropods called crustaceans*, the same group to which crabs* and shrimps* belong. They live in damp places under stones and leaves, and come out at night to feed on dead plants. They have 14 legs for walking and two more for feeding. When disturbed, many roll up into balls for protection.

Woodlouse

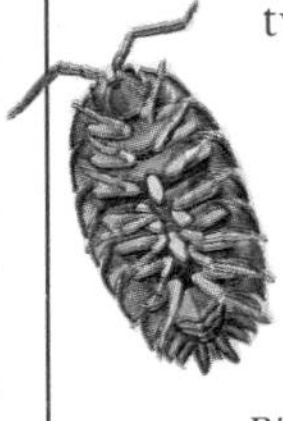

Left: female woodlice carry their young in pouches under their bodies.

Right: as woodlice grow, they shed their skins and grow new, larger ones.

SEE FOR YOURSELF

Woodlice like dark, damp places. If you put a few on one side of a dish and cover the other side with a piece of cloth, the woodlice will soon move to the dark side. After the experiment, carefully put them back where you found them.

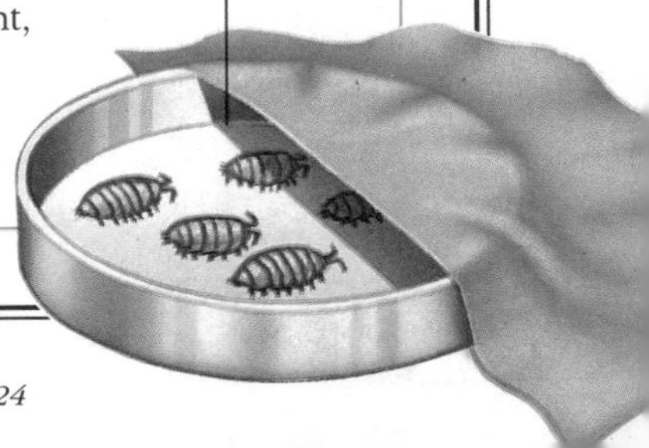

Woodlice move to dark area.

*Gastropods, 88; Arthropods, 88; Molluscs, 88

*Crustaceans, 24; Crabs, 24; Shrimps, 24

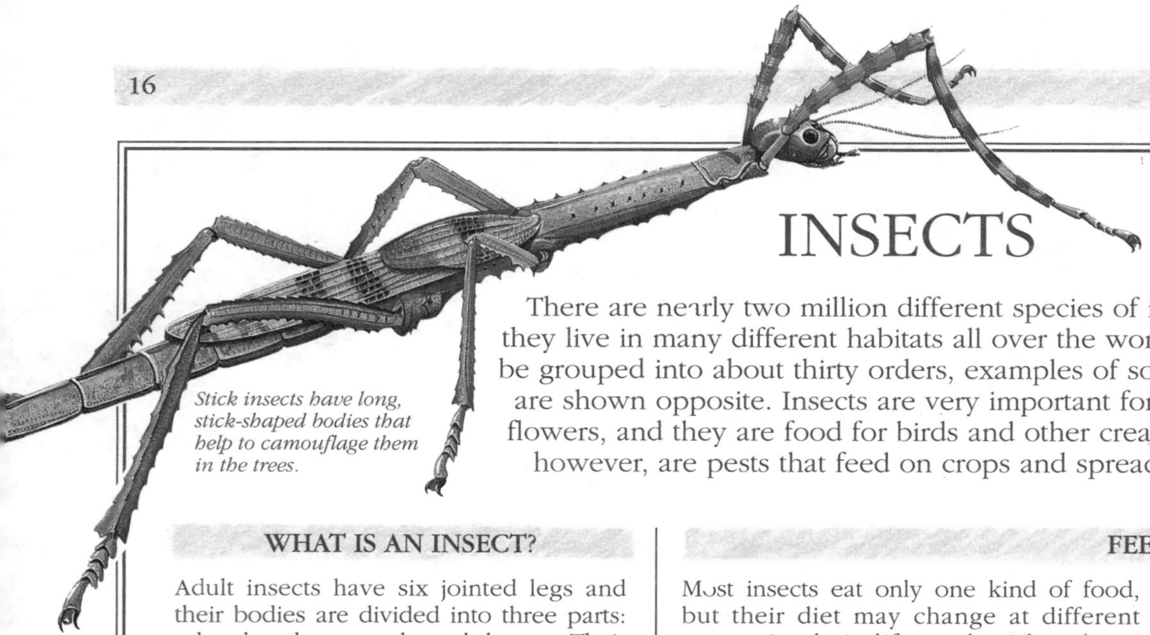

INSECTS

There are nearly two million different species of insects and they live in many different habitats all over the world. They can be grouped into about thirty orders, examples of some of which are shown opposite. Insects are very important for pollinating flowers, and they are food for birds and other creatures. Many, however, are pests that feed on crops and spread diseases.

Stick insects have long, stick-shaped bodies that help to camouflage them in the trees.

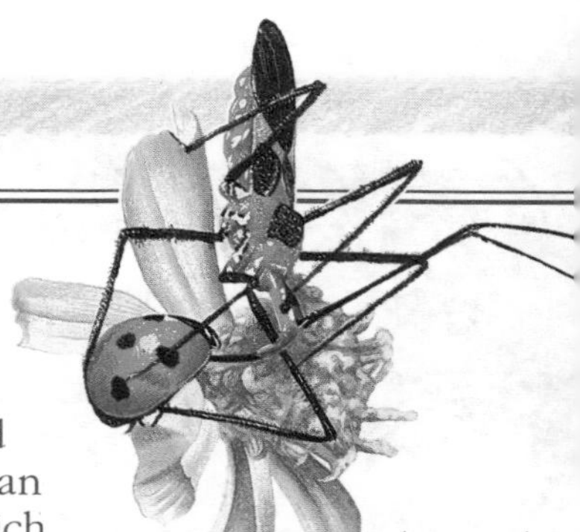

An assassin bug injects saliva into its prey, then sucks its juices.

WHAT IS AN INSECT?

Adult insects have six jointed legs and their bodies are divided into three parts: a head, a thorax and an abdomen. Their legs are attached to the thorax and on their heads they have a pair of antennae. Most adult insects have two pairs of wings and their bodies are covered with a hard skin called an exoskeleton.

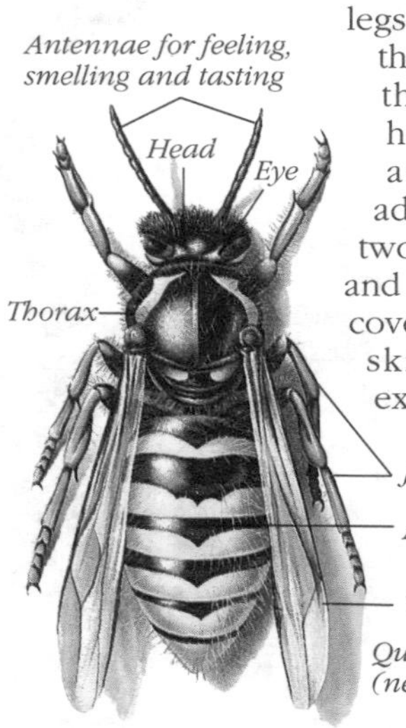

Antennae for feeling, smelling and tasting
Head
Eye
Thorax
Jointed legs
Abdomen
Wing

Queen tree wasp 2cm (nearly 1in) long

FEEDING

Most insects eat only one kind of food, but their diet may change at different stages in their life cycle. They have different shaped mouth parts depending on the food they eat.

More than half of all insects feed on plants and may damage them. But insects that feed on dead plants and animals play an important role in helping to break down the dead matter so the minerals can return to the soil and be recycled (see Nitrogen Cycle*).

Burying beetle

Burying beetles feed on dead animals. They bury them by digging out the soil from under them.

Insects that eat plants may feed on the leaves, roots or seeds, suck sap from the stems or take nectar or pollen from the flowers. The mouth part of insects that suck sap or nectar is a long tube called a proboscis (pronounced "pro-boss-kiss").

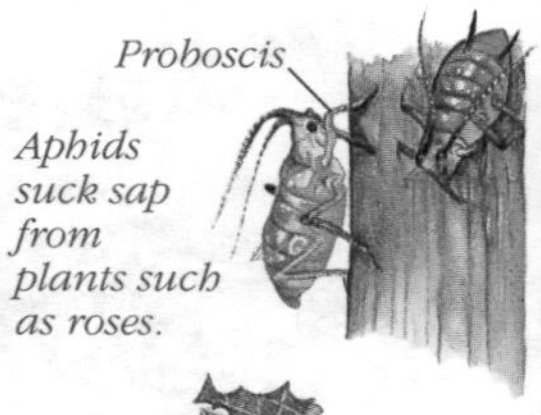

Proboscis

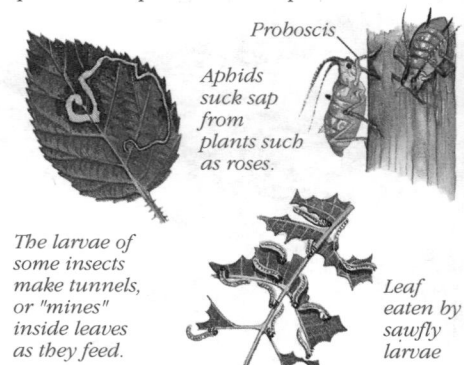

Aphids suck sap from plants such as roses.

The larvae of some insects make tunnels, or "mines" inside leaves as they feed.

Leaf eaten by sawfly larvae

Insects that feed on animals may suck blood like mosquitoes, eat other insects or feed on dead animal matter. Bloodsuckers have a mouth part called a stylet and insects that eat solid matter have biting mouth parts called mandibles.

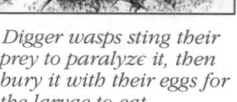

Female mosquitoes suck animal blood. Males suck nectar from flowers.

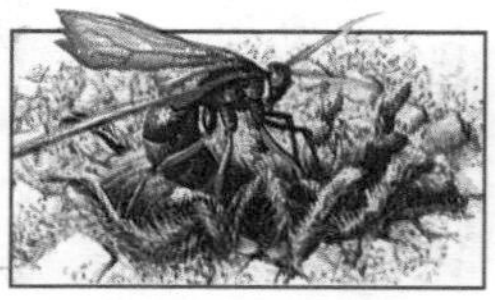

Digger wasps sting their prey to paralyze it, then bury it with their eggs for the larvae to eat.

Dung beetles feed on animal droppings. They also roll the dung into balls which they store in their underground burrows.

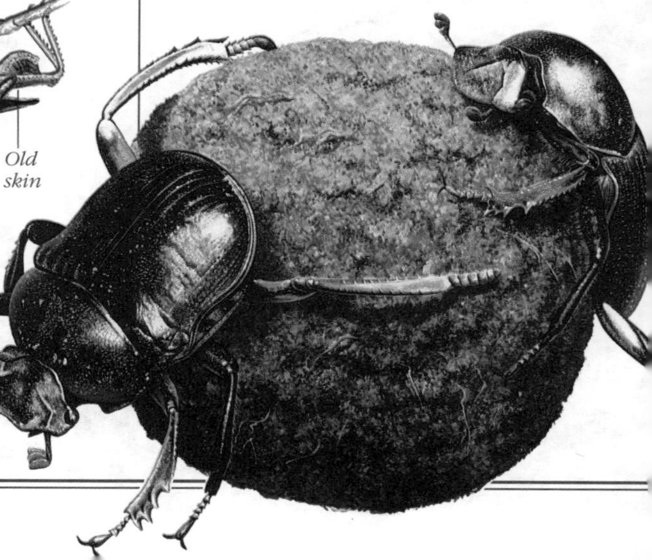

INSECT LIFE CYCLE

Insects hatch from eggs. The young may not look like their parents and they pass through several stages before becoming adults. Insects are divided into two groups according to the stages in their life cycle. The young of one group are called larvae. The larvae feed and grow and then become pupae. Inside the pupae, they change and become adults. This change is called metamorphosis.

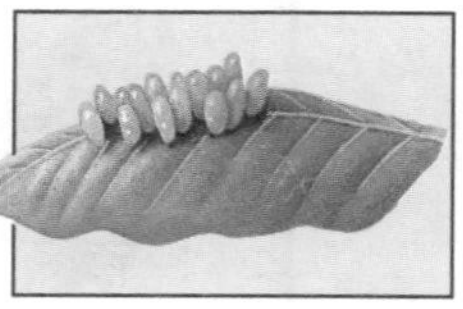

After mating, a female ladybird (ladybug) lays a cluster of tiny eggs on a leaf. A few days later, a larva hatches from each egg.

The larvae feed on tiny insects called aphids, and they grow very rapidly. As they grow, they shed their hard skins several times.

Pupa

After several weeks, the larvae stop feeding and become pupae. Inside the pupae, they gradually change to become adult insects.

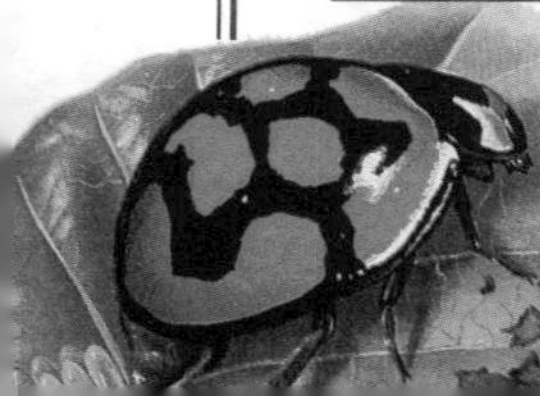

Adult five-spotted ladybird (ladybug) laying eggs

The young of the second group of insects, which includes grasshoppers and earwigs, are called nymphs. When they hatch, many look like their parents but they have no wings. Nymphs do not become pupae. As they grow, they shed their skins several times and their wings gradually grow until they are adults. This change is called incomplete metamorphosis.

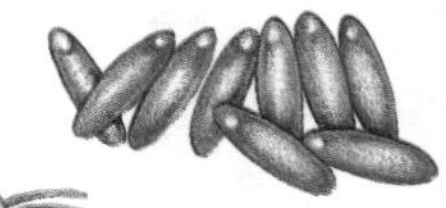

Locust eggs

Locust nymphs are called hoppers. A hopper has no wings.

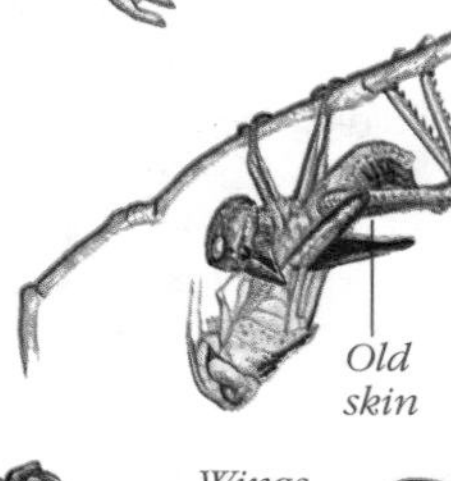

Old skin

Hoppers shed their hard skins several times as they grow.

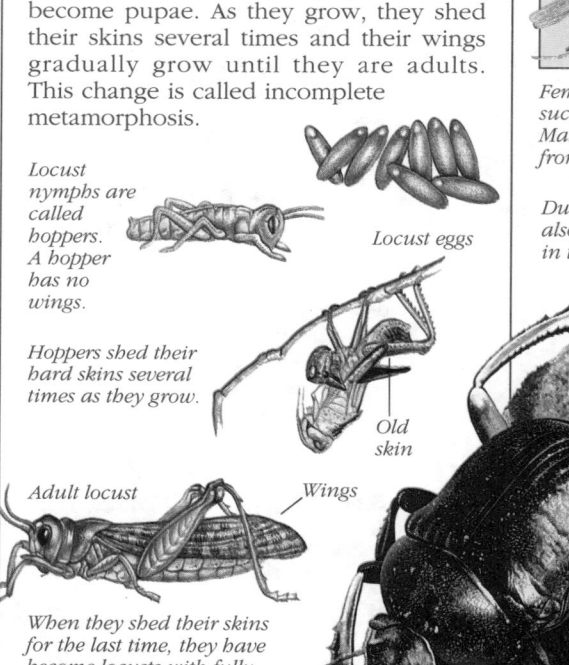

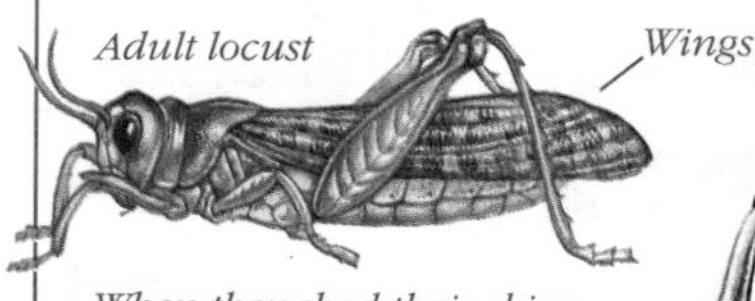

Adult locust
Wings

When they shed their skins for the last time, they have become locusts with fully-grown wings.

*Nitrogen Cycle, 69

THE WORLD OF INSECTS

There are nearly two million known species of insects, but scientists believe there may be several million more yet to be discovered. These pictures show insects from some of the main orders (groups). They are not to scale.

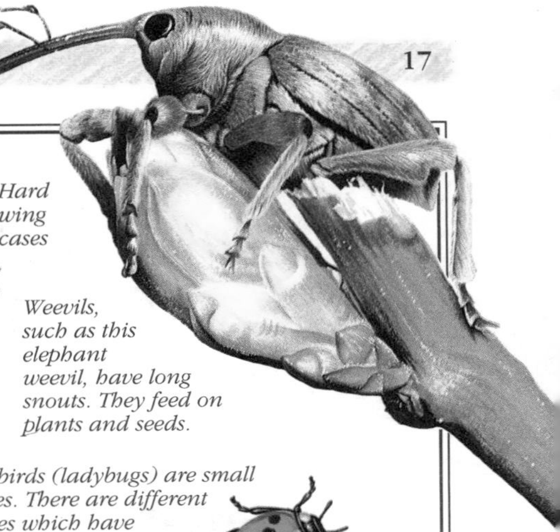

Weevils, such as this elephant weevil, have long snouts. They feed on plants and seeds.

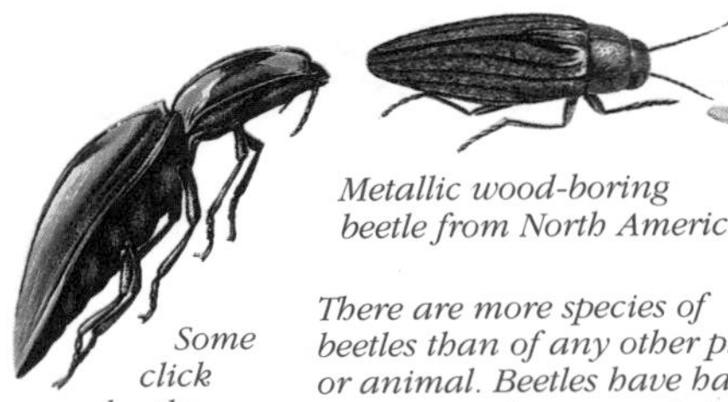

Some click beetles can jump 30cm (12in) into the air.

Metallic wood-boring beetle from North America

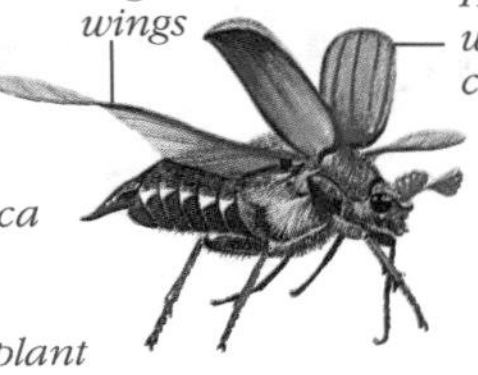
Flight wings
Hard wing cases

Cockchafer beetle

There are more species of beetles than of any other plant or animal. Beetles have hard wing cases that cover their wings. Their mouth parts are adapted for biting and chewing. Some species eat plants and others are predators.

Banded demoiselle damselfly

Common hawker dragonfly

Dragonflies and damselflies* live near water and their nymphs live in the water. They are predators and eat other insects and even tadpoles and small fish.

Glow-worms and firefly beetles produce light from a special organ in their abdomens. The light helps them to attract a mate.

Female glow-worms (left) have no wings.

Ladybirds (ladybugs) are small beetles. There are different species which have different numbers of spots. They mainly eat aphids.

The Goliath beetle (left) is the heaviest flying insect. It is 13cm (5in) long and weighs 100gm (3.5oz).

There are about 1,200 species of earwigs. They eat plants or small flies. The pincers on their abdomens are for grasping their prey, and defending themselves.

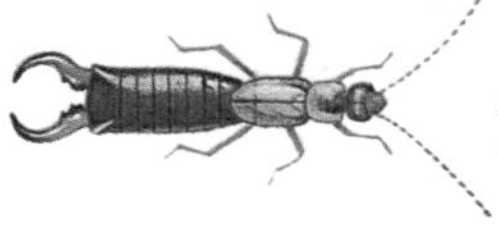

European earwig

Common cockroach

Most cockroaches live in the tropics, but they are found in buildings all over the world. There are about 4,000 different species of cockroaches.

Butterflies and moths* belong to the same order and are called lepidopterans. They have scaly wings, often with bright patterns to camouflage them or to warn that they are poisonous.

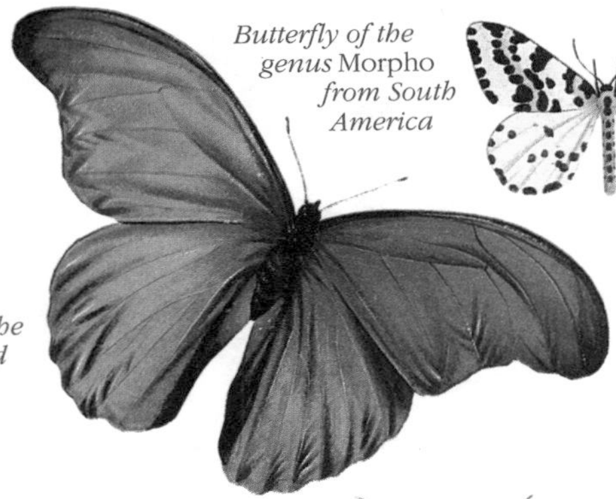

Butterfly of the genus Morpho from South America

Magpie moth

There are 85,000 known species of flies. They have one main pair of wings and a second, very small pair called halteres, to help them balance.

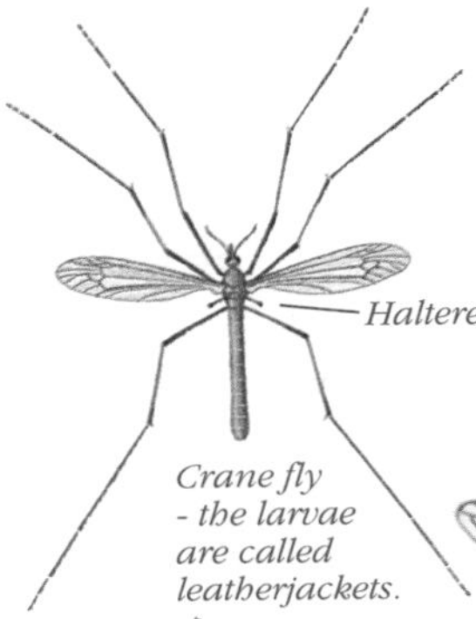
Halteres

Crane fly - the larvae are called leatherjackets.

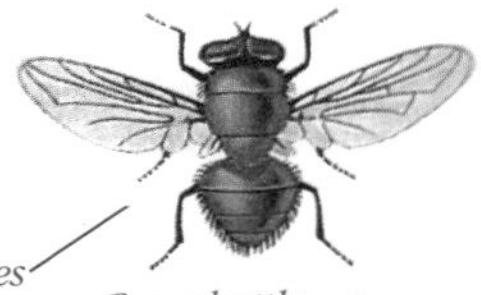

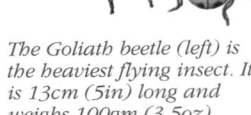

Greenbottle - a species of blowfly

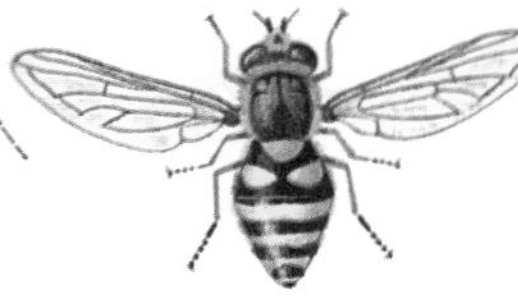

Hoverfly

Housefly - the larvae are maggots.

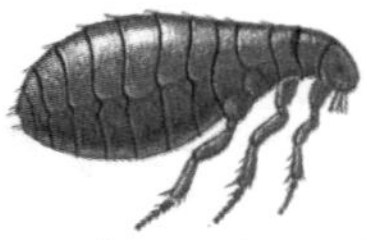

Cat flea - 2-3mm (0.1in) long

There are 1,400 different species of fleas. They suck animal blood and their bodies are flattened sideways so they can pass between hairs. They have strong back legs for jumping.

Froghopper

Hawthorn shield bug

Capsid bug

There are 60,000 different species of bugs. Some suck plant juices and others are blood-suckers.

Grasshoppers and crickets leap and can glide with their wings open, but they cannot fly. They make sounds by rubbing their wings together. Locusts* can fly They make a noise by rubbing their legs and wings together.

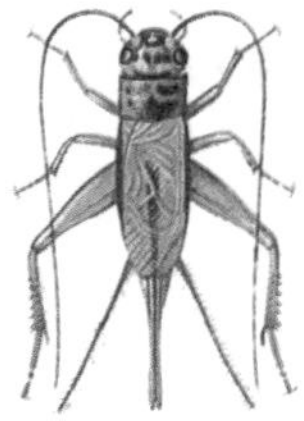

Crickets have long antennae.

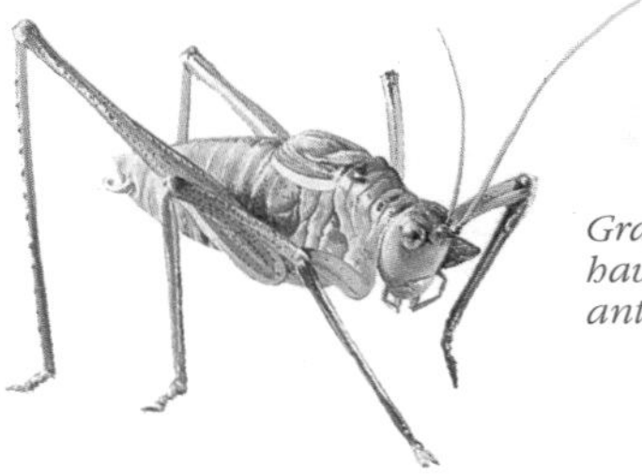

Grasshoppers have short antennae.

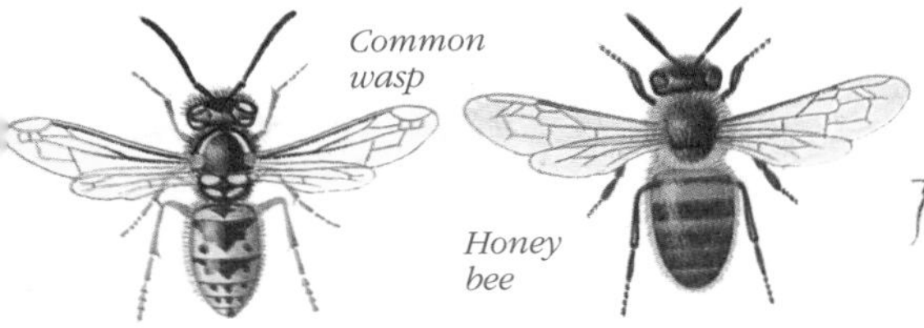

Common wasp

Honey bee

Bees* feed on pollen and nectar. Wasps* eat other insects or plants. Some species live alone and others are social insects that live in groups, or colonies, of thousands of insects.

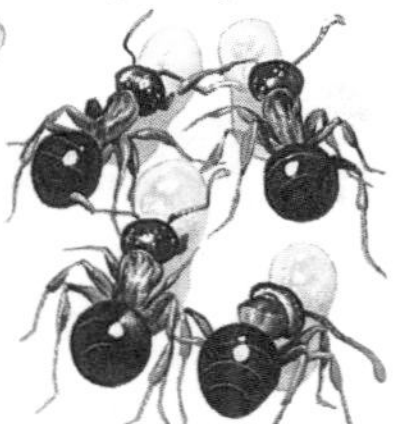

There are 10,000 different species of ants*. They are social insects and live together in nests, sharing the work of getting food and raising the young.

Velvet ants are not ants, but very hairy wasps. They lay their eggs in the nests of other bees or wasps.

Leaf insects have flat, leaf-like bodies. They live in Southeast Asian forests.

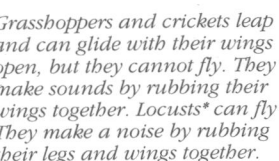

Soldier termite grasping an ant

Termites* build huge nests where thousands of termites live together.

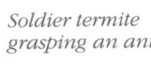

Termite nest

* Bees, 20; Wasps, 20; Butterflies and Moths, 18; Dragonflies and Damselflies, 71

*Ants, 21; Termites, 21; Locusts, 75

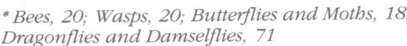

Wall butterfly

Common blue butterfly

BUTTERFLIES AND MOTHS

Magpie moth

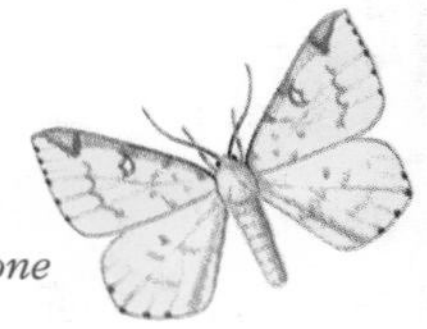

Brimstone moth

Butterflies and moths belong to a group of insects called lepidopterans, which means "scaly wings". Most feed on nectar, the sweet syrup produced by flowers. Butterflies feed during the day and moths feed at night. Like all insects, butterflies and moths go through several different stages during their life cycle* and their young are called caterpillars.

BUTTERFLIES

Butterflies, like other insects, have six legs and three body parts: head, thorax and abdomen. Their legs are attached to the thorax. On their heads they have a pair of antennae with which they feel and smell.

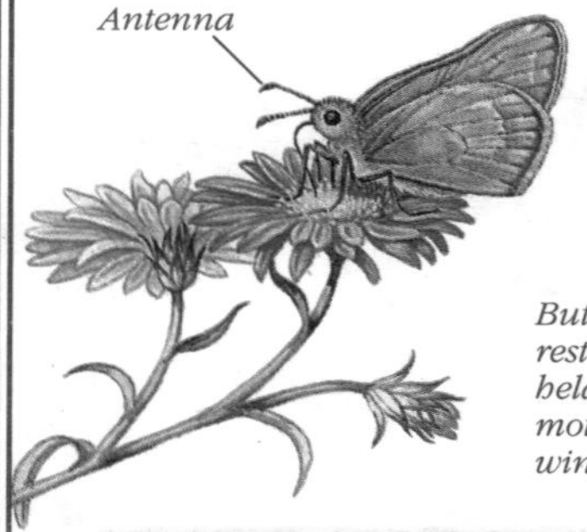
Antenna

Most butterflies have knobs at the tips of their antennae.

Butterflies usually rest with their wings held upright. Most moths rest with their wings open flat.

MOTHS

There is no biological difference between moths and butterflies, but moths are adapted to fly at night. Their bodies are hairy to keep them warm, and they have sensitive antennae with feathery tips. Most moths are not so brightly patterned as butterflies.

Moths usually have feathery antennae.

FEEDING

Both butterflies and moths have a long tube called a proboscis (pronounced "pro-boss-kiss") with which they suck nectar from flowers. The proboscis is curled up when they are not feeding. Some moths also drink sap from plants, and one type of moth sucks animals' blood.

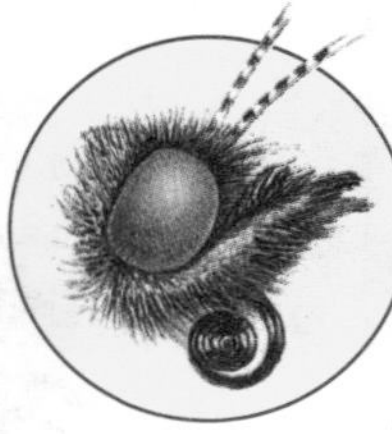

Butterflies and moths suck nectar through a tube called a proboscis. When they are not feeding, the tube is curled up.

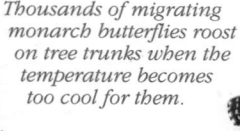

Thousands of migrating monarch butterflies roost on tree trunks when the temperature becomes too cool for them.

LIFE CYCLE

Most butterflies and moths live for a few weeks and then mate and lay eggs that hatch into larvae called caterpillars. In cold countries, some butterflies and moths hibernate and lay their eggs in the spring. Others pass the winter months as caterpillars or in a resting stage called a pupa (see below right).

Butterfly and moth eggs

In the spring, male and female spotted fritillary butterflies of southern Europe pair up and mate. Then the female butterfly lays her eggs on a small plant.

After a few days, the eggs hatch into caterpillars. During the summer, the brown, hairy caterpillars feed on leaves and grow large and fat.

In the autumn, each caterpillar grows a hard outer coating called a pupa (see right). This protects it during the harsh winter months.

Inside the pupa, the caterpillar slowly changes into a butterfly. In spring, the butterfly comes out of the pupa and searches for a mate.

To avoid the cold in the winter, some butterflies migrate to warmer climates. Monarch butterflies (see far left) migrate 4,000km (about 2,500 miles) from North America to Mexico. Thousands of these butterflies roost together on tree trunks when the temperature drops below 15°C (59°F). Painted lady butterflies migrate about 5,000km (3,100 miles) from Europe to spend the winter in Africa.

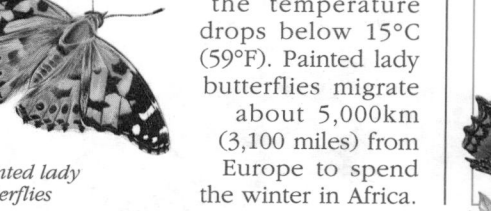

Painted lady butterflies

CATERPILLARS

Caterpillars are the young of butterflies and moths. When they are fully grown, they become pupae (see below) and change into adult butterflies or moths.

Most caterpillars feed on leaves, but some moth caterpillars feed on cotton and wool and damage clothes. As they grow, they shed their skins because their skin does not grow. When it is too small, the skin splits and the caterpillar wriggles out in a new skin. This happens several times until the caterpillar is fully grown and becomes a pupa.

Privet hawk moth caterpillar

Mandibles (mouth parts) for chewing
Three pairs of front legs for gripping food
Air holes through which caterpillar breathes
Five pairs of fleshy claspers

PUPAE

A pupa, or chrysalis, is a resting stage during which a caterpillar changes into a moth or butterfly. This change is called metamorphosis*. After feeding for several weeks, a caterpillar buries itself in the ground, or hangs from a twig or leaf. It sheds its skin and becomes a pupa. Inside the pupa, the caterpillar slowly turns into a butterfly or moth. The pupa has a hard case and some, such as those of silkworm moths, are covered with cocoons of silk.

Butterfly emerging from its pupa

SEE FOR YOURSELF

Most butterflies prefer to visit one particular type of flower. If you are in a garden or the countryside in spring or summer, watch the butterflies to see which flowers they visit.

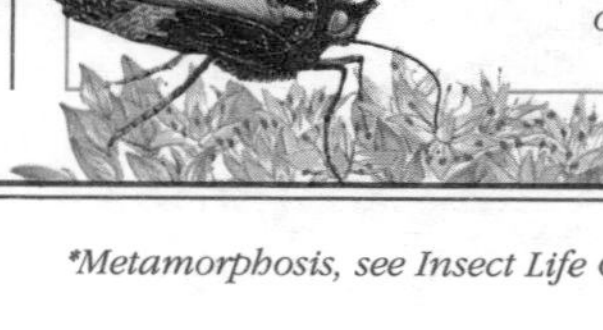

Small tortoiseshell butterfly feeding on ice plant

*Life cycle, see Insect Life Cycle, 16

*Metamorphosis, see Insect Life Cycle, 16

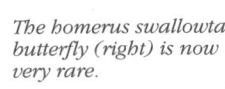

False head and antennae of hairstreak butterfly

Hairstreak butterflies (above) have a false head at the back of their wings. Birds are confused and peck the false head.

WORLD BUTTERFLIES, MOTHS AND CATERPILLARS

There are about 150,000 different species of butterflies and moths. Many have patterns to camouflage them, or to warn predators to leave them alone because they are poisonous. The patterns are made by tiny, overlapping scales on their wings, which reflect the light.

Mocker swallowtail butterflies have evolved to look like poisonous species, such as the poisonous friar butterfly and African monarch shown on the right. Birds quickly learn to recognize the poisonous butterflies and leave them alone - so they avoid the mocker butterflies too.

Poisonous friar butterfly

Mocker swallowtail

Poisonous African monarch butterfly

Mocker swallowtail

The homerus swallowtail butterfly (right) is now very rare.

Rare orange forester butterfly

Many species of butterflies are now very rare. The wild areas where they lived have been destroyed, and the flowers from which they fed have been killed by pesticides. Some are rare because they are collected.

Many butterflies, moths and caterpillars have markings that help to camouflage them against the plants on which they usually feed or rest. This makes it much harder for predators such as birds to spot them.

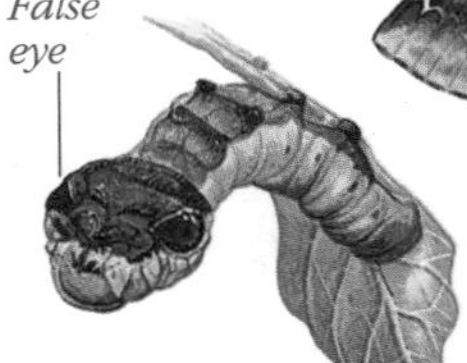

False eye

Hawkmoth caterpillar

Io moth

Owl butterfly

Many butterflies and moths, and even some caterpillars, defend themselves with false eyes that fool birds and other attackers into leaving them alone.

The patterns on the wings of buff-tip moths make them very hard to see against tree bark.

False eye mark

Meadow brown butterfly

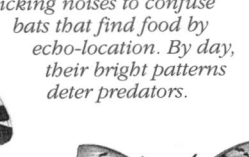

A bird attacked this butterfly (above), but it pecked its false eye mark and not its body, so the butterfly survived.

Peacock butterfly

False eye marks

Emperor moths live on heaths and moorland.

The dark wings of the Arctic ringlet (right) absorb warmth in the cold areas where it lives.

There are so many butterflies in the rainforest that many do not have common names, only scientific ones. Six examples are shown below.

Callicore cyllene

Papilio karna

Callithea optima

Callicore mengeli

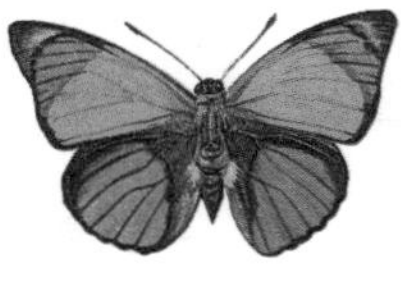

Agrias claudina

The green wings of a forester moth help to camouflage it.

The brown, ragged wings of a comma butterfly look like dead leaves on the forest floor.

Tiger moths make high-pitched clicking noises to confuse bats that find food by echo-location. By day, their bright patterns deter predators.

Caterpillars also have ways to deter and distract birds, for whom they make a good meal. Some are hairy, which birds find distasteful, some are camouflaged to look like twigs or leaves, and some even look like bird droppings.

The woolly bear caterpillar is protected by tickly hairs. It is the larva of the tiger moth (above).

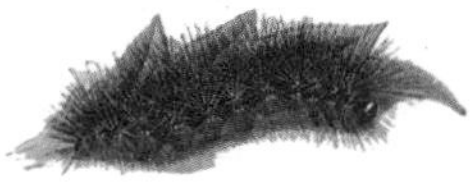

Agrias aedon

In the picture below, the world's largest and smallest butterflies are shown in proportion to each other, but not life-size.

When attacked, puss moth caterpillars (below) spit out their stomach contents.

Puss moth caterpillars also have false eye marks on their heads and long "whips" on their tails to make them look fierce.

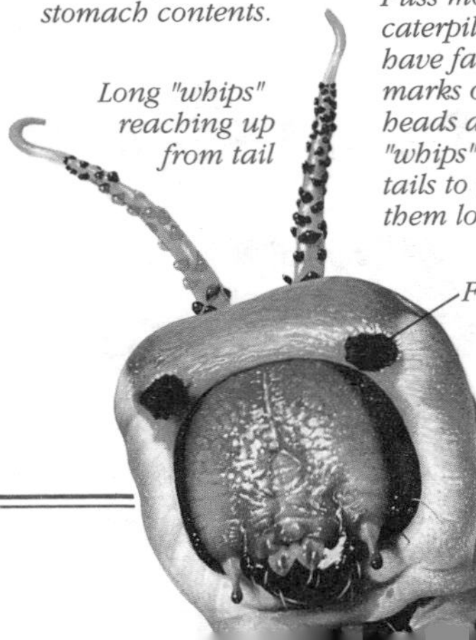

Long "whips" reaching up from tail

False eye mark

Cinnabar moth caterpillars are poisonous. They have bright stripes to warn birds not to eat them. They make their poison from the ragwort plants on which they feed.

The poplar hawk moth (right) matches the leaves on which it feeds.

Dwarf blue butterfly

Queen Alexandra's birdwing butterfly has a wing span of 28cm (11in).

BEES AND WASPS

There are many different species of bees and wasps. Some, such as honeybees and common wasps, are social insects: they live together in colonies of thousands of insects and share the work of getting food and looking after the young. Others, such as leaf-cutter bees, live alone. Like all insects, bees and wasps have several stages in their life cycle*. They lay eggs that hatch into larvae which metamorphose and become adult insects.

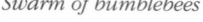

Swarm of bumblebees

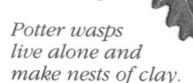

Potter wasps live alone and make nests of clay.

BEES

Bees feed on nectar and pollen that they gather from flowers. Social bees (bees that live in nests) take the nectar and pollen back to their nests and make the nectar into honey.

Bumblebee gathering pollen and nectar

In the nest, different types of bees have different jobs to do: drones are males whose only job is to mate with the queen bee, after which they die. The queen lays eggs and the workers, who are undeveloped females, find food and look after the young.

Honeybees

Drone
Worker
Queen

Honeybees build nests in walls or tree trunks - or in hives provided by people who want to collect their honey. The nests are made of thousands of wax cells where food is stored and the young are reared.

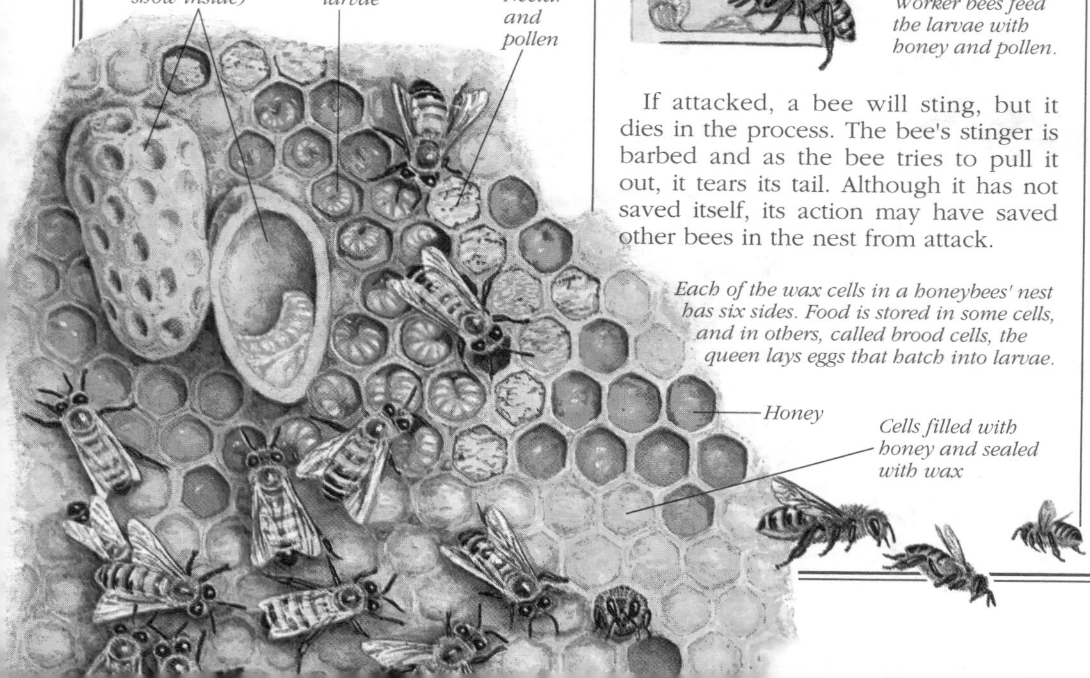
Cells containing queen bee larvae (one cut away to show inside)
Brood cells containing worker bee larvae
Nectar and pollen
Honey
Cells filled with honey and sealed with wax

Each of the wax cells in a honeybees' nest has six sides. Food is stored in some cells, and in others, called brood cells, the queen lays eggs that hatch into larvae.

The bees you see flying around are the worker bees. They tell each other where there is food by "dancing". They move around in circles and wiggle their bodies to show the other bees the distance and direction of the food from the nest. Different dances carry different information.

A "round dance" shows the other bees that the food is less than 80m (87yd) from the nest.

In the spring, the queen bee lays up to 1,500 eggs a day. The eggs hatch into larvae and are fed honey and pollen by the workers. After about six days, the larvae are big and fat and the workers seal their cells with caps of wax. Inside the cells, the larvae become pupae and metamorphose, or change, to become adult bees.

Queen bee larvae are fed a special substance, called royal jelly, which is produced by the worker bees. When they are fully grown, each new queen flies away with a swarm of workers who build a new nest.

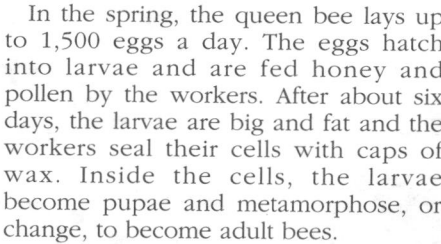

The queen bee lays an egg in each cell.

The eggs hatch into larvae.

Worker bees feed the larvae with honey and pollen.

If attacked, a bee will sting, but it dies in the process. The bee's stinger is barbed and as the bee tries to pull it out, it tears its tail. Although it has not saved itself, its action may have saved other bees in the nest from attack.

WASPS

Wasps do not make honey. Some feed their young on pellets of chewed-up insects and some are parasites that live in the bodies of other animals.

Sand wasp stinging a caterpillar to paralyze it before storing it in its nest.

Some wasps, such as gall wasps, lay their eggs in plants. The larvae then feed on the plant and cause it to produce a growth called a gall.

Galls made by oak apple gall wasps.

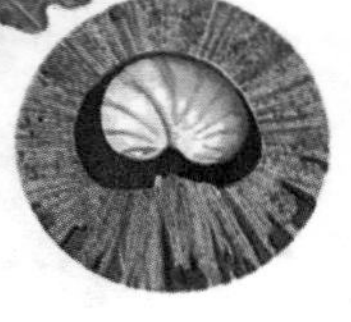

The larvae metamorphose and become adult wasps inside the galls.

Gall cut away to show larva inside.

Common wasps are social insects. They build a nest the size of a soccer ball with a papery substance made from chewed-up wood. A large nest may have 15,000 cells where larvae are reared and food is stored. Like bees, the wasp colony is divided into drones who mate with the queen, and workers who collect insects to feed the young.

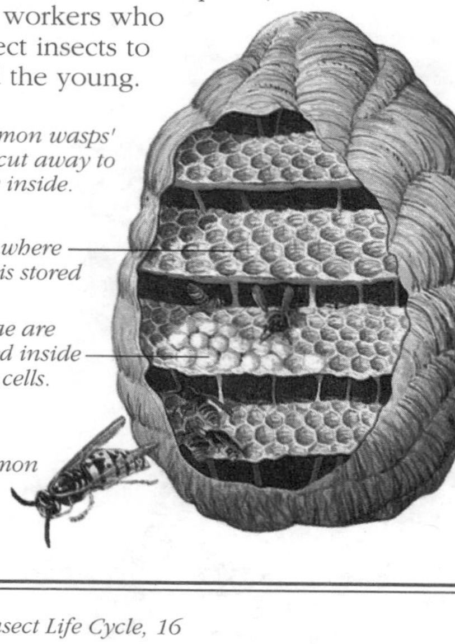
Cells where food is stored
Larvae are reared inside these cells.
Common wasp

Common wasps' nest cut away to show inside.

*Insect Life Cycle, 16

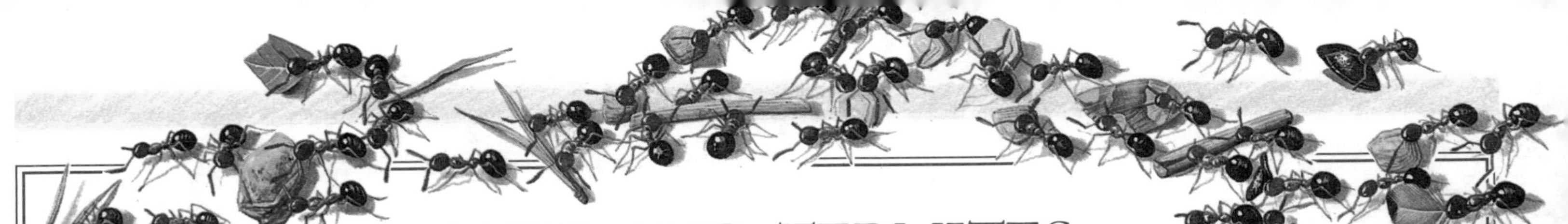

ANTS AND TERMITES

Ants and termites are social insects: they live in colonies made up of thousands of insects. Like other insects* they lay eggs that hatch into larvae, which then metamorphose and become adults. In each nest, the insects are divided into groups, or castes, that have different body shapes and different jobs to do: the queen lays eggs, workers collect food and look after the larvae, and soldiers guard the nest.

When worker ants leave the nest, they leave a scent trail for other workers to follow.

Wood ants collect seeds, leaves, insects and worms to eat.

ANTS

There are over 10,000 different species of ants and they are found all over the world, except in very cold places, such as Antarctica, Iceland and Greenland, and on some remote islands.

Wood ants live in cool woods and forests. They eat insects and can carry prey much larger than themselves.

Honey-pot ants live in dry grasslands and feed on nectar. Some of the worker ants eat nectar until they swell up. They hang from the roof of the nest storing food for when no more nectar is available.

Army ants live in tropical rainforests and eat insects and small animals.

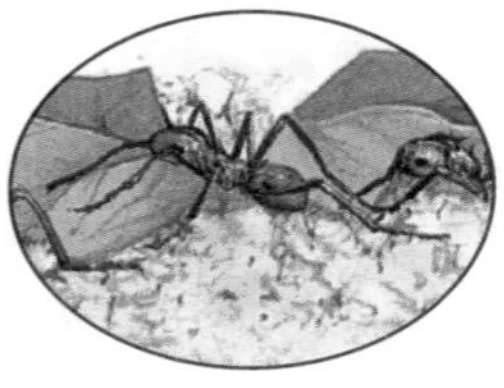

Leaf-cutter ants collect pieces of leaves and chew them until they are soft. They store them in their nest and eat the fungi that grow on them.

All species of ants live in colonies of large numbers of insects. Each nest has one queen who lays all the eggs. Workers and soldiers, which are all undeveloped females, collect food and guard the nest by waiting by the entrance with their jaws open. Other workers remove rubbish and open passageways to keep the nest cool.

Worker ant moving rubbish

Worker ant about to squirt poison to defend the nest from enemies.

Winged male ants mate with the queen.

In summer or the wet season, winged male ants leave the nest. After mating with young queens, they die and the queens lay eggs and start new nests. The eggs hatch into larvae and are fed by the worker ants until they pupate and change into adults.

Cut-away view inside a wood ants' nest, showing the chambers where eggs, larvae and food are stored

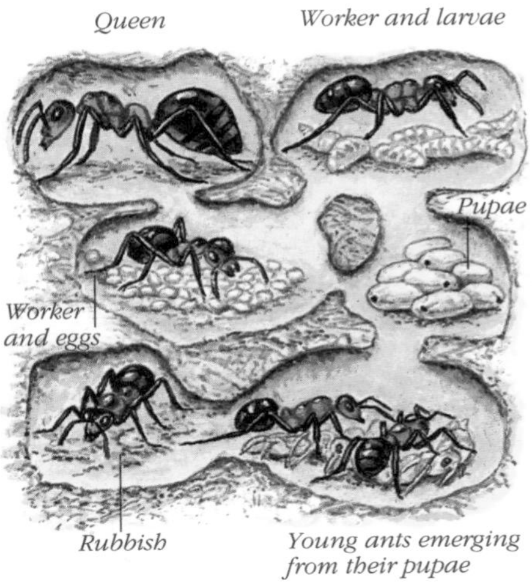
Queen
Worker and larvae
Pupae
Worker and eggs
Rubbish
Young ants emerging from their pupae

TERMITES

Termites live in tropical forests and grasslands. Some live in rotting wood and others build huge mounds of sand and clay cemented together with saliva (spit). Over a million termites may live in one mound and on the African grasslands, some termite nests are taller than giraffes. Inside the mound there are many passageways and chambers, and a complicated system of channels and air vents helps to keep the nest cool.

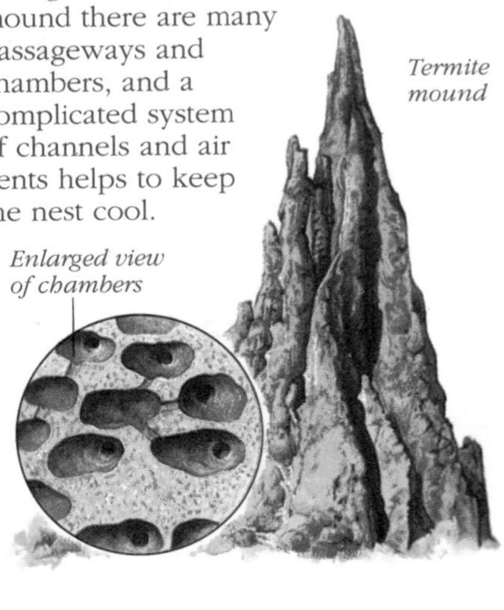
Termite mound
Enlarged view of chambers

Unlike other social insects, termites have a king who is the only insect to mate with the queen. The king and queen live in a chamber deep inside the mound. The queen may produce as many as 36,000 eggs a day and her body is swollen with eggs. Worker termites clean and feed the queen and take the eggs to nursery chambers nearby. Soldiers, who have bigger heads and jaws than workers, defend the nest.

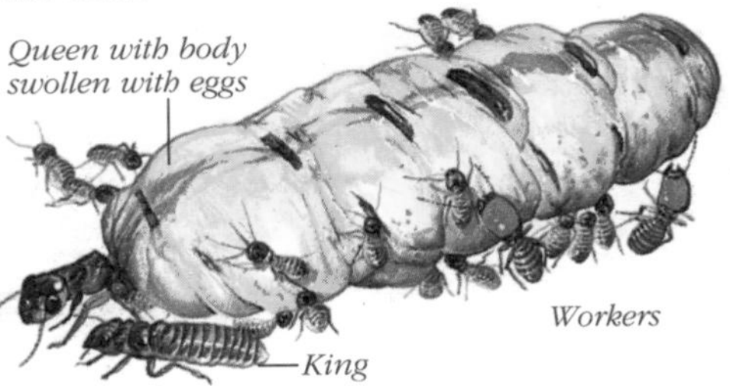
Queen with body swollen with eggs
Workers
King

The worker termites are blind and sterile (unable to breed). They feed and look after the soldiers, the queen and king and the young. Termites eat chewed-up wood and insects, and some grow fungi inside their nests for food. They build their droppings into structures, called combs, on which the fungi grow. The termites eat both the fungus and the comb.

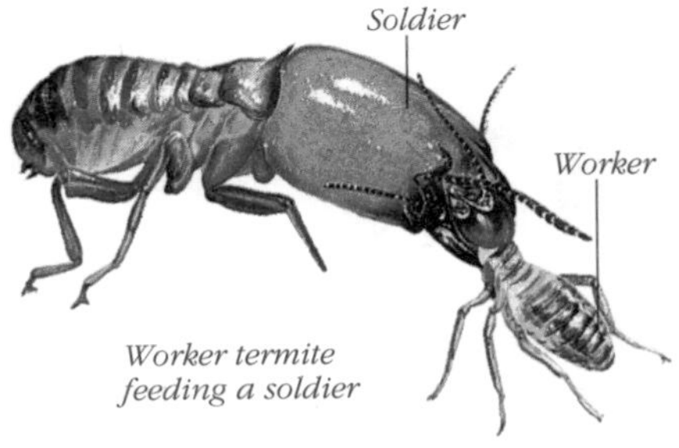
Soldier
Worker

Worker termite feeding a soldier

SEE FOR YOURSELF

To see how worker ants leave a trail for other ants to follow, put a piece of paper with food on it near an ants' nest. Watch the ants find the food, then move it and watch what the ants do.

Ants' nest
New position
First position of food

*Insects, 16

Jumping spiders have eight eyes and use different sets as they stalk their prey.

SPIDERS, MITES AND SCORPIONS

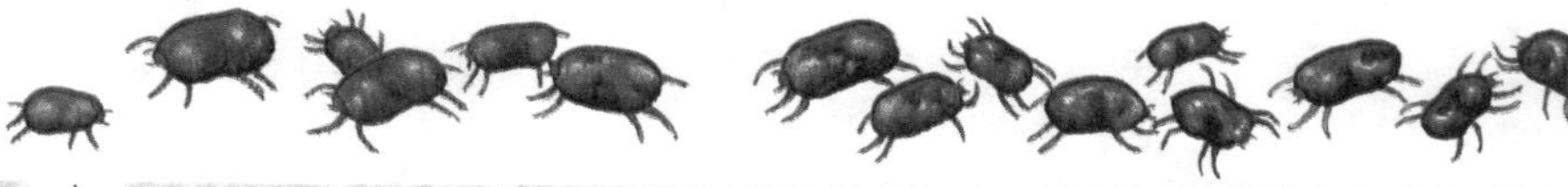

Red spider mites

Spiders, mites and scorpions belong to a group of animals called arachnids. Spiders and mites are common all over the world, but scorpions are found mostly in hot, dry places. They are all carnivores and eat other arachnids, insects and even birds.

SPIDERS

Spiders are often thought to be insects, but they have eight legs and only two body parts: head and abdomen. Insects have six legs and three body parts. All spiders are predators and they eat flies and other insects. They sting their prey to paralyze it, but only a few spiders have a sting that is dangerous for people.

Head
Abdomen

Garden cross spider

Most spiders spin webs to catch their prey, but a few, such as the jumping spider (see picture at the top of this page), catch insects without the aid of webs. Jumping spiders have very good eyesight and leap on their prey. Crab spiders lie in wait in flowers and ambush their prey. They are well camouflaged among the petals.

Crab spider hiding in a flower

After catching an insect, the spider bites it and the poison from its fangs paralyzes it. To feed, the spider sucks the body juices from the insect and leaves the dry skeleton in its web. Some spiders bind their prey with silken threads.

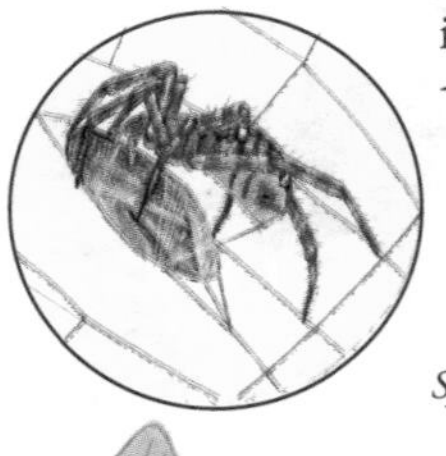

Spider binding an insect

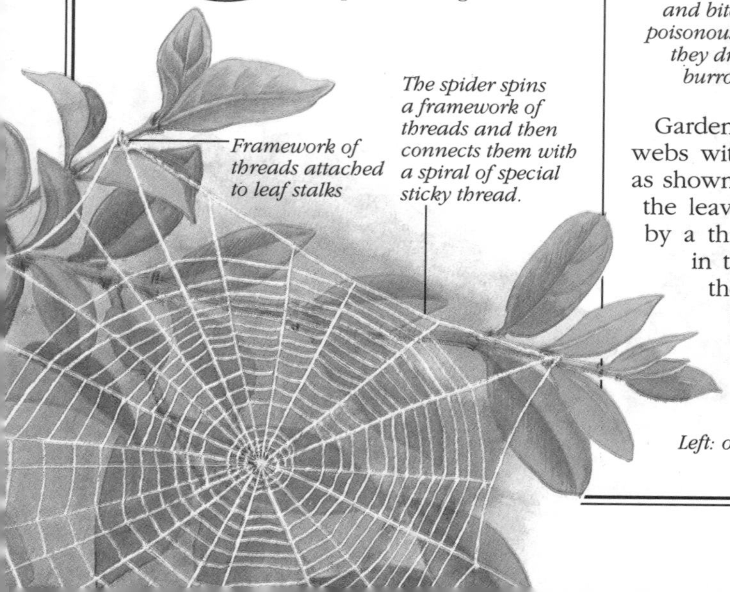
Framework of threads attached to leaf stalks
The spider spins a framework of threads and then connects them with a spiral of special sticky thread.

SPIDER WEBS

Spider webs are made from silk-like threads of protein produced by glands in the spider's abdomen. Spiders have several different glands for producing different threads: sticky threads for building webs, dry threads for anchoring the web and for the spider to travel on, and cocoon threads for wrapping their eggs. Different spiders build different kinds of webs, or use their threads in other ways to catch their prey.

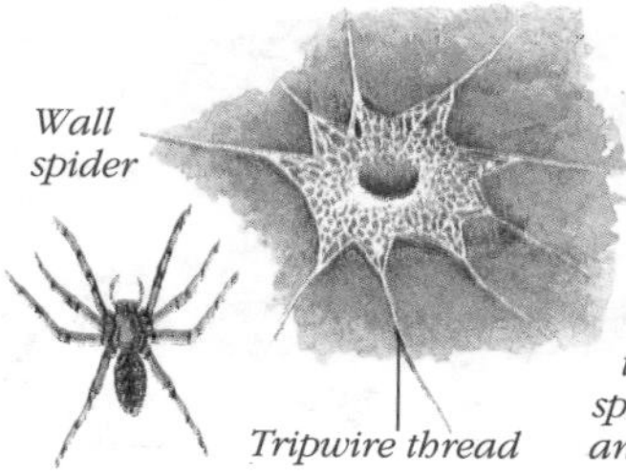
Wall spider
Tripwire thread

Wall spiders spin web tubes in cracks in walls. When an insect touches a tripwire thread, the spider dashes out and seizes it.

Trap-door spiders live in warm countries all over the world. They dig small, narrow burrows with lids, or "trap doors". They line the inside of the burrows with silk.

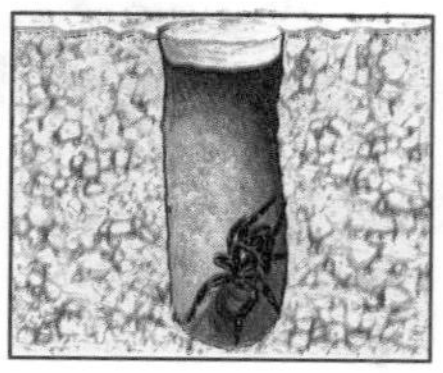

The spiders hide in their burrows with only their legs showing. They wait for an insect such as a beetle to pass nearby. Some place tripwire threads near their burrows.

When they feel the vibrations of an insect walking near their burrow, they rush out and bite it with their poisonous fangs. Then they drag it into the burrow and eat it.

Garden spiders spin orb webs: circular webs with spokes like a bicycle wheel, as shown on the left. The spider hides in the leaves nearby, attached to the web by a thread. When it feels movements in the web, it rushes out and bites the insect. Spiders usually have to spin a new web each day as webs become dry and dusty and are easily damaged.

Left: orb web of a garden spider

SPIDER REPRODUCTION

Spiders lay eggs and cover them with a cocoon of threads. When the young hatch, they feed on their egg yolk until they are ready to come out of the cocoon. As they grow, they shed their skin several times until they are fully grown. You may find old skins on webs.

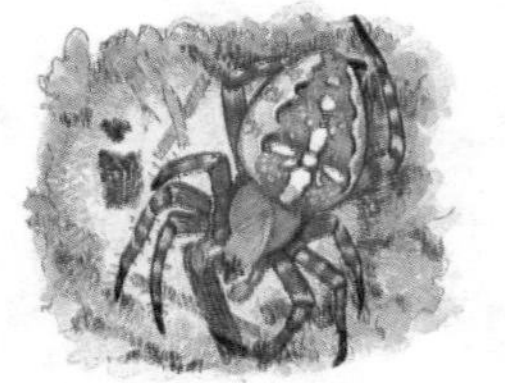

Female garden spiders lay their eggs in a cocoon of yellow threads which they disguise with pieces of bark and dust.

Hunting spiders spin a silk tent around their cocoon of eggs to protect them. When the eggs are ready to hatch, they tear the tent open.

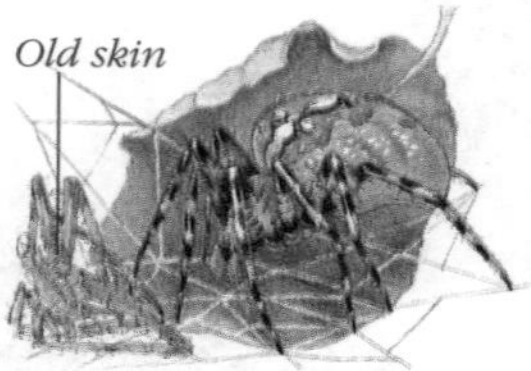
Old skin

This garden spider has just shed its skin and can now grow larger in its new skin. Spiders shed their skins several times as they grow.

Before mating, male spiders perform courtship rituals and some offer the females food wrapped in silk to persuade them not to eat the males as prey.

SEE FOR YOURSELF

To watch a spider spin its web, you could carefully catch a house or garden spider. Cut the front off a cereal box and put the spider in the box with some twigs taped upright to the side of the box. Cover the box with cling film and leave for several days. Then put the spider back where you found it.

Cereal box with front cut off
Cling film
Damp kitchen towel to provide moisture

WORLD SPIDERS

There are over 30,000 different species of spiders and they are found all over the world. Most spiders are very useful as they eat flies and other insect pests.

Black widows are small, very poisonous spiders whose bite can kill people. They live in Europe, North America, Africa and Australia.

Black widow spider

The poisonous red back of Australia (left) is called a night stinger in New Zealand.

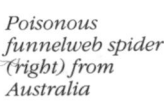

Poisonous funnelweb spider (right) from Australia

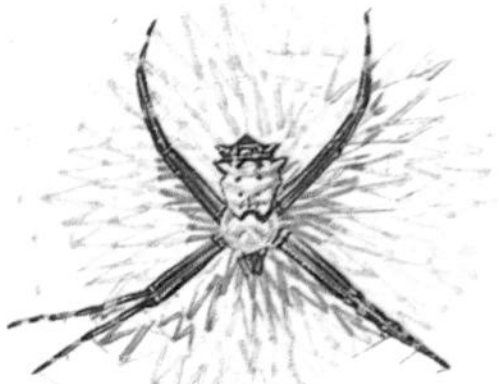

Some species of Argiope spiders (left), which live in rainforests, spin patterned webs that insects mistake for flowers.

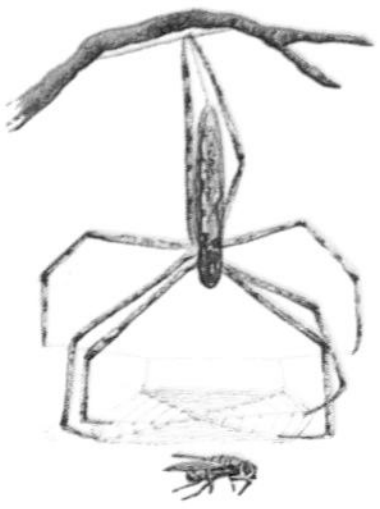

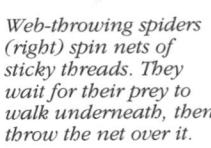

Web-throwing spiders (right) spin nets of sticky threads. They wait for their prey to walk underneath, then throw the net over it.

Tarantulas live in hot regions of North and South America. They capture small mammals, insects and snakes. Their sting is poisonous for humans, but not deadly.

Tarantula eating a locust

Cocoon

The wolf spider carries her cocoon of eggs with her wherever she goes.

Drysdera spiders (right) have large fangs with which they spear woodlice. They hunt at night.

House spiders (left) spin tangled webs in undisturbed corners.

Zebra spiders (right) have striped markings to camouflage them. They jump on their prey to catch it and do not spin webs.

Bird-eating spiders of South America eat small birds, mammals and insects. They measure about 25cm (10in) across.

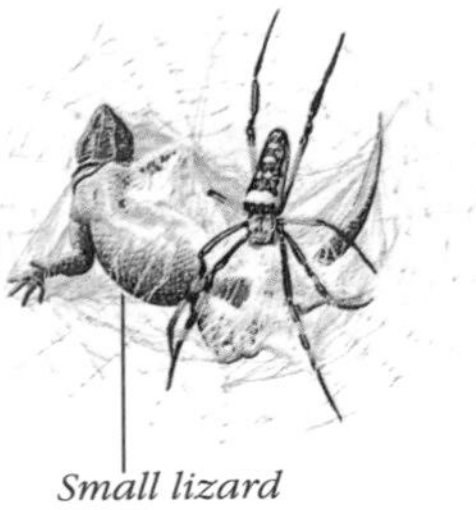
Small lizard

Golden orb web spiders, of Central and South America, spin very strong silk threads which can even trap small animals. The silk is sometimes used by local fishermen to make fishing nets and even for making shopping baskets.

Water spiders carry bubbles of air under the water in "nets" of silk. They catch pond insects, tadpoles and small fish and eat them inside the air bubbles, or on dry land.

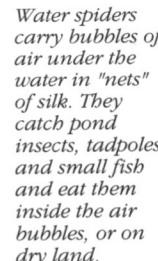

Water spider

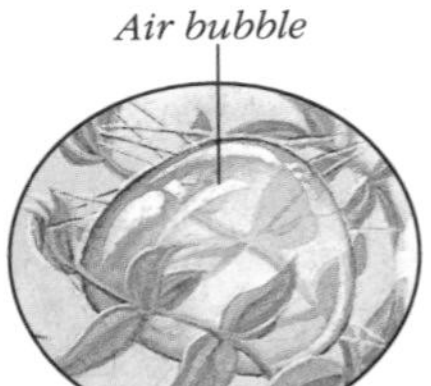
Air bubble

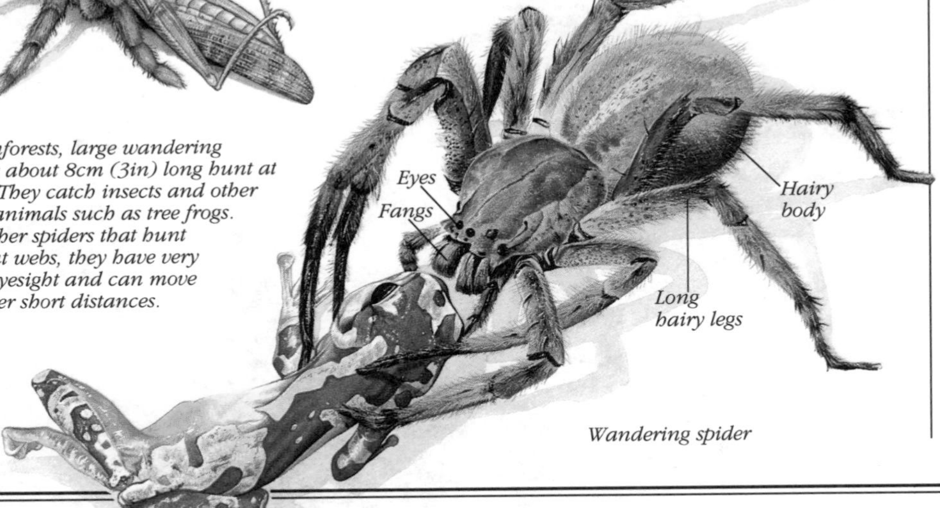
Eyes
Fangs
Hairy body
Long hairy legs
Tree frog

In rainforests, large wandering spiders about 8cm (3in) long hunt at night. They catch insects and other small animals such as tree frogs. Like other spiders that hunt without webs, they have very good eyesight and can move fast over short distances.

Wandering spider

MITES AND TICKS

There are thousands of different species of mites and ticks. They are mostly very tiny and have eight legs and one part to their body. Some mites feed on dead leaves and soil and help decompose plant matter, but most are parasites and suck blood from animals, or cell sap from plants.

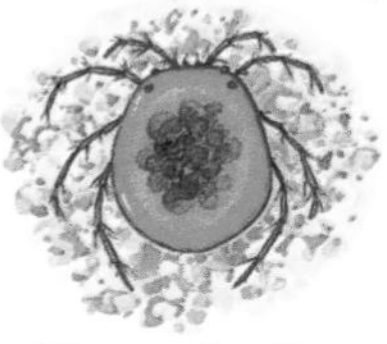

Water mites live in ponds and eat water insects.

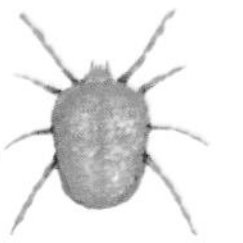

Red velvet mite - actual size about 2mm (0.1in) across

Ticks are parasites. They live on other animals and suck their blood, and often carry disease from animal to animal. After a meal, their abdomens grow very large. Then the ticks drop off their hosts and digest their food on the ground. They can go for long periods without a meal.

Magnified view of a deer tick embedded in deer's skin. Deer ticks are common wherever deer are found and they spread Lyme disease.

SCORPIONS

Scorpions live mainly in deserts and warm countries. They have eight legs and a large pair of pincers with which they grasp their prey. They hunt at night and hide under stones and plants during the day. They sit and wait for their prey and then seize it and paralyze it with a sting from their tail. The sting of some types of scorpion is also deadly for people.

Most scorpions perform elaborate courtship dances as the male is afraid to go near the female in case she stings him. The young are born live and are carried on the mother's back.

Scorpions performing a courtship ritual

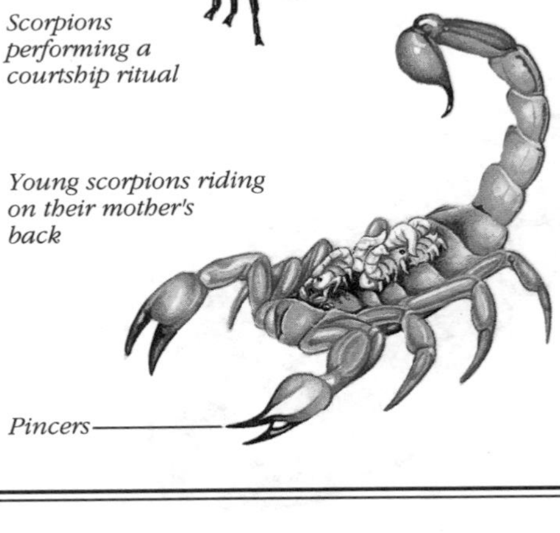
Pincers

Young scorpions riding on their mother's back

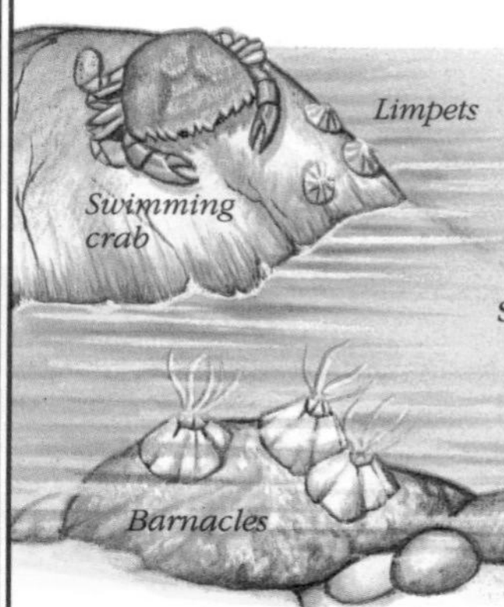
Limpets
Swimming crab
Barnacles

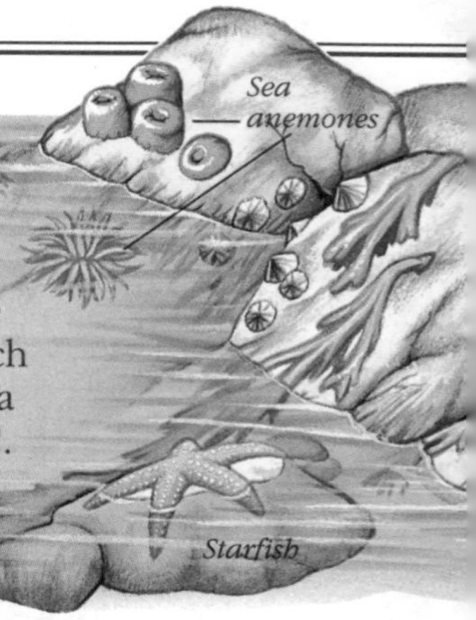
Sea anemones

SEASHORE LIFE

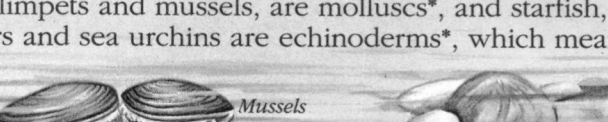

The plants and animals shown on these two pages live in shallow sea and on the seashore. Animals that have jointed legs and hard, shell-like skeletons, like crabs, belong to a group called crustaceans*. Shellfish, such as clams, limpets and mussels, are molluscs*, and starfish, brittlestars, sea cucumbers and sea urchins are echinoderms*, which means "spiny skin".

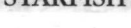

Mussels
Starfish

CRABS

Crabs belong to a group of crustaceans* called decapods, which means "ten legs". They have a hard case, called a carapace, which is their skeleton. On their first pair of legs they have large pincers. They use their pincers for feeding, digging and to defend themselves. Crabs live on the seabed, or in rock pools, and eat small fish, shellfish and other sea creatures.

Crabs lay eggs that hatch into tiny larvae that later develop into crabs. The larvae form part of the plankton* that many fish eat. As they grow, crabs, and other crustaceans, shed their carapaces and their skin gradually hardens to form a new, larger one.

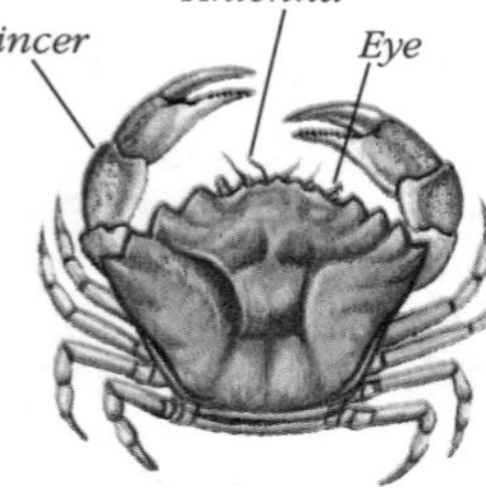
Antenna
Pincer
Eye

Shore crabs (right) live on the sand or rocks in shallow water.

The fiddler crab's extra-large claw is for fighting, and for attracting females.

Hermit crabs have soft carapaces. They live in old seashells. When the shells get too small, they find bigger ones.

LOBSTERS

Lobsters, like crabs, have ten legs and the first pair of legs have large pincers. They live under rocks in shallow water and crawl along the seabed looking for dead fish and other animal remains to eat.

Crayfish and crawfish are different kinds of lobsters that live in rivers and estuaries.

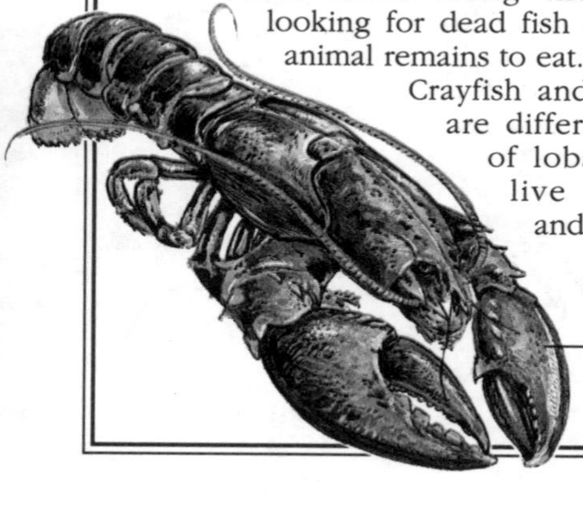
Pincer for feeding

Lobster

SHRIMPS AND PRAWNS

Shrimps and prawns are ten-legged crustaceans*, like crabs and lobsters. They are scavengers and feed on dead plant and animal matter. Like crabs, they shed their hard, external skeletons and grow new, larger ones. Many species are almost transparent to camouflage them against the pale sand.

Common prawn

Antenna
Pincer

Banded, or cleaner shrimps, live in coral reefs and eat the parasites off fish.

BARNACLES

Barnacles are crustaceans* that live attached to rocks, or sometimes to other sea creatures such as whales. When covered with water, they put out feathery legs with which they filter tiny plants to eat from the water. Their young are larvae that swim freely in the sea. When they become adults, they attach themselves to rocks and grow shells to protect their soft bodies.

Acorn barnacles

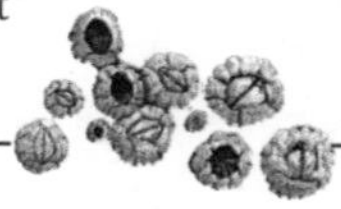

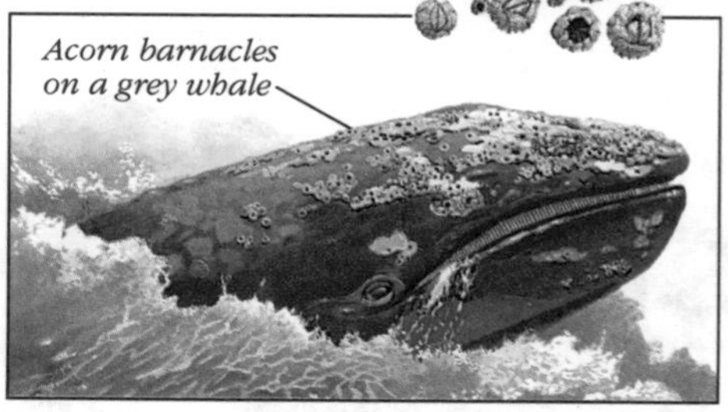
Acorn barnacles on a grey whale

STARFISH

Most starfish have five legs, which underneath are covered with suckers called tube feet. They walk and grip food with their tube feet and force open shells, such as clams, to eat the creatures inside. To feed, they turn their stomachs inside out and push them into the shells. If their arms break off, they can grow new ones.

Sunstar

Spiny starfish

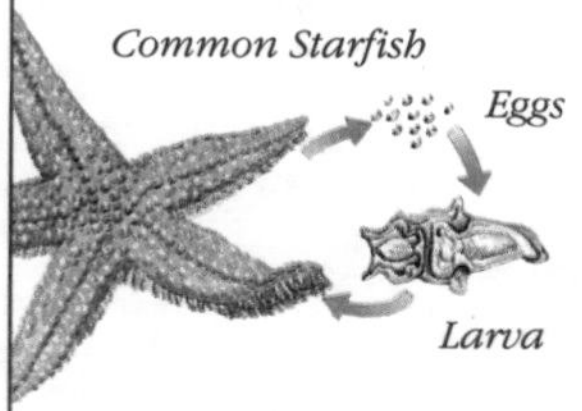
Common Starfish
Eggs
Larva

Starfish lay thousands of eggs that hatch into larvae. The larvae float in the plankton until they grow and become starfish.*

Starfish grip shells with their sucker-like tube feet and pull them apart to eat the shellfish inside.

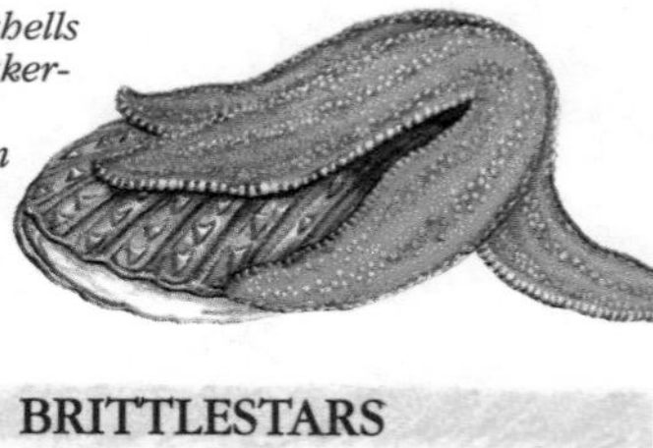

BRITTLESTARS

Brittlestars have long, thin, bendy arms surrounding their mouths. They live in deep and shallow water and swim with their arms. If attacked, they can shed their arms and grow new ones. They feed on dead plant or animal matter that floats in the water or on the seabed.

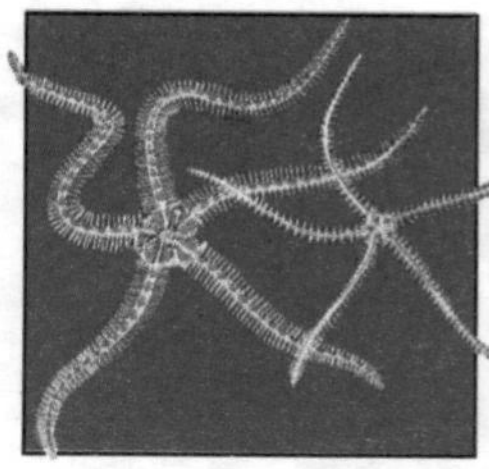

Most brittlestars feed at night.

SEA CUCUMBERS

These are animals related to starfish. They have soft bodies with tube feet with which they can move along the seabed. They feed on plant and animal matter that they catch with their long, sticky tentacles.

Sea cucumber defending itself against a crab

Tentacle
Tube feet

*Crustaceans, 88; Molluscs, 88; Echinoderms, 88; Plankton,82

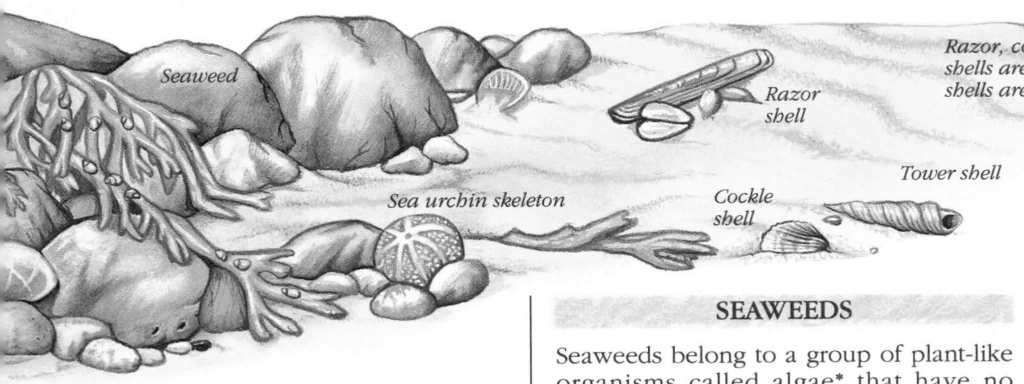
Seaweed
Razor shell
Sea urchin skeleton
Cockle shell
Tower shell

Razor, cockle and oyster shells are bivalves. Tower shells are univalves.

Oyster shell

SEA URCHINS

Sea urchins belong to the same group of animals as starfish. They have globe- or disc-shaped skeletons, called tests, covered with spines. Underneath the test they have a "mouth" with five chisel-like teeth with which they scrape algae off the rocks or coral.

Marks left by spines

Above: living sea urchin with spines
Right: the skeleton, or test, of a dead sea urchin

SEA ANEMONES

Sea anemones are animals related to jellyfish and corals*. Their simple, sac-shaped bodies are called polyps. They anchor themselves to rocks and wave their tentacles around in search of small fish or shrimps to eat. They sting the fish and push it into their mouths with their tentacles. When disturbed, or not covered with water, they draw in their tentacles and look like blobs of jelly.

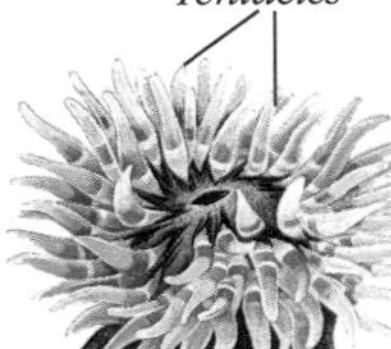
Tentacles

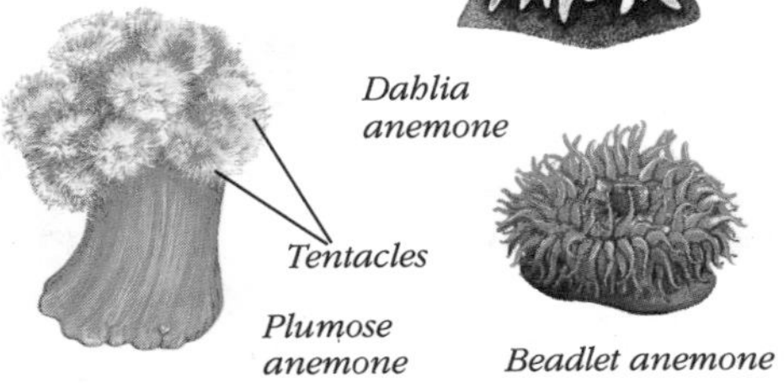
Dahlia anemone
Tentacles
Plumose anemone
Beadlet anemone

Sea anemones catch food with their tentacles. | *They sting the food and pull it into their mouths.* | *When they are disturbed, they draw in their tentacles.*

SEAWEEDS

Seaweeds belong to a group of plant-like organisms called algae* that have no roots or stems. They absorb all the substances they need from the water. They contain the green pigment, chlorophyll, so they can make their own food by photosynthesis*. Some seaweeds also contain other pigments that make them look red or brown. Instead of roots, seaweeds have holdfasts that anchor them to rocks. Their leaves are called fronds, and some types have air bladders that help them float upright in the water.

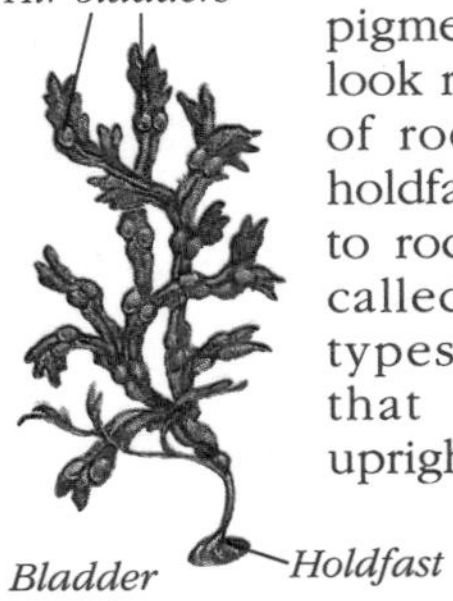
Air bladders
Holdfast

Bladder wrack

Edible dulse

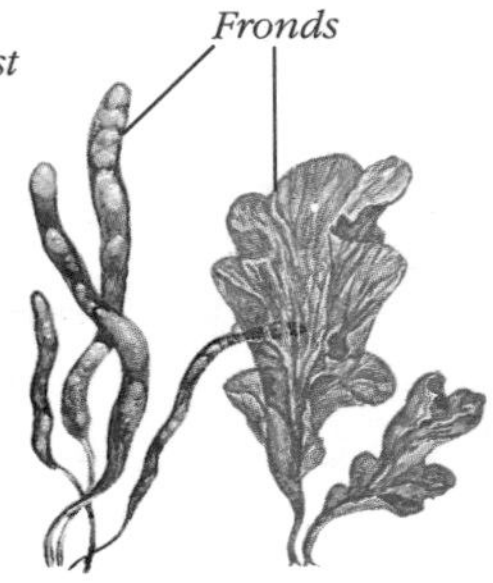
Fronds

Gut laver *Sea lettuce*

SPONGES

Sponges are very simple animals that attach themselves to rocks, corals or the seabed, and filter food out of the water. They also grow in rivers and lakes. Sponges are made up of minute, single-celled organisms that live in a "skeleton" made of a soft protein called spongin.

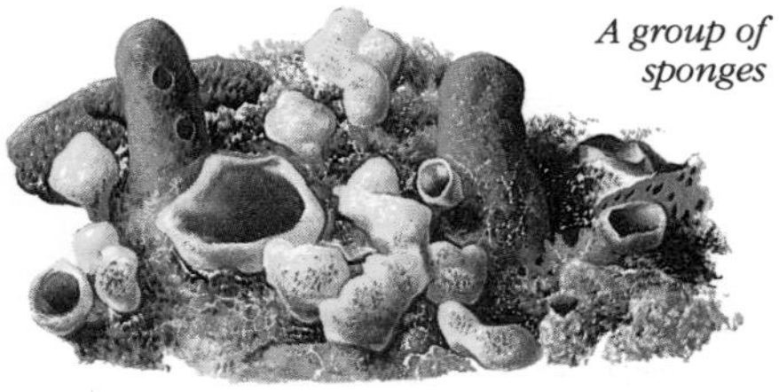

A group of sponges

Each of the minute organisms has a whip-like hair, or flagellum, with which it wafts water through the sponge so that particles of food can be filtered out. Sponges reproduce by producing larvae that form part of the plankton* until they become adult sponges and attach themselves to rocks. New sponges can also grow from pieces of broken sponge.

SHELLS AND SHELLFISH

Shells are the protective cases of a group of soft-bodied creatures called molluscs*. The shell may be a single shell, called a univalve, like that of a limpet, or a bivalve - a pair of shells that fit together like those of a clam or mussel.

Blue-rayed limpet: a univalve

Mussels are bivalves. They have a pair of shells that fit together.

A univalve mollusc, such as a limpet, periwinkle or whelk, has a muscular foot with which it clings to the rocks. When covered with water, it slides over the rock, scraping off algae with its rough tongue. When the tide goes out it clamps down hard on a rock so it does not dry out.

Siphon for sucking water over gills

Dog whelk

Some bivalve molluscs, such as mussels, anchor themselves to rocks and stay in one place. Others, for example, razor shells and cockles, bury themselves in the sand using a single muscular foot. When covered with water, the shells open up and the molluscs absorb microscopic sea creatures from the sea water.

Cockle
Muscular foot

Molluscs lay eggs that hatch into tiny shelled molluscs or into larvae. As a mollusc grows, it grows new sections of shell. The shell is made of a limy substance secreted by the mollusc's skin. Some are lined with mother-of-pearl.

SEE FOR YOURSELF

To see how limpets glide slowly over the rock, paint letters on their positions and shells with oil or acrylic paint. Next time the tide goes out, check their positions. Some will have moved, others will have returned to their places.

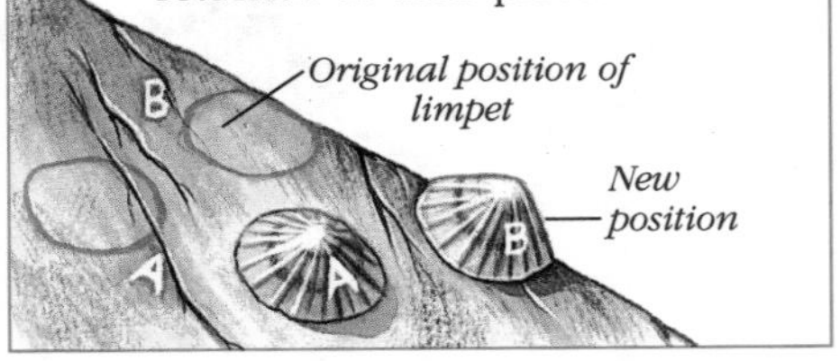
Original position of limpet
New position
B
A
A
B

*Corals, 82

*Algae, 11; Photosynthesis, 5; Plankton, 82

*Molluscs, 88

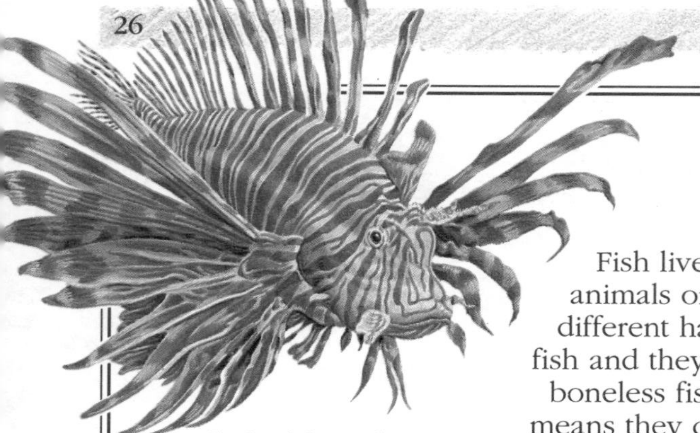

The lionfish's markings warn predators that it is poisonous.

FISH

Fish live in seas, oceans, rivers, lakes and ponds. Like animals on the land, different fish are adapted to living in different habitats. There are over 25,000 different species of fish and they can be divided into three main groups: bony fish, boneless fish and jawless fish. Fish are cold-blooded*, which means they cannot make their own body heat, and their bodies are about the same temperature as the water around them.

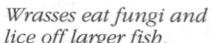

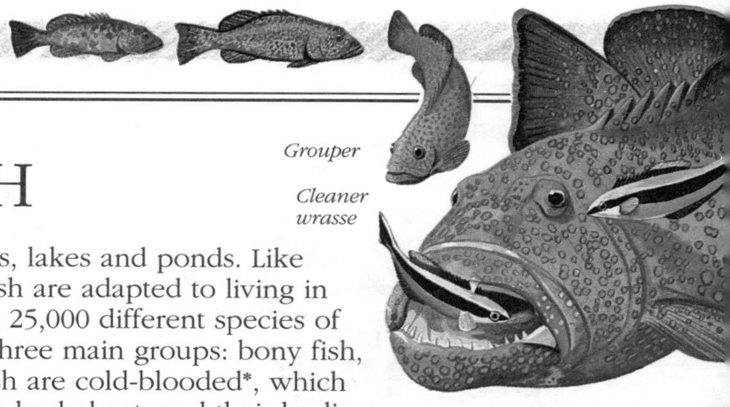
Grouper
Cleaner wrasse

Wrasses eat fungi and lice off larger fish.

BONY FISH

Most fish belong to this group. They have skeletons made of bone, and thin pieces of overlapping bone, called scales, in their skin. Their gill slits (see How Fish Breathe) are covered with flaps called operculae. Boneless and jawless fish do not have operculae.

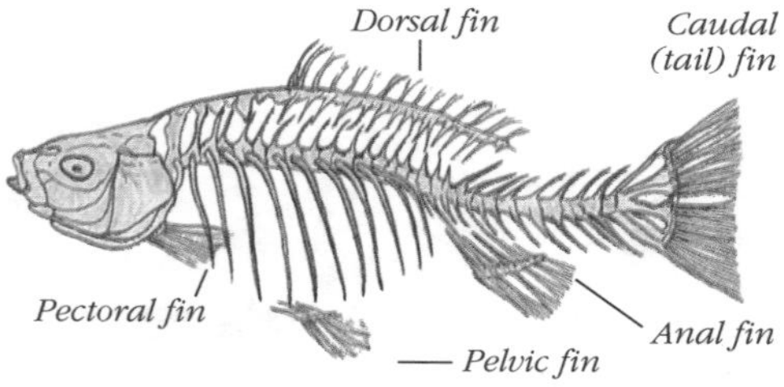
Dorsal fin
Caudal (tail) fin
Pectoral fin
Pelvic fin
Anal fin

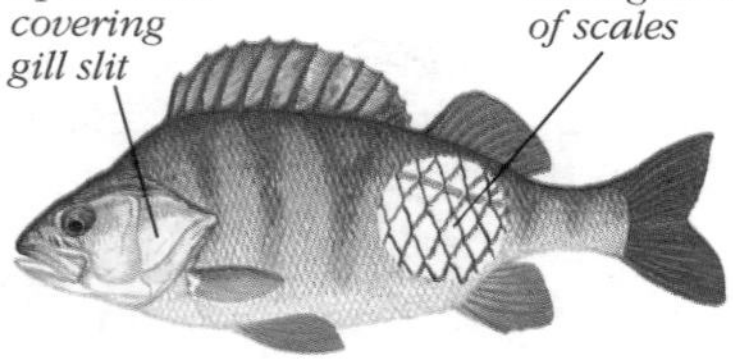
Operculum covering gill slit
Enlarged view of scales

This species of bony fish is called a perch.

BONELESS FISH

Boneless fish have skeletons made of a gristly material called cartilage. Their proper name is cartilaginous fish. Cartilage is very strong but it is not stiff like bone. Sharks* and rays* are types of cartilaginous fish. Their skin is covered with sharp, backward-pointing scales, and, unlike bony fish, they have no flaps covering their gill slits.

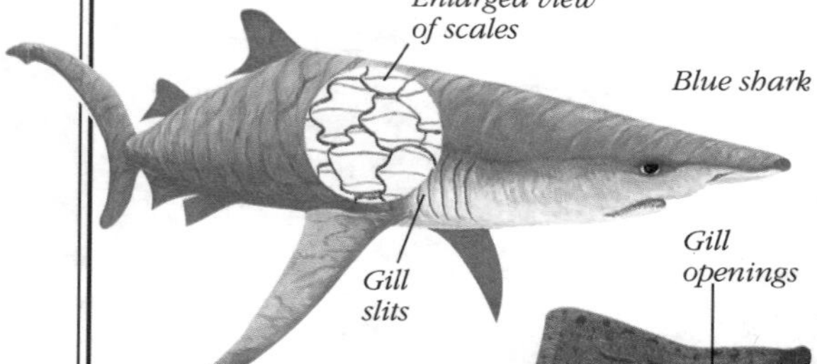
Enlarged view of scales
Gill slits

Blue shark

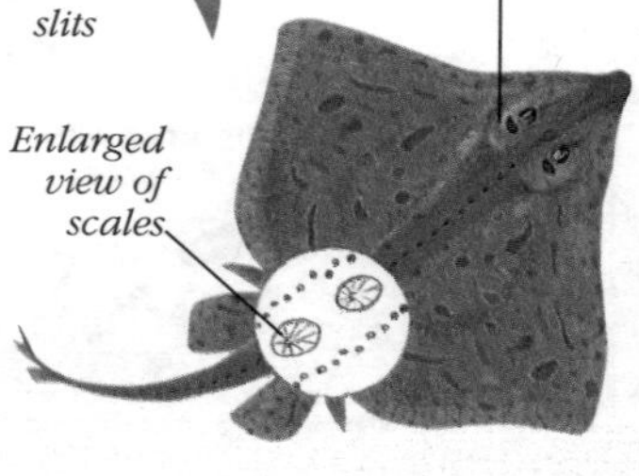
Gill openings
Enlarged view of scales

This is a species of ray called a skate.

JAWLESS FISH

Jawless fish are still very like the first fish that lived 500 million years ago. Their mouths are suckers with which they suck body fluids from other sea creatures. They have no scales and no gill flaps, and their skeletons are made of cartilage, like boneless fish.

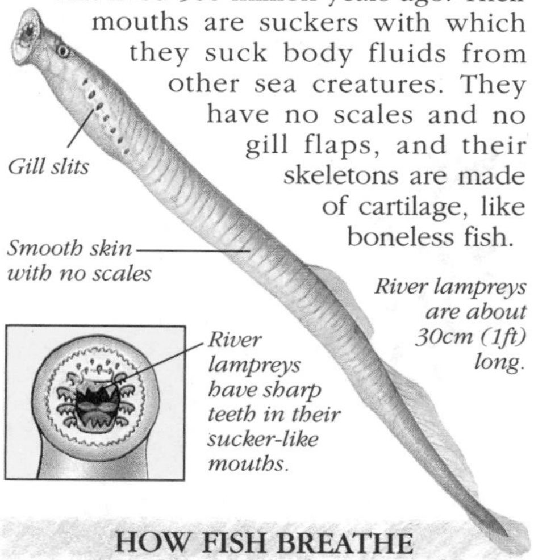
Gill slits
Smooth skin with no scales

River lampreys are about 30cm (1ft) long.

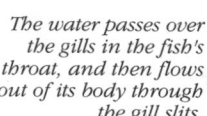

River lampreys have sharp teeth in their sucker-like mouths.

HOW FISH BREATHE

Fish need oxygen just like other animals. Most fish have gills to take the oxygen they need from the water. A very few fish, such as lungfish, which live in rivers and lakes in Africa, Australia and South America, have gills and lungs.

As a fish swims along, it takes big mouthfuls of water. After each mouthful, it closes its mouth.

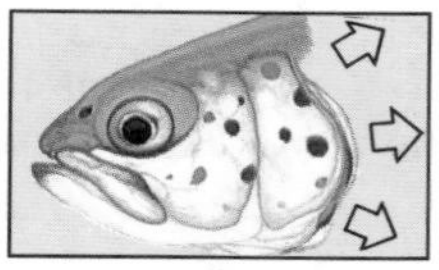

The water passes over the gills in the fish's throat, and then flows out of its body through the gill slits.

Cut-away view of gills

Gills are made of thin skin with many blood vessels. As water passes over them, oxygen passes into the blood.

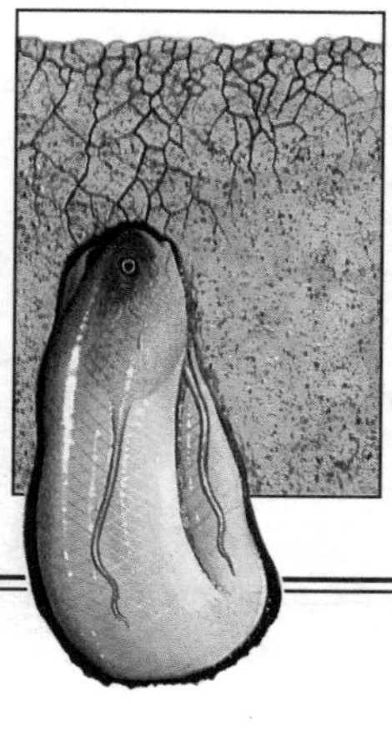

When the lakes where they live dry up in the dry season, African lungfish bury themselves in the mud. They absorb air through their lungs from cracks in the mud. Lungfishes may be related to the first animals that lived on land about 400 million years ago.

FEEDING

Some fish eat only plants, others eat small fish, snails, shrimps and even ducks. Some of the largest fish eat only zooplankton - microscopic animals that float near the surface of the water. Most fish have teeth, but jawless fish (see left) have sucker-shaped mouths and suck blood from other sea creatures.

Archer fish shoot drops of water at insects to knock them into the water so they can eat them. They can hit insects over 1.8m (6ft) away. They live in tropical rivers.

Luminous lure

The luminous lure on the heads of deep-sea angler fish attracts prey to their large jaws.

The gudgeon, a river fish, sucks up insects, worms and shellfish from the riverbed and crushes them with teeth in its throat.

HOW FISH SWIM

Fish swim by swinging their tails from side to side. This drives them forward through the water. To steer, they change the angles of their fins, and their fins also help them to brake and balance in the water.

The streamlined shape of a fish's body helps it move easily through the water.

Bony fish (see left) have a sac of air, called a swim bladder, in their bodies. By filling the sac with air, or emptying it, they can float at different levels in the water. Boneless and jawless fish do not have swim bladders and they have to keep swimming to stay afloat.

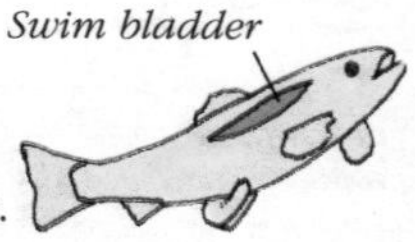
Swim bladder

*Sharks and Rays, 28

FISH SENSES

Most fish can smell, see, taste and hear underwater, and they also have other senses that help them detect objects and find their way around.

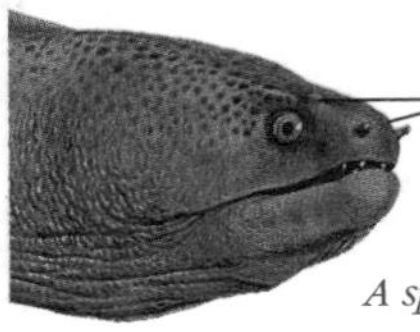

Most fish have two pairs of nostrils for smelling, not breathing.

A species of moray eel

Fish can detect the slightest movements in the water around them. Along each side of their body, most fish have a line called the lateral line. Along the line, there are small holes that allow the water to flow into a tube behind the holes. Movements in the water around the fish cause the water in the tube to move and this is detected by the fish's nerves.

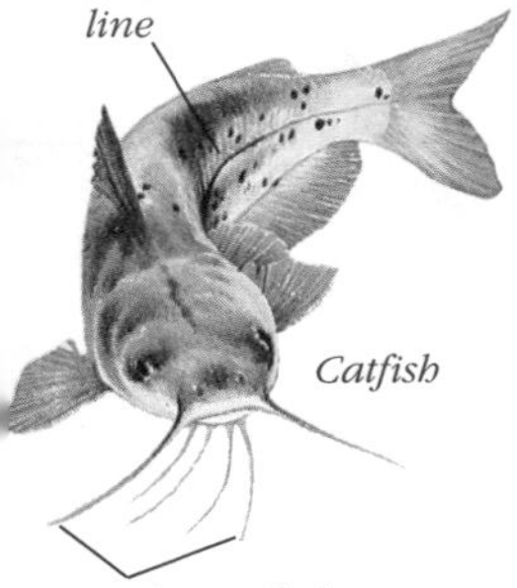

Lateral line

Catfish

Feelers called barbels are for tasting and feeling

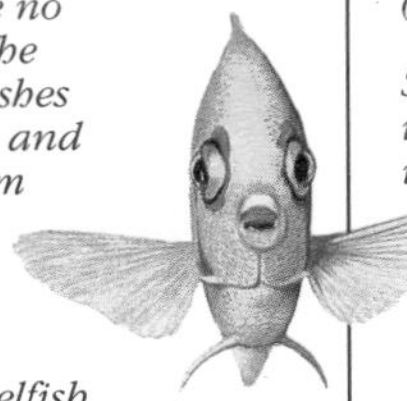

Fish have no eyelids. The water washes their eyes and keeps them clean and moist.

Sea angelfish

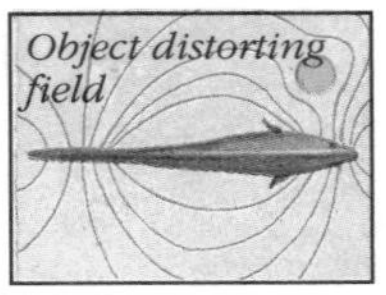

Object distorting field

Knife fish live in muddy rivers where vision is useless. They send out pulses of electricity and can detect objects that distort the field of electricity around them.

FISH REPRODUCTION

Most fish lay eggs, called spawn, although a few, such as the guppy fish, give birth to live young. Baby fish are called fry. Female fish lay many very small eggs. These may float in the water, or become attached to a plant. Most fish do not look after their eggs and young, but a few do make nests.

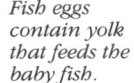

Fish eggs contain yolk that feeds the baby fish.

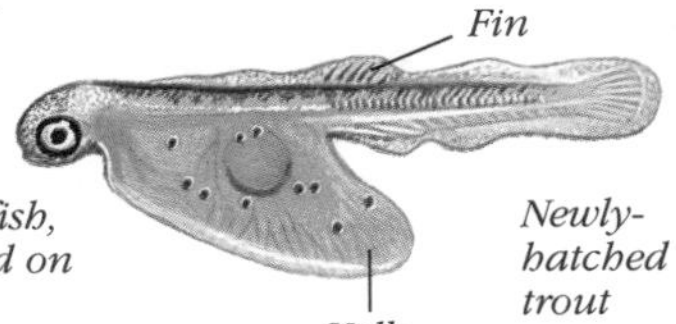

Fin
Yolk

After hatching, the baby fish, or fry, feed on the yolk.

Newly-hatched trout

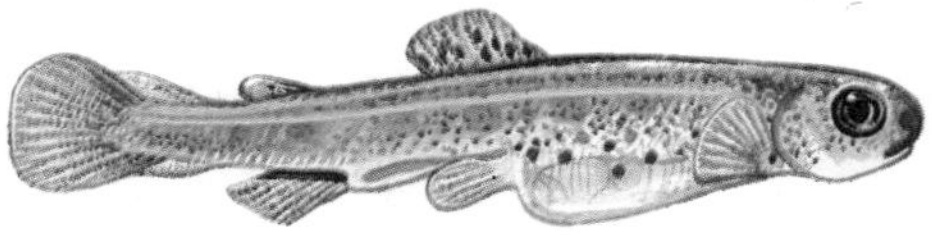

The yolk lasts until the fish's fins are fully grown.

SEA AND FRESHWATER FISH

To survive in the salty water of the sea, most seafish have to drink lots of water. The sea is saltier than their bodies, so water seeps out of them and into the sea by osmosis*. Freshwater fish are fish that live in rivers, lakes and ponds.

Flying fish can spread out their fins and glide 400m (1,300ft) along the surface of the water.

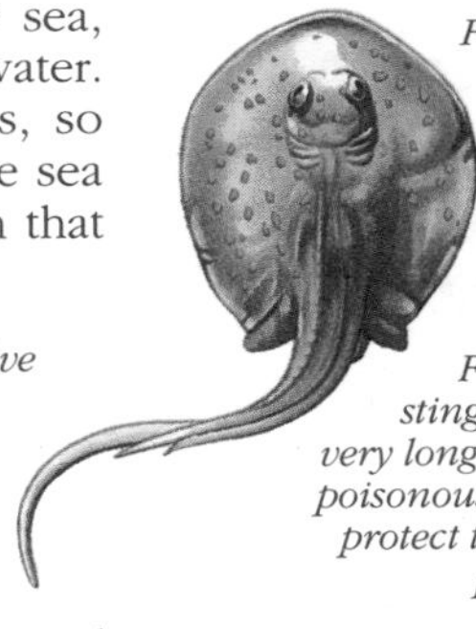

Freshwater stingrays have very long tails with poisonous spines to protect them from predators.

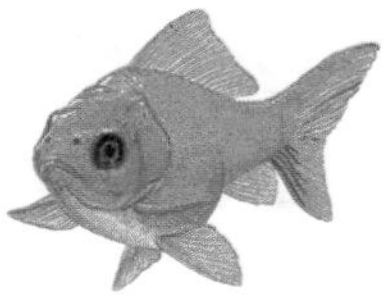

Goldfish originally lived in rivers in Europe and Russia.

Blind cave characins live in underwater caves in Mexico. They have lost their sense of sight and find food by sensing vibrations in the water.

Fast swimming fish like the swordfish (above left) and tuna (right) have crescent-shaped tails.

Trout lay their eggs in streams and then migrate to the sea. They eat insects and other fish.

Stone loaches hide under stones or in weeds on riverbeds and hunt for insects at night.

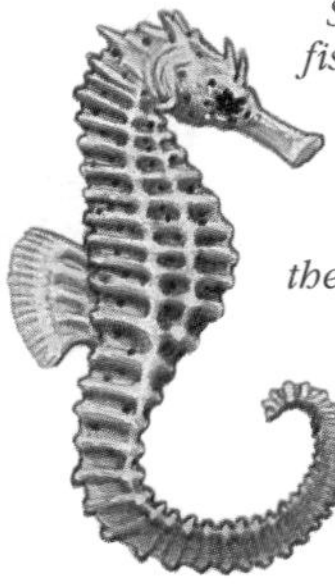

Sea horses are fish. They swim upright and their thick scales form a shell around their bodies. The male carries the fertilized eggs in a pouch on his belly.

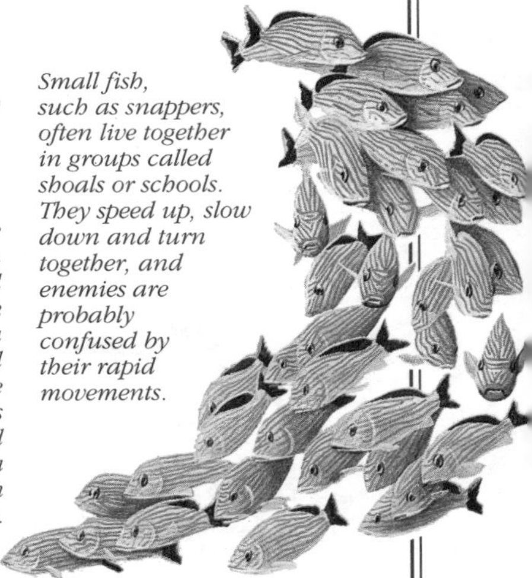

Small fish, such as snappers, often live together in groups called shoals or schools. They speed up, slow down and turn together, and enemies are probably confused by their rapid movements.

SALMON

Salmon spend part of their lives in the Atlantic Ocean, but return to streams in Europe and North America to breed. Some even return to the same streams where they were born, finding their way by their sense of smell. They have to swim upstream against the flow of water and leap over waterfalls to reach the streams where they were born.

Salmon return to the rivers where they were born to breed. They leap over rocks and waterfalls, jumping 3m (10ft) in the air.

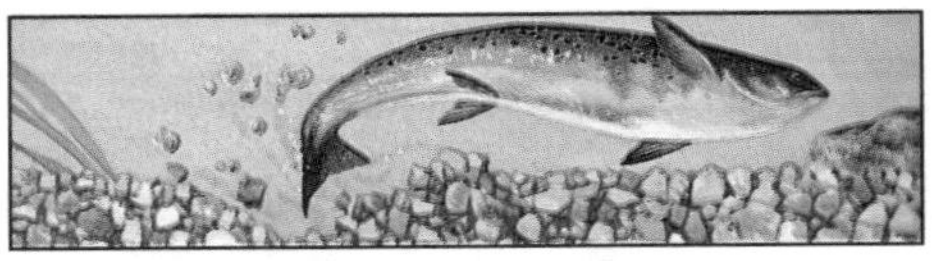

When they arrive at their home streams, the females lay up to 15,000 eggs in hollows in the riverbed that they make with their tails.

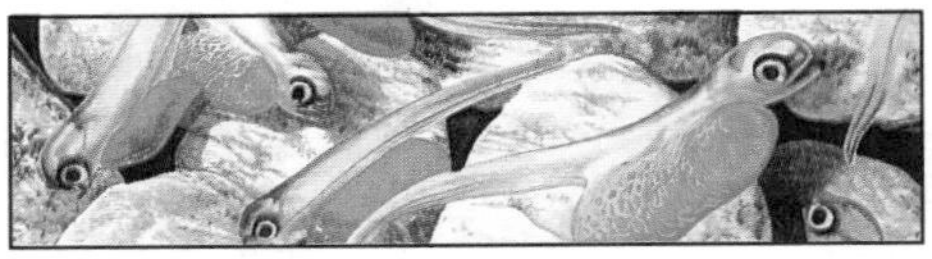

The salmon fry (baby salmon) live in the streams for about three years before migrating to the Atlantic Ocean to feed.

EELS

Atlantic eels live in rivers in Europe and North America until they are about ten years old. Then they swim to the sea to breed and die. They swim all the way to the Sargasso Sea, in the western Atlantic Ocean, where the females lay their eggs.

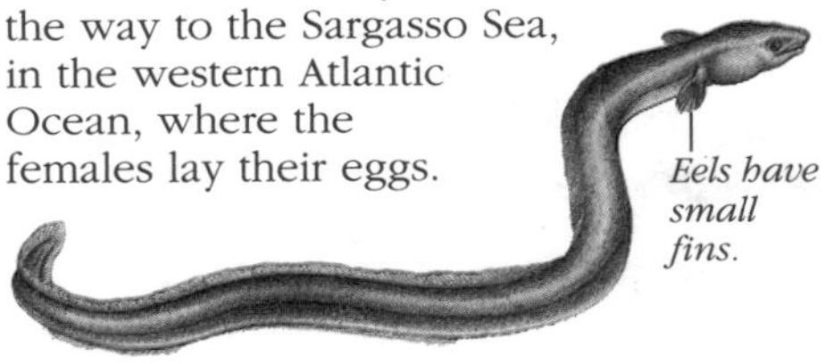

Eels have small fins.

The eggs hatch into tiny larvae and these are carried back to the rivers by ocean currents - a trip that takes three years. During this time, the larvae change into young eels, called elvers, and the elvers swim up the rivers and grow into adult eels.

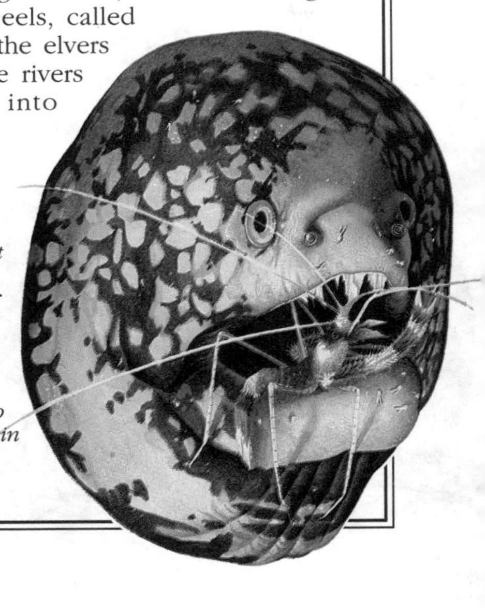

There are many different species of eels, including over a hundred species of moray eels. This one has a cleaner shrimp eating dead skin from its head.

*Osmosis, 5

SHARKS AND RAYS

Sharks and rays belong to a group of fish called boneless or cartilaginous fish*. Their skeletons are made of cartilage, the same substance that our noses and ear lobes are made of. Not all sharks are fierce. The whale shark is the largest fish in the sea, but it only eats plankton*.

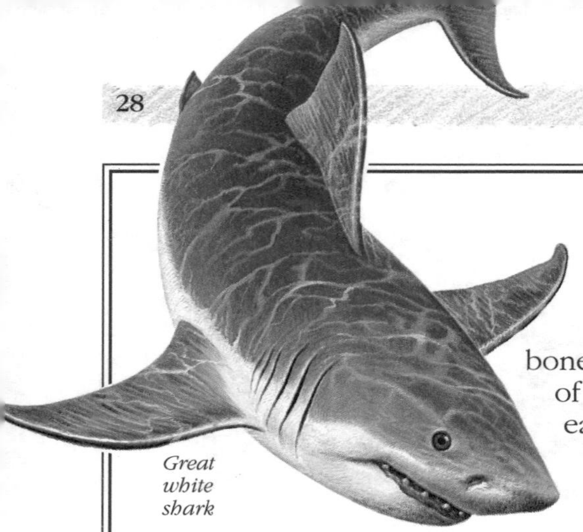

Great white shark

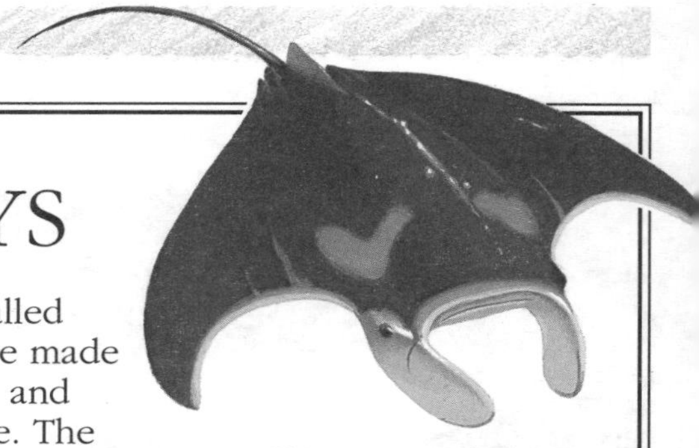

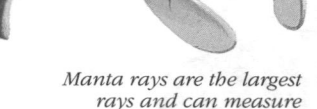

Manta rays are the largest rays and can measure 6.5m (21ft) across.

SHARKS

There are over 350 different species of sharks, but only 12 are dangerous for people. The smallest shark is only 15cm (6in) long. Most sharks eat fish and squid but some also eat seals, turtles, small whales and other sharks, and some only eat plankton*.

Gills

Tiger shark

Sharks have very sharp, backward-pointing scales in their skin that tear anything they touch. Like other fish, they take oxygen from the water with their gills*, but they do not have gill covers. They do not have a swim bladder* either, so they have to keep swimming all the time to stay afloat.

A shark's teeth are its weapons for catching and killing prey. They quickly wear down or fall out, and sharks have rows of new teeth that grow behind the old ones. Nurse sharks grow a new set of teeth every eight days.

Left: a tiger shark's teeth. The top two rows are in use. Those below are reserves.

Great white sharks grow to 9m (30ft) and live for 50 years. They eat turtles, and mammals such as seals, otters, dolphins and sea lions.

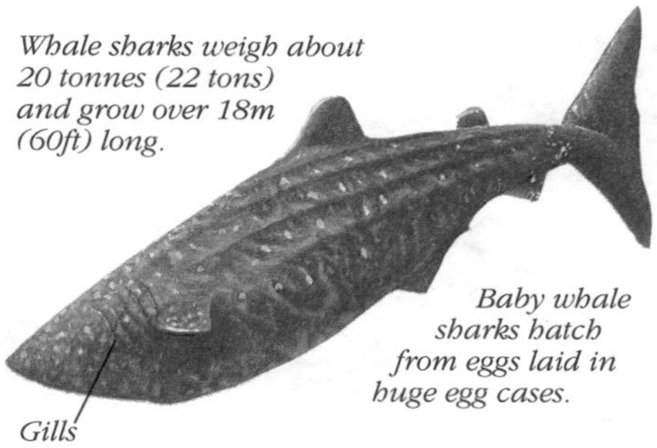
Gills

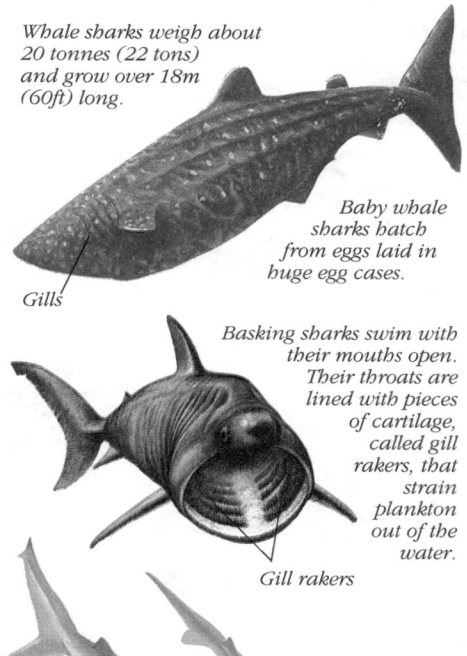

Whale sharks weigh about 20 tonnes (22 tons) and grow over 18m (60ft) long.

Baby whale sharks hatch from eggs laid in huge egg cases.

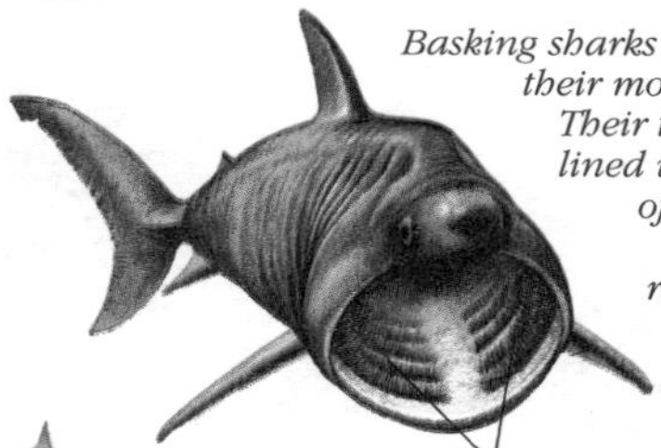
Gill rakers

Basking sharks swim with their mouths open. Their throats are lined with pieces of cartilage, called gill rakers, that strain plankton out of the water.

Nostrils

Hammerhead sharks have nostrils at either end of their hammer-shaped heads. They have an excellent sense of smell.

Blue sharks are common in northern seas. They feed on fish and squid, and garbage thrown from ships. They are about 3.8m (12.5ft) long.

The monkfish, or angel shark, lives in sand or mud at the bottom of the sea. It eats flatfish and rays.

Great white sharks have rows of sharp, saw-edged teeth over 7.5cm (3in) long. They have an excellent sense of smell and can scent a single drop of blood in the water. They hunt alone, but several sharks often gather around a kill.

RAYS

There are about 350 different species of rays, including manta rays, stingrays and skates. Most, apart from manta rays, live on the seafloor and eat shellfish and dead plants and animals. Their teeth are fused together to form strong ridges with which they crush shells. They swim by flapping their wing-like fins.

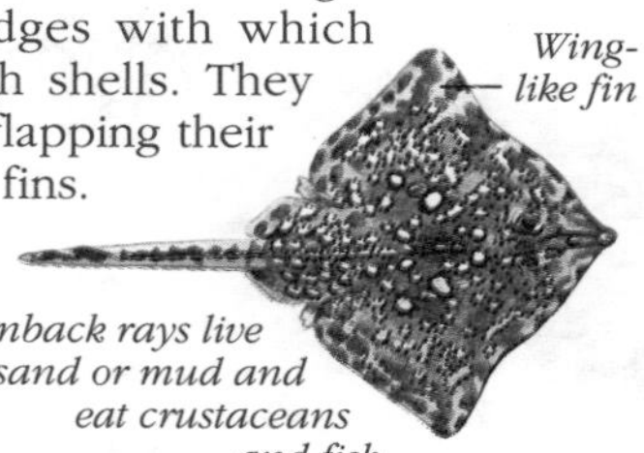
Wing-like fin

Thornback rays live in sand or mud and eat crustaceans and fish

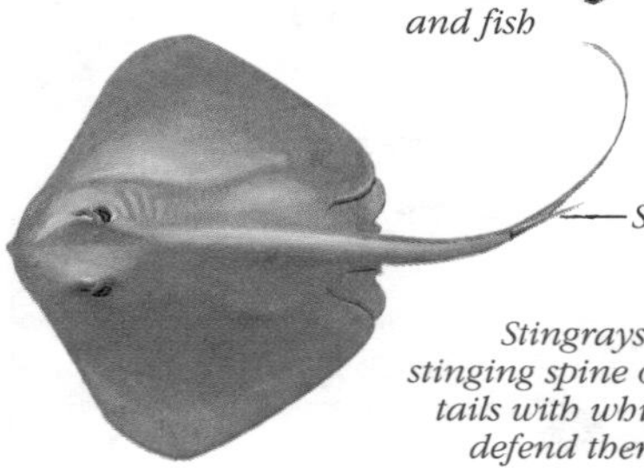
Stinging spine

Stingrays have a stinging spine on their tails with which they defend themselves.

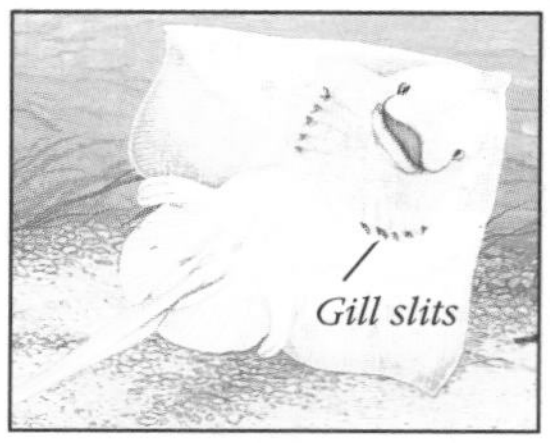
Gill slits

A ray's mouth and gill slits are positioned on the underside of its body, so it can suck up food as it swims along the sea bed.

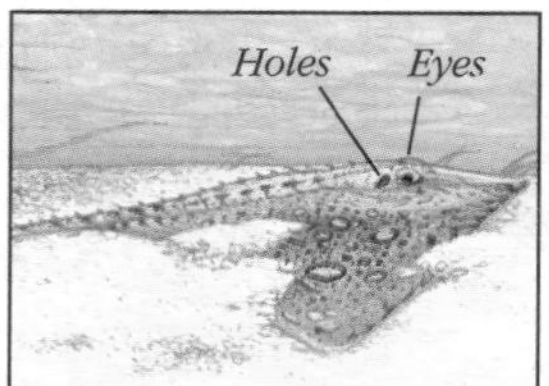
Holes
Eyes

To take in the water from which they extract oxygen, rays have two holes near their eyes on the top of their heads.

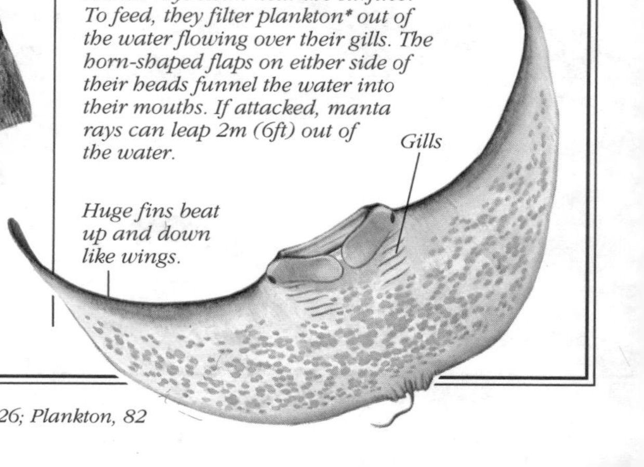
Gills

Manta rays swim near the surface. To feed, they filter plankton out of the water flowing over their gills. The horn-shaped flaps on either side of their heads funnel the water into their mouths. If attacked, manta rays can leap 2m (6ft) out of the water.*

Huge fins beat up and down like wings.

*Plankton, 82; Gills, see How Fish Breathe, 26; Swim bladder, see How Fish Swim, 26

*Boneless or cartilaginous fish, 26; Plankton, 82

Turtles, sea snakes, iguanas and salt-water crocodiles are the only reptiles that live in the sea but all, except sea snakes, nest on the land.

REPTILES

Reptiles are animals with scaly skin, such as snakes, lizards and crocodiles. They lay eggs and they are called "cold-blooded" animals because they do not produce their own body heat. There are four main groups of reptiles: lizards, snakes, turtles and crocodiles. Most reptiles live in warm and hot countries, although a few snakes and lizards live in cooler areas.

All reptiles have scaly skin, like that of this milk snake which lives in North America.

COLD-BLOODED ANIMALS

Unlike mammals and birds, cold-blooded animals cannot make their own body heat. The temperature of their blood is about the same as the air or water around them. The blood of mammals and birds is warmed by chemical reactions in their cells, but cold-blooded animals need the heat of the sun to warm them. Reptiles, fish and amphibians are cold-blooded.

Day gecko (a type of lizard) basking in the sun to warm up

At night, or when it is cold, cold-blooded animals are sluggish as their temperature falls below its ideal level. In the morning, or when the weather warms up, they bask in the sun until their blood is warm. Then they become active and search for food.

A lizard lying in the shade of a rock to keep its body at the correct temperature.

In deserts, cold-blooded animals, such as lizards, may become too hot. They cool down by lying in the shade, or in a breezy place where air passing over their bodies helps to cool their blood. Reptiles can survive in very dry places as they do not lose much water through their skin.

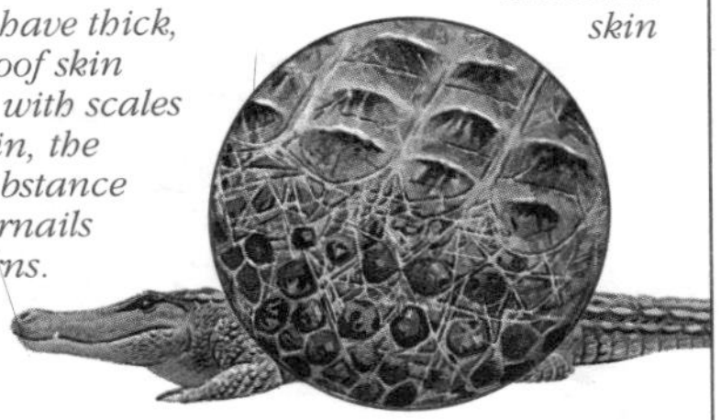

Crocodile skin

Reptiles have thick, waterproof skin covered with scales of keratin, the same substance as fingernails and horns.

Most reptiles live in warm places, but there are snakes and lizards that can survive very cold temperatures near freezing point.

FEEDING

Crocodiles, snakes and some lizards and turtles are carnivores, while tortoises eat mainly plants. Compared to mammals, however, reptiles need very little food. This is because reptiles do not use their food to keep their bodies warm.

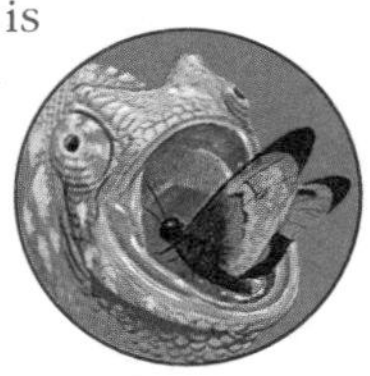

Chameleons (a kind of lizard) catch insects with their long, sticky tongues.

Crocodiles (below) lie in wait for their prey and then drag it under the water to drown it.

Mammals and birds use about 90 percent of their food to maintain their body temperature, and they spend most of their time searching for food. Snakes and crocodiles need a good meal only about once every six weeks and crocodiles often store their food underwater to eat later.

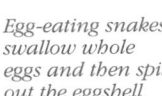

Egg-eating snakes swallow whole eggs and then spit out the eggshell.

Because they do not need so much food, reptiles can live in places where food is scarce. Snakes and lizards can also survive with very little water.

In the African grasslands, snakes and lizards, like those on the right, warm themselves by basking on the rocks in the morning sun. When it gets too hot, they hide in the shadows between the rocks.

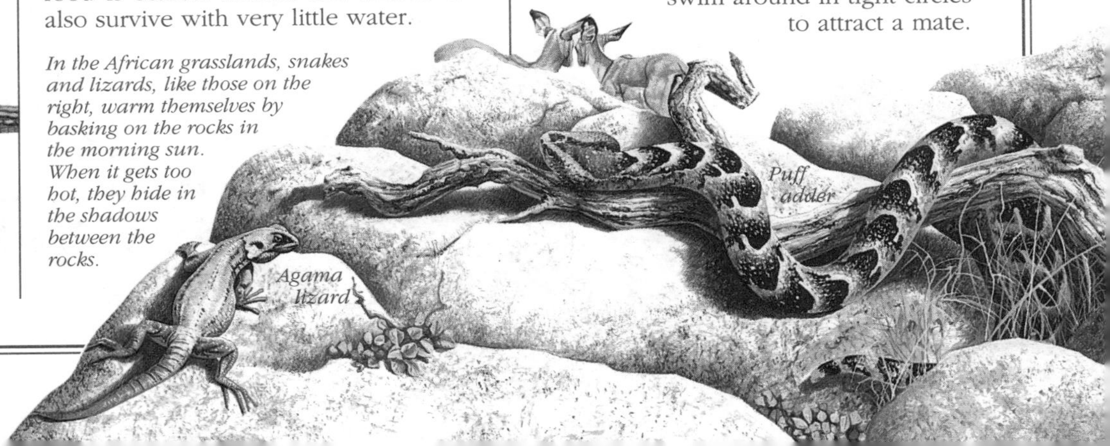
Puff adder
Agama lizard

REPTILE REPRODUCTION

Reptiles reproduce by laying eggs. Snake and lizard eggs have leathery shells, and turtle and crocodile eggs have hard shells, like those of birds.

Snakes lay their eggs in shallow holes, cover them with soil and leave them to hatch. After they hatch, the baby snakes have to look after themselves. This picture shows poisonous Australian taipan snakes hatching.

Most reptiles build some form of nest to protect their eggs. Crocodiles and some snakes stay with their eggs, but turtles bury them in the sand and when the young hatch, they have to dig their way out and crawl to the sea.

Alligators build nests of mud and plants. They look after the young for up to three years.

Frilled lizards display their neck frills to attract females and frighten enemies. The frills contain many blood vessels and may also help to keep the lizards cool.

During the breeding season, male reptiles may fight for territory and females, and some also perform courtship displays to attract a mate. Snakes may wrestle in tests of strength to win females, and crocodiles roar and bellow, snap their strong jaws and swim around in tight circles to attract a mate.

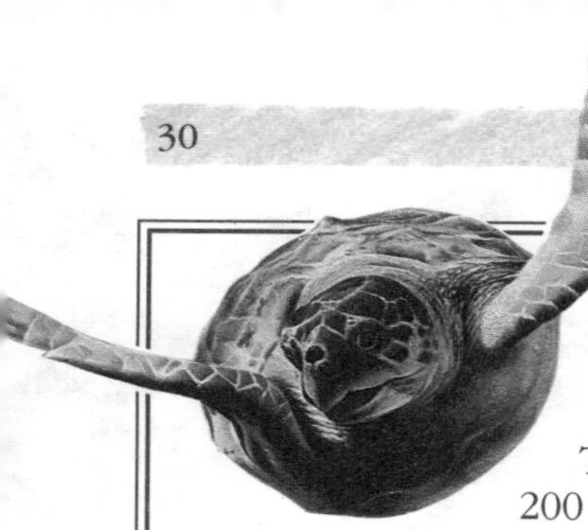

Hawksbill turtles live in tropical seas.

TURTLES AND TORTOISES

Leopard tortoises often travel long distances in search of food.

Turtles and tortoises are reptiles*. They have survived unchanged for over 200 million years, perhaps because they are so well protected inside their shells. There are over 200 different species of turtles and tortoises. Turtles live in water and tortoises live on the land. Terrapins are turtles that live in rivers and lakes.

TURTLES

Several species of turtles live in the sea, and many others live in ponds, rivers and lakes. Green turtles live in warm, shallow seas all around the world, but have been hunted almost to extinction. They eat mainly seaweed and algae.

At the beginning of the breeding season, green turtles migrate long distances to their nesting beaches. Turtles from Brazil, in South America, swim about 4,500km (2,300 miles) to Ascension Island, in the Atlantic Ocean. After mating in the water, the female turtles lay over a hundred eggs on the beach.

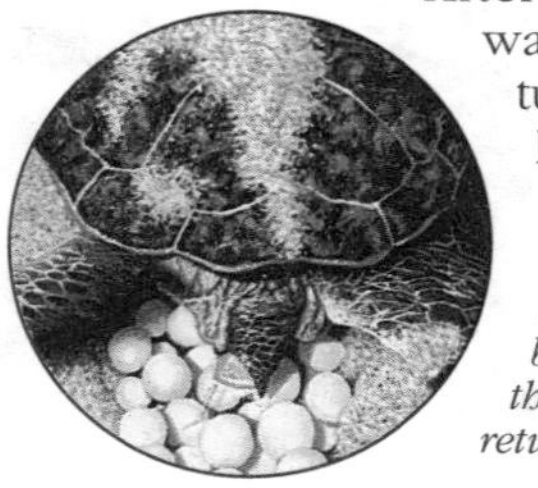

Female turtles bury their eggs in the sand and then return to the sea.

Two or three months later, the eggs hatch and the young turtles dig their way to the surface and crawl down to the sea. Hatching takes place at night when the young turtles are safer from predators such as rats and cats.

European pond terrapins live in ponds and marshes in Europe. During the winter they hibernate in the mud.

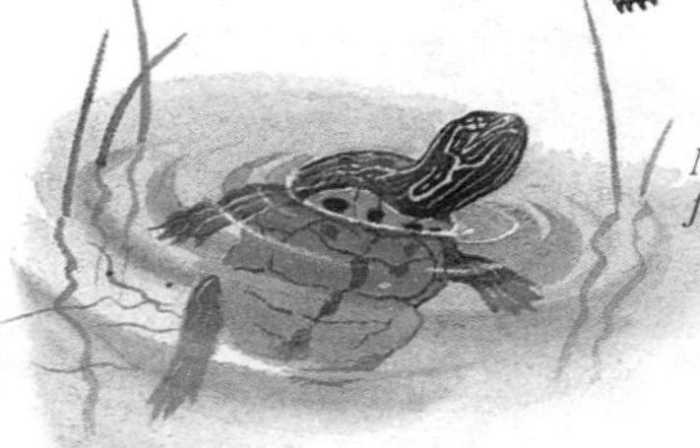

Red-bellied turtles from North America forage for food at the edges of lakes.

Matamata turtles lie in wait on riverbeds. When they feel ripples, they open their jaws and the fish are sucked into their mouths.

TORTOISES

Tortoises eat mainly plants and insects. They move very slowly, covering a distance of about 8m (less than 9yds) each minute. Most tortoises live in hot, dry regions of the world. In cooler countries, they hibernate in the winter.

During the mating season, male tortoises wander around looking for females. They butt anything they meet and if challenged by another male, they fight by banging their shells together.

The male Greek tortoise hisses and butts the female in a courtship ritual before they mate.

When the male tortoise finds a female, he butts her and bites her legs. After mating, the female tortoise lays her eggs in a hollow in the ground, and then leaves the eggs to hatch.

Giant tortoises in the Galapagos Islands, off the coast of South America, weigh over 150kg (330lbs) and their shells are up to 1.5m (5ft) long. Some of the tortoises are over a hundred years old. They live in the lowlands along the coast but travel to the hills to find water. They wander slowly along paths made by the scraping of the shells of many generations of tortoises.

Galapagos giant tortoises are kept free of fleas and lice by finches. The tortoise stretches its neck and stiffens its legs so the birds can reach under its shell.

SHELLS

Turtleshells and tortoiseshells are made of bony plates covered with layers of horn. Baby tortoises are born with complete shells and as they grow, each of the plates in their shells grows too.

The shell is joined to the animal's body at its ribs, spine, shoulders and hips. The rounded top of the shell is called the carapace and the flat bottom part is the plastron.

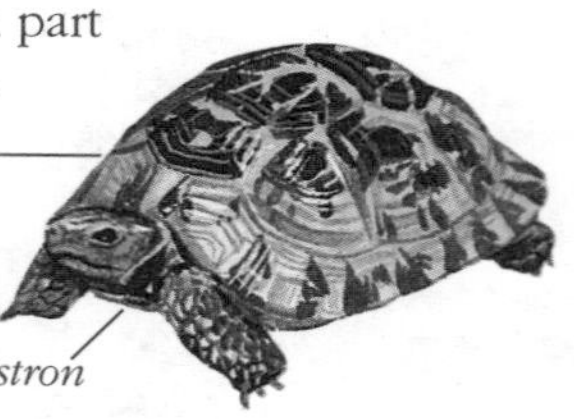
Carapace
Plastron

Hermann's tortoise

Most turtles and tortoises can withdraw their heads and legs into their shells. Once inside, they are almost completely safe from any attack. The box tortoise can even draw up the ends of its plastron (the bottom of the shell) so it is sealed inside. The big-headed turtle, however, cannot withdraw its head.

Tortoises cannot rely on speed to escape, but they are well protected by their hard shells.

Turtles are hunted for their shells from which tortoiseshell items such as combs, earrings and ornaments are made. Because of this, hawksbill turtles are in great danger of becoming extinct.

Many items are now made of plastic rather than tortoiseshell.

Hawksbill turtle

At the start of the breeding season, South American freshwater turtles make very long journeys along the rivers to the sandbanks or river islands where they will breed.

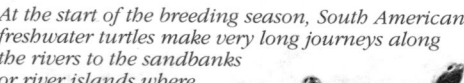

South American freshwater turtles sunbathing on a tree trunk

*Reptiles, 29

CROCODILES AND ALLIGATORS

Baby crocodiles can swim and hunt as soon as they hatch from their eggs.

Crocodiles, alligators, and their relatives, caimans and gavials, are reptiles*. They are descended from the same prehistoric reptiles as the dinosaurs. They are all carnivores and they live on the banks of tropical rivers and eat fish, animals, or even people who may come down to the riverside.

American alligator

CROCODILES

There are thirteen different species of crocodiles. The Nile crocodile, which lives in tropical rivers in Africa, is the largest of the crocodiles. It grows up to 6m (20ft) long and can weigh up to 1,000kg (2,200lbs).

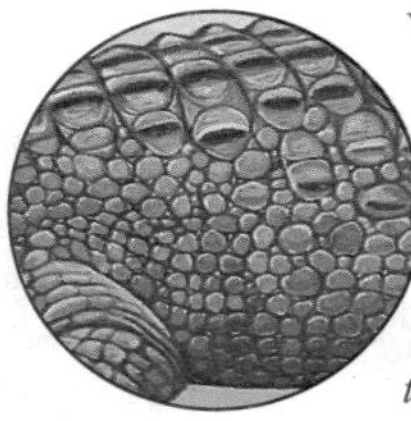

Crocodiles have protective bony plates, called scutes, in their skin. The scutes on their bellies are smaller than those on their backs.

Crocodiles live alone or gather in small groups. During the hottest part of the day, they lie in the water or in the shade of the riverbank to keep cool. They feed in the evening.

Crocodiles swim by paddling with their webbed feet and swinging their strong tails from side to side. Their eyes and nostrils are on the tops of their heads.

They have a second pair of see-through eyelids so they can see underwater, and a flap of skin in their throats stops them from swallowing water.

Female crocodiles build their nests on the riverbanks. The nests are made of mud and may be 2-3m (6-10ft) high.

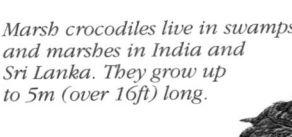

Marsh crocodiles live in swamps and marshes in India and Sri Lanka. They grow up to 5m (over 16ft) long.

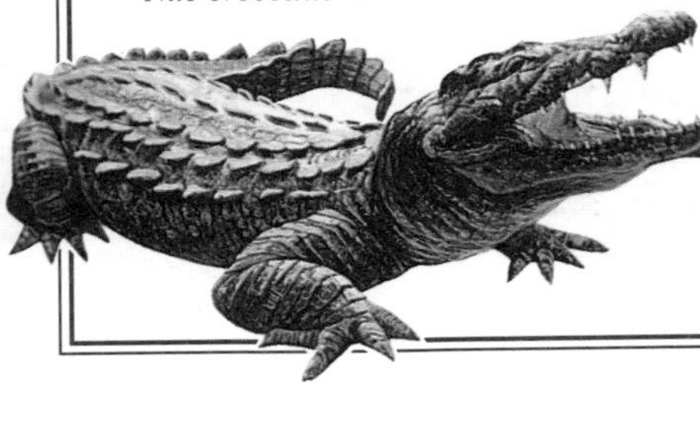

Nile crocodile

To catch their prey, which may be a zebra, fish, gazelle or even a lion, crocodiles lie very still until the animal is close enough to grab with their huge jaws. Then they pull it under the water to drown it. They eat all their prey, including fur, bones, hoofs and horns, which they tear up with their sharp teeth. They have very strong digestion and also swallow pebbles to help grind the food in their stomachs.

Crocodiles are well camouflaged against the muddy waters and riverbank.

After mating, female Nile crocodiles lay up to a hundred eggs and bury them in a nest on the riverbank. They guard the eggs for 6-14 weeks. When the baby crocodiles begin to croak, they dig up the eggs, crack the shells and carry the babies to the water.

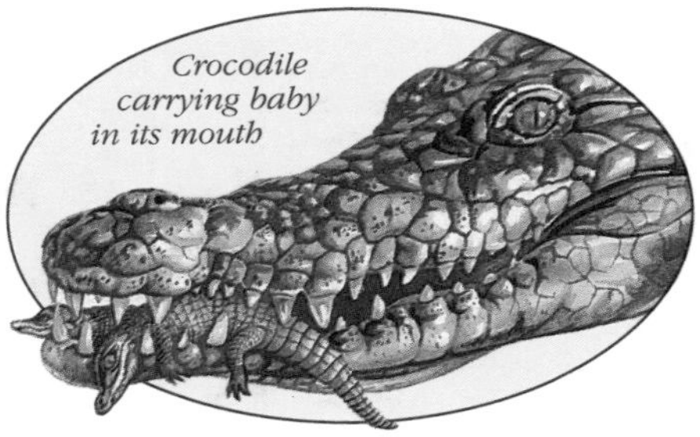

Crocodile carrying baby in its mouth

The young crocodiles are about 30cm (nearly 12in) long. They can swim and hunt for food as soon as they hatch, but they may stay near their mothers for protection from predators for up to two years. However, many of the eggs and young are eaten by mongooses, snakes, eagles or large fish.

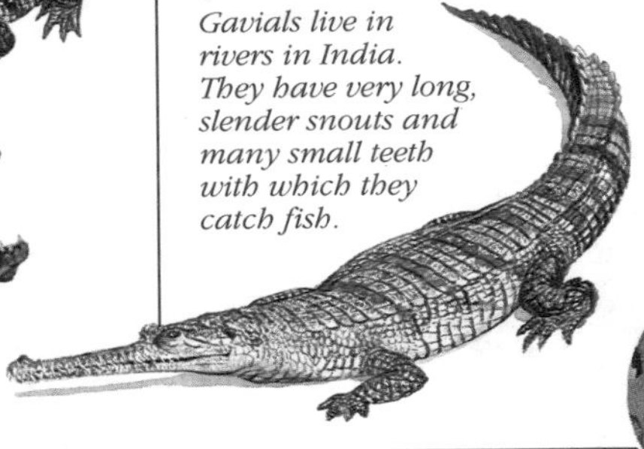

Gavials live in rivers in India. They have very long, slender snouts and many small teeth with which they catch fish.

ALLIGATORS

There are two species of alligators. American alligators live in the swamps in southeastern USA. Chinese alligators live in the Yangtze River in China, but may be extinct in the wild.

Young Chinese alligator bred in a zoo

American alligators were endangered by the draining of the swamps where they lived, and because they were hunted for their skins. In 1969, it became illegal to sell the skins of wild alligators and now the number of alligators has increased. They are kept on farms for their skins, which are made into bags and shoes.

CAIMANS

There are at least five species of caimans. They live along the banks of the River Amazon, in South America. Caimans are related to alligators, but they are smaller. They are now rare as they are hunted for their skins and eggs.

Anaconda constrictor snake eating a caiman

*Reptiles, 29

SNAKES AND LIZARDS

AND THE TUATARA

Boomslang snakes climb trees and snatch birds from their nests.

Boomslang snakes live in grasslands in southern Africa.

Geckos, such as this tokay gecko, have huge eyes and hunt for insects at night.

Snakes and lizards are perhaps the most successful of the reptiles*. There are several thousand different species of both of them and, unlike other reptiles, they have also adapted to live in cooler parts of the world. Snakes are believed to have evolved from lizards about 120 million years ago. The tuatara, which lives only in New Zealand, is the sole survivor of a group of reptiles that lived about 220-150 million years ago.

SNAKES

There are over 2,400 species of snakes and they live in every continent except Antarctica. They are skilled hunters and in many areas, they are useful to farmers as they help control pests.

The fer-de-lance is the most poisonous snake in South America.

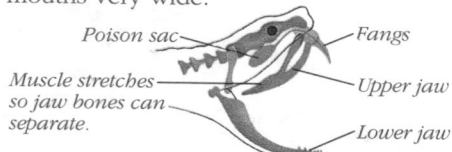

All snakes are carnivores. Small snakes eat insects and worms, but larger snakes eat eggs, birds, small mammals and even gazelles and crocodiles. They swallow their prey whole and can separate their jaw bones and stretch their mouths very wide.

Poison sac
Fangs
Muscle stretches so jaw bones can separate.
Upper jaw
Lower jaw

Some snakes kill their prey with venom (poison). Others, such as boas and pythons, are constrictors: they wrap themselves around their prey and slowly squeeze it until it suffocates. Poisonous snakes have hollow teeth, called fangs, through which the venom is injected into their prey. The venom may paralyze the victim, or cause internal bleeding.

Rock pythons coil around their prey and tighten the coils until the animal suffocates. Then they swallow it head first. Their skin stretches easily so large food fits inside.

Weaverbird in nest

Snakes have very poor eyesight and no eyelids or external ears. They find their prey by smell, and by feeling its vibrations through the ground. They also pick up scents in the air by flicking their forked tongues in and out. Rattlesnakes can sense tiny changes in temperature caused by the heat from the body of another animal nearby.

Rattlesnakes have small pits containing heat sensors on either side of their heads and they can hunt in total darkness. This rattlesnake has sensed the heat given off by a small mouse nearby.

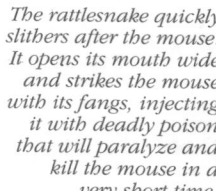

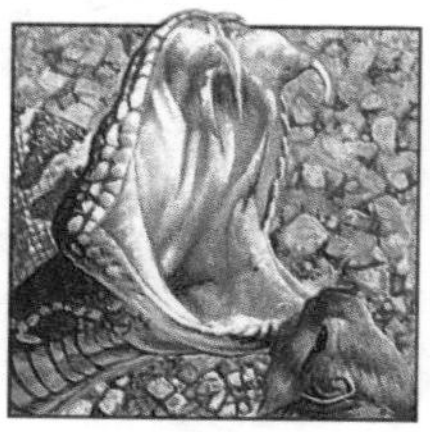

The rattlesnake quickly slithers after the mouse. It opens its mouth wide and strikes the mouse with its fangs, injecting it with deadly poison that will paralyze and kill the mouse in a very short time.

The mouse may try to run away, but it soon dies. The snake waits for the poison to work and then searches for its prey with its heat sensors. When it finds the mouse, the snake swallows it whole.

Snakes are cold-blooded* and do not need to eat a lot of food to make heat to keep their bodies warm. After a large meal, a snake may not eat again for several days - or even weeks.

Snakes move in a series of S-shaped curves, pushing back on each curve to move their bodies forward. On their bellies, they have large, overlapping scales called scutes that help them to grip the ground.

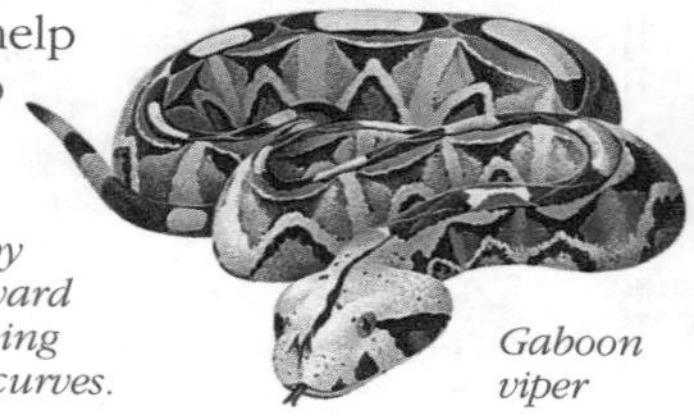

Snakes move by stretching forward and then pushing back on their curves.

Gaboon viper

A snake's patterned skin helps to camouflage it against the leaves, ground or rocks where it lives. Some snakes, though, have bright markings to warn other animals not to eat them because they are poisonous.

Milk snake

Milk snakes have bright markings but they are not poisonous. They look like poisonous coral snakes, so enemies leave them alone.

Coral snake

Many snakes also have other means of defending themselves. Poisonous snakes will bite an attacker, and the African spitting cobra can spit blinding venom. Rattlesnakes shake the rattle at the end of their tails to warn predators to go away.

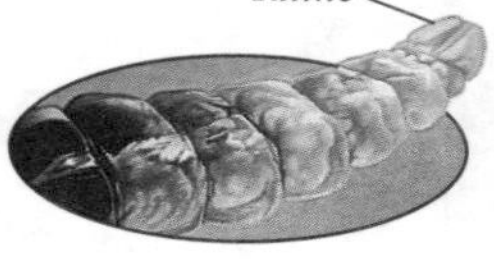
Rattle

A rattlesnake's rattle is made of sections of hard, dead skin.

When they are two or three years old, snakes mate and the females lay eggs. In cooler climates, the eggs hatch inside the female's body and she gives birth to live young. Snakes do not look after their young, but some boas and pythons curl around their eggs to protect them.

European grass snake with eggs

*Reptiles, 29; Cold-blooded Animals, 29

LIZARDS

Most lizards are small, agile little reptiles that live on the ground among rocks, or in trees, but the Komodo dragon, a type of monitor lizard that lives in Indonesia, grows up to 3m (10ft) long and eats goats and buffaloes.

Chameleons are lizards that live mainly in trees. They catch insects in the hollow tips of their long, sticky tongues.

Most small lizards eat insects, spiders and worms, while larger lizards, such as some iguanas, are usually herbivores. Like snakes (see left), lizards can open their mouths very wide as the bones in their skulls are not fused together.

There are many different species of iguanas. Most live in trees and eat insects, snails and worms, but larger iguanas are herbivores.

Lizards lay soft-shelled eggs in holes in the ground or among the rocks. In cool climates, the eggs may hatch inside the female's body, so she gives birth to live young.

To defend themselves, most lizards can shed their tails. Special fracture planes in the bones enable them to cast off the end of their tails and run away, leaving the enemy confused. A new tail grows again within a few weeks.

A young, five-lined skink can break off its blue tail. The tail keeps twitching to confuse the predator.

Most lizards are green or brown to camouflage them among tree leaves or in the grass. Chameleons can even change the patterns on their skin to match their surroundings. This helps them hide from predators - and from the insects they eat.

The pattern of yellow and green on a chameleon's skin changes according to its surroundings. It even takes on the pattern of leaves in the trees around it.

SNAKES AND LIZARDS OF THE WORLD

Prickly spines

Thorny devils live in the desert in Australia. Their skin is covered with spines that protect them from snakes and other predators. When attacked, they tuck their heads between their legs and arch their backs.

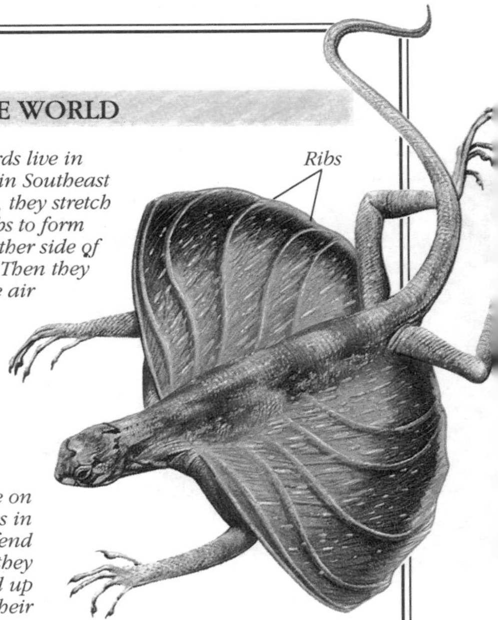
Ribs

Flying lizards live in rainforests in Southeast Asia. To fly, they stretch out their ribs to form stiff flaps either side of their body. Then they jump in the air and can glide up to 15m (50ft) between trees.

A ringed snake pretending to be dead

Ringed snakes live on boggy hillsides in Europe. To defend themselves, they lie coiled up with their long tongues hanging out, pretending to be dead.

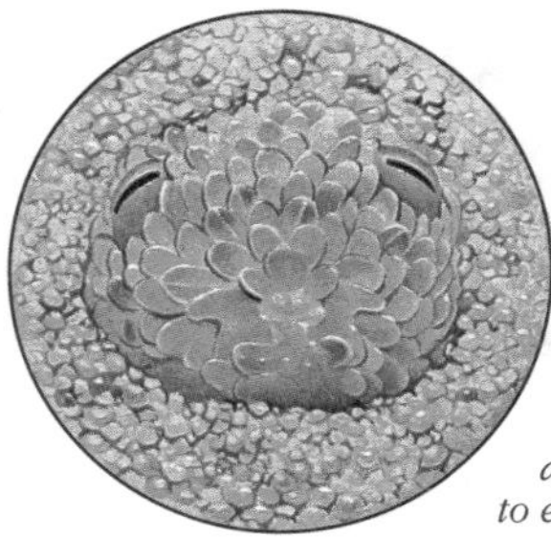

Dwarf puff adders (a species of snake) bury themselves in the desert sand to keep cool, and also to ambush small animals to eat.

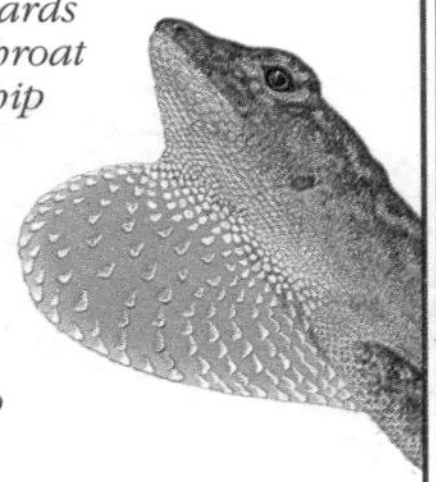

Male anole lizards display their throat sacs in courtship rituals to attract females, and also to challenge male lizards that come into their territory.

Gila monsters store fat in their tails.

Gila (pronounced "heel-ya") monsters are good swimmers.

The Gila monster lives in North America. It eats small mammals, such as mice, which it poisons with venom from a gland in its mouth.

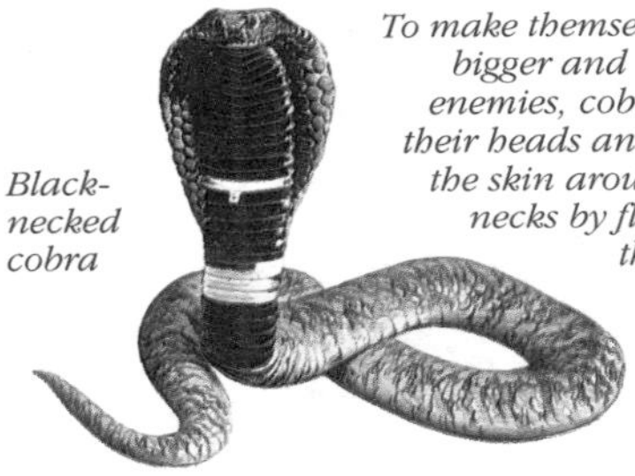

Black-necked cobra

To make themselves look bigger and threaten enemies, cobras raise their heads and stretch the skin around their necks by flattening their ribs.

Skinks and other lizards can shed their tails to defend themselves.

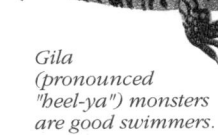

Ornate flying snakes live in rainforests. They can climb trees and glide between branches.

Flying snake's ribs when resting

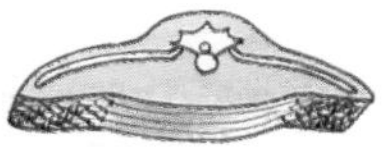

Flying snake's ribs when flying

To glide, flying snakes raise their rib-cages up and out. This flattens out their bodies which then act like parachutes. Using S-shaped movements, they can glide as far as 50m (165ft).

THE TUATARA

The tuatara is a lizard-like reptile that lives on small islands off the coast of New Zealand. Unusually for a reptile, it feeds at night and is active when its body temperature is only about 12°C (53°F). During the day, it rests in its burrow. It eats snails, worms and sometimes seabirds. Because its body is so cool, the tuatara is very slow. It breathes about once every seven seconds, and only once an hour when it is not moving. It also grows very slowly and takes up to 20 years to reach a length of about 60cm (2ft).

Tuataras

FROGS, TOADS AND SALAMANDERS

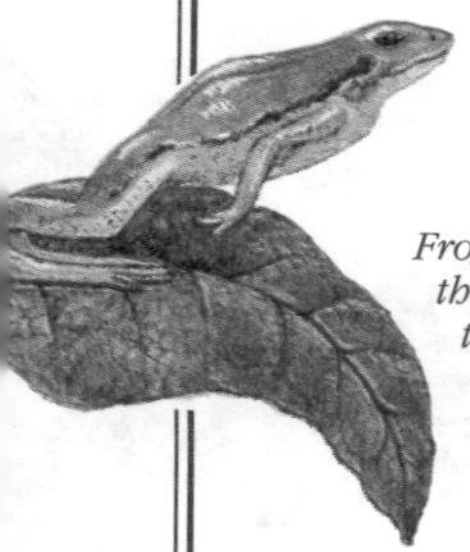

Frogs, such as this European tree frog, leap to catch flies and escape enemies.

Frogs, toads and salamanders belong to a group of animals called amphibians. Amphibians live in water when they are young and move onto land when they grow up. They are called cold-blooded animals*, which means they cannot make their own body heat, and their bodies are about the same temperature as the air or water.

LIFE CYCLE OF AMPHIBIANS

Frogs, toads and newts lay their eggs, called spawn, in water. The eggs hatch into tadpoles that do not look at all like their parents. They have tails for swimming and gills for taking oxygen from the water for breathing. The way tadpoles, and other animals such as insects, grow and change to become adults like their parents is called metamorphosis. A typical frog life cycle is shown in the pictures below.

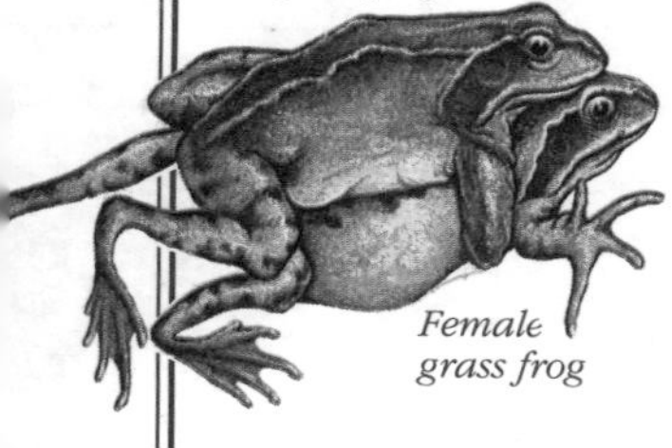

Male grass frog
Female grass frog

When mating, the male frog holds onto the female with his spiky thumb pads. The female lays a large clump of frogspawn in the water.

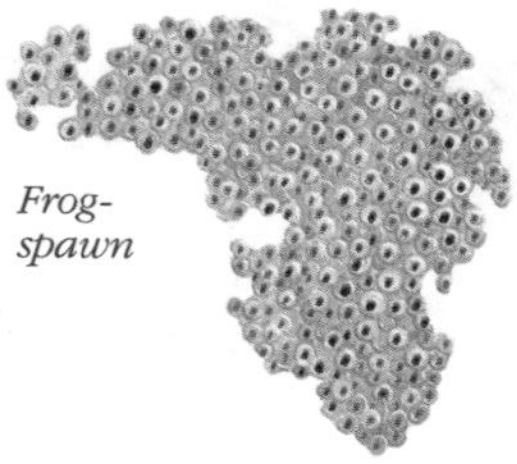

Frog-spawn

The tadpoles grow inside the eggs and feed on their yolk. After about ten days they wriggle out and cling to water plants.

Gills for breathing

After four more days, the tadpoles can swim. At first they eat small plants and then insects and small fish.

As the tadpoles grow, their gills disappear and lungs form inside their bodies. They go to the surface of the water to breathe.

After about eight weeks, the back legs form.

At 10 or 11 weeks, the front legs develop.

Grass frog

At 12 or 13 weeks, the tail disappears and the tiny frog, 1cm (0.4in) long, is ready to leave the water. It will be fully grown in three years. Few tadpoles survive to this stage. Most are eaten by other pond creatures.

FROGS

Frogs are found all over the world, except in Antarctica and Greenland. They have long, strong back legs for jumping, and large webbed feet for swimming. Although they have lungs, much of the oxygen gas that they need is absorbed through their skin, which has to be kept moist. Frogs have no earholes, but they have excellent hearing. A small circular mark under their eyes shows the position of their eardrums.

Position of eardrum

Webbed feet
Suckers
South American gliding tree frog

Tree frogs have suckers on their toes and can cling to bark and leaves. Some can glide up to 12m (40ft).

Frogs eat mainly insects and spiders, although they also eat slugs, snails and worms. They tend to sit still, waiting for their prey, and then catch it with their long, sticky tongues. Some of the larger species of frogs eat lizards, small mammals such as mice and voles, and even birds.

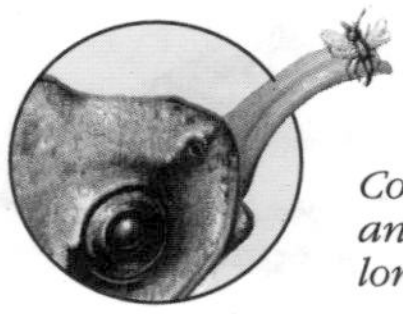

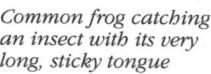

Common frog catching an insect with its very long, sticky tongue

In countries with a cold or dry season, frogs hibernate by burying themselves in the mud at the bottom of a pool. In the spring, or after the first rains, they come out to mate. Frogs usually return to the pond or pool where they were born to mate and lay their eggs. The male may attract the female by croaking, or by his bright markings.

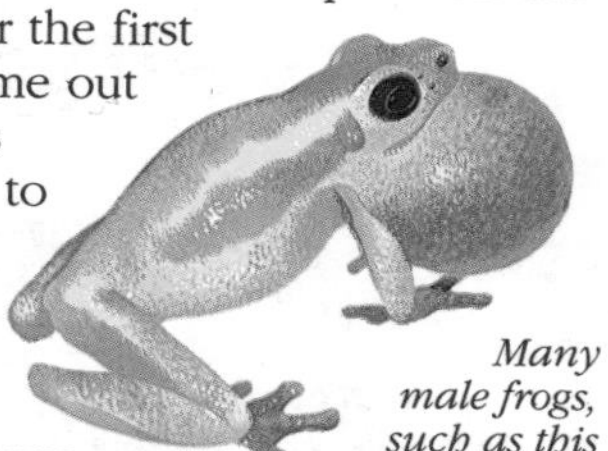

Many male frogs, such as this New Guinea tree frog, have large vocal sacs to make the sound of their croaking louder.

Most female frogs lay clumps of several thousand eggs. They do not look after the eggs or tadpoles and many of them are eaten by other creatures. A few species, such as arrow-poison frogs, lay fewer eggs, and look after them carefully.

Arrow-poison frogs, which live in rainforests in South America, carry their tadpoles to bromeliad plants. The leaves form cups that hold tiny pools of water.

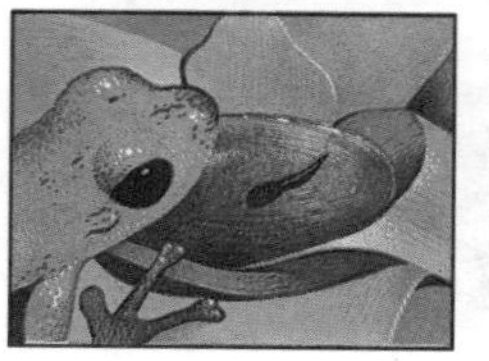

The female frog puts each tadpole into a separate, water-filled bromeliad plant. She feeds them each week with some of the frogspawn that has not developed.

The tadpoles grow and, after six to eight weeks, change into tiny frogs in the pools in the plants. When they are fully grown, they leave the pools and live in the forest.

Arrow-poison frogs have very bright patterns to warn predators that they are poisonous. Other species of frogs are very well camouflaged with the surroundings where they live to protect themselves from predators.

Hoods of skin

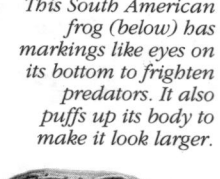

Horned frogs (above) in the Malaysian rain-forests have pointed hoods of skin over their eyes.They blend in with dead leaves on the forest floor.

This South American frog (below) has markings like eyes on its bottom to frighten predators. It also puffs up its body to make it look larger.

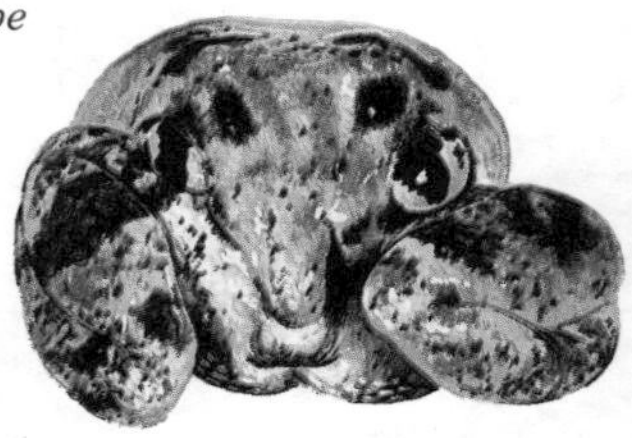

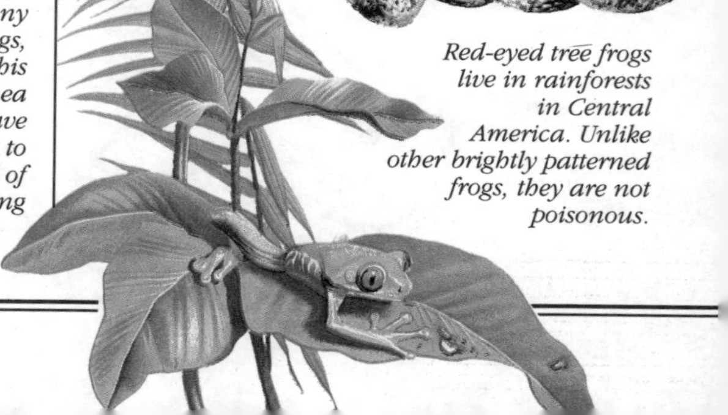

Red-eyed tree frogs live in rainforests in Central America. Unlike other brightly patterned frogs, they are not poisonous.

*Cold-blooded Animals, 29

TOADS

There is little biological difference between toads and frogs, but toads are usually squatter and have shorter legs and drier, warty skin. Like frogs, toads sit in wait for their prey and catch insects or small animals with their long, sticky tongues. Some are active at night and others hunt during the day.

Warty skin

Common toads hunt after dusk and eat snails, worms and insects.

Like frogs, adult toads live on land. They often travel far from water and in the cold or dry season, hibernate in mud or in old animal burrows. In the spring, or the rainy season, they return to the pools where they were born, to mate and lay their eggs. They often travel for several days to reach their pools.

In some countries, there are signs warning drivers to look out for toads that travel along the same routes to their breeding grounds every year.

At the beginning of the mating season, the male toads arrive at the pool first. They usually attract the females by croaking, and each species has a different type of croak.

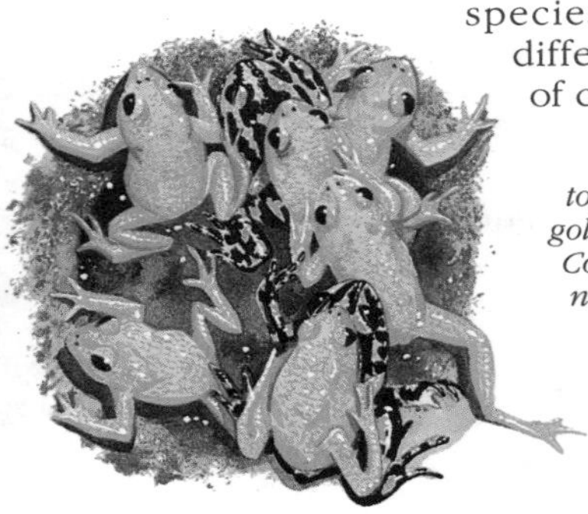

Some male toads, such as golden toads of Costa Rica, do not croak.The females are attracted by their shiny, golden skin.

After mating, female toads lay long strings of eggs, or toadspawn, in the water. In some species, the male toads look after the eggs. The eggs hatch into tadpoles and then take several months to metamorphose into young toads (see Life Cycle, left).

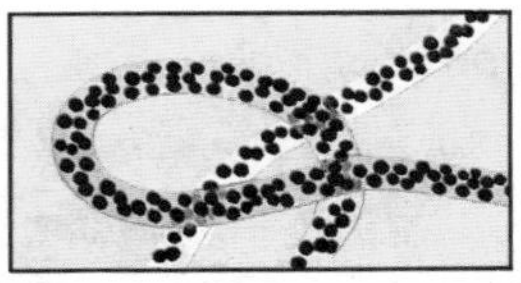

Toadspawn is in long strings, unlike frogspawn, which is in clumps.

Toadspawn

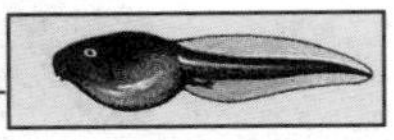
Tadpole

If a toad is threatened by a grass snake, it stands up straight and puffs its body up to make it look bigger and frighten the snake away.

Toads are well camouflaged with their surroundings and to defend themselves, most also secrete poison from glands in their skin. They can also suck in air to make their bodies look large and round, and stand up straight on their legs to frighten enemies.

Natterjack toads hunt at night and catch insects. The male toad has a very loud croak.

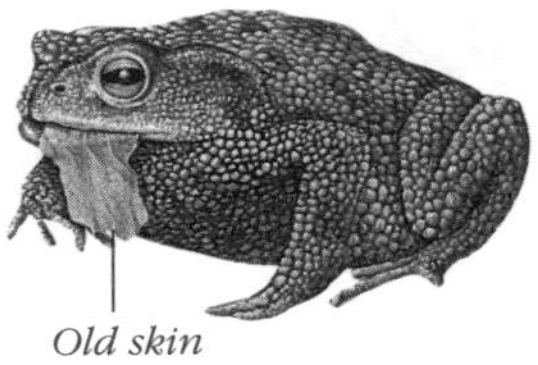
Old skin

European common toads shed their skins several times in the summer. They scrape off the old skin and eat it.

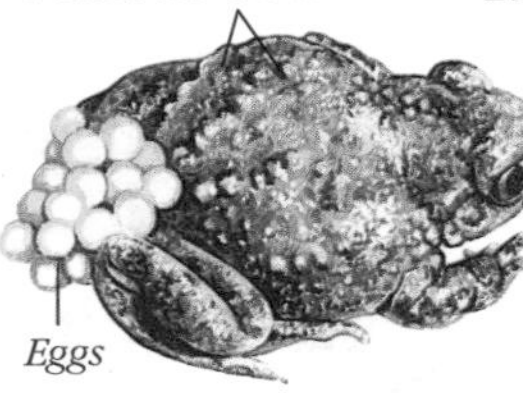
Poisonous warts
Eggs

Male midwife toads of Europe and North Africa carry eggs from several females wrapped around their legs. When the eggs are ready to hatch, they take them to water.

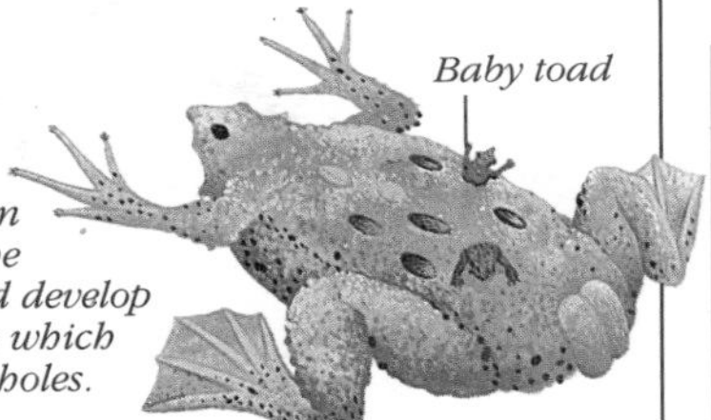
Baby toad

Male Surinam toads carry the female's eggs in holes on their backs. The eggs hatch and develop into tiny toads which hop out of the holes.

Water surface

Yellow-bellied European toads live in water all the time. They live in shallow puddles as well as in ponds and lakes.

Strong legs for burrowing in the sand

Spadefoot toads live in deserts. They can survive for nine months buried in the sand. After it rains, they come out to find a mate.

SALAMANDERS

Salamanders look rather like lizards, but they do not have scaly skin. Newts are salamanders that spend all their lives in water. Salamanders are found near water, but they hibernate under stones and other dry places. They are carnivores and eat insects and slugs.

Alpine salamander

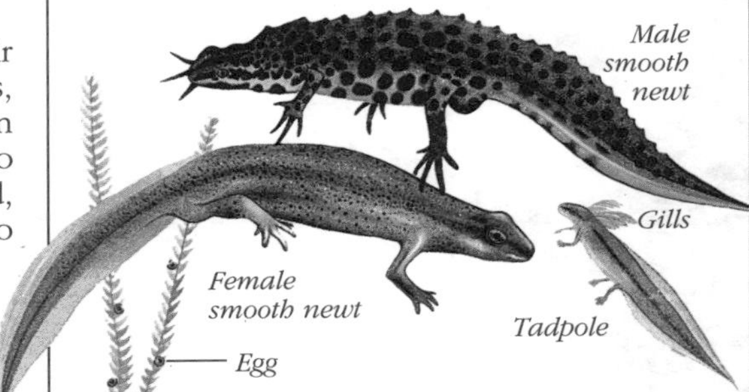
Male smooth newt
Gills
Female smooth newt
Tadpole
Egg

Like frogs and toads, newts and salamanders often return to the pools where they were born to lay their eggs. The males cannot croak and they perform elaborate courtship rituals to attract the females. Newts lay their eggs singly on water plants. The leaves are often bent over to protect the eggs. The tadpoles hatch after about two weeks. The young newts, called efts, are ready to leave the water in late summer, but some stay in the water until the next spring. Unlike frogs and toads, salamander and newt tadpoles do not lose their tails.

Tiger salamander

SEE FOR YOURSELF

You can keep tadpoles in a large tank, or bowl, and watch them develop into adult amphibians. In the spring, collect a small amount of spawn (or a few tadpoles) and some pond plants. After about a week, hang small pieces of raw meat in the water. Replace the meat every two days and if the water smells bad, change it (you can use tap water). After two or three months, the small frogs or toads will need a brick or stone so they can reach the surface to breathe. You should then return them to their pond.

Tadpoles cling to water plants.

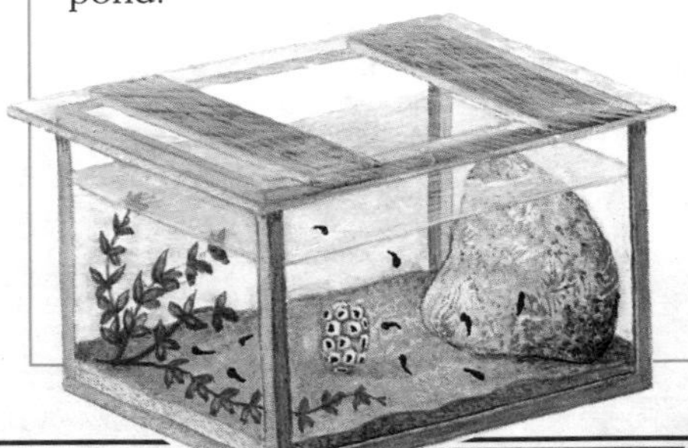

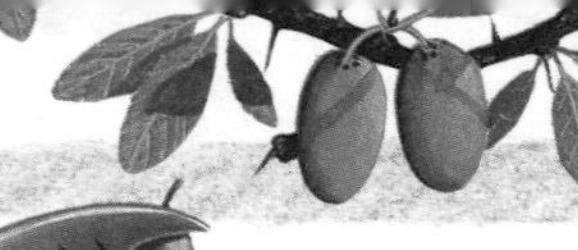

BIRDS

Birds may have evolved from small dinosaurs that lived 150 million years ago. Nearly all birds can fly, and they all have feathers, a beak and wings. They have streamlined bodies, powerful flight muscles and large hearts that beat up to 600 times a minute to pump blood to their flight muscles.

Toucans live in rainforests.

Rufous fantail

HOW BIRDS FLY

A bird's wings are curved on top and flat underneath, like the wings of an aircraft. This shape is called an aerofoil and it creates a force called uplift in the air that helps to keep the birds airborne. Birds' bones are hollow, which makes them very light, and they have a large breastbone to support their powerful flight muscles. Large birds, such as eagles and gulls, hold their wings out straight. They soar up on rising air currents and glide down.

Air flows faster over the curve above the wing.

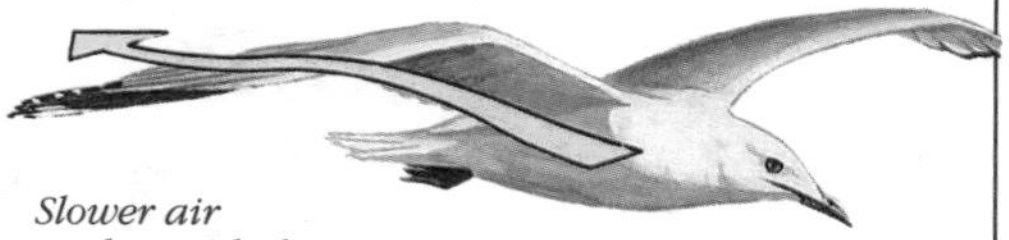

Slower air underneath the wing pushes upward.

Herring gull

Most small birds fly by flapping their wings. This increases the force of uplift under the wings. Hummingbirds hover in front of flowers by moving their wings very fast in the shape of an eight.

Goldcrest flapping

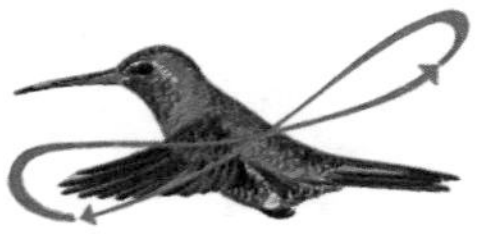

Hummingbirds hover by moving their wings in the shape of an eight.

Kittiwake gliding on an air current with its wings held out flat

To turn, birds use their tail feathers as a rudder. To slow down and land, they alter the angle of their wings and spread out the feathers. This allows air to pass through the wings and reduces the force of uplift under the wings.

Herring gull about to land with its wing feathers spread out, its feet lowered, and its tail held down and spread out as a brake

FEATHERS

A bird's feathers enable it to fly and also keep it warm and dry. Feathers are made of keratin, the same material as the hair and nails of mammals. The flight feathers of the wings and tail are long and stiff. Contour feathers on the body give the bird a very smooth and streamlined shape. Under the contour feathers, there are soft down feathers that help to keep the bird warm.

Flight feathers
Contour feathers

Kingfisher diving

Flight feathers have a central shaft and two vanes of barbs. The barbs have tiny barbules on either side and the barbules have hooks that knit together and hold the feather smooth. Feathers gradually become worn and are replaced by new ones that push out the old ones as they grow. Most birds change their feathers once a year.

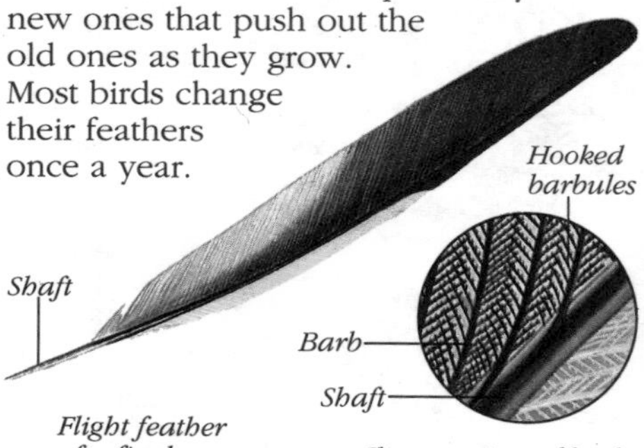

Hooked barbules
Shaft
Barb
Shaft

Flight feather of a finch

Close-up view of barbs

A bird's feathers are called its plumage. Its plumage may help a bird blend with the surroundings or attract a mate. Some birds have striking markings, such as wing or tail stripes, to help them recognize each other.

Greylag geese follow each other's white rumps.

Semi-palmated plovers have markings that break up their outline so they are hard to see.

FEEDING

The shape of a bird's beak shows the kind of food it eats. Insect-eaters have thin, pointed beaks and seed-eaters, such as finches, have strong, chunky beaks. Meat-eaters, such as hawks and kestrels, have hooked beaks for tearing flesh.

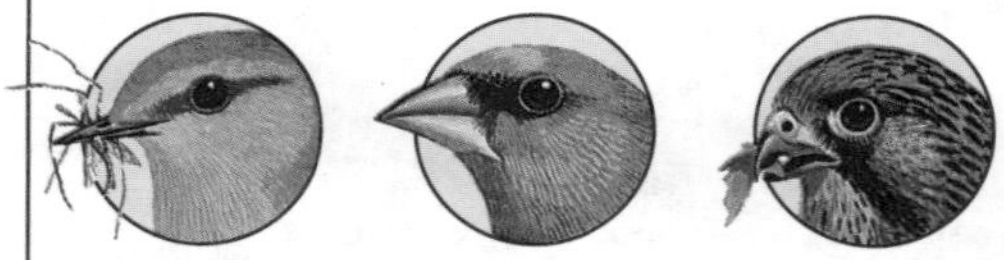

Wood warblers eat insects. *Greenfinches eat seeds.* *Kestrels are meat-eaters.*

Teals eat water plants. *Honey-eaters suck nectar.* *Arctic terns catch fish.*

Geese, swans and ducks, such as teals, have flattish bills for sucking tiny plants, animals and seeds from the water. Nectar-feeders, such as honey-eaters and hummingbirds, have thin, pointed bills for reaching into flowers. Herons, cranes and terns have long, straight, dagger-shaped bills for catching fish.

Birds have no teeth. Instead, their food is broken up in a sac called the gizzard at the beginning of their digestive system, and some swallow small stones to help the grinding process. They also have a sac called a crop where food can be stored before going into the gizzard.

Crop where food is stored
Gizzard where food is broken up

Digestive system of a pigeon

Many birds cough up food that cannot be digested, such as bones and fur, in a compact shape called a pellet. Owls, gulls and starlings produce pellets.

Grit and plant remains in a rook pellet

Feathers and bones in a barn owl pellet

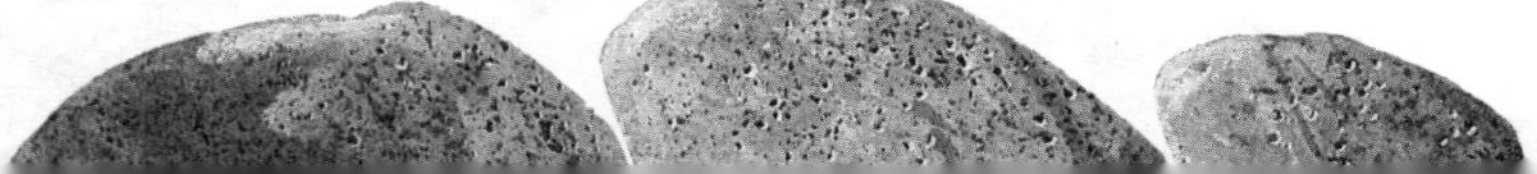

COURTSHIP

Some species of birds perform elaborate courtship rituals to attract a mate. Many other animals use their sense of smell to find each other, but birds have a very poor sense of smell. Courtship rituals, and the bright plumage of some male birds, may help male and female birds of the same species to find each other.

Male bowerbirds make elaborate bowers from sticks and grasses. They decorate them with shells, feathers and flowers. Satin bowerbirds prefer blue objects. Females visit at least three bowers before choosing a mate.

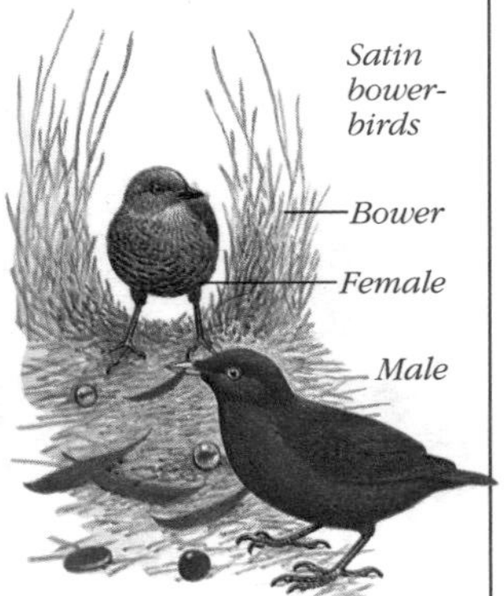
Satin bower-birds
Bower
Female
Male

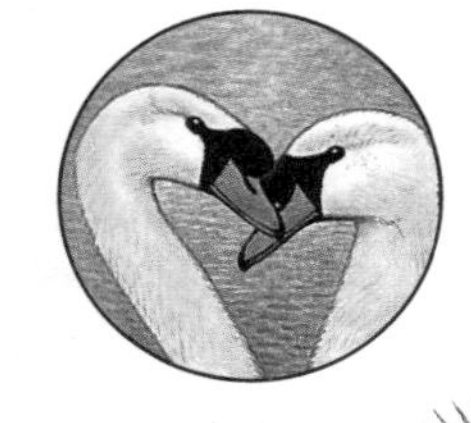

A pair of mute swans stays together for life. At the beginning of each breeding season, they perform graceful courtship ceremonies.

During courtship, birds of paradise shriek, puff out their chests and show off their tail plumes.

During the breeding season, male birds also compete aggressively for an area of land, or territory, which can supply nesting materials and food for the young.

When faced with a rival, starlings use their beaks in fights and warning displays. A European robin holds his head back and puffs out his breast tc make himself bigger.

European robins

BREEDING

After mating, the female bird lays eggs*. The eggs are usually laid in a nest* built by one or both parents. The number of eggs depends on the species of bird, the time of year and how much food is available. Blue tits have been known to lay as many as 19 eggs.

A male bee-eater hovers above the female and lands on her back to mate. He flaps his wings to keep his balance.

Parents sit on the eggs to keep them warm. This is called incubation and lasts about two weeks for small birds. The parents lose feathers from patches on their bellies so their warm skin touches the eggs. Usually both parents share the care of eggs and young, although over 70 species, including cuckoos and some cowbirds, deposit their eggs in other birds' nests and do not look after their young.

A marsh tit with a brood patch - a bare patch of skin for keeping its eggs warm

When a bird is ready to hatch, it chips its way out of its egg. Many birds have an "egg tooth" on their beaks to help them. This drops off soon after hatching.

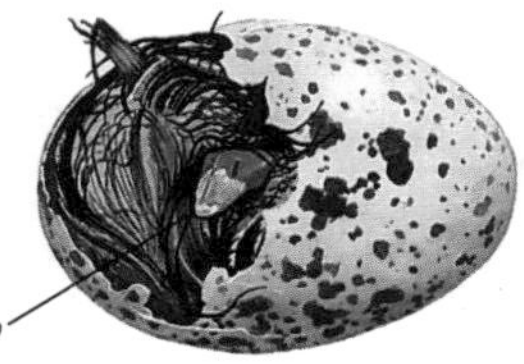
Egg tooth

Moorhen chick hatching

The young of most birds are blind and naked when they hatch. They are called nestlings and are fed and looked after by both parents. When they can leave the nest they are called fledglings. The young of birds such as hens and ducks that are born with their eyes open and with soft down or feathers, are usually called chicks. They can leave the nest and feed soon after they hatch.

Chick with soft feathers

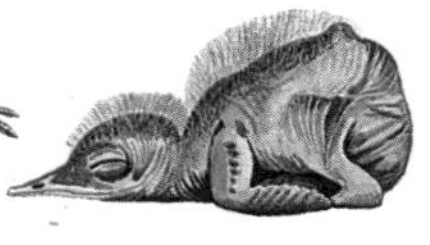

Nestlings are blind and naked

Above left: lapwing chicks can leave the nest and run about soon after hatching. Above right: blackbird nestlings stay in the nest for about two weeks.

BIRDSONG AND CALLS

All birds use calls to communicate with each other, and some can produce more complicated, tuneful sounds. In most species, only the males sing. They sing in the breeding season to attract a mate and claim their territory. Most birds also have different calls for specific purposes. Alarm calls warn other birds of a predator, and birds that live in flocks make contact calls to keep in touch with each other.

Many birds regularly sing from the same positions around their territory. These positions are called song posts. A song may be repeated over a thousand times every day.

Meadow-lark

BIRD MIGRATION

About half of all the different species of birds regularly travel to different habitats to find more food or better breeding conditions. As the days become longer (or shorter) the birds become restless and some species gather in large groups. Before migrating, birds build up layers of fat that will be the "fuel" for their journeys.

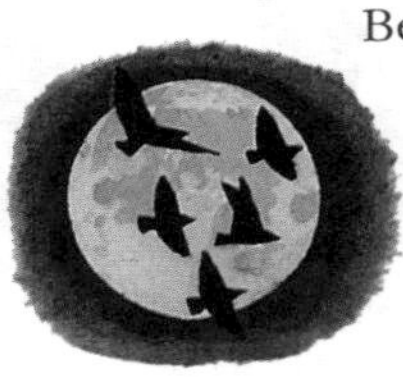

It is not fully understood how birds find their way over long distances. During the day, they may follow landmarks, such as rivers and mountains, or use the Sun. At night, some species may use the position of the moon and stars for navigation.

SEE FOR YOURSELF

To attract birds near your home, put out food such as unsalted peanuts, wild birdseed, breadcrumbs, cheese and lumps of fat. Birds also like some water to drink or bathe in. Do not feed birds during the breeding season, though, as the food may not be suitable for the nestlings.

In the nesting season, you could hang out nesting materials such as yarn, string, straw and feathers.

Experiment with different foods to attract different species of birds.

*Birds' Eggs, 38; Birds' Nests, 39

BIRDS OF THE WORLD

There are over 9,000 different species of birds and they have adapted to survive in almost every environment around the world, from desolate mountainsides to Arctic wastes, desert sands and cities. But at least a thousand species of birds are in danger of extinction. The main threats to birds are loss of habitat, pollution and hunting.

Count Raggia's bird of paradise

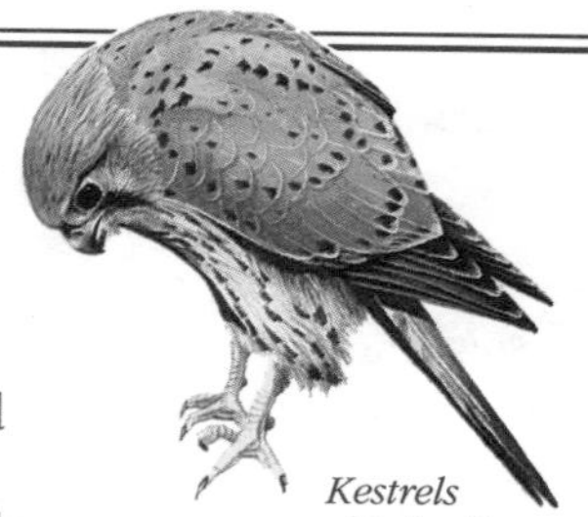

Kestrels are birds of prey. They hover in the air and then swoop down on small mammals or insects.

To attract female birds, Count Raggia's birds of paradise from Australia and New Guinea, clear leaves off branches to let the light shine on their brilliant feathers. They lean over, spread out their feathers and clap their wings together.

During the breeding season, many species of birds have very bright feathers, and some perform elaborate courtship rituals to help them find a mate.*

Flap of skin called a lappet

Male Temminck's tragopan birds open out their chest feathers to show bright blue and red flaps of skin called lappets. Two soft horns stand up on their heads.

Blue herons stand in shallow water, waiting to catch fish or frogs with their long beaks.

Jacanas live in tropical wetlands and walk on lily leaves looking for insects to eat.

During courtship, cranes clatter their beaks and hop up and down in a complicated dance.

Males
Female crane

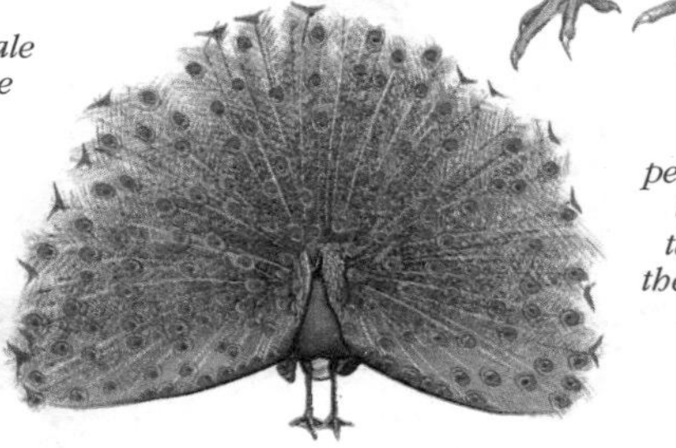

Indian male peacocks have long, brightly patterned tail feathers which they spread out and shake to attract a mate.

Many birds live near rivers, lakes and wetlands and feed on fish and insects.

Pelicans scoop up fish with the pouch in the lower part of their beaks.

Birds of prey are birds such as owls and hawks that hunt other animals for food. They have excellent eyesight and strong beaks and claws. Some, such as owls, hunt at night.

Philippine eagles (below) fly above the canopy in rainforests in Southeast Asia, hunting for birds and small animals to eat. They are an endangered species and only about 63 birds remain. This one has raised the feathers on its head to frighten an enemy.

Strong claws

Owls have big eyes and can see well in dim light, but they depend mainly on hearing to locate their prey. They can pinpoint the position of a mouse from the sound of leaves rustling as it moves.

The eyes of most birds are on the sides of their heads, but birds of prey have forward-facing eyes. This enables them to judge distances very accurately.

Owls have soft feathers and can fly almost noiselessly.

Egyptian vultures break ostrich eggs by dropping stones on them, and then eat the insides.

BIRDS' EGGS

The shape of a bird's egg and its markings help to keep it safe*. Birds that nest on the ground lay camouflaged eggs. Birds that nest in holes, such as owls, have pale eggs that can be seen in dim light.

Albatross egg
Emu egg
American robin egg
Common snipe egg
Herring gull egg
Little owl egg
Spotted flycatcher eggs
Broad-billed hummingbird egg

Guillemots lay their eggs on cliff ledges. The eggs are pointed and if they are knocked, they spin around in a circle.

*Courtship, 37

*Do not touch or take birds' eggs.

Gulls, such as glaucous gulls, live along coasts all over the world and scavenge for food.

Skuas fly over the oceans catching fish to eat.

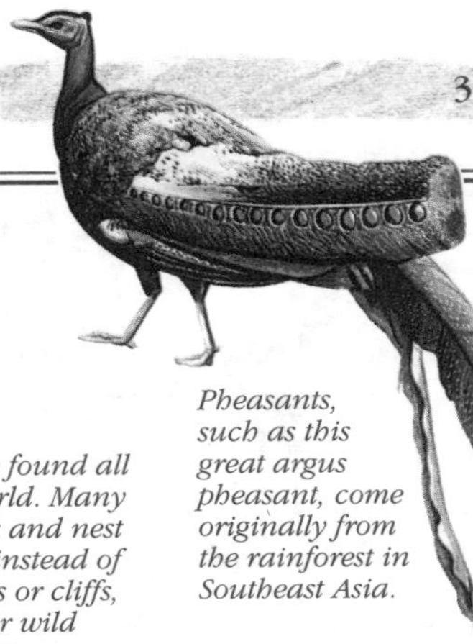

Pheasants, such as this great argus pheasant, come originally from the rainforest in Southeast Asia.

Gannets feed on fish and squid, which they catch by diving into the water.

Pigeons are found all over the world. Many live in cities and nest on ledges, instead of in the trees or cliffs, where their wild relatives live.

Shags live in colonies on rocky coasts and dive for fish.

Seabirds nest on cliffs and beaches and fly over the sea catching fish to eat. They often soar on rising air currents, holding their wings out stiffly.

Terns (left) are related to gulls, but they are smaller. They dive into the water to catch fish.

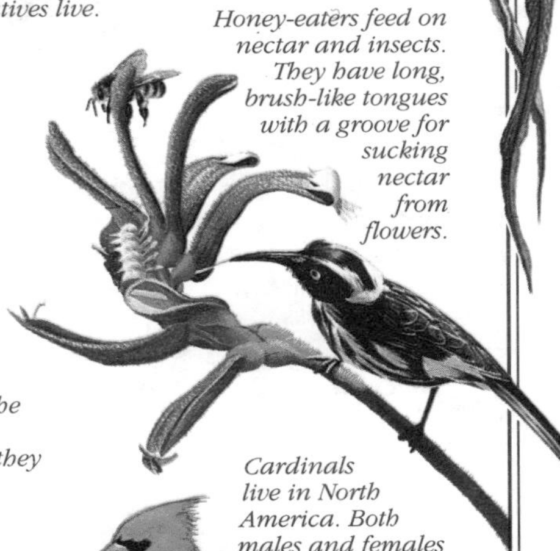

Honey-eaters feed on nectar and insects. They have long, brush-like tongues with a groove for sucking nectar from flowers.

Many birds spend part of the year in one place, and then migrate* thousands of miles to find better feeding and breeding conditions.

Swallows spend part of the year in southern Africa. In March, they fly north to Europe to breed. The journey takes about two months.

The largest group, or order, of birds are the perching birds. They have three toes that point forward and one pointing back so they can grip branches. The largest group of perching birds are the songbirds.

European robins live in woods and gardens and sing in winter and spring. American robins are a different species.

Blue jays live in woods and in towns in North America. This one is doing a threat display with its crest raised to scare off a rival.

Cardinals live in North America. Both males and females sing throughout the year.

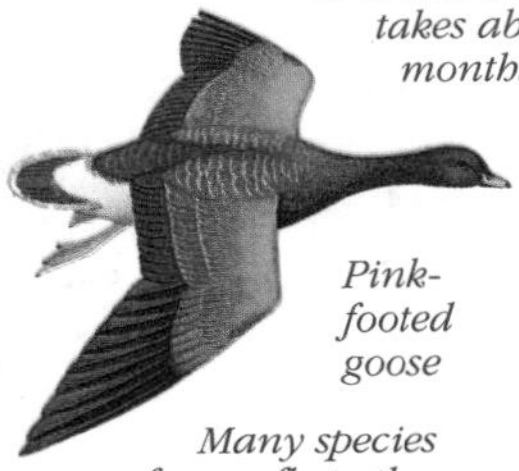

Pink-footed goose

Many species of geese fly to the Arctic to breed. At the end of the summer, they return to warmer places farther south. They fly in flocks for safety.

Each spring, hoopoes fly to Europe from Africa, and then return to Africa in the autumn. Hoopoes dig up insects with their long beaks.

BIRDS' NESTS

Each species of bird has its own design and method of nest-building. Some nests are little more than loose piles of twigs. Others are skilfully woven from twigs, grass, moss and even silk from spider webs. Many birds make cup-shaped nests that they line with mud or feathers.

Nests are usually built above the ground for safety. Most birds only use their nest in the breeding season and build a new nest each year.

Weaverbird knotting grasses onto twigs with its beak and claws

Rufous ovenbirds of South America build nests of wet mud which is baked hard by the hot sun. Behind the entrance hole there is a low wall to stop predators from reaching the eggs.

In tropical grasslands, a male weaverbird knots and weaves pieces of grass to make a nest hanging from a branch. If no female likes the nest, he destroys it and starts again.

Blue grosbeaks build cup-shaped nests of twigs, leaves, paper and snakeskins.

Golden eagles build their nests, called eyries, on rocky mountain ledges. The eyrie is made of sticks and lined with dry grass.

Penguins lay their eggs on piles of stones or in hollows in the ground. This gentoo penguin is trying to stop a skua from snatching her chick.

SEE FOR YOURSELF

To find out more about birds and learn to identify them, you need a field guide of the birds in your area. Try to visit places such as reservoirs, estuaries and nature reserves where you may see some unusual birds.

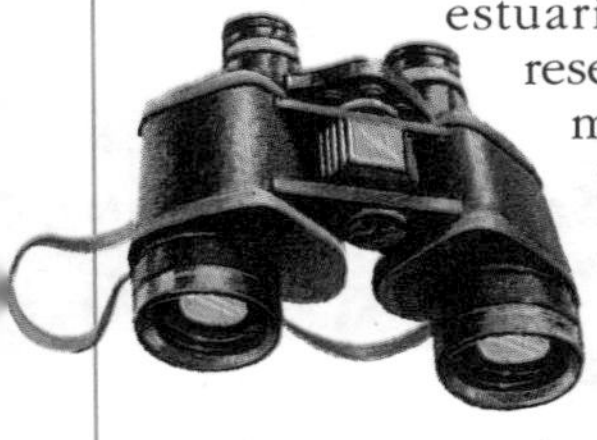

A pair of binoculars of magnification 8 x 30 or 8 x 40 is useful for birdwatching.

Make notes about the birds you see and write down when and where you spotted them.

Keep feathers flat by taping them in a notebook, and try to identify which birds they come from.

*Bird Migration, 37

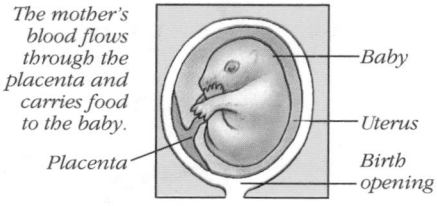

Deer suckling her fawn

MAMMALS

Mammals are animals that give birth to live young and the mother feeds them with her milk. They are warm-blooded animals, which means their bodies make their own body warmth, and most have fur or hair to help keep them warm. There are three main types of mammals: placental, marsupial and monotreme.

Siberian tigers play and gently bite each other before they mate.

PLACENTAL MAMMALS

Placental mammals, such as rabbits, give birth to fully-formed young, although the babies may be deaf, blind and hairless for the first few days. Most mammals are placental mammals. The young develop inside the mother's uterus (the womb), attached to her body by the placenta.

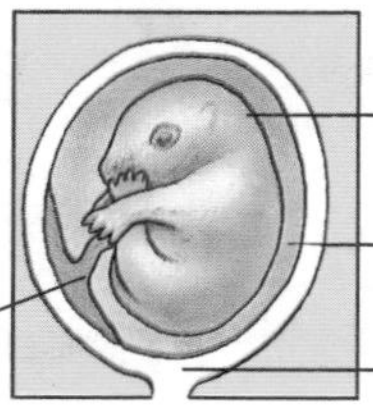
The mother's blood flows through the placenta and carries food to the baby.
Baby
Uterus
Placenta
Birth opening

MONOTREME MAMMALS

Monotreme mammals, such as the duck-billed platypus*, lay eggs. There are only three different species of monotreme mammals and they all live in Australia and Southeast Asia. Female monotremes look after their eggs in a pouch on their abdomens, or in a nest. The babies lick up milk that trickles out of glands in their mother's skin.

Duck-billed platypus

MARSUPIAL MAMMALS

Marsupial mammals, such as kangaroos*, give birth to tiny, unformed young that crawl into the mother's pouch and stay there for several months while they continue to develop.

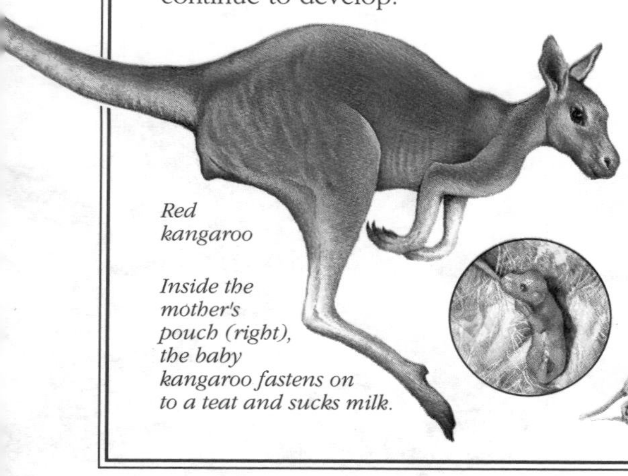

Red kangaroo

Inside the mother's pouch (right), the baby kangaroo fastens on to a teat and sucks milk.

LOOKING AFTER THE YOUNG

All mammals look after their young and the mother feeds, or suckles, them with her milk. The milk is produced by glands, called mammary glands, on her chest or abdomen. When they are old enough, the mother brings them solid food. The young learn the skills they need to survive by following and copying their mother, and by playing together.

White deer

The mother licks the newborn animals to clean and comfort them. Licking and grooming help to form a bond between the mother and her young.

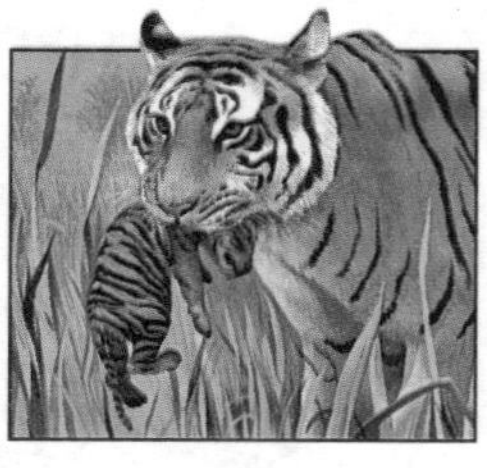

Cats, such as this tigress, pick up their cubs in their mouths to carry them to a safe place. Wild dogs carry their pups like this when the pack moves on to new hunting grounds.

This Japanese macaque baby is suckling milk from its mother. The milk is rich in nutrients the baby needs. The baby stays with its mother for two or three years.

Small mammals, such as mice, give birth to large numbers of young that are born after only two or three weeks. Larger mammals give birth to only one or two young that take longer to develop in the mother's uterus. In general, the larger mammals look after their young for longer than smaller mammals. Baby elephants stay with their mothers for up to ten years and chimpanzees stay with their parents for about seven years.

A white-toothed shrew takes her young with her, holding on to each other's tails, until they are three weeks old.

WARM-BLOODED ANIMALS

Mammals' bodies are warm both when they are active and when they are asleep. The heat that keeps them warm comes from chemical reactions in their cells. The hair or fur and fat on their bodies stops the heat from escaping. When they get too hot, mammals can cool down by panting and sweating.

Musk oxen live in the Arctic and have very thick, shaggy coats.

HIBERNATION

During the winter, mammals need to eat a lot of food to keep warm and food may be scarce. Some animals survive by hibernating - going into a deep sleep. In the autumn, the animals eat a lot of food so they can survive on their fat reserves. During hibernation their heartbeat and breathing slows down, and they do not need to eat.

During hibernation, a hedgehog's heart beats only 20 times a minute.

NOCTURNAL MAMMALS

Big eyes

Night monkeys

More than half of all the different species of mammals are nocturnal, that is, they wake up and feed and are active at night. Nocturnal animals have very good senses of smell and hearing and they can see very well in the dim light at night.

Badgers and other nocturnal mammals have a special layer at the back of their eyes that helps them see in the dark. It makes their eyes look red when a bright light shines on them.

*Duck-billed Platypus, 67; Kangaroos, 66

THE WORLD OF MAMMALS

All the different species of mammals can be organized into 21 groups, or orders*. The mammals in each order share certain characteristics. For example, all carnivores eat meat and all rodents have gnawing teeth. These pictures show the main orders.

Water bat

Bats are the only mammals that can fly. They belong to an order called Chiroptera.

Killer whale

Mediterranean monk seal

Whales and seals are mammals that live in the sea. Whales belong to an order called cetaceans and seals are pinnipeds.

Sika deer

Ungulates, such as deer and horses, are mammals that have hoofs on their toes.

Deer have two toes on each foot. They belong to the order called even-toed ungulates.

Red squirrel

Rodents, such as squirrels, have chisel-like incisor teeth with which they nibble and gnaw plants and nuts.

Mole

Mammals that eat mainly insects, such as moles and shrews, belong to an order called insectivores.

Horse

Horses have only one toe on each foot. They belong to the order called odd-toed ungulates.

Wolf

Mammals such as wolves, tigers, bears and weasels, which hunt and eat other animals, belong to the order called carnivores.

Koala

Marsupial mammals, such as koalas, give birth to tiny, unformed young that develop in the mother's pouch.

Blue hare

Rabbits and hares belong to the order called lagomorphs, which means "shaped like a hare".

African elephants

Elephants are the only animals in the order called proboscids, which means "animals with trunks".

Duck-billed platypus

Monotreme mammals, such as the duck-billed platypus, lay eggs.

Chimps

Monkeys and apes belong to the order called primates. Primates are the only mammals that have hands that can grip.

Giant anteater

Anteaters belong to the order called edentates, which means "toothless mammals".

HERBIVORES

Herbivores are animals that eat plants. Several different orders (see above) of mammals are herbivores. Plants such as grass and leaves are much more difficult to digest than meat, and herbivores have specially adapted digestive systems to break down the plant matter.

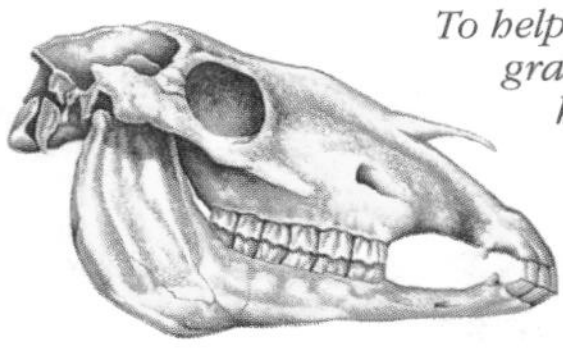

To help them chew tough grasses and leaves, herbivores have large, flat grinding teeth as seen on this skull of a zebra.

Most herbivores, such as this kangaroo, have eyes on the sides of their heads so they can look out for predators while they are grazing.

Herbivores need to eat large quantities of plants to survive and they spend much of their time grazing. Different species eat different plants, or different parts of the same plant, so many different herbivores can survive in the same place.

CARNIVORES

Carnivores are mammals that eat meat or fish. As well as describing an animal's diet, carnivore is also the name of the order (see above) to which meat-eating mammals belong. All carnivores have sharp teeth for tearing meat. They have strong, sharp claws for catching and holding on to their prey and a very good sense of smell.

Carnivores are expert hunters. Different species use different hunting techniques, such as ambushing, chasing or stalking their prey. Some, such as hyenas, are scavengers. They do not catch their own prey, but pick the remains off the bones that other animals leave behind.

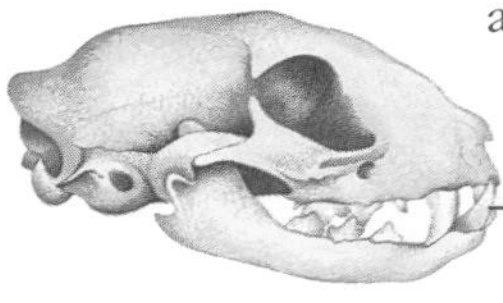
Canine tooth

Carnivores have long canine teeth for biting and killing, as seen on this skull of a wild cat.

Cougars are big cats that live in North and South America. They have a very good sense of smell and excellent sight and hearing, which helps them track down their prey. They can run fast and often chase their prey for long distances.

*Orders, 88

Lioness chasing prey

LIONS AND TIGERS

AND OTHER WILD CATS

There are about 40 different kinds of wild cats, including lions and tigers. Most of them live in the tropical forests and grasslands of Africa, Asia and South America, but they are also found in remote mountain areas. Many are now very rare, as their hunting grounds have been taken over for farming and mining.

Leopards are good climbers.

HOW CATS HUNT

All cats are carnivores - they eat only meat. They have sharp claws and strong jaws with very sharp, long canine teeth for stabbing and holding their prey. Most cats have retractable claws, that is, they can pull their claws up into their paws. This helps to keep their claws sharp.

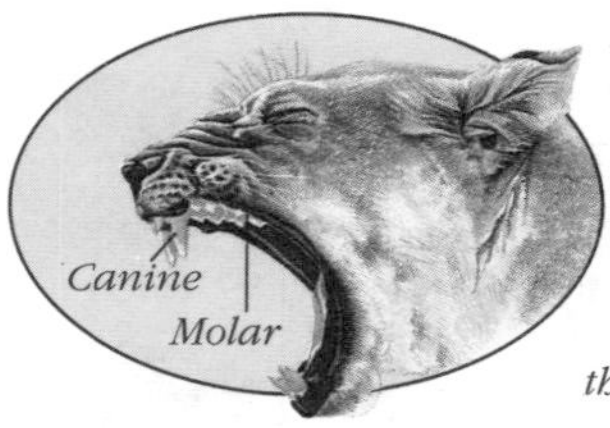
Canine
Molar

Lions kill their prey with their long canine teeth, and slice the meat with their molars. Big cats can bite through bones.

Cats are fast and expert hunters, using different techniques such as ambushing, stalking and chasing their prey. They usually hunt at night and can see about six times better than people can in the dark. Cheetahs, which rely on speed to catch their prey, hunt in the day, and all cats, except lions, hunt alone.

LIONS

Today, lions live only on the grasslands of Africa and northwest India. In the past, they also lived in southern Europe and the Middle East. Their sandy yellow coats help camouflage them against dry grass, and young lion cubs have spots that make them harder to see.

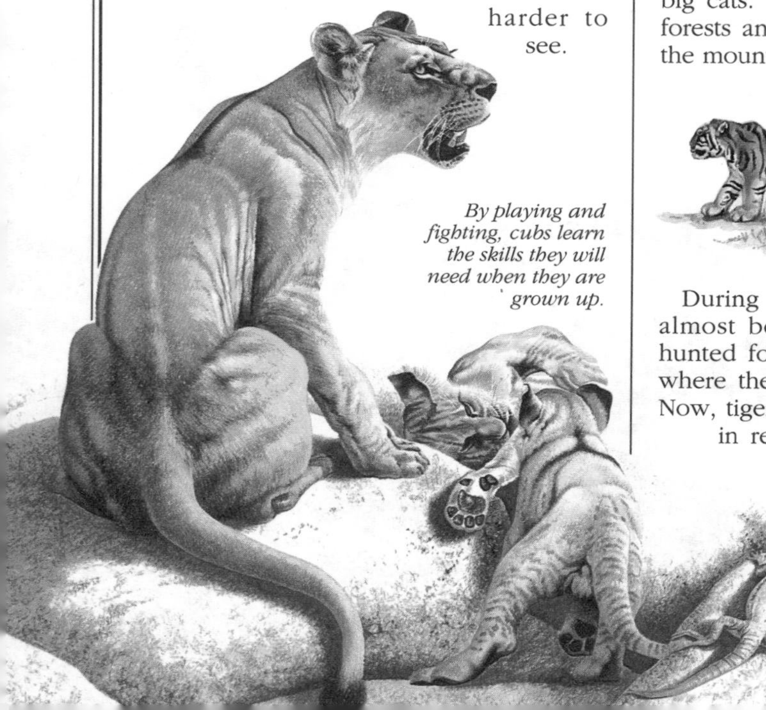

By playing and fighting, cubs learn the skills they will need when they are grown up.

Lions are the only cats that live together in groups. A group of lions is called a pride. It is made up of two or three adult lions and five or six lionesses and their cubs.

Lionesses bringing down a wildebeest

Each pride of lions has its own hunting area and the lions defend the territory. The lionesses do most of the hunting. Usually, they hunt in groups of two or three, creeping up on, and then leaping on their prey, which may be a gazelle, zebra or other large animal. The lions usually feed first and then the lionesses and cubs.

Lions and lionesses spend most of their time lying down, doing nothing.

TIGERS

Tigers are the largest and strongest of the big cats. They live in India and Asia, in forests and grasslands, and even high in the mountains of Siberia (Northeast Asia).

Young tigers learning to hunt with their mother

During the last hundred years, tigers almost became extinct as they were hunted for their fur, and the forests where they lived were cut down. Now, tigers in India are protected in reserves and, since 1970, all hunting has been forbidden. There are now probably about 3,000 tigers in India.

Tigers hunt alone at night, and often travel 10-20km (6-12 miles) to find food. If they cannot find big animals, such as deer, pigs, buffalo or baby elephants, they eat frogs, lizards and even ants. They are very strong and can drag a large animal to a safe place to eat it.

Tigers hunt by stalking and then ambushing their prey, as shown in the three pictures on the right. They kill their prey by biting it in the neck or throat. Only about one attack in twenty is successful. Each tiger has its own hunting territory that it marks with its droppings, and by scratching tree trunks and spraying them with urine.

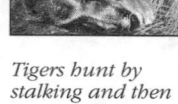

Tigers hunt by stalking and then leaping on their prey.

Tigers, and other big cats, communicate by roaring. Males roar to tell other tigers to go away, and tigresses roar to call their cubs, or to attract a mate. When angry, they snarl and twist their ears around to show two white marks on the back of their ears.

A tigress has three or four cubs and looks after them for about two years until they can hunt for themselves.

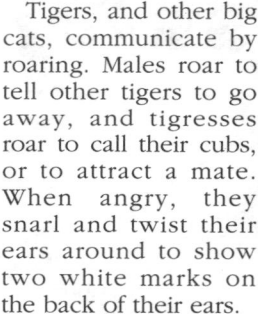

A tiger's stripes break up the outline of its shape and make it hard to see in long grass.

LEOPARDS

Leopards live in the rainforests and grasslands of Africa, India and Asia. The dark spots on their coats are called rosettes and they provide good camouflage in the dappled light of the forest. Black panthers are leopards with dark fur and black spots. They live mainly in thick rainforest.

Leopards often lie in trees and leap down on their prey, which may be an antelope, baboon or porcupine. They drag the carcass up a tree and feed on it whenever they are hungry.

Unlike the other big cats, leopards are usually silent, but the male may make a coughing noise. They live alone and only come together to mate.

Above: snow leopard in its winter coat, and left, in its summer coat.

Snow leopards live high in the mountains of Asia. They have thick fur, and in winter, their coats turn grey to help camouflage them against the snow.

JAGUARS

Jaguars are strong swimmers.

Jaguars live in rainforests in Central and South America, and in the southwest of the USA. They live near rivers in thick forests, and attack animals that come down to the rivers to drink. They mainly eat small mammals such as pig-like peccaries, small deer and rodents called capybaras. They are good swimmers and also catch fish, frogs and small alligators.

Jaguars live and hunt alone and, like other cats, mark out their territory by leaving smells or claw marks on trees. Each jaguar needs about 250sq km (155sq miles) of hunting ground in order to find enough prey to survive.

Most jaguars have spotted fur, like leopards, but their spots are darker and larger. Every jaguar has a different pattern of markings.

Some jaguars are born with black fur.

In the past, jaguars were much hunted for their fur. They are now nearly extinct, both because of hunting, and because large areas of the forest where they lived have been cut down.

CHEETAHS

Cheetahs live on the grasslands of Africa and a few still exist in southern Asia. They can run faster than any other animal, reaching speeds of over 110kph (68mph) over short distances.

When hunting, cheetahs creep up on their prey and then sprint after it as it runs away, as shown in these three pictures.

The chase is very exhausting and if the cheetah does not catch its prey within about a minute, it gives up and rests for half an hour.

Cheetahs hunt small animals that can run very fast, such as impala, Thomson's gazelles, and wildebeest calves.

Cheetahs are smaller and thinner than leopards, and have longer legs. They need to be very fast to catch their prey. Their claws do not fully retract into their paws and this helps them to grip the ground as they run.

OTHER WILD CATS

Clouded leopards (left) live in the rainforest in Southeast Asia. They are now very rare. They have long, thick tails that help them balance.

The northern lynx (right) lives in remote parts of North America, northern Europe and Asia. It has two tufts of fur on its throat that stick out when it is angry.

Ocelots (left) live in the grasslands and forests of Central and South America. They are excellent swimmers and climbers.

Servals (right) live in grasslands in Africa. They can run fast over short distances and have very good hearing.

Caracals (left) live in dry grasslands in Africa and the Middle East. They have tufts of hair on their ears that may help to camouflage them in long grass.

Pumas (right), also called cougars, or mountain lions, live in the mountains of North and South America. They creep up on, and then pounce on, their prey.

Wild cats, like the one on the left, are the ancestors of pet cats. They still live in Africa, Asia and remote parts of Europe. This one is in a zoo.

Cheetah running

Grey, or timber, wolf

WOLVES, FOXES AND WILD DOGS

An Arctic fox smashing the burrow of a lemming

Wolves, foxes and wild dogs all belong to the dog family. They have long, lean bodies and they can run fast to catch their prey. They also have long noses and a good sense of smell. Wolves and wild dogs hunt in packs and they are the ancestors of all the different types of domestic dogs.

WOLVES

Wolves live in remote parts of northern Europe and Asia, and in Canada and North America. They have thick, shaggy coats and live together in packs of about 20 wolves. Each pack has a leader and each wolf has its own position in the pack's order of importance. This affects the way it behaves with other wolves in the pack and even the way it stands and holds its tail when it meets them.

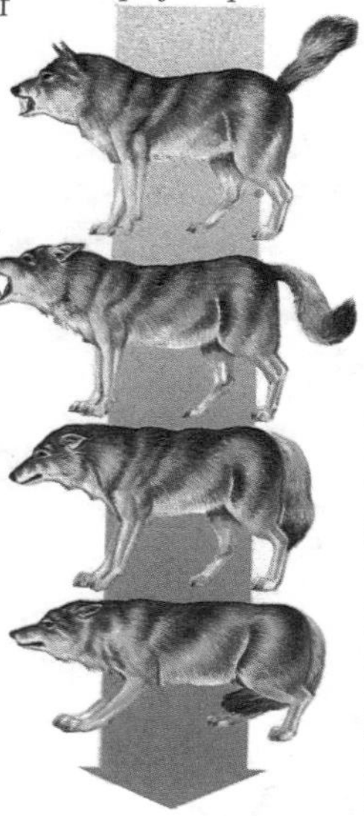

Top of the pack
Bottom of the pack

This picture shows how wolves stand and hold their tails depending on their place in the pack.

By hunting together in small groups, the wolves can catch animals, such as caribou and musk oxen, that are much larger and can run faster than themselves. They usually pick off the older or less able members of a herd. They also catch small mammals and scavenge for food.

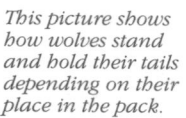

These wolves, seen from above, have surrounded a young caribou. The mother has escaped.

Despite their fearsome reputation, wolves rarely attack people, although they sometimes take animals from farms. Because of this, they have been hunted nearly to extinction.

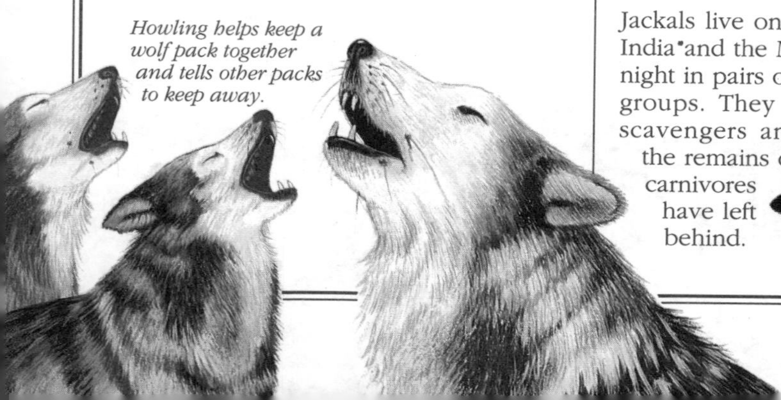

Howling helps keep a wolf pack together and tells other packs to keep away.

AFRICAN WILD DOGS

African wild dogs live on the grasslands of Africa and follow herds of zebra or wildebeest. When the herd moves to new grazing grounds, the dogs follow. About 20 dogs and their pups live together in a pack. Like wolves, each dog has its position of importance in the pack. They hunt in small groups, chasing and surrounding animals that have become separated from the herd.

African wild dogs can run up to 50kph (30mph) to bring down prey such as a wildebeest.

DINGOES

Dingoes have short brown hair.

Dingoes are wild dogs that live in Australia. Like other wild dogs, they live and hunt in small packs. There were no dogs originally in Australia. Dingoes are descended from dogs brought to Australia in prehistoric times by Aboriginal settlers.

JACKALS

Jackals live on the grasslands of Africa, India and the Middle East. They hunt at night in pairs or small family groups. They are also scavengers and eat the remains other carnivores have left behind.

COYOTES

Coyotes are wild dogs that live on the North American prairies. They live in pairs or, when there is enough food, in small family packs. In recent years, thousands of coyotes have been killed as pests, but despite this, they are surviving.

FOXES

There are over 20 different species of foxes, including red foxes, grey foxes, fennec and kit foxes, which live in deserts, and Arctic and blue foxes, which live in very cold places. Most foxes hunt alone at night, pouncing on their prey with their front paws. They eat rats, mice, rabbits, frogs and insects.

Fennec foxes live in deserts in Africa and Arabia. Air flowing over the blood vessels in their large ears helps to cool them.

Arctic foxes start shivering at -70°C (-94°F), while red foxes shiver at -13°C (9°F).

Red foxes are found in northern Europe, Asia, North America and Australia. They live mainly in woods and bushy country, although many now live in towns and scavenge on garbage.

Playing helps fox cubs learn to fight and hunt.

Red foxes build dens, called earths, in banks or under tree roots. The female, called the vixen, has four or five cubs in the spring.

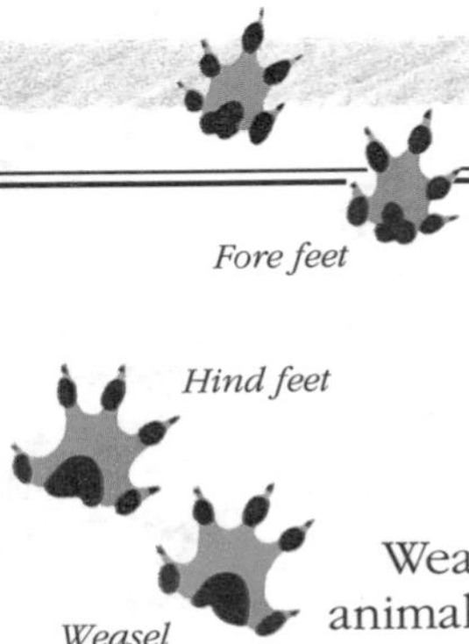
Fore feet
Hind feet

Weasel tracks

Stoat

WEASELS AND STOATS

AND OTHER SMALL CARNIVORES

Weasels and stoats are slim, agile little carnivores - animals that hunt and eat other animals. They have very good hearing and sense of smell and can catch animals bigger than themselves. Badgers, martens, skunks and polecats are related to weasels.

WEASELS

Weasels are found all over the world, except in Australia. With their long, slender bodies they can chase rabbits, mice and voles down their burrows, and even turn around in the narrow tunnels.

A weasel measures about 20cm (8in) to the base of its tail.

Weasels kill their prey by biting it in the neck. They hunt alone, at night, and have very good sight, hearing and sense of smell.

In the day, weasels sleep in nests in trees or logs, or old animal burrows. The male defends the territory around his nest.

These four-week-old weasels eat the meat their mother brings them. By the time they are eight weeks old, they can hunt alone.

STOATS

Stoats look like weasels, but they are larger and the tips of their tails are black. At the end of the summer, stoats that live in the far north grow white fur to camouflage them against the snow. Their brown fur returns again in the spring. In their winter coats, stoats are called ermine and they have been much hunted for their beautiful fur. Like weasels, stoats eat rabbits, rats, mice and voles and also take birds' and chickens' eggs.

A stoat measures about 28cm (11in) to the base of its tail.

An ermine (stoat in its winter coat)

POLECATS AND FERRETS

Polecats are also called ferrets and are found in Europe, North America and northern Asia. They eat frogs, birds, rodents and rabbits and have strong claws for digging out their prey. Tame ferrets are sometimes used for hunting rabbits.

Polecat

Black-footed ferrets live on the grasslands of North America, but are now nearly extinct.

MARTENS

Martens are nocturnal. In the day they sleep in tree hollows, rocky crevices or even in birds' nests. They eat birds, mice, insects, fruit and berries and sometimes even catch squirrels. Pine martens live in remote coniferous forests and beech martens live on farmland.

Pine martens are expert climbers.

BADGERS

Badgers are stocky animals with short legs and strong claws for digging out insects, worms and small mammals. Most are nocturnal. American badgers dig out mice and prairie dogs from their burrows, while the honey badger, or ratel, which lives in Africa and southern Asia, feeds mainly on honey. Its thick, loose coat helps protect it against bee stings.

American badger

Honey badgers are often led to bees' nests by the singing of honey guide birds that feed on beeswax.

European badgers mainly eat worms, insects, mice and voles. About 12 badgers live together in a series of tunnels called a sett. There are a number of chambers which are used for sleeping and rearing the young. The badgers keep the sett clean and use a hole outside as a dung pit.

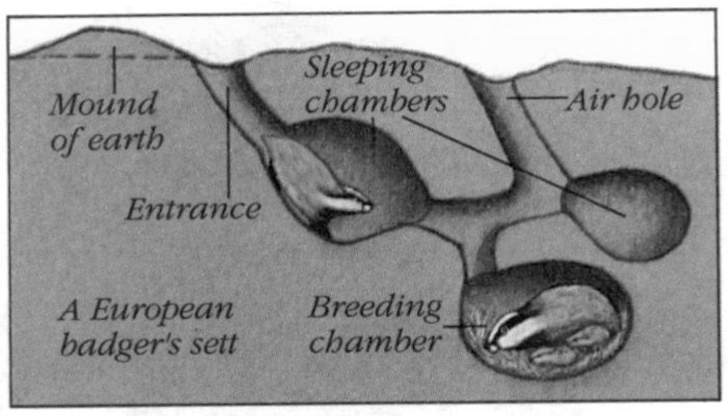
Mound of earth
Sleeping chambers
Air hole
Entrance
Breeding chamber

A European badger's sett

SKUNKS

Skunks live in North and South America. There are three main species of skunks: striped, spotted and hog-nosed. They have black and white patterned fur that helps to camouflage them at night when they hunt for food.

To protect themselves, skunks can squirt a foul-smelling liquid from glands under their tails. This can cause temporary blindness, but, before squirting, they stamp their feet, raise their tails and growl and hiss to warn their enemies to go away.

Above: spotted skunk warning enemy to go away

Right: striped skunk

Brown bear catching salmon

BEARS, PANDAS
AND RACCOONS

Bears are among the largest and strongest of land animals. Although they are carnivores*, they all, except for polar bears, eat mainly leaves, roots and berries. Pandas and raccoons are related to bears. The most famous panda species is the giant panda that lives in China, but there are also red pandas that live in the Himalayas.

Transporting a polar bear away from a town in Canada

BROWN BEARS

Brown bears are the largest of the bears. They eat small animals, berries, leaves, roots and honey, but when salmon are swimming up the rivers, they eat mainly fish, which they catch with their paws. They usually walk on all-fours, but rear up on their hind legs to show how strong they are, and to frighten enemies.

Brown bear

Fore foot
Hind foot

There are several different kinds of brown bears. Grizzly bears live in the Rocky Mountains in the USA. Their brown fur is tipped with white, giving them a grizzled appearance. Kodiak bears live in Alaska, and other brown bears live in northern Asia and remote, mountainous parts of Europe.

In the winter, brown bears hibernate in caves, or hollows dug out under tree roots. The female gives birth to two cubs in the snow-covered den.

BLACK BEARS

Black bears are smaller than brown bears. They can run fast and they are good climbers. They climb trees to look for bees' nests to raid for their honey. They also eat small animals, leaves, berries and roots. Black bears live in central and eastern Asia and also in North America. Like brown bears, they hibernate in the winter.

Black bears are protected in America's national parks. This one is in a zoo.

POLAR BEARS

Polar bears live on the pack ice that floats on the sea near the North Pole. They are strong swimmers but prefer to ride on pieces of ice. They have very thick fur and a thick layer of fat under their skin to keep them warm.

Adult polar bears live alone. During the short summers in the Arctic, they travel long distances looking for food. They are skilled hunters and feed on seals, fish and birds.

An adult polar bear weighs up to 800kg (1,764lb).

Sometimes, polar bears wander into towns in northern Canada and scavenge from garbage dumps. They have to be transported away as the garbage may be dangerous for them and they may harm, or be harmed by, frightened people.

To catch a seal, a polar bear waits by the seal's breathing hole. It creeps up very quietly, so the seal does not hear the sound of its feet through the ice.

The polar bear lies without moving for up to four hours. Its thick fur and fat help to keep it warm. It waits until a seal pokes its head out of the hole to breathe.

It quickly kills the seal with a powerful swipe of its paw, and pulls it out of the water with its sharp claws. It eats the fat and skin first and then the meat.

Polar bears do not usually hibernate. During the winter, female bears dig dens in the ice where they give birth to two or three cubs. The cubs feed on their mother's milk, but the mother does not eat until the spring. The cubs stay with their mother for two years.

Brown bears line their dens with leaves and twigs.

On warmer days, the bears may wake up and look for food.

Bear cubs are born blind with no teeth or hair. By early spring, they leave the den and play in the snow outside.

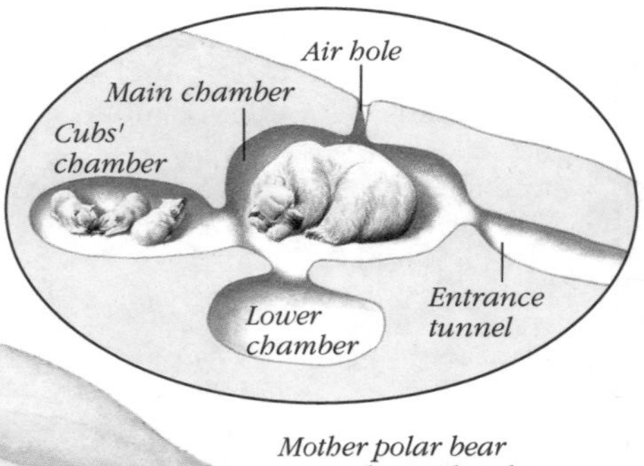
Air hole
Main chamber
Cubs' chamber
Lower chamber
Entrance tunnel

Mother polar bear in den with cubs

*Carnivores, 41

SUN BEARS

Sun bears live in tropical rainforests in India and Southeast Asia. They are good climbers and sleep in nests built in trees. Smaller than the other bears, they grow to a height of about 1.4m (4.5ft). Sun bears eat plants, honey, ants and termites. They do not hibernate as there is no cold season in the areas where they live.

Sun bears eat termites by licking them up with their long tongues.

SPECTACLED BEARS

Spectacled bears live in forests in the high mountains of the Andes in South America. They have pale markings around their eyes. They are very rare because many of the mountain forests where they lived and found their food have been cut down.

GIANT PANDAS

Giant pandas live only in bamboo forests in the high mountains of Sichuan in western China (see map above right). Their name means "bamboo eater" and they live almost entirely on bamboo shoots. Occasionally, they eat other plants and rats, birds, snakes and fish. Pandas spend most of their time eating and sleeping. They do not hibernate, but when it is very cold, they shelter in caves or hollow trees.

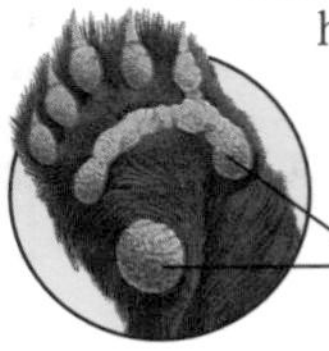
Pads

Pandas have special pads on their paws that help them grip bamboo shoots.

Bamboo leaves

Giant pandas

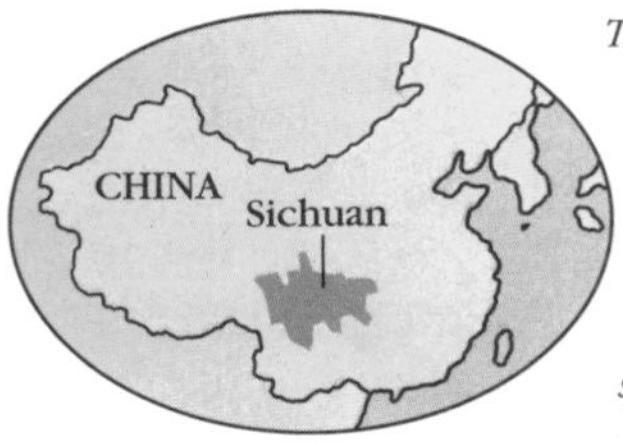
CHINA
Sichuan

This map shows the mountains of Sichuan, in China, where most giant pandas live. They are a protected species.

Much of the forest where giant pandas lived has been cut down for farmland, and the panda is in very great danger of becoming extinct. There are now only about 700 giant pandas left in the wild.

Pandas live alone and only come together to mate. Females are not ready to breed until they are four years old, so pandas have a very slow rate of reproduction. This makes it difficult for their numbers to increase.

Five months after mating, the female panda gives birth to one or two cubs in a den she has made in a cave. At birth, the tiny cubs are blind and naked but, within about ten days, they grow fur and their eyes open.

Usually, the mother only manages to look after one of the cubs and the other one dies. Young pandas are very playful. They stay with their mothers for about 18 months until they are old enough to fend for themselves.

Another reason why there are so few pandas is that bamboo trees flower only every hundred years, and after flowering, they die. In 1983, a large area of bamboo in Sichuan flowered and died. The pandas living there could not find food and many starved and died.

The giant panda is the symbol of the WWF - World Wide Fund for Nature (formerly World Wildlife Fund) - one of the world's largest nature conservation organizations.

RED PANDAS

Red pandas live in forests on the slopes of the Himalayas, the mountains in Asia. They belong to the same family as raccoons, and are also related to the giant panda.

Red pandas build their nests in trees and spend much of the day sleeping. They are nocturnal and feed at night on fruit, roots and bamboo, and also eat snakes, insects and eggs. Red pandas are in grave danger of becoming extinct because the forests where they live are being cut down.

Red pandas are good climbers.

RACCOONS

Raccoons live only in North and South America. They are nocturnal and their dark fur with black and white markings helps to camouflage them. In the day, they usually sleep in trees and they feed mainly at night.

Berries
Dead vole
Fish

Raccoons can pick up food and hold it with their front paws.

Although raccoons are carnivores, they also eat berries and fruit, and hook fish out of streams with their paws.

Raccoons do not hibernate, but in the winter, their coats become very thick and they stay in their nests. In North America, raccoons are hunted for their fur.

Raccoons often live near towns and scavenge from garbage.

Whale leaping out of the water

WHALES AND DOLPHINS

Whales are mammals that live in the sea. There are nearly 80 different species of whales and they can be grouped into two types: baleen whales and toothed whales. Dolphins and porpoises are toothed whales. Whales have a thick layer of fat, called blubber, under their skin, which helps keep them warm. For centuries, whales have been hunted for their blubber and meat and now many of the large whales are in danger of becoming extinct.

Bottlenose dolphin leaping

BALEEN WHALES

Baleen whales have fringes of tough skin, called baleen, inside their mouths. They have no teeth. They feed on small, shrimp-like animals called krill*. To feed, they take a mouthful of water full of krill. Then they force the water out through the sieve-like fringes of baleen and swallow the krill.

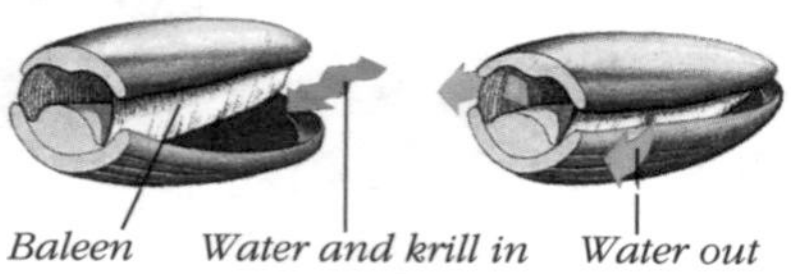
Mouth open
Mouth closed
Baleen
Water and krill in
Water out

A large whale eats 4 tonnes (4.4 tons) of krill a day. Most baleen whales feed in the cool seas near the Arctic and Antarctica. In the winter, they migrate to warmer waters nearer the equator to breed.

Blue whales, right whales, minke whales and humpback whales are all baleen whales. They are all nearly extinct, except for the minke whale.

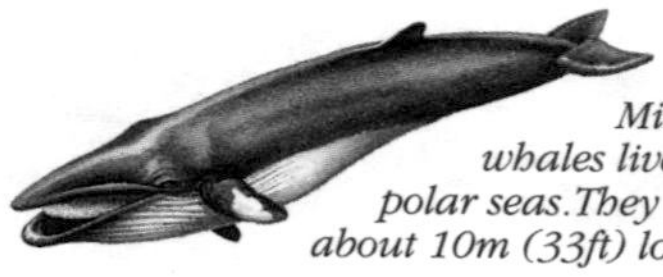

Minke whales live in polar seas. They are about 10m (33ft) long.

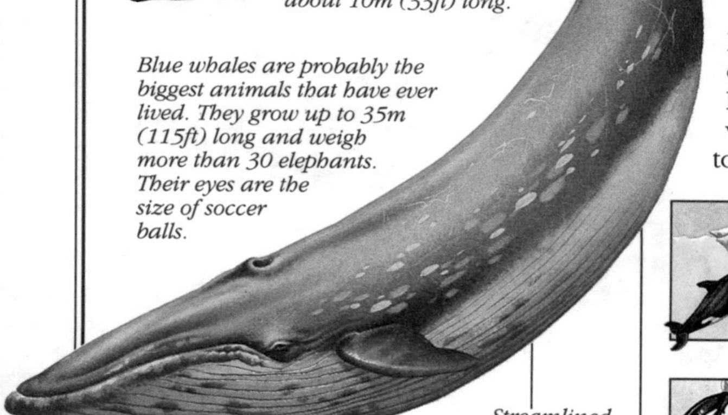
Streamlined body shape

Blue whales are probably the biggest animals that have ever lived. They grow up to 35m (115ft) long and weigh more than 30 elephants. Their eyes are the size of soccer balls.

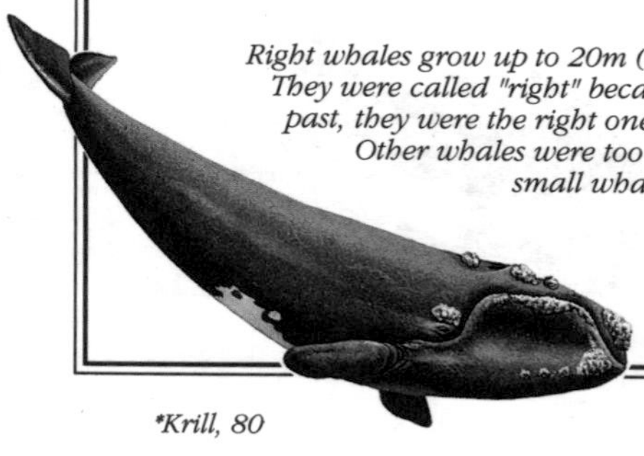

Right whales grow up to 20m (66ft) long. They were called "right" because, in the past, they were the right ones to catch. Other whales were too big for the small whaling boats.

TOOTHED WHALES

Toothed whales eat mainly fish and squid. They grip the slippery fish with their rows of sharp teeth and then swallow them whole. Toothed whales often live together in groups, called pods. Members of a pod "talk" to each other in whistles and clicks and often share their food.

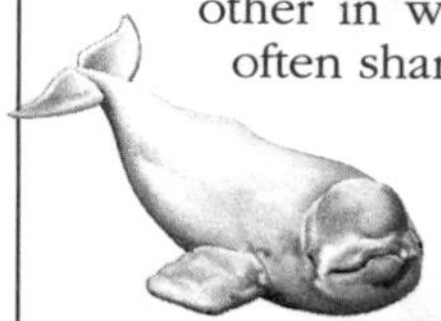

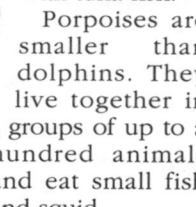

Beluga whales live in the Arctic Ocean.

Narwhals live in the Arctic Ocean. Males, and some females, have a spiral tusk about 2m (7ft) long on their upper lips.

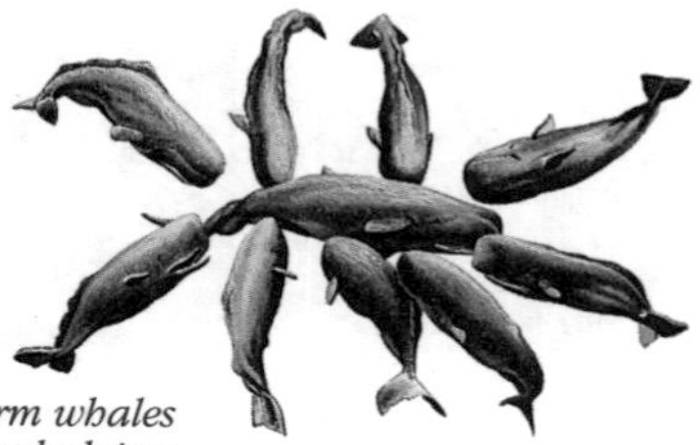

Sperm whales have bulging heads full of waxy oil, called spermaceti, that helps them float. These sperm whales are helping an injured whale.

Most toothed whales use echo-location to find fish and avoid obstacles (see Dolphins and Porpoises above right). Sperm whales can dive over 1km (3,300ft) to catch giant squid on the seabed.

Killer whales hunt together to catch seals. Here, they are surrounding a crabeater seal on an ice floe.

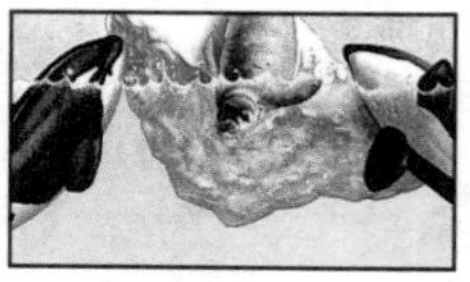

One whale leans on the ice floe and another tips it up to tip the sleeping seal into the water.

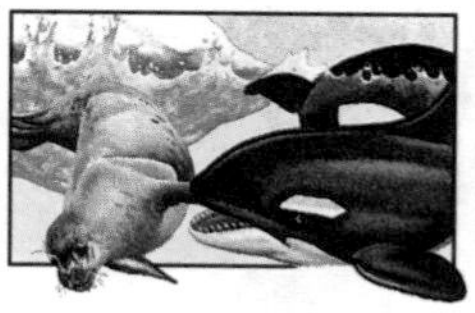

As the seal slips off, one whale grabs it in its jaws. The other whales will share the food.

DOLPHINS AND PORPOISES

Dolphins live in warm seas. They are intelligent, sociable creatures and very fast swimmers. The bottlenose dolphin can reach speeds of 50kph (31mph). They often follow boats and many are caught in nets with tuna fish.

Dolphins are a type of toothed whale.

Porpoises are smaller than dolphins. They live together in groups of up to a hundred animals and eat small fish and squid.

Dolphins, and other toothed whales, use echo-location to find fish and avoid obstacles. They make high-pitched clicking noises as they swim along. These noises bounce off objects such as fish, and echo back to the dolphins. From these echoes, the dolphins can tell the exact position of the fish.

Clicking noises
Echoes

Dolphins send out streams of up to 700 clicks a second by forcing air through special passages in their heads. They also "talk" to other dolphins in a language of clicks. They live and hunt together in large groups called schools, and frequently help each other or injured members of the school.

HOW WHALES BREATHE

Whales have lungs, like all mammals, and have to come to the surface to breathe air. They suck in fresh air and blow out used air through a blowhole in the top of their heads. The warm air they blow out is full of moisture. The moisture condenses to form a spray of water droplets. You can tell the species of whale by the shape of its spray.

Minke whale
Right whale
Sperm whale

*Krill, 80

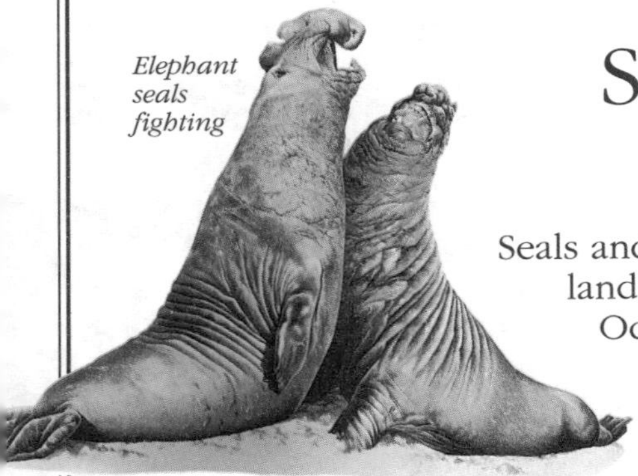

Elephant seals fighting

SEALS AND SEA LIONS
AND OTHER SEA MAMMALS

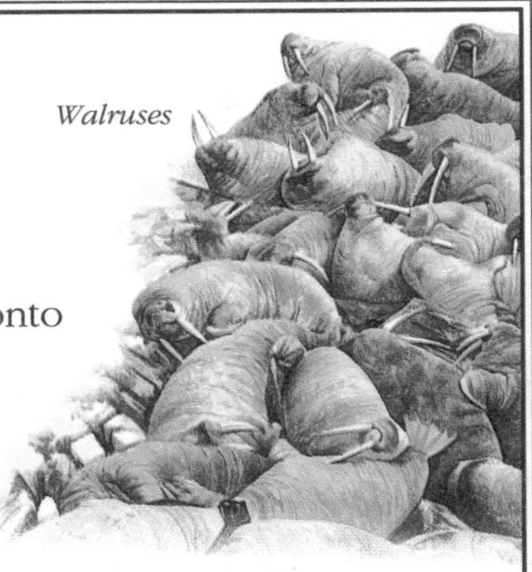

Walruses

Seals and sea lions are mammals that live in the sea, but come onto land to give birth. Most live in the cold Arctic and Southern Oceans, and on the shores of the North Atlantic Ocean. They have oily fur and a thick layer of blubber (fat) under their skin to keep them warm.

SEALS

Seals are very good swimmers, but when on land or ice, they can only drag themselves along on their bellies. They have smooth, streamlined bodies and webbed flippers. They swim by kicking their hind flippers up and down, and steer with their front flippers. They come to the surface to breathe and in winter, when the sea is frozen over, they scratch breathing holes in the ice. They eat mainly fish, squid and small shrimps called krill.

Weddell seal swimming

In the spring, seals come onto the land or pack ice to give birth to their babies, which are called pups. During the breeding season, they gather in large groups in an area called a rookery, but some, such as ringed seals, dig dens in the ice.

Ringed seal and pup in den

Crabeater seals live in Antarctica. They eat krill, not crabs.

Harp seals live in the Arctic. The pups have fluffy white fur to camouflage them against the ice.

In the past, seals (especially harp seal pups) were hunted for their fur and many species were in danger of becoming extinct. Now it is forbidden to hunt most types of seals.

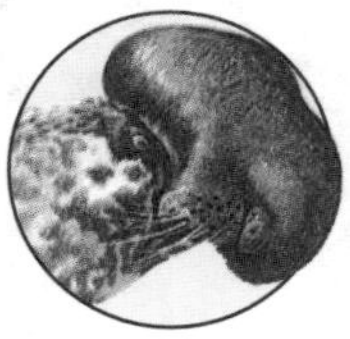

Hooded seal with top part of head inflated

Antarctic leopard seals eat penguins.

SEA LIONS

Sea lions belong to a group called eared seals because they have small ear flaps on their heads. True seals, such as those described on the left, do not have ear flaps.

True seal

Eared seal

Californian sea lion

Sea lions, and all other eared seals, can turn their back flippers forward and waddle on land more easily than true seals. They are good acrobats and have even been trained to take tools to divers on the seabed. They are very fast swimmers and good divers. They swim with their front flippers and steer with their back flippers. They eat fish and squid.

Antarctic fur seals are eared seals. They were hunted for their very thick fur, but are now a protected species.

WALRUSES

Walruses are related to seals. Males and females have two long, sharp ivory tusks with which they dig for clams and other shellfish. A large walrus can eat 3,000 clams a day. They also eat fish, birds and seals.

Walruses live in the Arctic and, like seals and sea lions, come onto land to give birth. In the breeding season, males fight with their tusks. Usually, the males with the longest tusks attract most females.

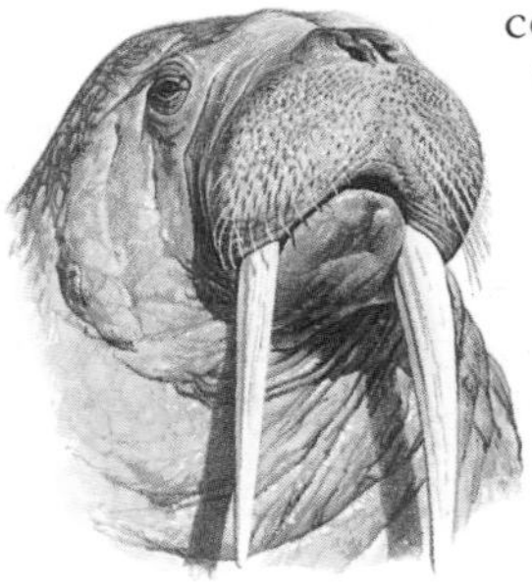

Walruses feed in shallow water, feeling for clams with their fleshy noses and sensitive whiskers.

They use their tusks to drag themselves out of the water.

In fights, walruses attack each other with their tusks.

SEA COWS

Sea cows are large, peaceful, plant-eating mammals. They eat seaweed and other sea plants. There are two main types of sea cows: manatees and dugongs. Manatees live on the shores of the Atlantic Ocean and are protected in reserves off the coast of Florida, USA. Dugongs are also very rare and live along the coasts of the Indian Ocean and the Red Sea.

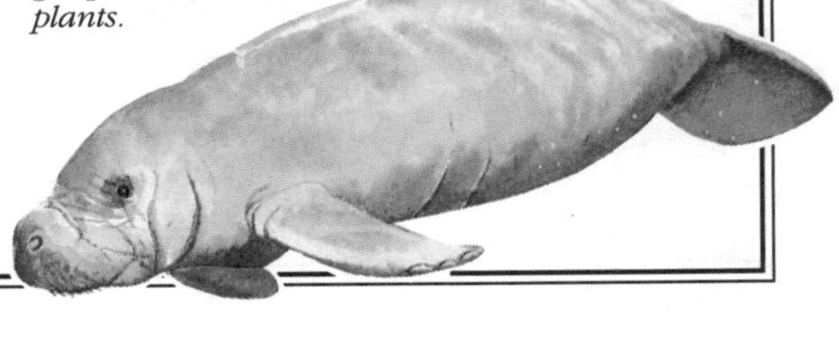

Manatees have a split upper lip that they use to grasp sea plants.

Black-handed spider monkeys live in the treetops in the South American rainforest.

MONKEYS AND APES

AND SMALL PRIMATES

Gibbons live in the rainforest in Southeast Asia.

Monkeys and apes belong to a group of animals called primates* - the same group to which people belong. As well as monkeys and apes, there are other small primates such as lemurs, tarsiers and bushbabies. There are about 120 species of monkeys and four species of apes: chimpanzees, gibbons, orangutans and gorillas. Most primates live in trees and have very good eyesight. They are the only group of animals that can press their thumbs against their fingers. This enables them to grip branches and pick leaves and fruit.

MONKEYS

Most monkeys live in the rainforests of Asia, Africa and South America but some, such as baboons, live on the African grasslands, and Japanese macaques live on snowy mountains.

Monkeys are smaller than apes and most of them have tails. Apes do not have tails. In the rainforest, monkeys live in the treetops and their tails help them balance. Many South American monkeys have long, strong tails with which they can grip branches. Some can even pick fruits and nuts with their tails. A tail that can grip is called a prehensile tail.

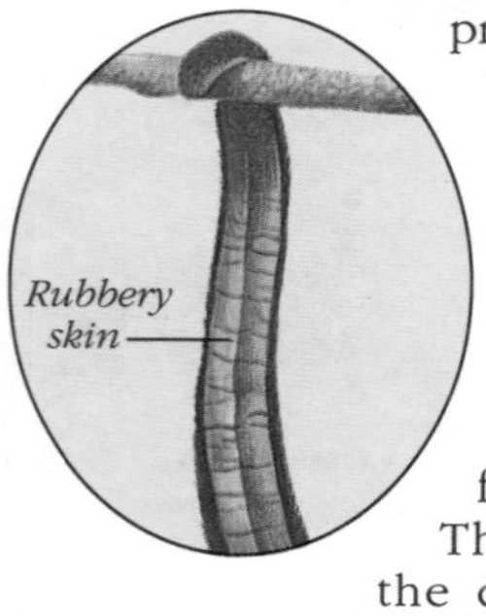
Rubbery skin

The rubbery skin on the back of a spider monkey's tail helps it grip the branches.

Most monkeys live in troops made up of small family groups. They are active in the day and sleep in the trees at night. They eat leaves and fruit and many also eat insects. Saki monkeys have special teeth for eating seeds, and marmosets gnaw holes in branches and eat the sap that drips out.

Mandrills have very bright faces and bottoms. Adult males are the most showy and become even more vivid when they are angry or excited. Mandrills live in West Africa.

Howler monkeys live in the South American rainforest. Their howling calls can be heard up to 3km (2 miles) away.

Golden monkeys live in the mountains of Sichuan, in China. The fur on their backs can be up to 10cm (4in) long.

Humboldt's woolly monkeys live in the South American rainforest. They have been hunted almost to extinction.

Night monkeys, or douroucoulis, live in the topmost layers of the South American rainforest. They live in small family groups and feed at night.

Long-tailed macaques live near rivers in Southeast Asia. They eat crabs and snails and are good swimmers.

Proboscis monkeys live on the island of Borneo, in Southeast Asia. Males have noses up to 18cm (7in) long and make loud honking noises.

Sakis of South America crack open hard seeds in a special gap between their teeth.

BABOONS

Baboons are large monkeys that live on the grasslands of Africa. They walk on all-fours, but climb trees to sleep and escape enemies. They mainly eat plants, but they hunt too. Baboons live together in troops of up to a hundred animals, and each troop has its own territory.

Grooming each other helps to strengthen friendships within the troop - it also helps to keep the fur clean.

Young baboons present their backsides to older males to show that they accept them as leaders.

Babies cling to their mothers for the first few weeks. Later, they play with other young baboons.

Each animal behaves according to its position of importance in the troop. Large, older males are the leaders and stronger, younger males act as scouts and chase away enemies.

Both male and female baboons look after the babies, and young baboons learn the skills they will need by playing chase and fighting.

A mother baboon grooming her baby

*Primates, 41

LEMURS

Lemurs are related to monkeys. They live in the rainforest on the island of Madagascar and the nearby Comoro Islands off the coast of Africa. There are 22 different kinds of lemurs, but most are in danger of extinction as the rainforests are being cut down.

Ring-tailed lemur rubbing scent from glands under its arms onto its tail

Ruffed lemurs are the largest lemurs.

Lemurs are active during the day and eat plants, insects and small animals. They live in the trees and, like most other primates, are very good climbers. They live together in small troops of about 20 animals led by the females.

Each troop of lemurs has its own territory, which the males mark with their scent. The males also have stink fights in which they wipe their tails over their scent glands and then wave their tails and waft the smell at their rivals.

TARSIERS AND BUSHBABIES

Tarsiers are small primates that live in the rainforest in Southeast Asia. Bushbabies (or galagos) live in the rainforests of Africa, India and Southeast Asia.

Tarsiers are nocturnal and have huge eyes to help them see at night. They can leap between trees and turn their heads right around to the back. They eat insects, birds, eggs and lizards.

Bushbabies eat insects, seeds and flowers. They are nocturnal and make a call like a baby crying. They live alone and mark their territory with their urine.

CHIMPANZEES

Chimpanzees live in Africa and there are two types: common chimps and pygmy chimps. They live on the grasslands and in woods, and also in the rainforest.

Chimps live together in small bands of several males and females and their young. They eat plants, insects and small mammals, and in the rainforest common chimps hunt together to catch larger animals, such as monkeys. They guard their territory and attack or throw rocks at strangers.

Chimps are our closest relatives and are believed to be the most intelligent of the primates. They have been observed shaping sticks to use as tools to help them poke out termites to eat.

Chimps use rocks and sticks as tools to help them get food.

GORILLAS

Gorillas are the largest of the primates. They live in small areas of rainforest in central and East Africa, and eat leaves, stems, fruit and berries. Gorillas stay mainly on the ground and walk on their knuckles on all-fours. At night, they sleep in nests made of leaves and broken branches. They live in family groups of several females and their young, led by a large, adult male called a silverback. They rarely fight, and to frighten their enemies, they stare at them and beat their chests, roar loudly and tear up plants.

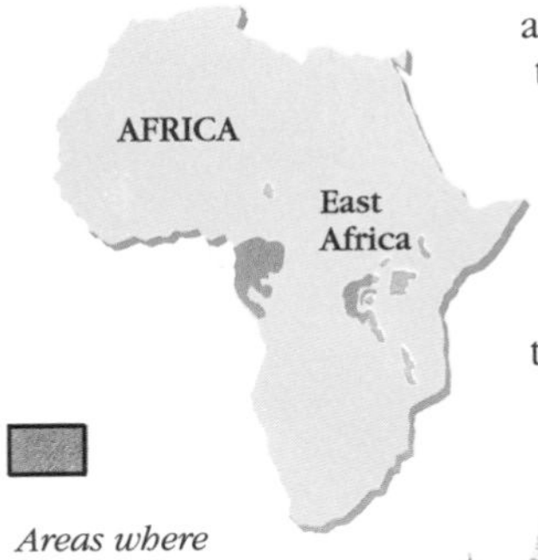
AFRICA
East Africa

Areas where gorillas live. Mountain gorillas live in the highlands in East Africa.

ORANGUTANS

Orangutans usually live alone, although babies live with their mothers for two or three years. The name orangutan means "person of the forest". They eat mainly fruit and leaves and rarely come down to the ground. They are found only in forests on the islands of Borneo and Sumatra, in Southeast Asia.

Orangutans can reach between branches over 2m (6.5ft) apart.

Female orangutan with baby clinging to her fur

Adult males have fatty lumps on either side of their faces. They guard their territory fiercely and roar to tell other males to stay away.

GIBBONS

Gibbons live in small family groups and eat plants, fruit, eggs, insects and other small animals. They are smaller than the other apes and swing effortlessly from branch to branch, calling tunefully to each other.

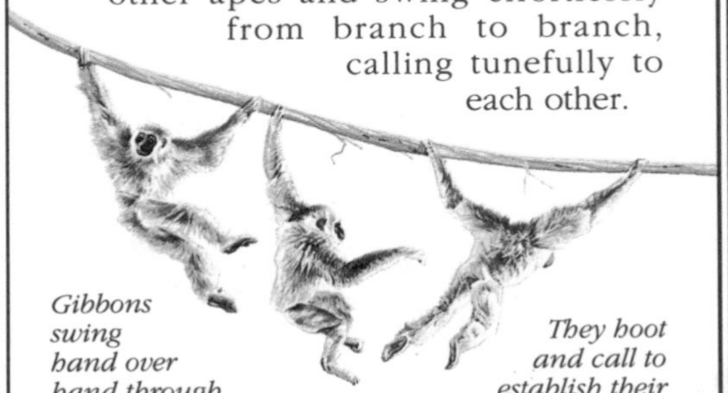

Gibbons swing hand over hand through the branches.

They hoot and call to establish their territory.

Young gorillas playing follow the leader

Female gorillas grooming each other

The silverback is a large male whose fur is turning grey.

A group of gorillas feeding in a clearing in the forest

Indian elephant and Sumatran rhino

ELEPHANTS AND RHINOS

Both these massive creatures are in danger of becoming extinct. Until 1990, over 100,000 elephants were killed each year for their ivory tusks. Rhinos are killed for their horns, which are made of matted hair and are believed by some people to have medicinal qualities.

Birds wait near rhinos to eat the insects disturbed by their feet.

ELEPHANTS

There are two different species of elephants. African elephants are the largest animals that live on land. They live in grasslands and forests in Africa. Indian elephants are smaller and live mostly in forests in India and Southeast Asia.

Above: Indian elephants have smaller ears and shorter tusks than African elephants.

Right: female African elephant with calf.

A herd of African elephants is made up of a number of small family groups. Each group consists of a female (called a cow), and her young sons and daughters. Big bull elephants live alone and join the females at mating time.

Elephant tusks are very long incisor teeth. They are made of dentine (ivory), the same substance of which teeth are made.

Elephants eat leaves, fruits and seed-heads such as millet. They eat up to 150kg (330lbs) of food a day and have very large stomachs. They use their trunks to pick food and put it into their mouths, and sometimes push over and destroy trees to reach the leaves.

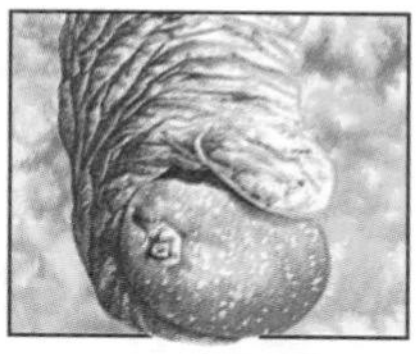

The two "lips" at the end of an elephant's trunk are used like fingers to pick things up, pluck grass and leaves and tear up roots and bark.

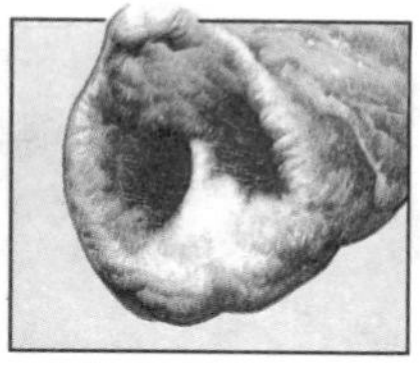

An elephant's trunk is its nose. It has two nostrils. Elephants smell with their trunks and also suck up water and squirt it into their mouths.

Elephants also use their trunks to spray themselves with water or dust. This cleans their almost hairless skin and keeps it in good condition.

Elephants keep cool by flapping their large ears. The ears have many blood vessels, and the blood cools down as the air passes over their ears. They have very good hearing and spread their ears wide to catch faint calls from other elephants up to 8km (5 miles) away. Their calls include barks, snorts, roars and low-pitched rumbles, some of which cannot be heard by people.

Female elephants are pregnant for about 22 months and give birth to one baby. Other female elephants in the family group help look after the baby and make sure it does not wander too far away.

Female elephants fondle and guide baby elephants with their trunks.

RHINOCEROSES

There are five different species of rhinoceroses. Black rhinos and white rhinos live on the grasslands of Africa. Indian rhinos have only one horn and their bumpy skin has several thick folds. Two other kinds of rhinos are smaller and live in rainforests in Sumatra and Borneo, in Southeast Asia.

Cattle egrets sometimes perch on a rhino's back.

Black rhino

Black rhinos and white rhinos both look greyish-brown, but black rhinos are slightly darker and have pointed upper lips for plucking leaves from bushes and trees. White rhinos have straight lips and eat only grass.

Black rhinos (right) have pointed lips and white rhinos (far right) have straight lips.

Rhinos live alone and feed during the night when it is cooler. They can run fast for short distances. They have very good senses of smell and hearing, but their eyesight is poor. Their eyes are on the sides of their heads so they can only see well to the sides.

Male rhinos fight with their horns and if a horn breaks off, a new one grows. In parts of Africa, people are trying to save rhinos by sawing off their horns. This does not hurt and may stop them from being killed by poachers.

In the day, rhinos sleep and wallow in mud to keep cool and get rid of insects.

ZEBRAS, HIPPOS AND GIRAFFES

Zebras, hippos and giraffes live on the grasslands of Africa. Herds of hippos wallow in the big rivers, and giraffes and zebras roam over the grassy plains. They all belong to the group of mammals called ungulates* (hoofed mammals) and they are all herbivores. Zebras and hippos eat grass and giraffes eat leaves.

Birds help animals like this zebra by eating insects off their skin.

ZEBRAS

Zebras belong to the horse family. Like horses, they have hoofs, long legs, manes and tails and they eat grass. There are three different species of zebras, one of which, the mountain zebra, is now very rare. Each of the species has a different pattern of stripes on its rump (bottom).

Zebras crop grass with their sharp front teeth.

In the heat haze of the African plains, a zebra's stripes blur its outline and make it more difficult to see.

Zebras live together in herds. This helps to protect them from meat-eaters such as lions or wild dogs. They have very good eyesight, and excellent hearing and sense of smell and, like horses, they can run very fast. They often live among other grazing animals, such as antelopes.

A family of zebras

Within the herd, the zebras stay in small family groups, usually led by one large male, called a stallion. He gives a barking alarm call if there is danger.

Zebras groom each other in pairs so they can both keep a look-out for predators.

HIPPOPOTAMUSES

Hippotamuses live only in Africa. Great African hippos are the second largest land animals after elephants. They live in central and southern Africa. Pygmy hippos are much smaller. They are now very rare and live only in rainforests in West Africa.

A great African hippo can weigh over 3,000kg (6,600lbs).

Pygmy hippos weigh about 180-275kg (396-606lbs).

The name hippopotamus means "river horse" and great hippos spend up to 16 hours a day lazing in rivers and swamps. They are good swimmers and can stay underwater for up to five minutes. They do not stay out of the water for long as their skin dries up in the sun. Pygmy hippos have oilier skin and can stay out of the water longer.

A hippo's ears, eyes and nostrils are on top of its head so it can watch for enemies.

At night, hippos come out of the water and feed on grass, leaves and roots. Night after night, they walk along the same trails, looking for food. They can run quite fast for short distances and when in danger, run to the water. Baby hippos are born in the water and can swim immediately.

To frighten enemies, or give a show of strength, male hippos open their mouths wide to show their teeth and short tusks. This is called gaping.

GIRAFFES

Giraffes are the tallest animals in the world. A tall male giraffe measures 5m (over 16ft) to the tips of its horns. Both male and female giraffes have two, three or four horns and some have another knob between their eyes.

Giraffes eat the leaves and shoots of trees and shrubs. They tear off leaves with their tongues, which may be up to 45cm (18in) long, and their thick, hairy lips. They browse together in small groups and spend most of the day wandering from tree to tree. To drink, giraffes have to splay their long forelegs wide apart so their mouths can reach the water.

With their long necks, giraffes can reach leaves in the treetops that other animals cannot reach.

Young male giraffes fight to establish who is the leader. They use their necks to push each other slowly from side to side, and bang their heads together.

Giraffes can run quite fast and when they are running, they close their nostrils to keep out the dust. With their bulging eyes, they can see well to the front and sides and they have very good hearing and sense of smell. Their patterned coat helps camouflage them in the dappled light under the trees. There are several different patterns found on giraffes in different geographical areas.

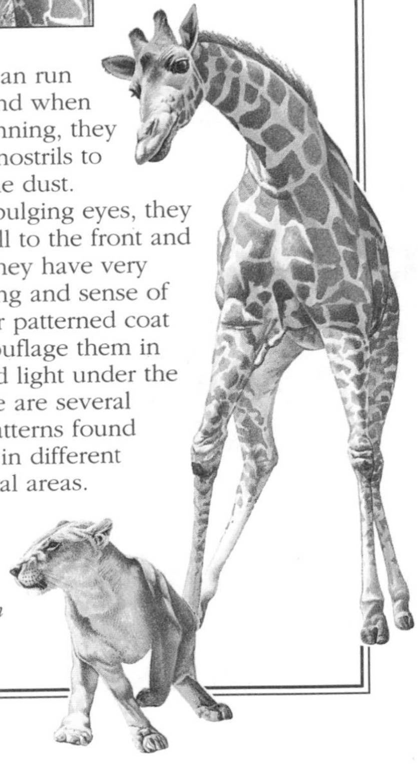

Giraffes kick predators to frighten them away.

*Ungulates, 41

Camels are kept as beasts of burden and herded for their milk, hair and meat.

CAMELS AND LLAMAS

AND WILD CATTLE

Yaks have thick, shaggy hair to keep them warm.

Most camels, llamas and cattle are domestic animals. They are kept for their meat and milk and there are very few left in the wild. They are all ruminants, that is, they have a special digestive system that helps them eat tough grass and leaves.

CAMELS

There are two kinds of camels. Dromedary camels have one hump and live in the Arabian Desert and the Sahara Desert in Africa. They have also been introduced to Australia. Bactrian camels have two humps and live in the Gobi Desert in Asia.

Dromedary camel

In the winter, Bactrian camels grow very thick hair as the winters are very cold in the Gobi Desert. In spring, they shed their winter coats.

Camels can go without water for many days. They store fat in their humps and after a long journey across the desert, their humps shrink and become soft and floppy. When they reach a well or oasis, they may drink up to 20 buckets (about 114 litres or 25 gallons) of water.

Camels eat tough, dry desert grasses and leaves.

To save water, camels sweat very little and a groove in their upper lips carries drips from their noses back into their mouths. They can close their nostrils to stop sand or dust from entering them.

In the Arabian Desert, camels are kept as beasts of burden and herded for their milk, hair and meat. In the Gobi Desert, Bactrian camels still run wild.

Dromedary camel

HOW RUMINANTS EAT

All plant matter contains a substance called cellulose that is very difficult to digest. Animals that are ruminants, such as cattle, camels, llamas, sheep and goats, "chew the cud". This means they regurgitate (bring up) the food (cud) from their stomachs and chew it a second time to help break down the fibrous matter. Deer* and antelopes* are also ruminants.

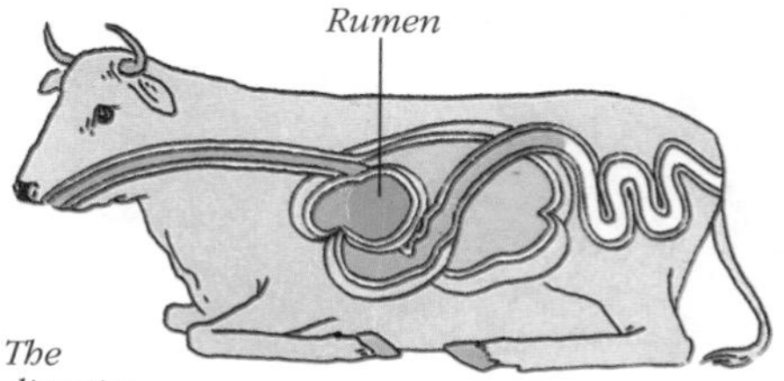
Rumen

The digestive system of a cow

Cows graze standing up and then lie down to chew the cud.

Ruminants have very large stomachs with several chambers. The first time they swallow their food it goes into the first stomach chamber, which is called the rumen. Then, after chewing the cud, the food goes through the other chambers. Their stomachs also contain harmless bacteria that help break down the tough plant matter. In this way, the animals are able to digest all the goodness in the food.

WILD CATTLE

Cattle is the common name for the group of mammals that includes cows, buffaloes, bison and yaks. Today, most cattle are kept as farm animals* and there are very few wild cattle. A hundred years ago, North American bison (called buffaloes in the USA) were hunted nearly to extinction. Now they are bred in zoos and also protected in national parks.

Male bison fight by putting their heads together and pushing hard.

African buffaloes still run wild on the grasslands, but the wild water buffalo of Asia is nearly extinct. The European bison, or wisent, is also very rare.

African buffaloes facing an enemy

LLAMAS

Llamas are related to camels and live in South America. They are domestic animals that are kept for their milk and wool, and also for carrying heavy loads. They are descended from guanacos.

Guanacos still live in the wild in the Andes in South America. Alpacos are also descended from guanacos. They are bred for their long, thick wool. Vicunas are another wild species that are protected on reserves as they were hunted for their fine wool.

Left: adult guanaco with a young guanaco

Vicuna

Llamas, guanacos and vicunas live in small groups of females led by a male.

Llama

*Deer, 56; Antelopes, 57

*Farm Cattle, 65

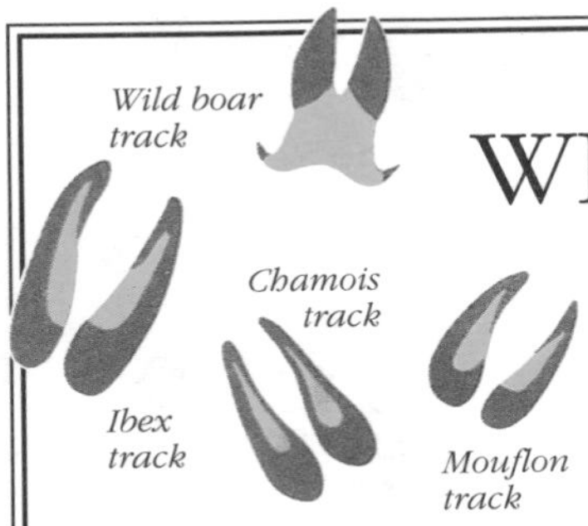
Wild boar track
Chamois track
Ibex track
Mouflon track

WILD SHEEP, GOATS AND PIGS

Most sheep, goats and pigs are kept as farm animals*, but there are still some species of wild sheep and goats living in high mountainous areas, and wild pigs, such as the wild boar of Europe and the warthog of Africa. Sheep and goats are ruminants - they chew the cud like cattle (see opposite).

Female wild boar with piglet

WILD SHEEP

Nowadays, wild sheep live only in remote mountainous regions. With their thick wool coats, they are well suited to surviving in extreme conditions. They live in flocks or herds, usually led by an older female.

Both rams (male sheep) and ewes (females) have horns, but those of the rams are longer.

Mouflon

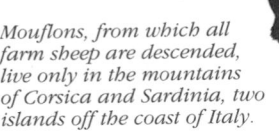

Mouflons, from which all farm sheep are descended, live only in the mountains of Corsica and Sardinia, two islands off the coast of Italy.

Bighorn sheep live in the Rocky Mountains in the USA. Rams fight for females by ramming each other with their bony skulls.

The sheeps' horns grow longer each year and curl around at the tips. The ram with longest horns usually wins in the fights for females.

GOATS

Wild bezoar goats still live in remote mountainous areas in the Middle East. Some other species of wild goats are the chamois, the ibex, and the rare markhor goats that live in the Himalayas.

Male ibexes showing off their strength

Ibexes live high in the mountains in Europe, North Africa and Asia. Adults leave their young among the rocks when they go to find food. Male ibexes show off their strength during the mating season by standing up on their back legs.

Wild goats spend the summer months feeding on the plants that grow on the rocky slopes high above the treeline. Their hoofs cling to the rocks and they can climb very steep slopes and leap from rock to rock.

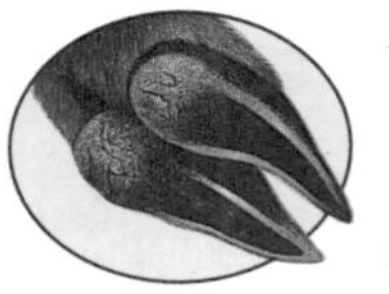

Ibexes have hoofs with narrow edges that dig into cracks in the rocks, and slightly hollow soles that help them cling to the rocks.

Goats eat tough grasses and can go without food for several days. In the winter, they move down the slopes to shelter in the mountain forests and feed on pine shoots and moss.

Chamois (pronounced "cham-wa") live on the mountains of Europe and Asia. They live in small herds and one of the herd looks out for danger and whistles and stamps to warn the others.

Female chamois and their young, called kids, live in small herds on the mountains of Europe and Asia. Kids stay with their mothers for about two years. Male chamois live alone.

Rocky Mountain goats (right) live in the Rocky Mountains in the USA. They are related to chamois.

MUSK OXEN

Musk oxen are related to goats. They live in herds in Arctic regions and have thick, shaggy coats, with finer hair underneath to keep out the cold. Their hoofed feet are large and wide to support them on the snow. They eat grass and the small tundra plants that grow in the Arctic.

During the mating season, male musk oxen give off a strong smell of musk.

WILD BOAR

Wild boar live mainly in remote forests in Europe, Asia and North Africa. They eat acorns, roots and worms, which they dig out of the soil with their snouts. The boars (males) have long canine teeth that form sharp, upward-pointing tusks.

The females (sows) live together in herds with their young and are joined by the boars at mating time. The females give birth to about 11 piglets, which at first are stripey to help them hide in the undergrowth.

All pigs are descended from wild boar.

WARTHOGS

Warthogs live on the grasslands of Africa. They have large tusks and wart-like growths on their faces. Their coarse, short hair is often covered in the mud that they wallow in to keep cool. They eat grasses and fruits, and dig for roots and bulbs. Warthogs live together in large family groups. They shelter in dens lined with grass among the rocks or in old animal burrows.

The wart-like growths may help protect the warthog's face.

*Farm Animals, 65

Reindeer (caribou) live in the Arctic.

DEER

Deer belong to the group of mammals called ungulates*, which means "hoofed mammals". Deer have cloven hoofs, that is, each hoof is divided to form two toes, and the males have antlers. There are about forty species of deer and they live mainly in northern forests and moorlands, although the small mouse deer lives in rainforests. Deer eat grass, moss, lichens, leaves and berries and, like sheep and cows, they are ruminants*: they have four chambers in their stomachs to help them digest plant matter.

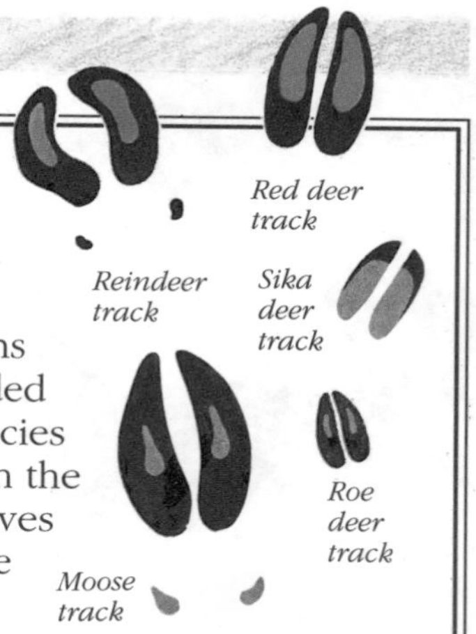
Red deer track
Reindeer track
Sika deer track
Roe deer track
Moose track

RED DEER AND WAPITI

Red deer live in herds in open country and woods. A similar kind of deer, called wapiti live in North America. Red deer eat grass, fruit, bark and heather and may also raid crops. In the spring and summer, they have rusty red coats, but in winter, they grow thicker, grey-brown fur. Male deer are called stags, females are called hinds or roes and the young are called fawns. Stags and hinds live in separate herds, but come together in the autumn to mate. This is called the rutting season.

Red deer stag roaring to establish his territory

At the beginning of the rutting season, a stag leaves his group and goes off on his own.

The stag thrashes his antlers against the trees and rounds up a group of hinds to mate with.

He fights off other stags by locking his antlers with theirs in a test of strength.

REINDEER OR CARIBOU

Reindeer are called caribou in North America. They live in cold Arctic lands. Reindeer live in Scandinavia and northern Asia and caribou live in the Arctic areas of North America. Reindeer and caribou are the only species of deer in which both males and females have antlers.

Reindeer and caribou have thick coats to help keep them warm.

Antlers are used for scratching under the snow for small plants to eat.

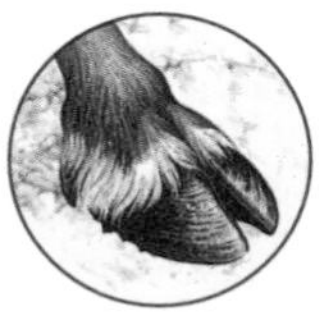

Wide hoofs fringed with fur support them on soft snow.

In winter, these deer live in forests on the edge of the Arctic. In summer, large herds travel north to feed on the tundra*, the regions where small plants grow when some of the snow melts in the summer.

ANTLERS

Antlers are made of a hard, bone-like substance. All deer lose their antlers in the winter and grow new ones in the spring. They often chew the old antlers and this provides them with minerals that their bodies need.

At first, the new antlers are covered with velvety hair, but this soon rubs off. Each year, the new antlers have an extra branch, until they have the maximum number of branches, or points, for that species.

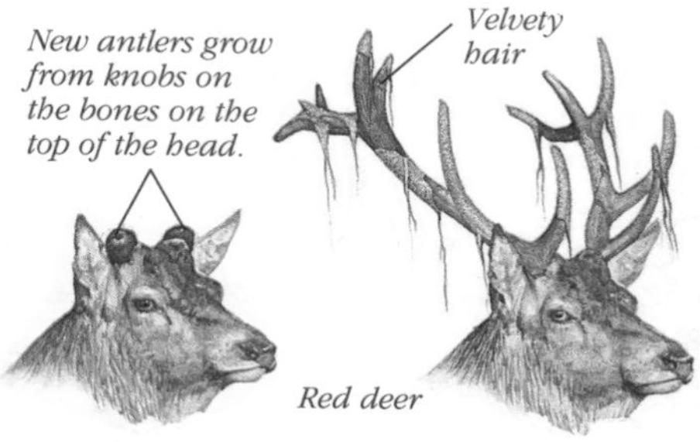
New antlers grow from knobs on the bones on the top of the head.
Velvety hair

Red deer

MOOSE OR ELKS

Moose are called elks in northern Europe. They are the largest species of deer and they live in the forests of North America and northern Europe and Asia. The antlers of a large bull moose (male) can measure up to 2m (6.5ft) across.

Moose live on their own in the summer and in herds in the winter. They are good swimmers and eat water plants, and grass, moss and leaves.

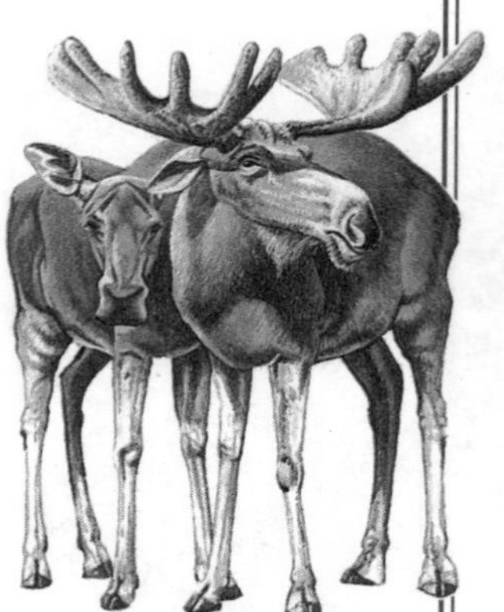

Female moose (left) and male (right)

OTHER DEER

Fallow deer live in herds in parks and woods. They eat grass, acorns, berries, bark, buds and fungi.

Muntjac deer live on their own, or in pairs, in thick undergrowth. They originally lived in China but have been introduced to European forests.

Musk deer live in forests in the Himalayas. They eat grass, leaves, mosses and lichens. The males have long, sharp front teeth with which they fight other males.

All four species of mouse deer are less than 35cm (14in) tall. They live in rainforests in Africa and Asia.

*Ungulates, 41; Ruminants, 54; Tundra, 81

ANTELOPES

Cheetah cub chasing a baby gazelle

Antelopes live in the dry grasslands and deserts of Africa, the Middle East, India and China. There are over a hundred different species of antelopes and they belong to the same family as cattle, sheep and goats. Like these animals, they are ungulates* (hoofed mammals) and their hoofs are divided to form two toes. They live together in herds as protection from predators and they are fast and graceful runners.

Springboks can leap 3m (10ft) up in the air.

GAZELLES

Gazelle is the common name for a group of about 18 different species of small antelopes, including springboks and gerenuks (see right). They are mostly browsers and feed on leaves. Male and female gazelles live in separate herds, but during the dry season they migrate together to find food and water.

Thomson's gazelle

Grant's gazelle

Gazelles, and other antelopes, have very good senses of smell and hearing. These gazelles have sensed a wild dog, or cheetah, which may be 1km (nearly a mile) away.

HORNS

Antelope horns, and those of cattle, sheep and goats, are made of a bony core covered with a layer of keratin, the same substance that fingernails are made of. Most antelopes have ridged horns that usually point backward.

In most species, both males and females have horns but the female's are smaller. The horns grow a little each year. In the mating season, males lock their horns together in contests for the females.

Kongoni antelope

Male topi antelope threatening each other

OTHER ANTELOPES

Dik-diks live on grasslands in Africa and browse on low bushes. Males have short horns.

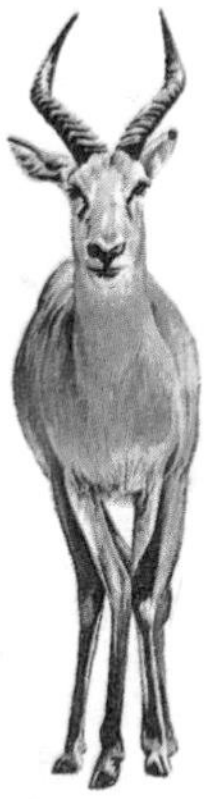

Many gazelles and antelopes have dark backs and pale bellies, like the gerenuk gazelle on the right. This is the opposite of the natural light and shadow and makes them harder to see.

Kob, left, live in wet grasslands in Africa and eat water plants.

Saiga antelope live on the dry grasslands of central Asia. They have thick, brown fur, as the winters are very cold, and broad noses.

WILDEBEEST OR GNUS

Wildebeest, which are also called gnus, are a kind of antelope. They live on the grassy plains of East Africa. During the rainy season, they live in scattered herds and feed on the lush grass. As the grass dries up, they gather together and herds of thousands of wildebeests travel across the plains in search of grass and water. Year after year, they follow the same trails, kicking up huge clouds of dust. In the rainy season, they return to their old feeding places to breed.

Wildebeests have manes like horses.

SPRINGBOKS

Springboks are small gazelles that live in herds on the dry grasslands of southern Africa. They eat mainly grass. When fleeing from an enemy, springboks, and other small antelopes such as impala, leap as they run and this may help to confuse their attackers. The animals that cannot leap so high are usually the ones that are caught.

During the mating season, male springboks fight to claim an area of land in a large mating area. They mark their area with their scent. Females prefer to mate with strong males that have their territories in the middle of the area. Many other species of antelopes and deer have mating areas like this, too.

Springboks fighting in the mating season

SEE FOR YOURSELF

You can make plaster casts of animal tracks using quick-drying plaster of Paris. You also need a container, water, an old spoon, strips of cardboard 30cm x 5cm (1ft x 2in), petroleum jelly and some paper clips.

Smear some petroleum jelly inside a strip of cardboard and clip the ends together to form a ring. Press the ring into the soil around the footprint. Mix some plaster, then pour it into the ring. Leave to set for about 20 minutes, then lift up the plaster.

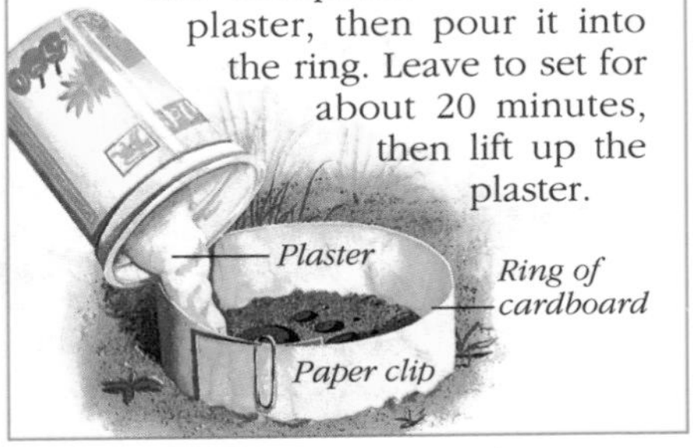
Plaster
Ring of cardboard
Paper clip

*Ungulates, 41

RODENTS

North American porcupine

Rodents* are a group of mammals that have long, chisel-like front teeth, like rats, mice, squirrels and beavers. They eat their food, which may be nuts, fruit, seeds, bark or roots, by gnawing at it. Their strong incisor teeth never stop growing and they are worn down by gnawing. Over a third of all the species of mammals are rodents. Most live in burrows in the ground, but some, such as squirrels, live in trees.

Harvest mice use their tails to help them climb.

MICE

There are over a thousand different species of mice, including house mice and field mice, and rats, gerbils, voles and lemmings*, which all belong to the same family as mice.

House mice are nocturnal. They are found all over the world and can adapt to almost any environment. They have even been found living in deepfreezes, feeding on the frozen food.

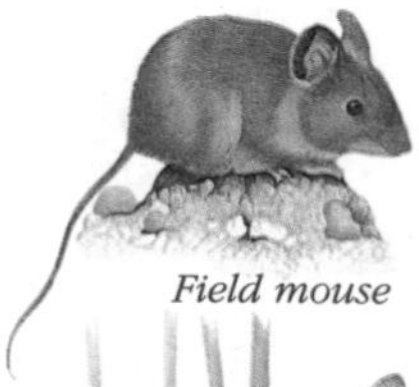

Field mouse

All mice have long, scaly tails and harvest mice can grip with their tails.

House mouse

Harvest mice rear their babies in nests of woven grass. They are active during the day.

Mice live in large groups, called colonies, and they breed very rapidly. A female house mouse can start having babies when she is two months old, and can have up to eight babies every three or four weeks. Baby mice are born in a nest and they are blind and naked.

Field mice, also called wood mice, live outdoors. They build their nests in cracks in walls or tree stumps, and eat seeds and nuts, which they store in their nests. When in danger, a field mouse can shed the end of its tail to escape.

Tooth marks

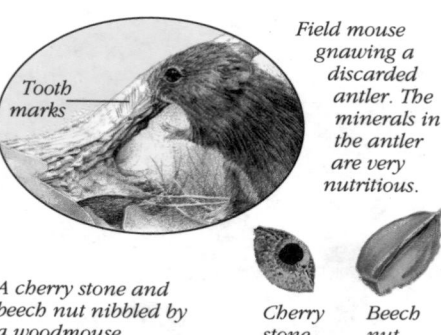

Field mouse gnawing a discarded antler. The minerals in the antler are very nutritious.

Cherry stone

Beech nut

A cherry stone and beech nut nibbled by a woodmouse

RATS

Rats eat almost anything and can even gnaw through metal and stone. Like house mice, they live in colonies and breed very rapidly. Rats can cause a lot of damage to stored foodstuffs and also spread disease. Bubonic plague (which killed a third of the people in Europe in the fourteenth century) is spread by the bite of rat fleas.

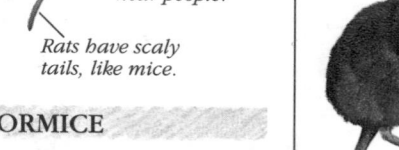

Common rats are brown. They live anywhere near people.

Ship rats are also called black rats, but they are not always black.

Rats have scaly tails, like mice.

DORMICE

Dormice are small, mouse-like rodents but, unlike mice, they have furry tails. They are nocturnal and live alone, climbing trees to look for insects, flowers, berries and seeds to eat. They live in Europe, Asia and Africa.

The fat dormouse lives in forests in Europe. They were called edible dormice by the Romans, who liked to eat them.

Garden dormouse

Common dormouse

European dormice spend nearly half their lives asleep. During the winter, when food is scarce, they hibernate in nests of straw. They survive on stores of fat that they build up during the summer, when they almost double their own body weight.

European dormouse hibernating in a nest of bark and straw

VOLES

Voles have blunter faces than rats and mice, with smaller ears and shorter tails. They live in burrows in the ground and are mainly active at night.

Field voles burrow under plants to eat the roots and can destroy crops. Bank voles eat grasses, nuts, buds, berries and seeds. They can swim and climb well. When food is scarce, they strip off the bark high up in trees and gnaw the wood underneath.

Bank vole

Water vole

Muskrat

Water voles live in the banks of rivers and streams, but are also found in burrows farther from the water. They swim with only their noses showing and may stay underwater for over 30 seconds. They eat waterside plants.

Muskrats are a kind of vole. They were brought to Europe from North America for their fur, called musquash. Animals that escaped from fur farms survived and bred in the wild. Muskrats have webbed hind feet and are good swimmers.

SEE FOR YOURSELF

Rodents, such as mice, hamsters, guinea pigs and gerbils, are often kept as pets and become very tame if they are handled gently and regularly. They are very playful and enjoy exploring objects such as boxes, tubes or wheels put in their cages.

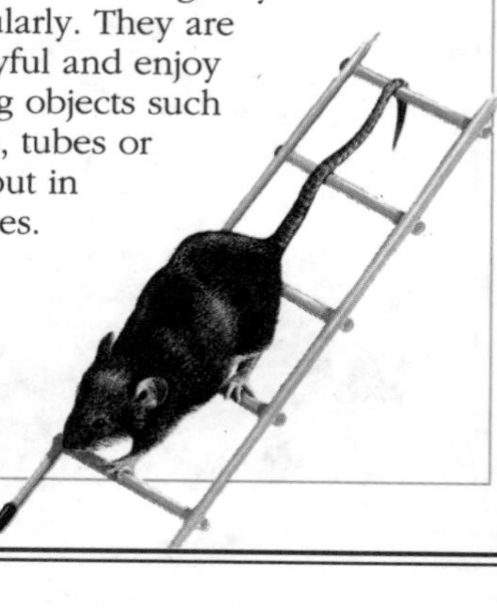

Pet mouse climbing a ladder

*Lemmings, 81

*Rodents, 41

PORCUPINES

Porcupines have stiff, pointed spines, called quills, which they can raise and rattle to frighten enemies. The quills have sharp tips and backward-pointing barbs. If an animal gets them in its flesh, they are very difficult to pull out.

When in danger, porcupines raise their quills as a warning sign. If the enemy does not go away, the porcupine backs into it and spikes it with its sharp, barbed quills.

African porcupines live on the ground and North American porcupines (see above left) live mainly in trees, although in summer, they feed on the ground. They eat leaves, fruit, seeds and bark.

BEAVERS

Beavers live in rivers in northern Europe, Asia and North America. They eat twigs, bark and leaves and build their homes, which are called lodges, underwater. They are very powerful swimmers and have waterproof fur, flat, paddle-like tails and webbed feet.

Beaver carrying a branch to store for food

To build a lodge, beavers cut sticks with their strong gnawing teeth, and even fell small trees. They dam a river to make a quiet pool, and then build the lodge on a pile of stones and mud. The entrance to the lodge is under the water. Near the lodge, they pile up twigs, leaves and bark as a food store.

Each family of beavers has its own lodge. The mother and father beaver stay together all their lives and have three or four babies, called kits, each year.

Beavers' lodge with side cut away to show inside

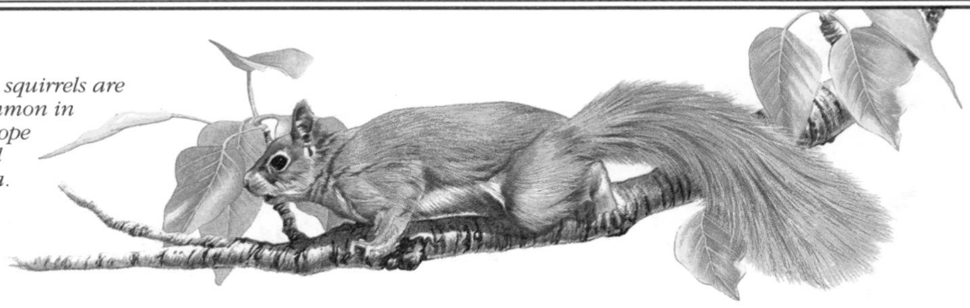

Red squirrels are common in Europe and Asia.

SQUIRRELS

Squirrels live in trees and eat seeds, buds, fungi, cones and fruits. They grip the branches with their sharp claws and their big, bushy tails help them to balance. They have very good eyesight and can judge distances well. There are 267 different species of squirrels that live in woods and forests all over the world, except in Australia.

Red and grey squirrels live alone. In the autumn, they hide nuts and seeds for the winter, some of which is eaten, but most is forgotten.

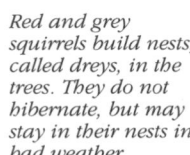

Grey squirrel

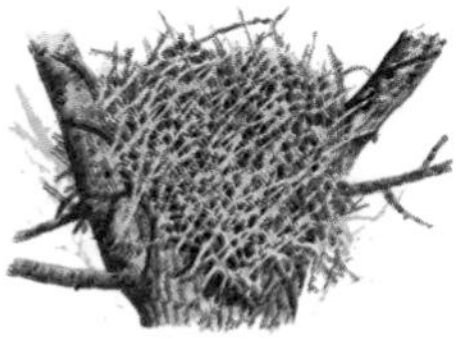

Red and grey squirrels build nests, called dreys, in the trees. They do not hibernate, but may stay in their nests in bad weather.

Flying squirrel jumping onto a tree trunk

North American flying squirrels have flaps of skin joining their arms and legs. When they jump, they stretch their arms and legs like wings and can glide up to 100m (328ft) between trees.

OTHER RODENTS

Chipmunks are related to squirrels. They have cheek pouches in which they carry nuts and seeds.

Hamsters live on grasslands in central Asia. They are nocturnal and hibernate in winter. They carry nuts and seeds in their cheek pouches.

Naked mole rats live in grasslands in Africa. They have very little hair and spend all their lives in their burrows.

Gophers live on the North American grasslands. Their long incisor teeth stick out of their mouths, so they can dig with their mouths closed.

Agoutis live in rainforests in South and Central America. They sniff around on the forest floor, looking for roots and seeds to gnaw.

The mara is related to the guinea pig. When moving fast, it hops like a rabbit. It lives in the South American pampas grasslands.

PRAIRIE DOGS

Prairie dogs are rodents, but they bark like dogs. They live on the prairies (grasslands) of North America, and feed on grass. Prairie dogs live together in extensive systems of burrows, called towns, and each family group has its own area. Sentries keep watch and bark as a warning if there is danger.

When prairie dogs meet they "kiss" to find out if they are from the same group. In fact they are smelling each other. If they are from the same group, they groom each other, but if they are strangers, the intruder is driven away.

Prairie dogs

Prairie dogs "kissing"

Males and females look after the young.

Hares run fast to escape danger.

HARES, RABBITS
AND PIKAS

Rabbits bolt down their holes when in danger.

Hares, rabbits, and pikas belong to a group of animals called lagomorphs*, which means "shaped like a hare". They eat grass, seeds, leaves and roots. To obtain all the goodness from the plants, which are difficult to digest, they eat their own droppings, so the food passes through them twice.

HARES

Hares live alone and feed at night. They eat mainly grass. In the daytime, they rest in a flattened area of grass or earth called a form. When disturbed, hares lie still with their ears flat, but to escape enemies, they can run very fast. Brown hares can reach speeds of up to 80kph (50mph). They also swerve and double back on their tracks to confuse the enemy. When they run, their long hind feet touch the ground in front of their forefeet, and this gives them a powerful push forward.

Leverets (baby hares) are born in a nest on the ground. They are born with fur and with their eyes open.

Baby hares are called leverets. Unlike rabbits, which are born underground, leverets have fur and their eyes are open at birth. Three days after birth, the mother moves them to separate forms. When she leaves them to find food, they lie absolutely still in the nest until she returns. In the breeding season, hares gather together to mate. They leap and kick, chase around in circles and box each other before they pair off and mate.

In the spring, brown hares are sometimes called "mad March hares" because of the way they box each other and chase around in circles during the breeding season.

Hares live in grassy areas all over the world, although Arctic hares, also called blue or mountain hares, live in northern forests, snowshoe hares live in the mountains of North America, and jack rabbits, a type of hare, live in desert areas in the south of the USA.

Black-tailed jack rabbits hop quickly across the desert sand to stop their feet from burning.

Arctic hares (right) have bluish-white fur in winter.

Left: Arctic hare in summer

PIKAS

Pikas have short legs and cannot run as fast as hares and rabbits. They live on rocky mountainsides in North America, and in northern Asia.

In summer, pikas collect green plants and dry them in the sun to make food for the winter. Each pika hides its food among the rocks, or builds a haystack near its burrow and guards it fiercely.

In summer, pikas lay grass on the rocks to dry in the sun. Dried plants, or hay, keep longer than fresh ones.

Each pika fiercely guards its food.

RABBITS

European rabbits often live together in groups of about ten adults and their young, in a maze of burrows called a warren. American rabbits, or cottontails, live alone.

European rabbits originally lived in southern Europe, but spread farther north and have been introduced into Australia and South America.

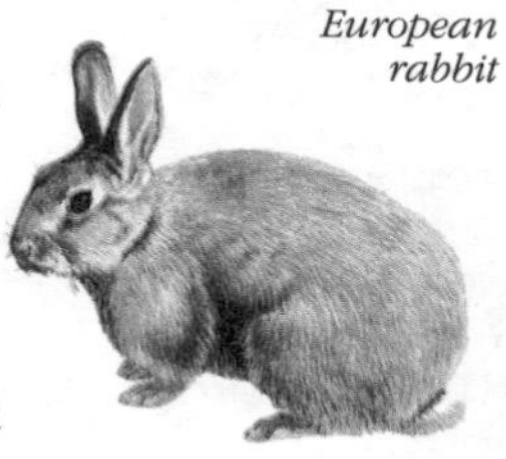

European rabbit

Rabbits usually feed at dawn or dusk. Their eyes stick out so they can see all around when they are grazing. They stay near their warrens as they can only defend themselves by kicking with their strong back legs or by running down a burrow to escape from enemies.

When rabbits run, their bobbing white tails are a danger signal for other rabbits.

Female rabbits are called does and males are called bucks. The does have about ten babies every year. Within three or four months, the young are old enough to breed, so the number of rabbits increases very rapidly.

SEE FOR YOURSELF

If you examine the crops at the edges of fields you may see tooth marks made by rabbits and hares on turnips and carrots. Look also for nibbled bark, buds and branches on nearby trees.

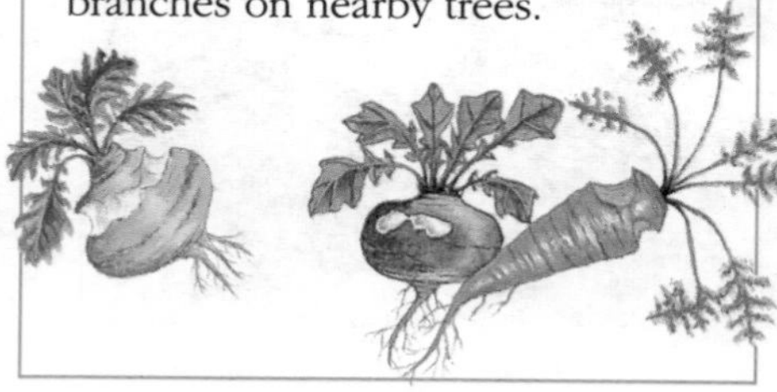

*Lagomorphs, 41

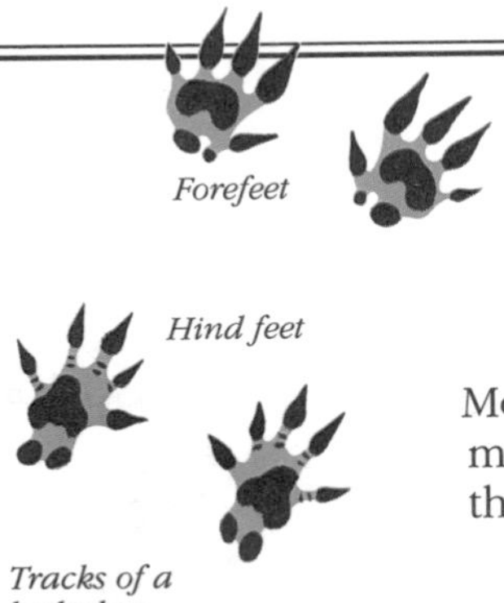
Forefeet
Hind feet
Tracks of a hedgehog

MOLES, HEDGEHOGS
AND SHREWS

Moles, hedgehogs and shrews are all insectivores* - animals that eat mainly insects. They need to eat a lot to survive and spend most of their time searching for food. They are all nocturnal. Their eyesight is not very good, but they have long, sensitive noses to help them find food, and whiskers to feel around in the dark.

Water shrew

MOLES

There are about 20 different kinds of moles found in Europe, Asia and North America. They live almost anywhere where the soil is soft enough to dig and there are earthworms to eat. They have very sensitive pink snouts and powerful shovel-shaped paws for digging. Their hearing is good and their small eyes are protected by their fur or, in some species, by a thin layer of skin.

Shovel-shaped paws
Sensitive snout
A mole's velvety fur lies smoothly in either direction so it can move easily along its narrow tunnels.

Moles live alone and spend most of their time underground. They dig tunnels just under the surface and push the earth out to make molehills. They run through the tunnels looking for worms and insects that fall through the walls. Moles eat at least fifty worms a day. They also bite the heads off worms to paralyze them so they can store them for later.

Desmans are related to moles. They live in mountain streams in Europe and Asia, but were hunted for their fur and are now very rare.

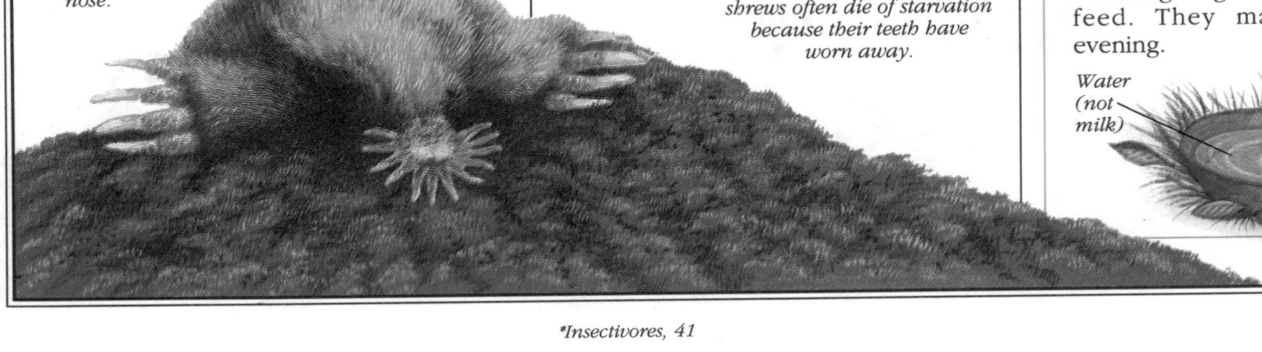
The North American star-nosed mole feels for grubs and worms with the feelers on its nose.

SHREWS

Shrews are found all over the world, except in Australia and Antarctica. There are about 270 different species of shrews and they live in many different habitats, including thick undergrowth, semi-desert and water.

Shrews are very small, with long, twitching, whiskered noses. They dig in leaves and soil to find beetles, slugs and worms to eat. Because they are so small, their bodies lose heat rapidly and they need to eat their own weight in food each day to keep warm. They are active day and night, only resting for a few minutes at a time.

Common shrew

Pygmy shrew

Pygmy shrews weigh about 3g (0.1oz)

Water shrew

Most shrews live alone. They defend their territory and they often fight when they meet other shrews. They have a musky smell and are rarely eaten by other animals. Many, including water shrews, have poisonous saliva, giving them a venomous bite that enables them to overcome prey that is larger than themselves.

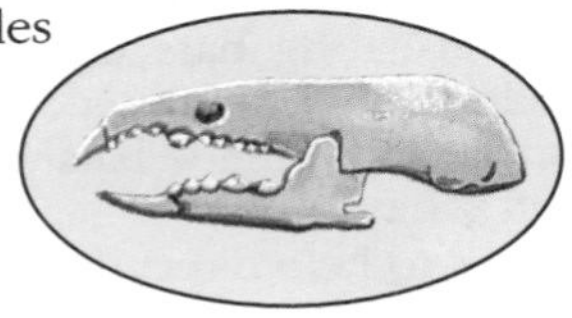
Shrews are born with only one set of teeth and older shrews often die of starvation because their teeth have worn away.

HEDGEHOGS

Hedgehogs have prickles on their backs but their bellies are soft and hairy. They have long noses with whiskers, and small eyes and ears. They live in fields and ditches in Europe, Asia and Africa.

Hedgehogs live alone but come together to mate.

Hedgehogs rest in burrows during the day and come out at night. They snort and grunt as they search for insects, worms, slugs and frogs to eat. When in danger, they roll up into a ball with their prickles sticking out to protect them. They are good climbers, but if they do fall they are cushioned by their prickles.

In the winter months, European hedgehogs hibernate in nests of grass and leaves. They live off the reserves of fat that they built up during the autumn, although on warm days, they may wake up and feed. Baby hedgehogs are born in the springtime.

Baby hedgehogs are born naked and blind, but within a few hours they have soft prickles.

SEE FOR YOURSELF

Hedgehogs are quite tame. If you leave a saucer of water or pet food outside in the evening, you may see hedgehogs coming to drink or feed. They may return each evening.

Water (not milk)

*Insectivores, 41

BATS

Bats are the only mammals that can fly, although some mammals, such as flying squirrels*, can glide. There are over 900 different species of bats. They can be divided into two groups: insect-eating bats and fruit bats. All bats are nocturnal - they feed at dusk and spend the day sleeping in caves, treetops or old buildings.

There are 60 different species of horseshoe bats. Their fleshy nose flaps help them find insects using echo-location.

A bat's wings are made of thin, leathery skin supported by long finger bones.

Malay fruit bat

Sharp claws

INSECT-EATING BATS

Insect-eating bats eat moths, gnats and mosquitoes. They usually live near rivers or lakes where there are lots of insects. They find the insects using echo-location (see below right), catch them with their mouths and eat them while they fly.

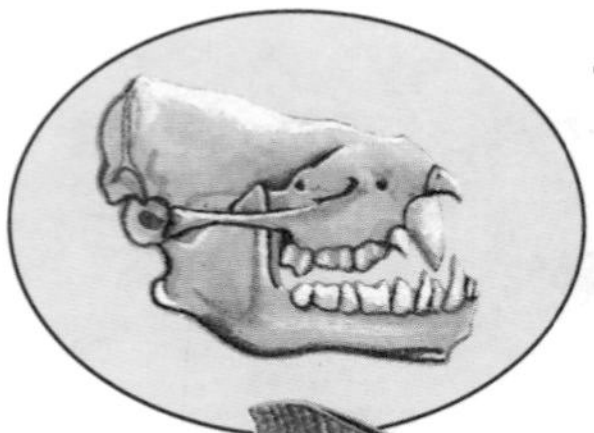

Skull of an insect-eating bat. Bats grasp insects with their sharp teeth.

In cooler parts of the world, most bats hibernate during the cold months. Thousands hibernate together in caves, disused buildings or hollow trees. They hang upside-down by their back claws, huddled together for warmth. Other bats migrate to warmer places to avoid the cold.

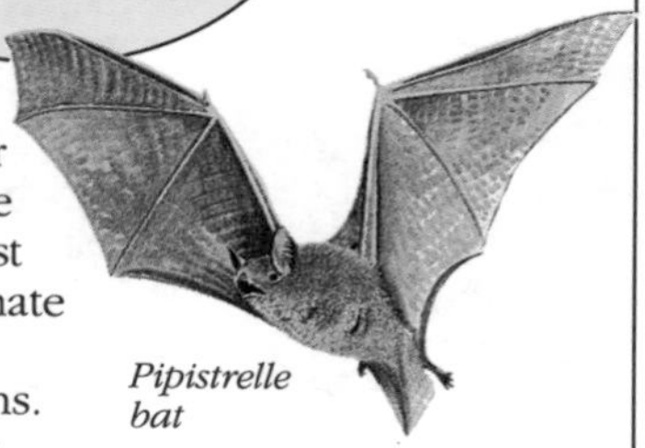

Pipistrelle bat

A long-eared bat's large ears help it pick up echoes.

Noctule bats (right) migrate 2,300km (1,400 miles) from Moscow to Bulgaria.

Daubenton's, or water bats (left), fly low and fast over the water, catching mosquitoes.

Natterer's bats (right) are found in woods and in towns.

FRUIT BATS OR FLYING FOXES

Fruit bats are also called flying foxes because of their fox-like faces. They eat fruit, and the nectar and pollen from flowers. They live in hot countries in Africa, Asia and Australia, but are in danger of extinction because the forests where they live are being cut down.

Most fruit bats do not use echo-location to find their way around. They feed at dusk and have good eyesight. They also have a very good sense of smell with which they find ripe fruit, and flowers that open at night.

Fruit bats help to pollinate flowers by carrying pollen from flower to flower. When they visit flowers, the pollen clings to their fur and then brushes off on other flowers. When they eat fruits, they also help to disperse the plant's seeds.

Long-nosed fruit bats reach inside flowers with their long, bristly tongues.

Fruit bat taking nectar from banana flowers

ECHO-LOCATION

Most insect-eating bats use echo-location to guide them as they fly. The bats make very high-pitched clicks or squeaks (too high for humans to hear). These sounds bounce off objects and echo back to the bats. Using this system, the bats can find their way in total darkness, and can also track and catch insects. Many insect-eating bats have large ears to help them locate the echoes and some, such as horseshoe bats (see picture top left), have folds of skin around their noses to help direct their sounds.

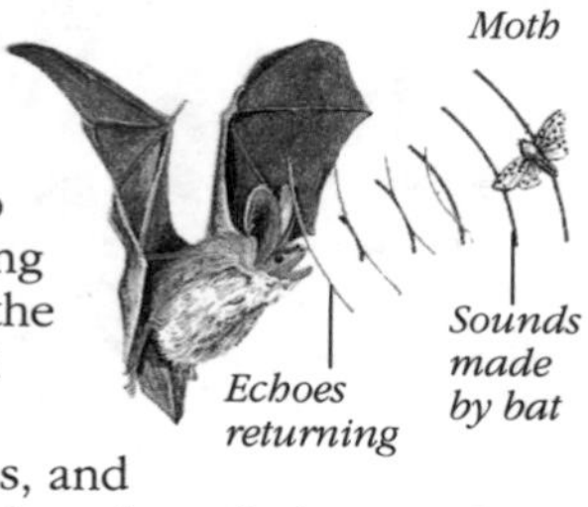
Moth
Sounds made by bat
Echoes returning

FISH-EATING BATS

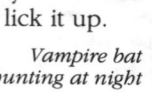

Fish-eating bats belong to the same group as insect-eating bats. They use echo-location to locate small fish swimming just below the surface. Then they swoop down and catch the fish.

VAMPIRE BATS

Vampire bats suck animals' blood and spread disease, but they do not usually bite people. They live in South America. They make a shallow bite with their razor-like teeth and their saliva prevents the animal's blood from clotting. The blood flows freely and the bats lick it up.

Vampire bat hunting at night

SEE FOR YOURSELF

Look for bats in old buildings or lofts, or flitting through the air at dusk near a river or lake. In forests and nature reserves, you may see bat boxes for bats to nest in, high on the trees. There may be up to 50 bats in one box. If you find bats hibernating, do not disturb them, as they may die if they wake.

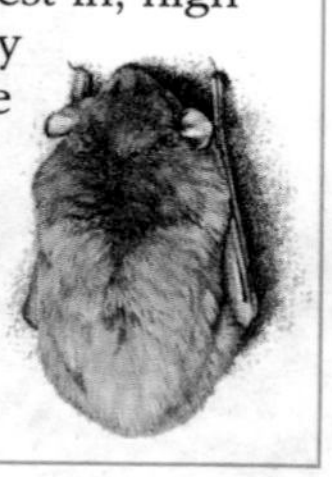

Roosting bat

*Flying squirrels, see Squirrels, 59

Tamandua (a type of anteater)

TOOTHLESS MAMMALS

Pangolins can grip with their tails.

The toothless mammals, or edentates*, are a strange group of animals that live in the forests and grasslands of South America. They include anteaters, armadillos and sloths, and all, except sloths, eat ants and termites. Only anteaters have no teeth at all. The others have small, peg-like teeth. Other "toothless" mammals, the aardvarks and pangolins, live in Africa. Some of them have chewing teeth at the back of their jaws, but none has any front teeth.

ANTEATERS

Giant anteaters live in the grasslands of South America and the lesser anteater, or tamandua, lives on grasslands and in the rainforest. Anteaters have strong front legs with three claws with which they tear open anthills and termites' nests. They lick up insects and crush them with their cheeks as they have no teeth. They eat about 30,000 insects a day.

Anteaters dig for ants with their long, sharp claws.

Anteaters can collect about 500 ants with each lick of their long tongues.

During the day, giant anteaters spend most of the time sleeping in hollows with their tails curled over them to protect them from the sun. When in danger, they move at a clumsy gallop and rear up on their back legs to frighten an enemy. Baby anteaters ride on their mothers' backs.

SLOTHS

Sloths live in the trees in rainforests in South and Central America. They do everything very slowly and move only 4m (13ft) a minute in the trees. They eat leaves, which take a long time to digest, so they need to save their energy. It takes a month for their food to pass through their large stomachs.

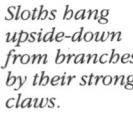

Sloths hang upside-down from branches by their strong claws.

On the ground, sloths cannot stand up on their arms and legs and they only come down from the trees once a week to defecate. They spend a lot of time sleeping, or hanging upside-down from branches. Their fur looks green because it is covered with blue-green algae. This helps to camouflage them in the trees.

Three-toed sloths have three, hook-like claws on their front paws for gripping branches. Two-toed sloths have only two.

PANGOLINS

Pangolins live in rainforests and grasslands in Africa and Southeast Asia. Their bodies are covered with thick scales made of keratin, the same substance as hair. Their scales are different from the scales of armadillos, (see below left), which are made of bone. When in danger, they roll into a ball and their enemies cannot hurt them.

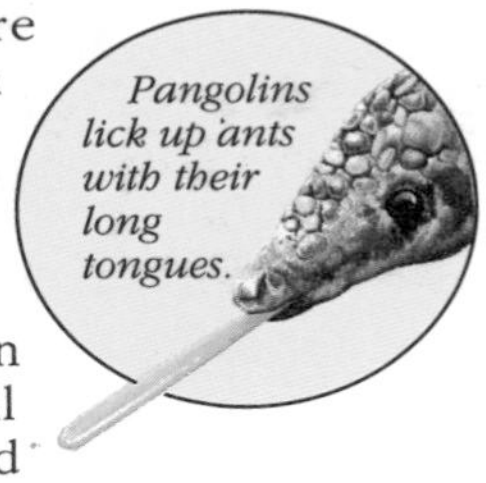

Pangolins lick up ants with their long tongues.

Pangolins eat up to 200,000 ants each night. Their stomachs have tough linings to crush the insects and help them digest them. Some types of pangolins live on the ground and others live in the trees. Ground-living pangolins are nocturnal and sleep in burrows during the day.

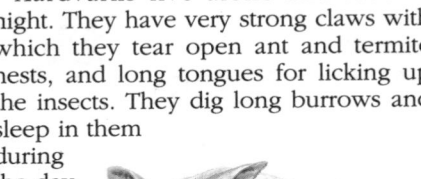

A pangolin is well protected by its sharp-edged, overlapping scales.

ARMADILLOS

Armadillos live in the grasslands and tropical forests of South America, and the nine-banded armadillo is also found in North America. Their leathery skin is covered with bony plates, called scutes, covered with horn. The hairy armadillo has hair growing between its scutes.

There are about 21 different species of armadillos. Some, such as small, three-banded armadillos, can roll into tight balls to protect themselves. Only jaguars are strong enough to force open their hard, bony plates and eat their soft bodies.

Armadillos are mainly nocturnal. They have poor eyesight but a very good sense of smell. In the day, they sleep in burrows and at night, they dig for ants and termites to eat.

Nine-banded armadillo

The three-banded armadillo (left) can roll itself into a tight ball.

AARDVARKS

Aardvarks live in forests and grasslands in Africa. They look a little like pigs but, in fact, they are a very distant relative of elephants. They grow nearly 2m (6ft) long and have almost hairless skin, very long ears and thin noses. They have no front teeth and feed mainly on ants and termites.

Aardvarks live alone and feed at night. They have very strong claws with which they tear open ant and termite nests, and long tongues for licking up the insects. They dig long burrows and sleep in them during the day.

Aardvarks grow up to 2m (6ft) long.

*Edentates, 41

HORSES AND DONKEYS

Horses and donkeys belong to the group of animals called ungulates* (hoofed mammals). They originally come from the grasslands of central Asia, but are now found all over the world. For over 5,000 years, horses and donkeys have been used for pulling and carrying heavy loads, and for riding. There are now very few left in the wild.

Knabstrup, far left, and Pinto, left

Strong workhorse

HORSES

The only wild horses left in the world are Przewalski (pronounced "che-val-ski") horses from the Gobi Desert. These horses have never been bred or trained and are still the same as their ancestors that roamed the plains.

No Przewalski horses have been seen in the wild since 1968, but there are some in zoos.

Herds of horses that now roam freely, such as mustangs in North America and Camargue horses in southern France, are descended from horses that were bred by people (see below). The herds are made up of a stallion (male) and a number of mares (females) and their foals. The stallion defends the territory in which the herd grazes.

Horses eat mainly grass. They crop the grass with their sharp front teeth. In the wild, they graze day and night. Their teeth never stop growing, but they are worn down by chewing.

Camargue horses live in wetlands in southern France.

Foals are born in the spring. They can stand within a few hours and rejoin the herd two or three days later. When colts (young males) are about three years old, the stallion forces them out of the herd. Colts roam together until they are strong enough to set up their own herds.

French Auxois mare suckling her foal

DONKEYS

Donkeys belong to the same family as horses, but they are smaller and sturdier and they have much rougher coats and longer ears.

Wild donkeys, such as the Nubian ass, still live on the grasslands of North Africa and central Asia, but domestic donkeys are now found all over the world. Donkeys have probably been domesticated for even longer than horses as they are very strong for their size and can carry or pull very heavy loads.

Nubian ass

Donkeys are calm and friendly and are often kept as companions for horses.

Horse
Donkey

BREEDS OF HORSES

There are over a hundred different breeds, or types, of horses. They have been bred by selective breeding (see opposite page) over hundreds of years. All the breeds are descended from two ancient types of horses. The ancient southern type was similar to the Arab breeds of today. It was light and fast with a fine coat. The northern type, from the mountains of Europe and Asia, was smaller with a thick coat, like the mountain ponies of today.

Standardbreds are usually bay (reddish-brown), black or brown.

Danish Knabstrup horses are always spotted.

Shire horses were bred to pull heavy loads, and to carry knights.

Palominos have golden brown coats and white manes and tails.

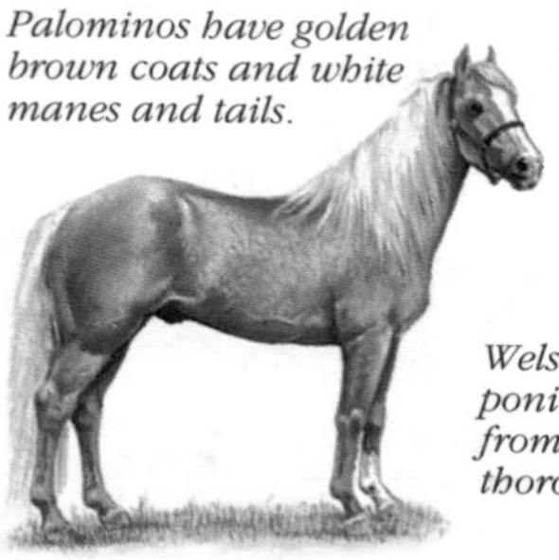

Welsh mountain ponies were bred from Arab and thoroughbred horses.

Thoroughbreds were bred from Arab horses.

SEE FOR YOURSELF

Here are some tips to help you recognize some of the main breeds of horses.

Mountain ponies, such as highland ponies, are small with rough coats.

Dished profile

If it has a dished profile (a face that curves in) and carries its tail high, it probably has some Arab blood.

Workhorses, such as Percherons or Shires are big and heavy with long hairs around their fetlocks.

Fetlock

Thoroughbreds are tall and lightly built. They have long legs and a fine coat.

*Ungulates, 41

Cow suckling her calf

FARM ANIMALS

Cattle, sheep, goats and pigs* originally lived in the wild and were hunted by our early ancestors. Some of the animals became tame, perhaps because they lost their mothers and grew up with people. Herds of sheep and goats were first kept about 10,000 years ago.

Chick hatching

FARM CATTLE

All the different breeds of cattle are descended from fierce wild cattle*, called aurochs, that once lived in parts of Europe, Asia and North Africa.

Aurochs are an extinct species of cattle.

Farm cattle still live together in herds, like their wild ancestors. The herd has a leader and the other cattle know their position of importance in the herd. When they are young, cattle may threaten each other to establish leadership.

Below: Fresian cow with calf

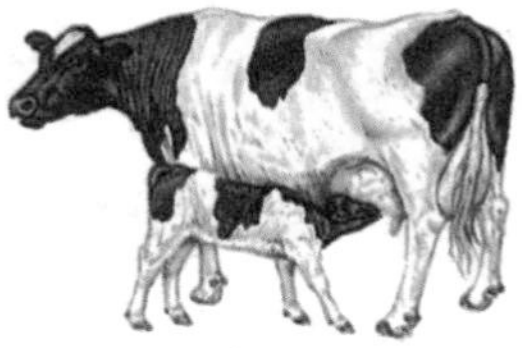

Above: a threatening cow stands with its head lowered and its hind legs forward, eyeing its rival.

SELECTIVE BREEDING

Since earliest times, farmers have chosen their best animals for breeding. Usually, the young of these animals have the good qualities (they grow faster or produce more milk) of their parents. Mating two animals of the same breed is called pure breeding. Crossbreeding is the mating of two animals of different breeds. The young are called cross-breeds, or hybrids.

Camborough 12 crossbred sows have large litters of strong piglets.

Duroc boar - a strong, hardy, outdoor breed

Landrace sows look after their large litters well.

PIGS

Pigs are descended from wild boar that still live in remote forests in Europe and Asia. As a result of selective breeding (see below left), a modern pig may weigh twice as much as a wild boar, and give birth to up to 20 piglets in each litter.

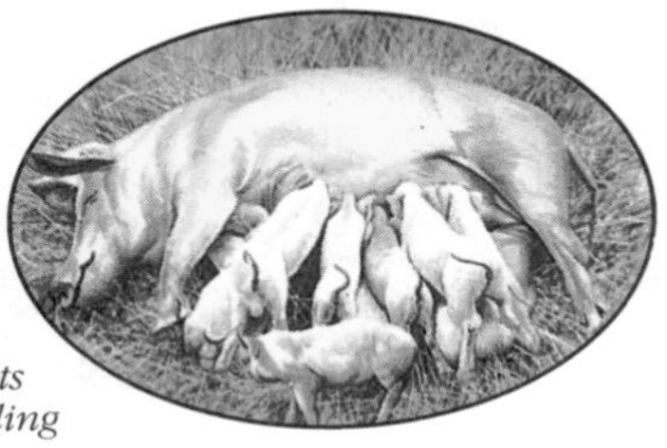

Piglets suckling

Pigs are clean animals. They eat, sleep and excrete in different parts of their pen.

Pigs have very sensitive noses. In France, they are used to search for truffles (fungi for cooking) in the ground.

SHEEP

All farm sheep are descended from mouflon sheep* that lived on grasslands in Europe and Asia. There are many different breeds of sheep. Each has been bred to suit a particular region.

Sheep live in flocks and usually they all eat together and rest together. Like cattle, they are ruminants* and have special stomachs to help digest the tough grass that they eat.

Right: Dalesbred sheep from Britain

Above: merino sheep from Spain

Left: Mongolian sheep from Asia

HENS

Hens are descended from red jungle fowl that live in rainforests in Southeast Asia. They were first domesticated in India and China about 4,000 years ago. In the wild, the fowl lay about 30 eggs a year, but if the eggs are taken away, they may lay as many as 80.

Red jungle fowl

Hens peck each other to show who is boss. The most aggressive hen is the one that pecks all the others and is recognized as the leader. The next hen pecks all the hens below it, but not the leader, and so on.

Each hen knows its position in the pecking order and knows who it can peck.

Before mating, a cock performs a courtship display for a hen. He waltzes around her with his neck feathers ruffled and one wing held out. The hen builds a nest of straw, and the eggs she lays for the next few days will be fertile (chicks will grow in them).

Some breeds of hens

White leghorn

Yokahama cock

Silver campine hen

Indian game hen

Hens kept in battery farms, where they are warm and well-fed, lay about 240 eggs a year. Some countries ban battery farming as they believe the cramped conditions are cruel.

*Wild Cattle, 54

*Wild Sheep, Goats and Pigs, 55; Mouflon sheep, see Wild Sheep, 55; Ruminants, 54

Sugar gliders (a type of possum) can glide up to 45m (150ft) between trees.

Mother and baby koala

MAMMALS OF AUSTRALIA

AND SOUTH AMERICA

Most of the mammals in Australia are different from those in the rest of the world. Many of them are marsupials* - they give birth to tiny, unformed young that complete their development in a pouch on their mother's abdomen. There are also monotreme mammals* that lay eggs. There are many different kinds of marsupial mammals, from koalas and kangaroos, to marsupial mice, moles and cats and there are also some marsupials in South America.

KANGAROOS AND WALLABIES

There are about 50 different kinds of kangaroos including wallabies, which belong to the same family as kangaroos. They live mainly in the grass and dry scrubland areas of Australia and Tasmania and eat grass. There are also a few tree kangaroos that live in forested areas in Australia, and on the island of New Guinea. They have strong claws and can climb trees to eat leaves.

Red kangaroos live mainly in the scrublands in central Australia and can go many days without water. Grey kangaroos live in the grasslands in eastern Australia.

Red-necked wallaby

Wallabies live in dry grasslands in southeastern Australia and Tasmania.

Kangaroos live together in small groups, called mobs, led by a strong male. They spend most of the day lying in the shade. In the evening when it is cooler, they look for food and water. To warn other kangaroos of danger, they thump their hind legs on the ground.

Grey kangaroo with a joey (young kangaroo) in its pouch

In the spring, male kangaroos fight for the right to mate with the females. Baby kangaroos are born about 30 days after mating, and then spend four or more months in the mother's pouch. Only female marsupials have pouches.

A newborn kangaroo is less than 2.5cm (1in) long at birth and is blind and naked. It slips out of the birth opening and crawls up through the mother's fur to the pouch on her abdomen.

Inside the pouch, the baby fastens on to one of its mother's teats and sucks milk. It stays in the pouch for about four months and grows to become a young kangaroo called a joey.

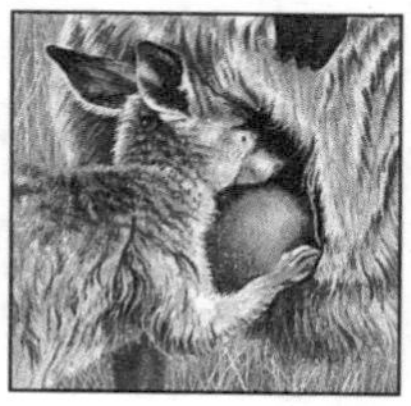

After four months, the joey begins to leave the pouch for short periods, but it continues to suck milk and returns to the pouch when it is tired or frightened until it is about a year old.

Kangaroos are considered pests by farmers as they eat the grass and drink the water the farmers need for their livestock. The kangaroos can jump over fences put up to keep them off grazing land. Each year, several million are shot by farmers and in the past, they were also hunted for their meat and fur. However, at present, none of the species of kangaroos or wallabies is in danger of becoming extinct.

With their strong back legs and tails, large adult kangaroos can jump 3m (10ft) in the air and 9m (30ft) along. They use their tails to help them balance and can travel at speeds up to 60kph (about 40mph). When grazing, or walking slowly, they walk on all-fours.

KOALAS

Koalas are marsupial mammals that live in forests in eastern Australia. They eat the leaves and bark of eucalyptus trees. They are very particular and will eat the leaves of only five of the 350 different kinds of eucalyptus trees. They feed at night and spend much of the day digesting their food while sleeping on branches in the treetops.

Koalas have long claws and two "thumbs" on each forepaw with which they grip the branches.

The name koala means "no drink" in the Australian Aboriginal language and koalas almost never drink. They get all their liquid from the leaves they eat.

Baby koalas are about the size of a bean when they are born. They crawl into their mother's pouch, which opens to the back, and then continue their development attached to a teat in the pouch. When the baby is about six months old, it leaves its mother's pouch and clings to the fur on her back. The mother koala feeds it with chewed-up leaves until it can feed itself.

WOMBATS

Wombats live in burrows in grassland areas of Australia and Tasmania. They have short, powerful legs and long, strong claws for digging their burrows. They are marsupials. The female's pouch opens at the back so earth does not go in as she moves along the tunnels of the burrow. Wombats live together in groups and are nocturnal. They sleep in their burrows in the day and come out at night to eat grass. They have poor eyesight but good senses of smell and hearing.

Wombats graze at night.

*Marsupial Mammals, 40; Monotreme Mammals, 40

OPOSSUMS

Opossums are small, rat-like marsupials that live in South and Central America, and some have also moved into North America. There are about 70 different kinds. The smallest is the size of a mouse, while the Virginia opossum of North America is as large as a cat.

Opossums give birth to about 18 young. When they are too big for the mother's pouch, they cling to her fur.

Most opossums are good climbers and can grip branches with their toes and tails. They are nocturnal and eat small animals, fruit and insects, and also scavenge in garbage.

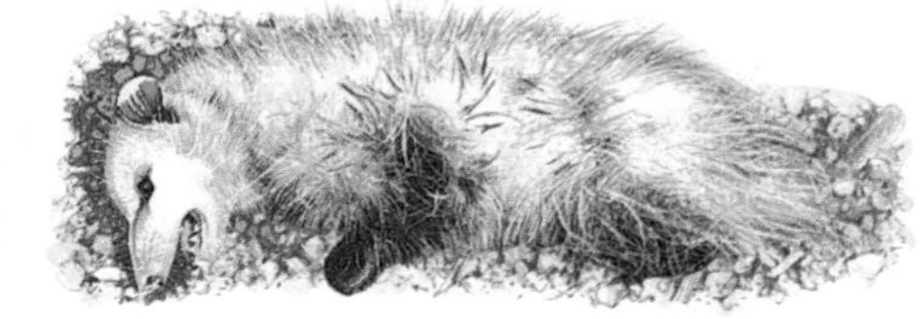

When frightened, an opossum may pretend to be dead. It lies completely still with its eyes and mouth open. Carnivores, such as cats, will not eat dead animals.

POSSUMS

Possums live in trees in the forests of Australia, Tasmania and New Guinea, and feed on nectar and insects. They are expert climbers and can grip the branches with their paws and tails. Possums are marsupials and there are many different kinds, including pygmy, honey and ringtail possums, and sugar gliders (see picture on opposite page).

Sugar gliders have flaps of furry skin along their sides. When they stretch out their arms and legs, they can glide up to 45m (150ft) between the trees. They carry their young in their pouches until they are two months old.

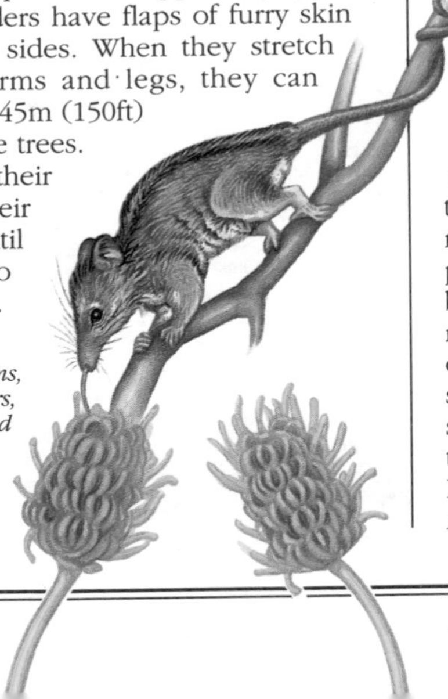

Honey possums, or noolbengers, eat nectar and pollen with their long, brush-like tongues.

OTHER MARSUPIALS

The small boodie (left) is a member of the rat kangaroo family. It eats plants and is nocturnal.

Numbats (right) are also called banded anteaters. They live in dry grasslands in Western Australia and eat termites.

The long-nosed potoroo (left) is another kind of rat kangaroo, like the boodie (top). It sleeps in a nest in the day.

Bandicoots (right) are small, rat-like marsupials. They eat fruit, insects and worms, and their pouches open to the rear.

Quolls or tiger cats (left), are small cat-like marsupials. They eat mainly wombats, small reptiles and sugar gliders.

WHY THEY ARE DIFFERENT

When mammals first evolved, about 200 million years ago, scientists think that all the land was joined up to make one huge continent. Marsupial mammals lived all over the land then.

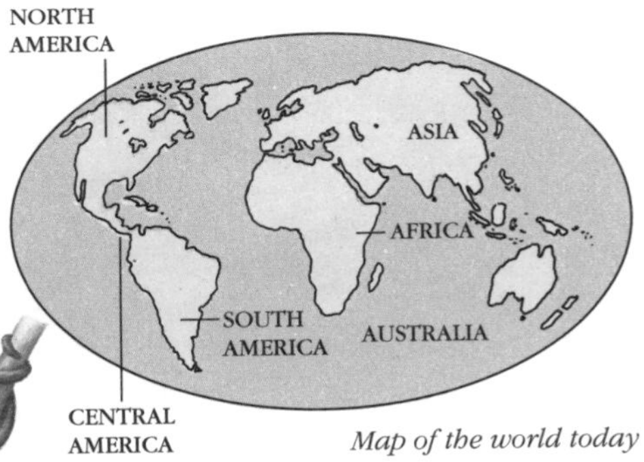
NORTH AMERICA
ASIA
AFRICA
SOUTH AMERICA
AUSTRALIA
CENTRAL AMERICA

Map of the world today

Over millions of years, the land split up to form the continents we know today. In Asia, Africa and North America, marsupial mammals were replaced by placental mammals* (mammals that give birth to fully-formed babies). Placental mammals could not cross into Australia or South America because they were separated from the rest of the land by sea, so marsupials continued to survive there. South America became joined to North America, by the land called Central America, about 3.5 million years ago.

SPINY ANTEATERS OR ECHIDNAS

Spiny anteaters are also called echidnas. They are monotreme mammals and the female lays one egg that she keeps in a pouch on her abdomen. When it hatches, the baby licks up the milk that seeps out of glands in the mother's skin. Echidnas do not have teats.

Short-beaked echidna

There are two species of echidnas. Short-beaked ones live in Australia, New Guinea and Tasmania and eat ants and termites. The rarer, long-beaked echidna eats worms as well as ants and termites.

Echidnas lick up insects with their long tongues. They have strong, sharp claws for digging out termites and ants. To protect themselves, they curl up into a ball or burrow quickly into the sand.

When in danger, spiny anteaters rapidly dig a shallow hollow in the ground, as shown in these two pictures. Only their sharp, protective spines show above the ground.

THE DUCK-BILLED PLATYPUS

The duck-billed platypus is a monotreme mammal that lives in Australia and Tasmania. The female lays two eggs in a nest of leaves and grass at the end of a long tunnel in a river bank. The eggs have soft shells and when they hatch, the babies cling to their mother and lick up the milk that oozes from her skin. The platypus does not have teats.

The platypus is a good swimmer and has webbed feet and a strong tail. Its beak is covered with sensitive skin that helps it find worms and shrimps in the muddy riverbed. It has pouches in its cheeks where it can store food to eat later.

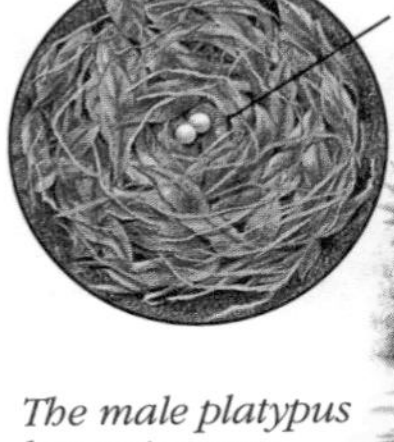

Platypus nest with two eggs

The male platypus has poisonous spines on its feet.

*Placental Mammals, 40

Living things depend on each other for their food.

ECOLOGY

Ecology is the study of living things in their natural surroundings, or habitat. It examines how animals and plants depend on each other, and on the non-living world - the soil, air and water - around them. The essential substances that plants and animals need, such as oxygen, carbon dioxide and water, are continually being recycled between animals and plants, and the land, sea and air. The study of ecology helps show how peoples' activities affect the delicate balance between living things and their environment and how wildlife can be protected.

WILDLIFE HABITATS

The particular place where a plant or animal lives is called its habitat. Each living thing is adapted to the conditions in its habitat. For example, cactus plants grow in deserts and have fleshy stems that store water.

The prickly pear cactus has fleshy stems with a thick waxy coating to reduce water loss. Instead of leaves, it has sharp spines.

The plants and animals that live together in a particular habitat are called a community. Within the community, each living thing has its own niche, or living conditions, so the animals and plants are not competing for the same food and space. If they were, one type would die out or be driven away. For example, many different species of animals can survive on the African grasslands because they eat different parts of the same plants.

On the African grasslands, giraffes and elephants reach up to pluck leaves from high branches, and antelopes and black rhinos browse on the lower branches. Many other species graze on the grass.

There is a natural balance between the numbers of animals and plants that can survive together in an area.

BIOMES AND ECOSYSTEMS

The world can be divided into a number of different regions, or biomes, that are the result of different climates. Deserts* and rainforests* are two very different biomes and each has its own wildlife. Each biome contains many ecosystems.

An ecosystem consists of a habitat and all the things that live there and depend on each other and their environment for their food. It can be as small as a rotting log, which in turn may be part of a larger ecosystem such as a forest.

Map showing main world biomes

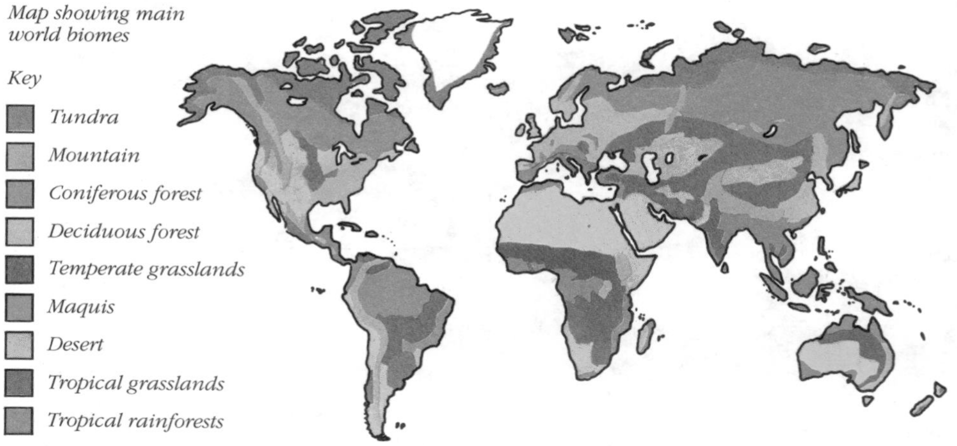
Key
Tundra
Mountain
Coniferous forest
Deciduous forest
Temperate grasslands
Maquis
Desert
Tropical grasslands
Tropical rainforests

FOOD CHAINS

All the living things in a particular area are linked by their feeding habits. A diagram showing who is eaten by who is called a food chain.

A typical woodland food chain

Plant
Beetle
Thrush
Hawk

Most food chains start with green plants because plants make their own food by photosynthesis*. Plants provide animals with all the energy they need to live. Herbivores (plant-eating animals) obtain the energy when they eat the plants. The energy is passed on to carnivores (meat-eating animals) when they catch and eat the herbivores.

FOOD WEBS

In any area, there are many interlinked food chains. The food chains form complex food webs that are delicately balanced. If one species of animal dies out, the whole web may change.

The arrows show the flow of food through the food chains.

A rainforest food web

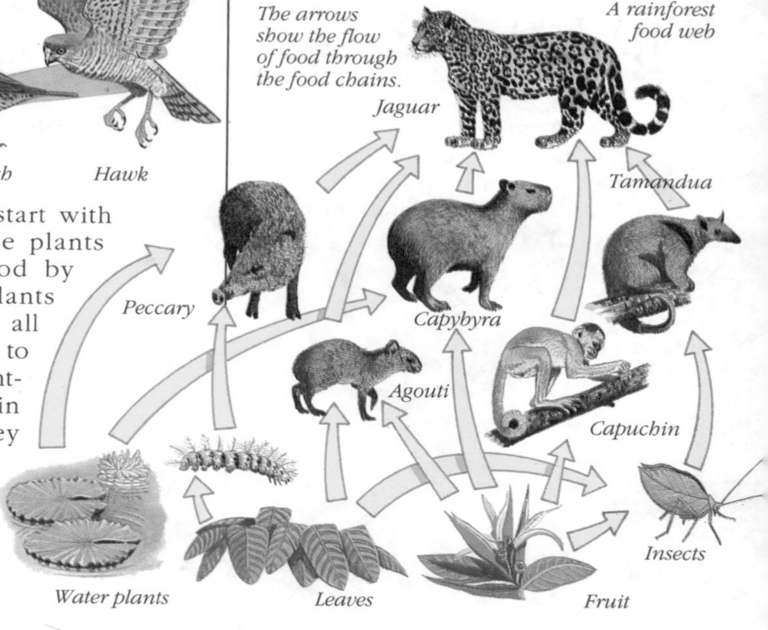
Jaguar
Tamandua
Peccary
Capybyra
Agouti
Capuchin
Insects
Water plants
Leaves
Fruit

*Deserts, 76-77; Tropical Rainforests, 78-79; Photosynthesis, 5

THE WATER CYCLE

The water that falls as rain drains into rivers and the sea. It gradually evaporates and then becomes tiny droplets of moisture in the air. The droplets form clouds and fall again as rain. In this way, water is continually recycled between the Earth and the air and this is called the water cycle.

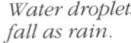

Water droplets form clouds.

Water droplets fall as rain.

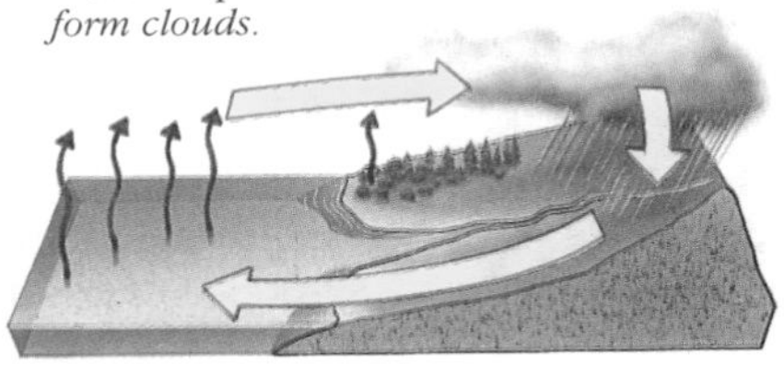

THE CARBON CYCLE

Carbon is one of the essential substances that all living things need to live and grow. It circulates through living things in many different forms. Plants take in carbon dioxide gas from the air and use it to make food by photosynthesis*. Animals eat plants and their bodies break down, or digest, the plant matter and use the carbon for their own growth.

Plants need sunlight for photosynthesis so they only make food, and take in carbon dioxide, in the day.

Animals build their bodies using carbon from plants, or from animals that have eaten plants.

Both plants and animals burn up food inside their bodies to release energy, and carbon dioxide is given off as a waste product. The carbon dioxide goes back into the air when animals breathe out. At night, when plants are not making food by photosynthesis, they also give off carbon dioxide. Carbon dioxide is also released back into the air when dead plants and animals decompose (rot).

Fossil fuels, such as oil and coal, are made of animals and plants that died many millions of years ago, but did not rot away. When they are burned, more carbon dioxide is released into the air.

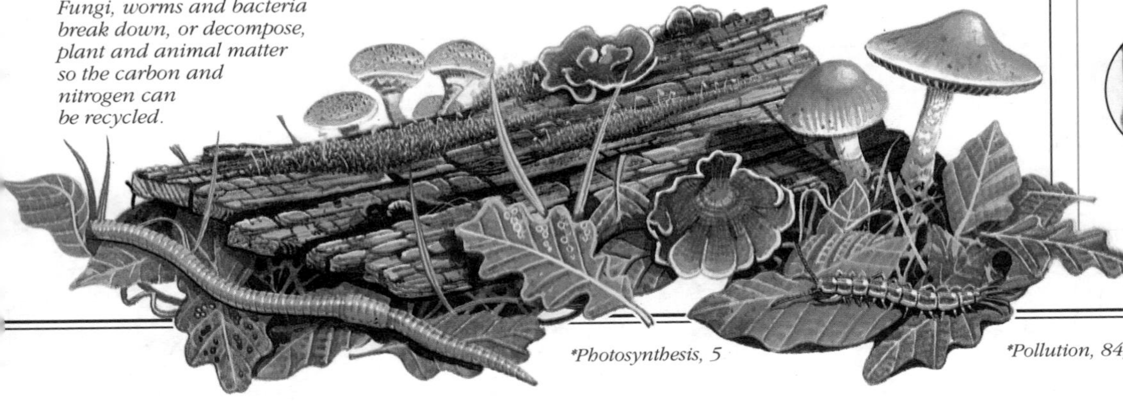

Fungi, worms and bacteria break down, or decompose, plant and animal matter so the carbon and nitrogen can be recycled.

THE NITROGEN CYCLE

Nitrogen is one of the many gases in the atmosphere. Plants and animals need nitrogen-based substances to build proteins for their bodies. Plants absorb nitrogen in the form of nitrates from the soil and use it to make plant matter. Animals obtain nitrogen by eating plants, or animals that have eaten plants.

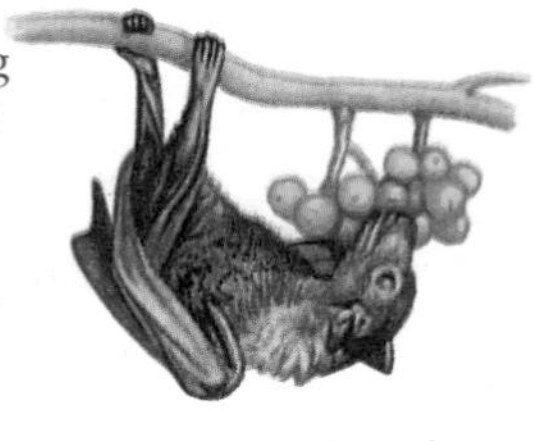

Fruit bat eating fruit

Insects, such as dor beetles that feed on animal dung, help break down plant and animal matter and release the nitrogen and carbon dioxide.

When plants and animals die, bacteria and fungi break down the plant and animal matter and the nitrogen is released back into the soil in the form of ammonia. In the soil, the ammonia is converted into nitrates again. The nitrates are then taken up by new plants and the cycle repeats itself.

THE GREENHOUSE EFFECT

The carbon dioxide in the air plays an important role in warming the Earth by trapping the Sun's heat. This is called the greenhouse effect, as the carbon dioxide is like the glass that traps the heat in a greenhouse.

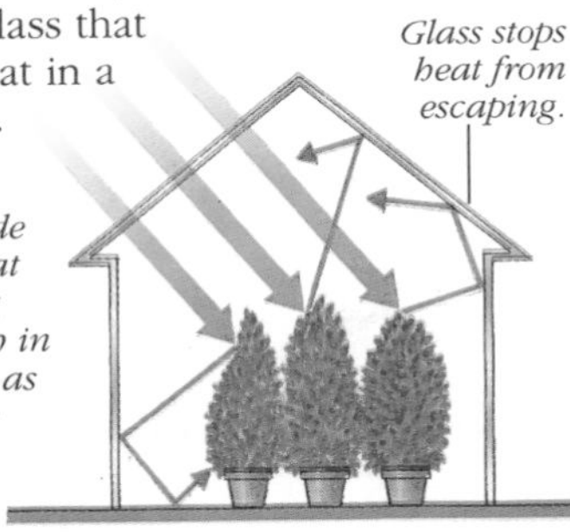

Glass stops heat from escaping.

Carbon dioxide stops some heat from escaping from the Earth in the same way as the glass traps the heat in a greenhouse.

More and more carbon dioxide is going into the air from the burning of fossil fuels, such as oil and coal, in cars and factories. Scientists believe this may cause climates around the world to become warmer, and some of the ice in the polar regions to melt. This is known as global warming.

ECOLOGICAL PROBLEMS

The natural balance between plants and animals and their surroundings is frequently upset by the activities of people. Pollution*, the destruction of habitats* and intensive farming methods all disturb the delicate balance between living things and their environment.

The destruction of the rainforest is causing severe ecological problems, as well as the extinction of thousands of different types of wildlife.

Scientists believe that carbon dioxide from the burning of the rainforest is upsetting the carbon cycle and increasing the greenhouse effect (see left).

If one particular species of animal becomes scarce due to pollution, hunting or fishing, the balance in food chains (see left) is upset. Other species in the chain may starve or they may increase in number because the animals that ate them no longer exist.

Sandeels

In the 1980s, many puffin chicks in the North Sea starved because the sandeels that they eat had been overfished.

The balance in nature is continually changing due to natural causes such as droughts, but now, peoples' activities are the most serious threat to wildlife.

SEE FOR YOURSELF

You can see how much pollution there is in your area by studying the growth of lichens* on trees and walls. In very polluted areas, there are no lichens and only green algae*. In cleaner areas, you may see shrubby lichens on trees.

Polluted | *Some pollution* | *Clean*

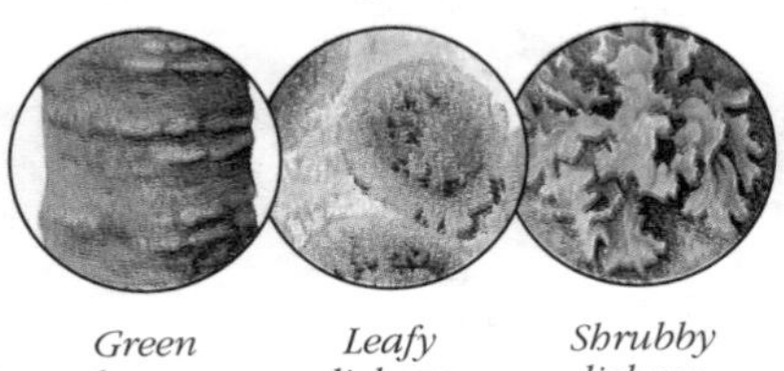

Green algae on tree trunks | *Leafy lichens on walls* | *Shrubby lichens on trees*

*Photosynthesis, 5

*Pollution, 84; Destroying Habitats, 84; Lichens, 73; Algae, 11

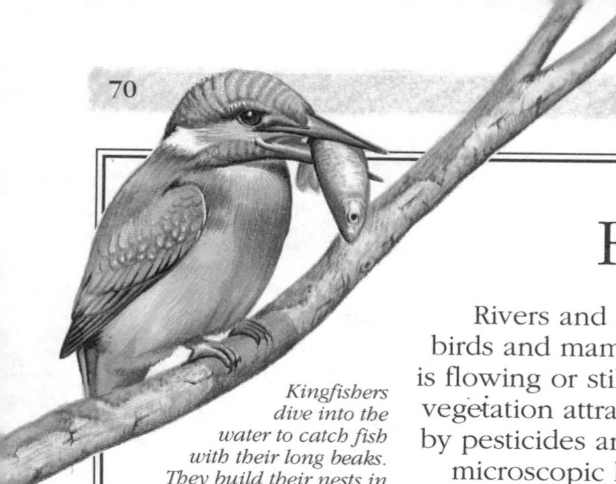

RIVERS AND LAKES

Smooth newts eat tadpoles, snails and insects.

Rivers and lakes are home to a wide variety of plants, fish, insects, birds and mammals. The particular species depend on whether the water is flowing or still. Plants root easily in the still water of a pond and the lush vegetation attracts many animals. Many rivers and lakes are badly polluted by pesticides and chemical fertilizers that drain off farmland. These kill the microscopic life on which many fish and animals feed. These pictures show the wildlife around a river or lake in a cool part of the world.

Kingfishers dive into the water to catch fish with their long beaks. They build their nests in burrows in the riverbank.

FRESHWATER FOOD CHAIN

The term "freshwater" describes the wildlife that lives in rivers and lakes, as opposed to the salty water of the sea. A food chain diagram, like the one below, shows how some of these animals and plants are linked by their feeding habits.

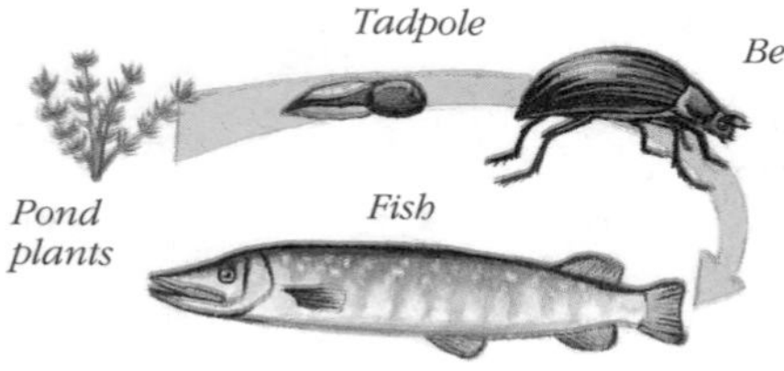
Tadpole
Beetle
Pond plants
Fish

The arrows in a food chain diagram show the flow of food through the "chain".

The different species are dependent on each other and if one is destroyed, for example, if pond plants are killed by pesticides, many other creatures in the food chain are affected.

LIFE ALONG A RIVER

This picture shows some of the plants, mammals, birds, insects and amphibians that live along a slow-moving river.

Great reedmace has dark-brown velvety seedheads. They are often wrongly called bulrushes.

WATER PLANTS

Water plants provide food and shelter and give off oxygen that fish, and other water animals, can absorb from the water. The oxygen is produced by photosynthesis, the process by which plants make their food.

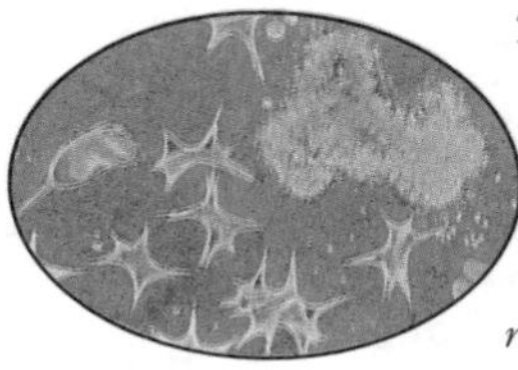

Tiny plant-like organisms, called algae, float in the water and are eaten by ducks, fish and insects. The green slime on rocks is also algae.

Plants that grow underwater have thin stems and leaves as the water supports the stems and the leaves do not need to hold water. Floating plants have large leaves with thick stems to support them.

Canadian pondweed grows underwater and spreads very rapidly. New plants can grow from pieces of broken stem.

Mare's tail grows partly underwater and has very small leaves.

Yellow water lilies have large leaves that float on the surface, and strong stems to anchor them to the riverbed.

WATER INSECTS

Many species of insects and their larvae (young) live in and on the water, feeding on microscopic plants and animals, and on tadpoles, other insects and even small fish. Insects that dive under the water, such as beetles and water boatmen, take in air at the surface and carry a bubble of air for breathing underwater. Insects are eaten by fish, frogs, toads, newts and birds.

Great diving beetles feed on young fish.

The nymph (young) of a stonefly

Water boatmen swim and take in air upside down at the surface.

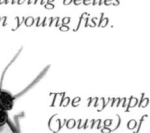

Adult stonefly

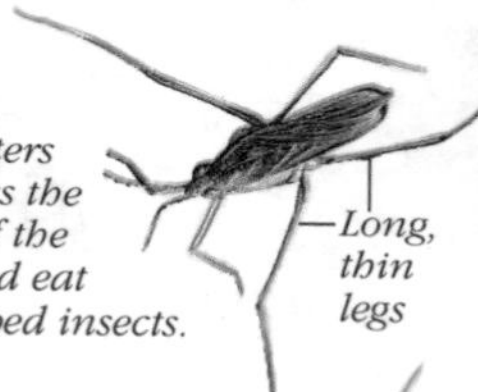
Long, thin legs

Pond skaters run across the surface of the water and eat trapped insects.

Caddis fly larvae protect themselves with cases of shells, stones and leaves.

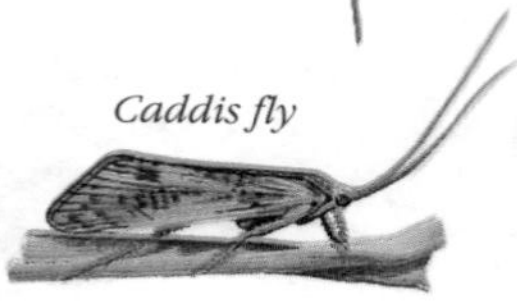

Caddis fly

Moorhen
Herons catch fish and frogs with their long beaks. They build their nests in trees.
Ducks dabbling for underwater plants
Mallard ducks
Bulrush
Reed warblers
Common European frogs
Water lilies often sink at night when the flowers close.

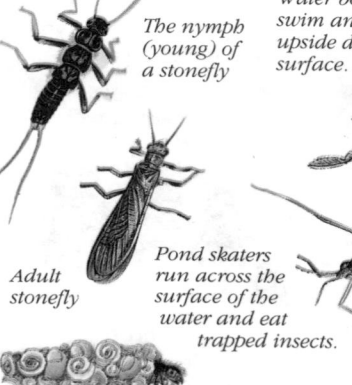

DRAGONFLIES AND DAMSELFLIES

Dragonflies and damselflies live near water and lay their eggs on water plants. They look similar, but damselflies can fold their wings over their bodies. They are both carnivores and eat other insects. Their young are called nymphs*.

The nymphs live for several years in the water, feeding on tadpoles and water insects, and shedding their skins as they grow. When they are fully grown, they climb the stems of water plants. They shed their skins and emerge as adult dragonflies or damselflies.

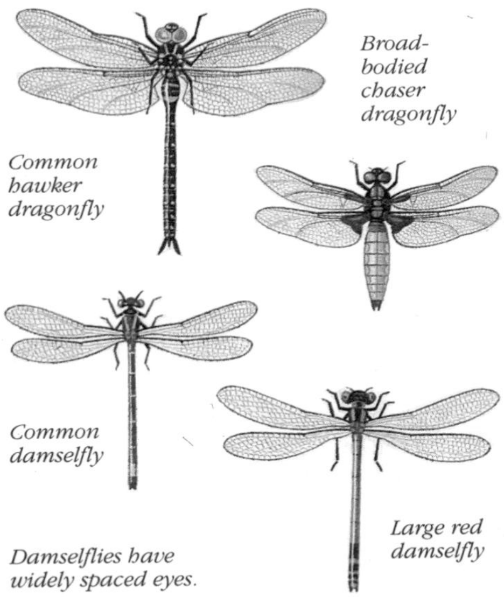

Broad-bodied chaser dragonfly
Common hawker dragonfly
Common damselfly
Large red damselfly

Damselflies have widely spaced eyes.

HYDRA

Hydra are small animals that cling to plants and sting prey, such as water fleas, with their long tentacles. They grow up to 2cm (0.75in) long and move by making loops and somersaults. If they are disturbed, they shrink into blobs.

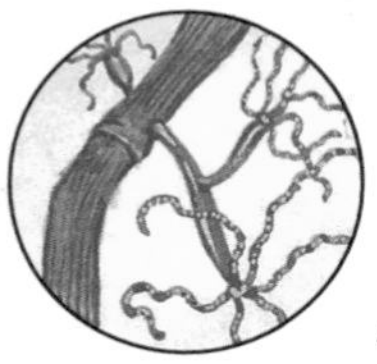

Hydra attached to a plant stem - and to each other

OTTERS

Otters are well adapted for life in the water. They have long, sleek bodies, webbed feet and strong tails which they use as rudders. When they dive, they shut their ears and nostrils. Freshwater otters live in rivers and lakes and eat fish, frogs and shellfish. Sea otters live in the northern Pacific Ocean and use stones to knock shellfish off the rocks.

Freshwater otters live in burrows, called holts, near streams and rivers. They feed at night.

SEE FOR YOURSELF

To look at underwater plants and animals you can make a pond viewer from a clear plastic bottle - but be very careful near deep water.

Cut the top and bottom off the bottle. Cover one end with clear plastic wrap held in place with an elastic band. Cover the other edge with some tape so it is not sharp.

Place the covered end of the viewer in the water and look through the open end. You may see fishes, newts, pond insects and snails.

Piece of plastic bottle
Plastic wrap

WATER BIRDS

Many different birds live on or near the water. Birds that eat insects, such as swallows, swifts and wagtails, fly over the water. Ducks feed on plants growing in and beside the water and some birds, such as mallards and swans, reach down for underwater plants. Herons and kingfishers eat fish, frogs and insects.

Grey wagtail

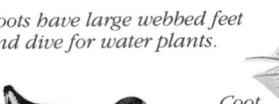

Wagtails nest near fast-flowing streams and catch insects.

Coot

Coots have large webbed feet and dive for water plants.

Moorhens live near ponds and streams and eat plants and small animals.

Sedge warblers often build their nests among the thick plants on riverbanks.

Shovelers filter plants out of the water with their long, flat bills.

Goosanders live on large lakes and dive for fish. Females have shaggy crests on their heads.

Mute swan

Vith their long necks, swans can reach down for underwater plants. They may also graze on land.

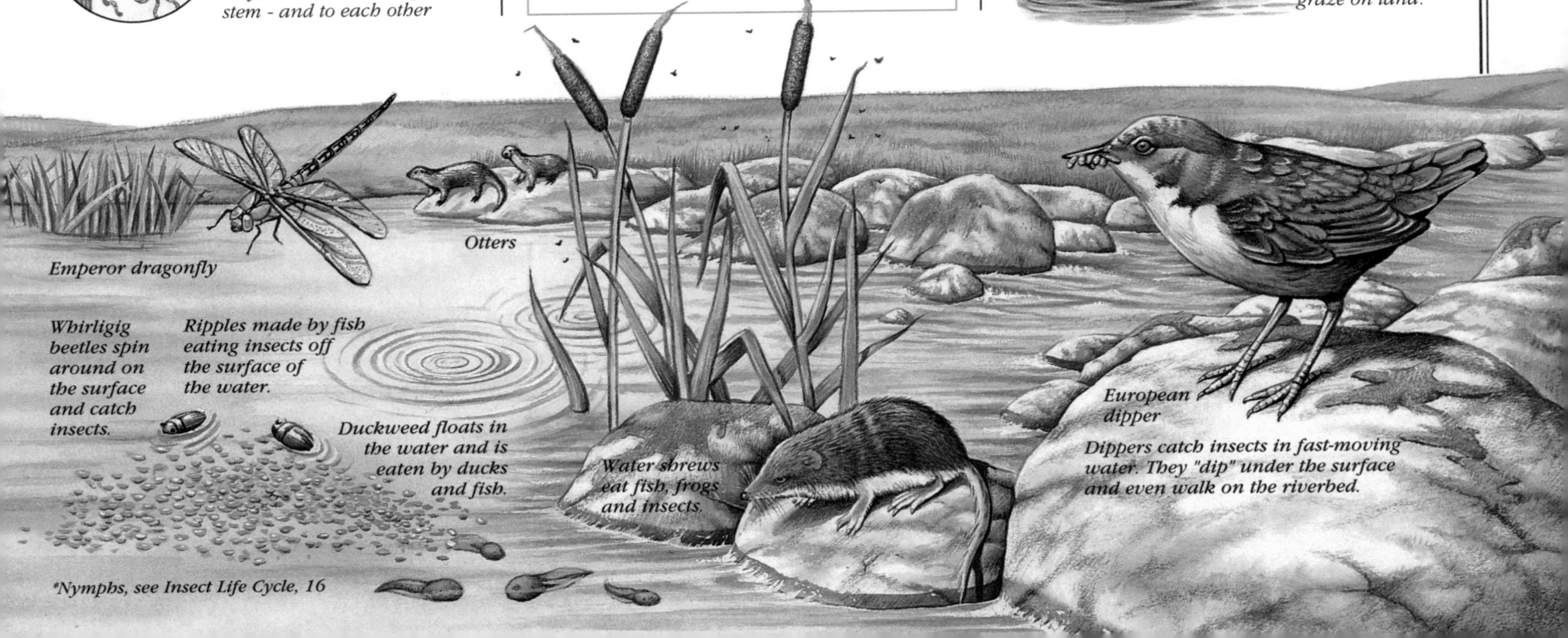

Emperor dragonfly
Otters
Whirligig beetles spin around on the surface and catch insects.
Ripples made by fish eating insects off the surface of the water.
Duckweed floats in the water and is eaten by ducks and fish.
Water shrews eat fish, frogs and insects.
European dipper
Dippers catch insects in fast-moving water. They "dip" under the surface and even walk on the riverbed.

*Nymphs, see Insect Life Cycle, 16

Eagle

MOUNTAIN WILDLIFE

Mountain hares (above) have white fur in winter.

Alpine marmots live on the grassy slopes above the treeline.

Mountains are some of the wildest places in the world. Thick forests and bare, rocky slopes make it hard for people to live on mountains, but many species of wildlife can survive. As you travel up a mountain, the air becomes cooler and drier and the species of plants and animals change. There are different plants and animals on mountains in different parts of the world, but they have all adapted to living in extreme conditions.

THE SNOWY PEAKS

Even near the equator, the tops of very high mountains may be covered with snow all through the year. Insects and arachnids have been found at these altitudes, feeding on pollen, seeds and dead insects blown by the wind from the valleys below.

Harvestmen can reach into hollows in the snow to pick up dead insects.

ALPINE ZONE

Below the snowy peaks there are usually bare rocks and steep slopes of loose stones. For much of the year, these slopes are also covered with snow, although the snow may melt for two or three months in the summer. Then lichens and small plants, such as mosses and grasses, grow between the rocks.

Few animals live here, but mountain goats and sheep come to the rocky slopes to graze on the grasses in the summer. Large birds, such as eagles, build their nests among the rocks and fly over the slopes looking for small animals to eat.

No plants or animals larger than insects live on the snowy peaks, but birds of prey fly over the icy slopes. The level where the snow ends is called the snowline.

Below the snowy peaks there are steep, rocky slopes. This area is called the alpine zone after the range of mountains in Europe called the Alps.

Rocky Mountain goat

Sure-footed mountain goats and sheep live in the alpine zone during the summer. They climb over the steep rocks looking for grass and small plants to eat. They can survive for several days without eating anything.

Below the rocky slopes, there are grassy meadows. Many animals live here in summer, but it is too cold for trees to grow. The level where trees begin to grow is called the treeline, or timberline.

Apollo butterfly

Purple saxifrage

Many bright flowers grow on the grassy slopes in spring and summer. Insects fly among the flowers gathering nectar, and birds feed on the plants and insects. Deer, rabbits and marmots come to the grassy slopes to graze.

MAP OF MOUNTAIN RANGES

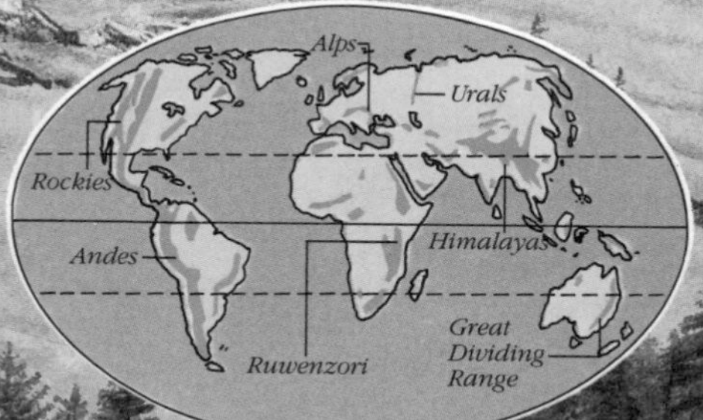

Alps
Urals
Rockies
Andes
Himalayas
Ruwenzori
Great Dividing Range

Cougar

Below the treeline, the mountain forests are home to many different kinds of wildlife, such as cougars, wolverines, porcupines, squirrels and martens.

THE GRASSY SLOPES

Below the alpine zone, there are grassy meadows. It is too cold for trees to grow, but there are small shrubs such as bilberries. In the winter, the slopes are covered with snow, and marmots and pikas hibernate or shelter in their burrows. In the spring, deer, goats and other mammals come to graze.

In spring, small mammals such as hares lose their white winter coats and grow brown hair to camouflage them among the rocks and grass.

Deer live on the meadows during the summer and move down to the forests in the winter. They travel in long lines of up to 500 animals.

TREELINE OR TIMBERLINE

The treeline, or timberline, is the height above which it is too cold, and the summers are too short, for trees to grow. The height varies according to where the mountains are. On mountains near the equator, such as the Andes in South America, the treeline occurs at 5,250m (17,250ft). On the Alps, in Europe, the treeline is at 2,600m (8,500ft).

Along the treeline the trees are small and shaped by the strong winds into weird and stunted shapes.

Below the treeline, the conditions are less harsh and cold. There is also a thicker layer of soil, so larger plants, such as coniferous trees, can grow.

MOUNTAIN FLOWERS

Mountain flowers grow mainly in the meadows and among the rocks. These pictures show some of the flowers that grow in the European Alps in spring. Many flowers, such as gentians and saxifrage, grow in short, round clumps for protection against the cold wind.

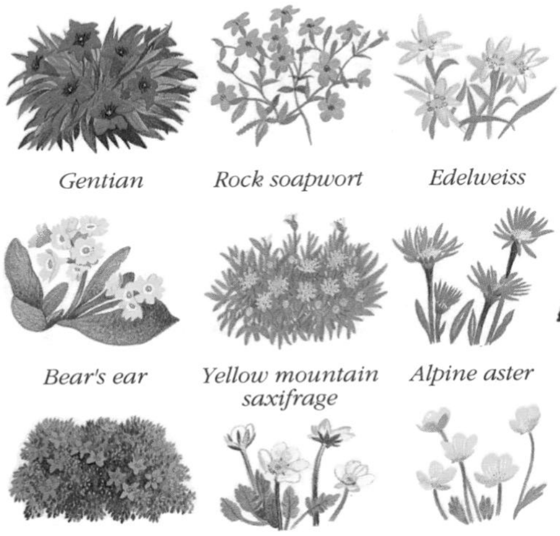
Gentian
Rock soapwort
Edelweiss
Bear's ear
Yellow mountain saxifrage
Alpine aster
Purple saxifrage
Mountain avens
Mountain buttercup

LICHENS

Lichens are made up of a simple plant-like organism, called an alga, and a fungus living together. They can grow on bare rocks and tree trunks.

There are many different types of lichens. Some are crust-like and others are shaggy.

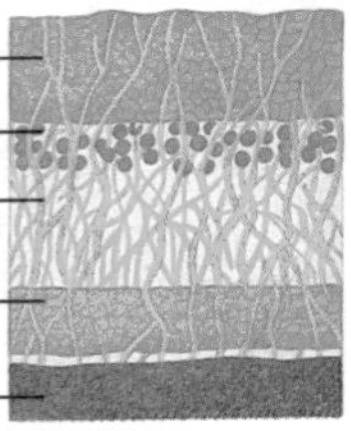
Fungus
Alga
Fungus strands
Lower fungus
Rock

The picture on the right shows how lichens are made up of an alga and a fungus living together.

MOUNTAIN BIRDS

Large birds of prey, such as falcons, eagles and vultures, live on the rocky slopes above the treeline. They have powerful wings and can fly in the strong winds. They hunt small mammals, reptiles and other birds.

Lammergeier vulture

Alpine swift

Smaller birds, such as wood warblers, siskins and pipits, spend the summer in the meadows and forests, then migrate to warmer parts of the world.

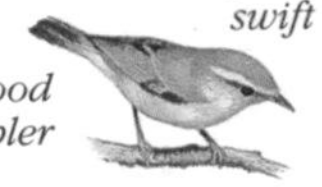

Wood warbler

Red-throated pipit

Ring ouzel

Siskin

Wallcreepers (right) grip the rocks with their large claws and search for insects between the rocks with their long beaks.

MOUNTAINS OF AFRICA

Mountains near the equator, such as the Ruwenzori Mountains in Africa, have different bands of vegetation from the mountains in cooler areas. On the grasslands at the foot of these mountains, there are elephants and rhinos. In the foothills, there is rainforest and above this, scrubland where leopards hunt. Above the treeline, at about 4,500m (15,000 ft), there are forests of giant flowers.

Groundsel and lobelia grow up to 9m (30ft) high.

Giant lobelia
Giant groundsel

MOUNTAIN FORESTS

The needle-shaped leaves of coniferous trees are tougher than the flat leaves of broadleaved trees, and their seeds are protected in hard cones.

Hard scales
Cone cut in half
Seed

Snow slides off sloping branches.

Wolf

Just below the treeline, only coniferous trees such as firs, spruces and pines can survive the extreme winter cold and the short summers. The forest is too thick and dark for flowers or grass to grow, but martens and squirrels live in the trees, and in winter, deer feed on the shoots of the pine trees.

Wolves and brown bears live in mountain forests in remote parts of Europe, Asia and North America.

Pine martens live in the trees and eat small animals and fruit and nuts. They are excellent climbers.

Red crossbills use the crossed tips of their beaks to break into cones and reach the seeds inside.

Pheasants live in mountain forests in Sichuan, China, and feed on seeds.

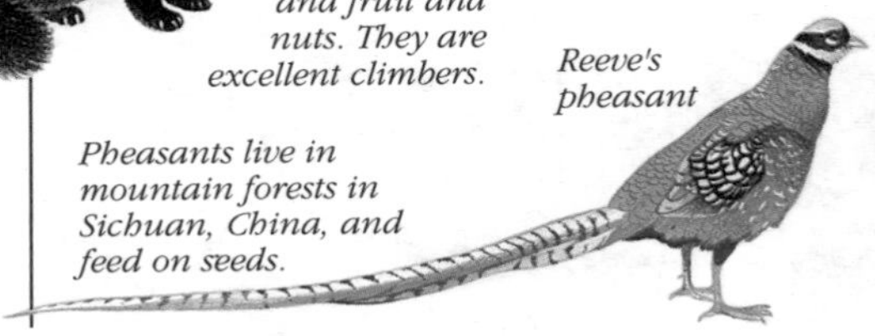

Reeve's pheasant

TROPICAL GRASSLANDS

In Africa and South America, there are vast areas of grasslands called tropical grasslands, or savanna. There are few trees because for most of the year it is very dry. There are two seasons in the savanna: a long, hot, dry season followed by about five months of rain. In the wet season, the grasses grow very tall and lush, and many large herbivores (plant-eating animals) live on these grasslands.

Vultures fly above the grasslands looking for dead animals to eat. They swoop down on a corpse before other scavengers arrive.

Cheetah sitting on a termite mound

TROPICAL GRASSLAND REGIONS

Tropical grasslands lie between the imaginary lines called the Tropic of Cancer and the Tropic of Capricorn. It is always warm, with about 60cm (24in) of rain in the wet season.

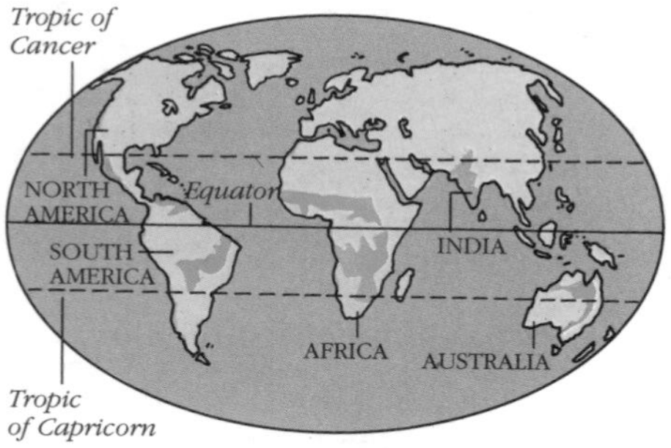
Tropic of Cancer
NORTH AMERICA
Equator
SOUTH AMERICA
INDIA
AFRICA
AUSTRALIA
Tropic of Capricorn

Map showing areas of tropical grasslands

GRASSES

Grasses belong to a group of flowering plants called monocotyledons*, of which there are over 9,000 species. They have fine, fibrous roots that spread a long way through the soil to find water.

Grasses have long straight leaves that grow up from the base of the plant. After being cropped short by grazing animals, the leaves grow up again - as long as there is enough water.

During the long dry season, the grasses become brown and dry. When it rains, new leaves grow up from the roots.

TREES

Trees need a lot of water, so few trees grow on the savanna. They have long roots that grow deep into the soil, and in the dry season they lose their leaves to help them survive. Baobab and acacia trees grow in Africa and eucalyptus trees grow on the grasslands of Australia.

Baobab trees take up water from the soil and store it in their enormous trunks. Elephants sometimes smash open the trunks and suck the water out of the wood.

Thorns

Acacia trees have small leaves to reduce water loss.

When an animal eats a tree's leaves, it eats the whole leaf, including the growing part. Many trees have thorns to stop animals from eating their leaves, and some taste nasty.

LIFE ON THE AFRICAN GRASSLANDS

Many large mammals, such as elephants, rhinos, hippos, giraffes, antelopes, zebras and wildebeest, live on the African grasslands. They can survive as the different species eat different plants, or even different parts of the same plants.

Zebras feed on the top parts of the grasses. Wildebeest eat the middle parts and gazelles eat the lowest parts.

Carnivores, such as cheetahs and wild dogs, prey on the plant-eating animals. Ants and termites, and many different species of birds, eat grass seeds. The picture below shows some of the animals that live on the grasslands of East Africa.

During the long dry season, the grasses become very dry. Plant-eating animals such as zebras and wildebeest migrate long distances to find fresh grass.

Huge herds of wildebeest travel over 1,500km (about 1,000 miles) to find grass and water.

At the beginning of the wet season, the animals return to their original grazing grounds to feed and breed.

Giraffes reach up to the leaves in the treetops. Adults are safe from most predators, but young giraffes are sometimes attacked.*

Buffaloes wallow in water to keep cool and clean insects off their skin.*

Cheetahs stalk their prey for up to three hours before sprinting and trying to catch it.*

Wild dogs attack the less able members of a herd, such as the old, sick or very young.*

*Monocotyledons, 88; Cheetahs, 43; Buffaloes, 54; Giraffes, 53; Wild Dogs, 44

GRASSLAND INSECTS

Many different species of insects live in the grasslands. They eat plants, suck animal blood or break down dead plant and animal matter and help return the minerals to the soil. Ants help disperse plant seeds, but other insects, such as tsetse flies and locusts, are serious pests.

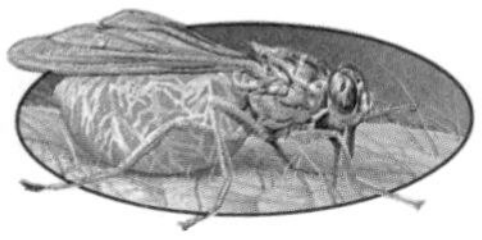

Tsetse flies bite people and farm animals and spread a disease called sleeping sickness.

Locusts are related to grasshoppers. When it rains, huge numbers swarm together to feed. There are hundreds of millions of locusts in a swarm and in farming areas, they do great damage to crops.

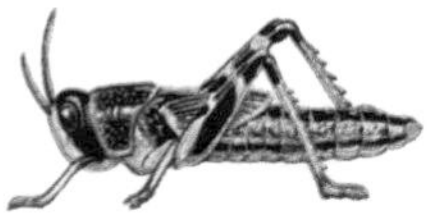

Swarming locust hopper

PROTECTING GRASSLAND SPECIES

Many of the animals that live in tropical grasslands are hunted for their horns, skins or tusks. The numbers of some have become so low that they are in danger of becoming extinct. Poachers sell skins from cheetahs, antelopes and snakes, horns from rhinos, tusks from elephants and feathers from ostriches.

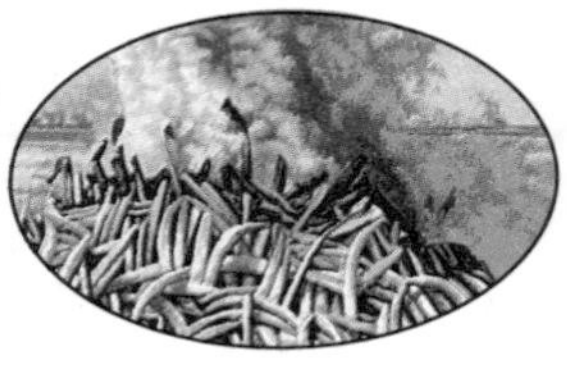

In 1989, to try to stop the ivory trade, the president of Kenya organized a huge bonfire of elephants' tusks confiscated from poachers.

There are now laws protecting certain species, such as elephants, and large areas of grassland have been made into reserves where the animals are protected.

OSTRICHES AND EMUS

Rhea

Ostriches and emus are large, flightless birds that live in tropical grasslands. Ostriches live in Africa and emus live in Australia. Another species of flightless birds, called rheas, live in the cool grasslands of South America. Although they all have small wings, their feathers are soft and downy and they cannot fly. They are beige, black or brown so they are hard to see among the dry grasses, and they lay their eggs in nests on the ground. They feed on grasses, leaves, flowers and seeds, and emus also eat insects, lizards and small mammals.

Emu

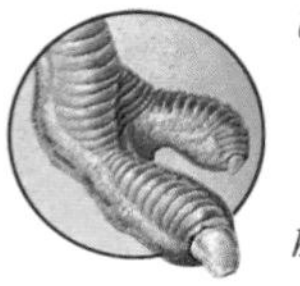

Unlike other birds, ostriches have only two toes on each foot. Rheas and emus have three and most other birds have four.

Both male and female ostriches look after their chicks, which are speckled and striped to help camouflage them in the grass.

Female ostrich

Male ostrich

To attract females, a male ostrich leans his head back and moves it from side to side in a courtship dance. He also beats his wings and flutters his tail.

The male may mate with several females, which all lay their eggs in one nest. There may be 40 eggs in a nest. Ostrich eggs are about 15cm (6 inches) long.

The male and one of the females take turns sitting on the nest to keep the eggs warm. Eggs left uncovered at the edge of the nest get cold and do not hatch.

Ostriches walk at 4kph (2.5mph) and run at about 30kph (18.5mph), but when fleeing from danger, they can race along at 80kph (50mph). They have very strong feet and leg muscles.

Running away is the most common way of escaping from predators on the grasslands.

Acacia trees provide food and shelter for animals and birds.

When it has not rained for a long time, many animals collect around areas of water called waterholes.

Elephants* spray themselves with water to keep cool.

Antelopes* can run up to 100kph (60mph) to escape from predators.

Ostriches have excellent eyesight and can see above the grasses to watch for predators.

Some species of birds called shrikes spike their prey onto thorns to hold it still while they feed on it.

Termites* build huge mounds of soil, saliva and droppings. The mounds are their nests.

Bat-eared foxes eat insects, especially termites. They have excellent hearing and can hear the insects moving in the grass.

Rufous-backed shrike

*Elephants, 52;
Termites, 21

*Antelopes, 57

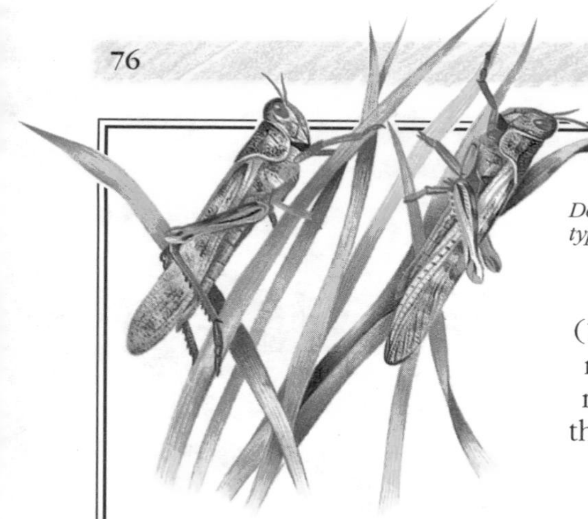

Desert locusts - a type of grasshopper

DESERTS

Kangaroo rats (a type of rodent) run and leap away from danger.

Deserts are very dry areas that have less than 25cm (10in) of rain each year - and in some deserts it has not rained for hundreds of years. The land is bare sand or rock and there is little wildlife. The plants and animals that do live in the desert have their own special ways of surviving with very little water in the intense heat.

DESERT REGIONS

Most deserts are very hot in the day and cold at night all through the year, but in the Gobi Desert, daytime temperatures drop to -20°C (-4°F) in the winter.

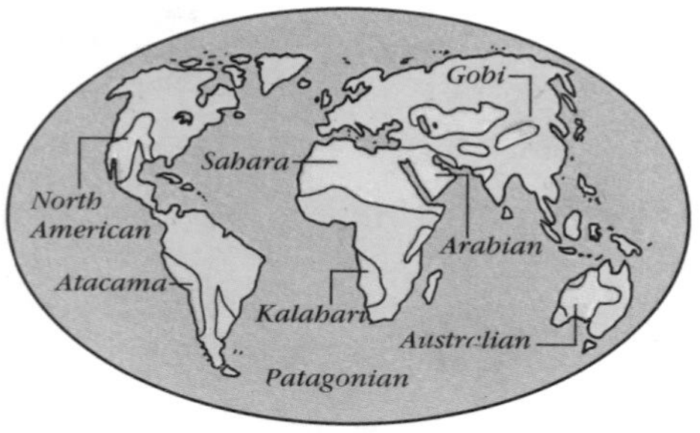
Gobi
Sahara
North American
Arabian
Atacama
Kalahari
Australian
Patagonian

Map showing main areas of desert

DESERTIFICATION

Over the last 50 years, the amount of desert in the world has been increasing. Land at the edges of desert areas, where some grass and trees used to grow, has become lifeless desert. This process is called desertification.

Many thousands of people and animals died when the land where they lived became true desert.

Desertification usually happens because people who live in these dry areas need the grass for their animals and wood to burn as fuel. Because it is so dry, the grass and trees do not grow again and gradually the area becomes true desert.

PLANTS IN THE DESERT

Desert plants have long roots to reach water deep under the ground, or many fine roots near the surface to absorb early morning dew. Many have thick, fleshy leaves with waxy skin so they do not lose water, or no leaves at all. They also have spines or thorns to discourage animals and birds from eating them.

North American century plants grow for about 15 years before flowering. Then when it rains, they flower, produce seeds and die.

After a rainfall, Australian sungold (right) grows quickly, covering the ground with its bright yellow flowers.

A North American desert after a rainfall

During long periods with no rain, many plants survive as dry stems, or as seeds. When it eventually rains, the plants turn green, or grow and flower and produce seeds in the short time before the water dries up. Some plants lie dormant for years waiting for rain.

Cacti have spongy stems that swell up full of water after a rainy period. Many have pleats in their stems that expand as the cacti take up water. There are over 800 different kinds of cacti, most of which grow in North America. They do not have leaves and they make their food in their green stems. Most cacti are covered with prickly spines.

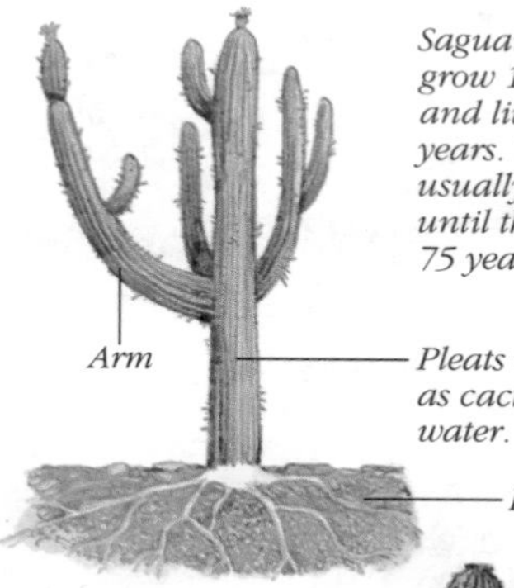
Arm
Pleats in stem expand as cactus takes up water.
Long roots

Saguaro cacti may grow 15m (50ft) tall and live for over 200 years. They do not usually grow "arms" until they are at least 75 years old.

Barrel cactus before rain
Barrel cactus after rain

The spongy stems of the barrel cactus swell up with water when it rains. After a long period with no rain, they are small and soft.

Leaves grow from the middle.

African welwitschia leaves have thick skin that stops them from losing too much water.

The plants in a desert are usually spaced wide apart as their roots compete for water. The roots of some, such as the creosote bush that grows in deserts in North and South America, even give off poisons that keep other plants away.

This scene shows the Sahara Desert in North Africa. The plants and animals are not shown to scale.

Date palms grow near oases where their roots can reach the water.

Euphorbia plants have thick, fleshy leaves.

Gerbils take all the water they need from their food. They lose very little water in their droppings.

Sand grouse fly long distances to find water. They soak their breast feathers in the water and carry droplets back to their chicks.

An oasis (plural: oases) is a pool in the desert. Here, more plants grow and animals and birds come to drink.

DESERT MAMMALS

Many of the mammals that live in the desert are nocturnal - they feed at night when it is cooler. During the heat of the day, they rest in the shade of rocks or plants, or in burrows in the ground. Most desert mammals have pale fur that reflects the bright sunlight and does not heat up as quickly as dark fur.

A jack rabbit's large ears help to keep it cool. The blood flowing through tiny blood vessels in the ears is cooled by the air around them.

Desert hedgehogs live in burrows in the sand. They hibernate during long periods with no rain when food is scarce.

Many small, mouse-like rodents, such as jerboas, live in deserts and eat seeds, roots, stems and leaves.*

Meerkats live in burrows in the Kalahari Desert in southern Africa. They live together in tightly-knit groups and share the work of looking after the young, scaring off predators and other tasks.

Most desert animals drink very little water. Some, such as the Arabian oryx (a species of antelope*) hardly ever need to drink, and small mammals, such as jerboas and gerbils, take all the moisture they need from the plants and seeds that they eat.

DESERT REPTILES

Most reptiles, such as snakes and lizards, are active in the day. Reptiles are cold-blooded animals* and they need the heat of the sun to keep them warm. Even in the desert, it is often too cold for them at night and they become sluggish because they cannot keep their blood warm. To keep cool during the hottest part of the day, they bury themselves in the sand, or climb plants to cool off in the breeze.

Desert tortoises keep cool by burying themselves in the sand.

Geckos hunt for insects in the cool of the evening. They cling to rocks with the suckers on their feet.

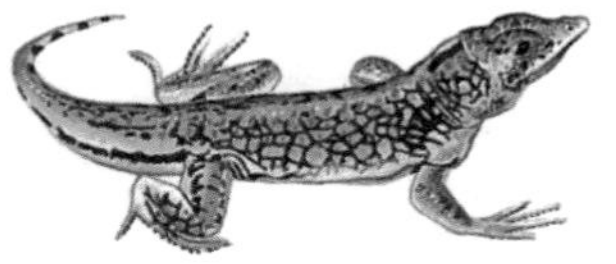

Fringe-toed lizards stand on two legs at a time to avoid touching the hot sand.

Rattle

In the hot season, rattlesnakes are active at night. They hunt birds and small mammals.

Many desert snakes use a side-winding movement to keep cool. They touch the sand near their head and tail and fling the rest of their body forward in a loop.

During the hottest time of the year, reptiles become active at night and rest in the day to avoid overheating. In deserts that have cold winters, such as the Gobi Desert in central Asia, snakes hibernate for several months in burrows in the ground.

DESERT BIRDS

Most desert birds are sandy brown to blend with their surroundings. They live near oases or waterholes, or fly there at dawn and dusk to drink. They feed mainly on insects and seeds and usually build their nests on the ground.

Budgerigars (parakeets) live in the desert in Australia and eat seeds and fruit. Huge flocks gather to drink at waterholes in the early morning. If the waterholes dry up, many of them die.

There are few nesting places in the desert for birds. Gila woodpeckers often build their nests in the stems of cactus plants, so their eggs are shielded from the sun. It can be up to 30°C (54°F) cooler inside.

American burrowing owls make nests in old animals' burrows. If a predator approaches, the owls hiss so the predator thinks there are snakes in the burrow and does not attack.

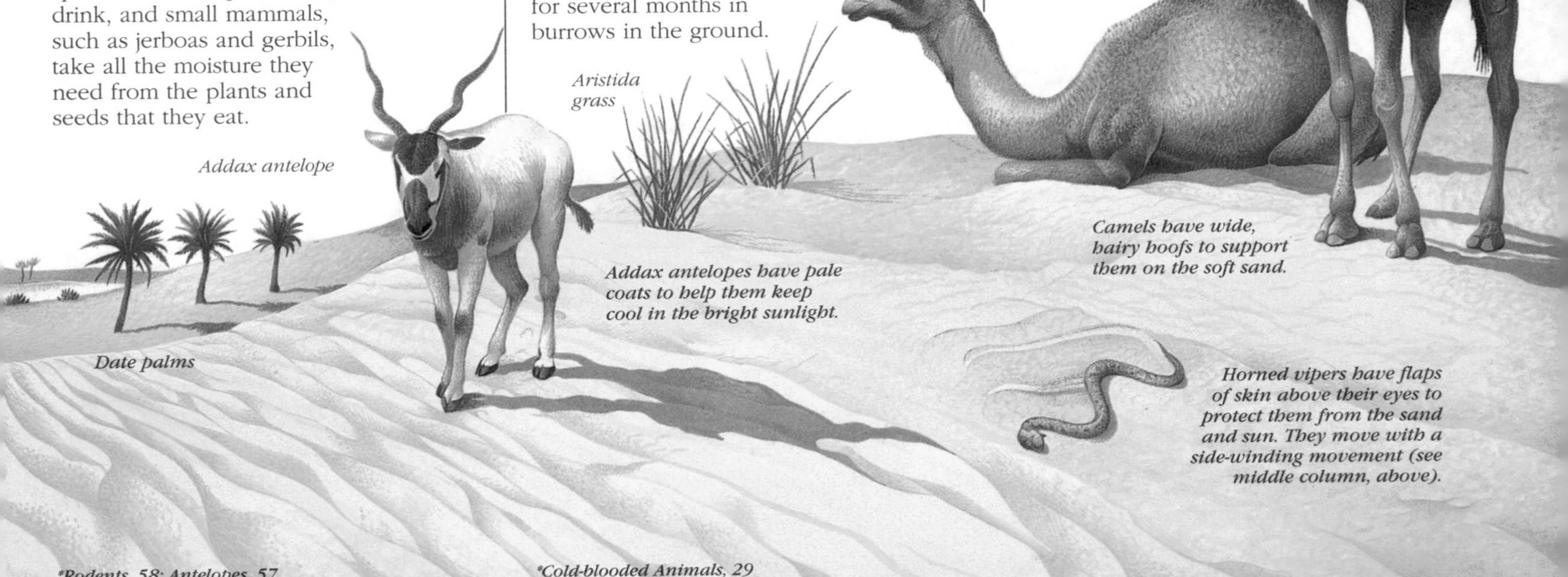
Aristida grass
Addax antelope
Date palms

Camels can survive for months without drinking if their food contains enough moisture. They have very dry droppings and this helps them save water.

Camels have wide, hairy hoofs to support them on the soft sand.

Addax antelopes have pale coats to help them keep cool in the bright sunlight.

Horned vipers have flaps of skin above their eyes to protect them from the sand and sun. They move with a side-winding movement (see middle column, above).

*Rodents, 58; Antelopes, 57

*Cold-blooded Animals, 29

The flowers and fruits of banana palm trees hang below the canopy of leaves.

Eagles fly above the treetops looking for small animals, such as baby monkeys, to grasp with their sharp claws.

TROPICAL RAINFORESTS

Tropical rainforests grow in lands near the equator where it is always warm and it rains nearly every day. As there is no dry or cold season, rainforests are always green and the trees grow very tall. Beneath the trees, it is hot, dark and damp. Over half of all the different species of plants and animals in the world live in rainforests, but each rainforest is different.

RAINFOREST TREES

The trees in rainforests grow very fast and very tall as they compete with each other for light. Many of them are broadleaved trees*, such as mahogany, teak, rubber trees and balsa, and there are also many species of palm trees*. There may be 2,500 species of trees in one region.

The tallest trees grow nearly 100m (330ft) tall. Below them, other trees, about 45m (150ft) tall, spread out their branches to form a thick canopy of leaves that shuts out the sunlight from the forest below. Shorter, narrower trees grow where some sunlight filters through the thick canopy.

The flowers of many trees grow below the thick tangle of branches and leaves in the canopy, so they can be reached more easily by the insects, birds and bats that spread their pollen and seeds.

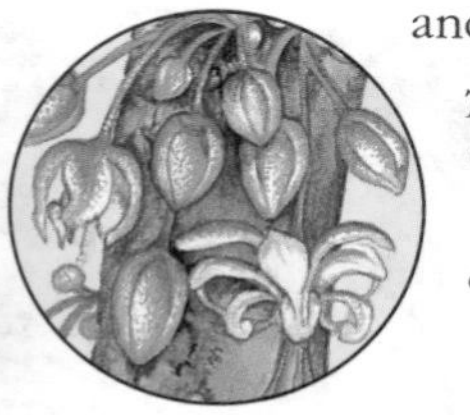

The flowers of the cacao tree grow out from the trunk. Cacao seeds are used for making chocolate.

Durian tree fruits hang down from the branches and are eaten by orangutans and other animals. The seeds are dispersed in the animals' droppings.

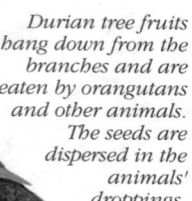

The tallest trees have very thick roots above the ground. These are called buttress roots and they help support the trees in the very thin soil.

RAINFOREST REGIONS

Tropical rainforests grow in places where the average temperature is about 24°C (75°F) and there is at least 400cm (160in) of rain a year.

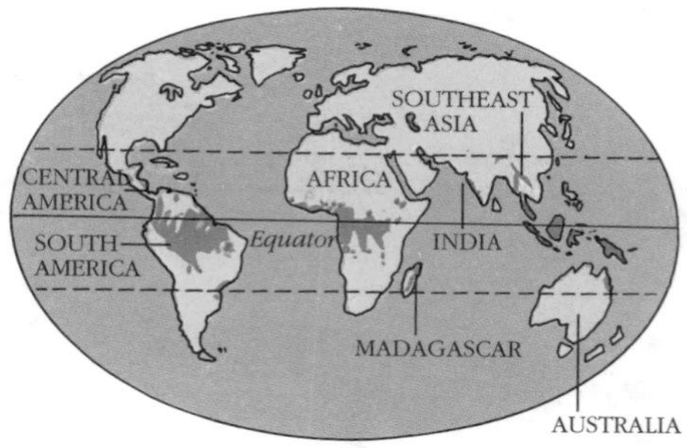
SOUTHEAST ASIA
CENTRAL AMERICA
AFRICA
SOUTH AMERICA
Equator
INDIA
MADAGASCAR
AUSTRALIA

Map showing areas of tropical rainforests

THE FOREST FLOOR

Very little light filters through to the forest floor, so few plants grow at ground level. Insects, such as ants and termites, and centipedes, millipedes and spiders feed on the dead leaves, plants and even animals that fall to the ground. The dead plant and animal matter rots very quickly in the warm, damp air in the forest.

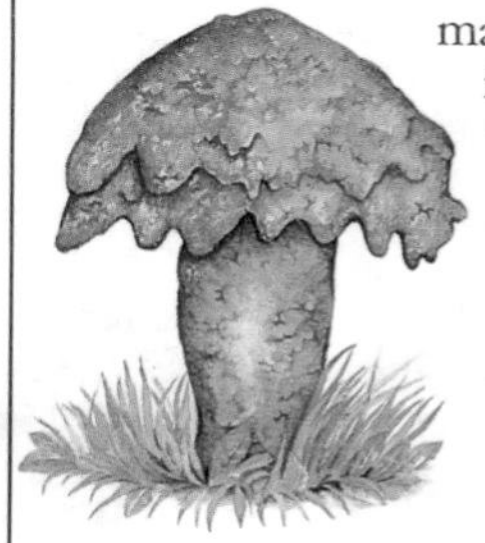

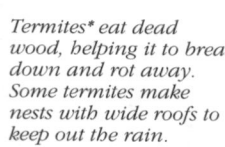

Termites eat dead wood, helping it to break down and rot away. Some termites make nests with wide roofs to keep out the rain.*

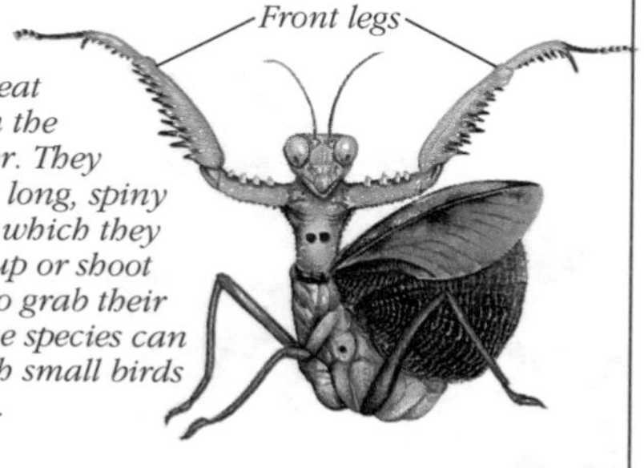
Front legs

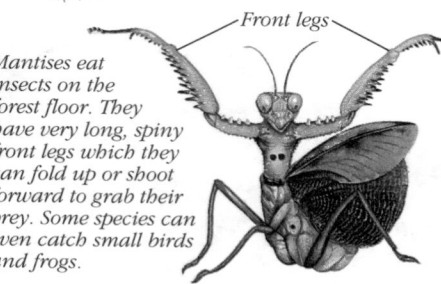

Mantises eat insects on the forest floor. They have very long, spiny front legs which they can fold up or shoot forward to grab their prey. Some species can even catch small birds and frogs.

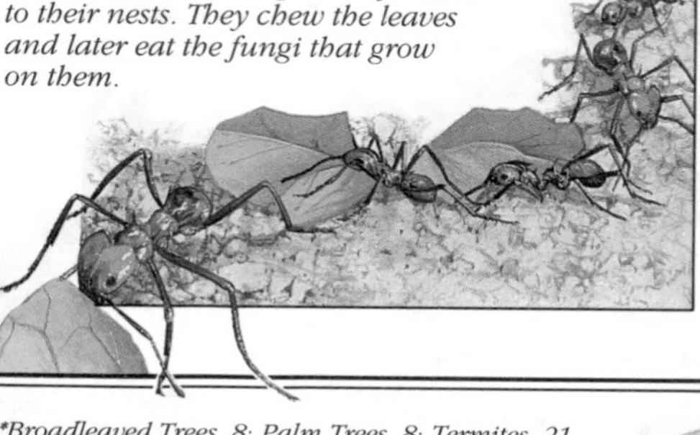

Leaf-cutter ants take pieces of leaves to their nests. They chew the leaves and later eat the fungi that grow on them.

RAINFOREST PLANTS

Many of the plants in the rainforest grow on the branches of the trees, as little sunlight reaches the ground. Ferns, orchids and other plants grow in rotting leaf matter that collects in cracks between the branches.

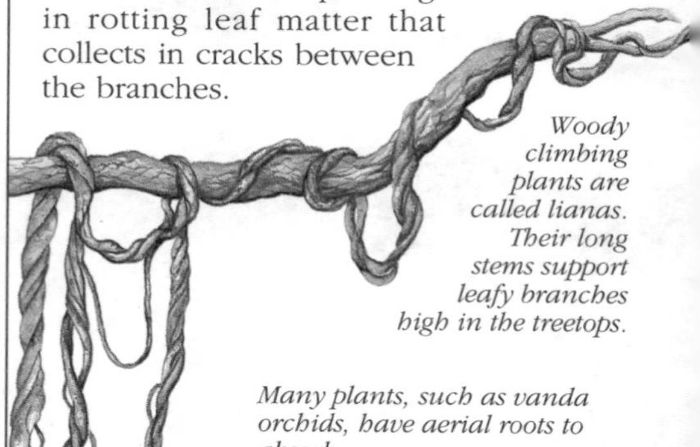

Woody climbing plants are called lianas. Their long stems support leafy branches high in the treetops.

Many plants, such as vanda orchids, have aerial roots to absorb moisture from the air.

Aerial roots

Thousands of different species of orchids grow in the rainforest.

LIFE IN THE RAINFOREST

There are more plants and animals in the rainforest than in any other habitat in the world. The plants grow thickly beside rivers where more sunshine reaches the forest floor, and many different species of birds and animals live along the riverbanks. The picture on these two pages shows some of the wildlife that lives along a river in the Amazon Rainforest in South America.

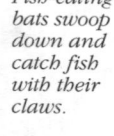

Fish-eating bats swoop down and catch fish with their claws.

*Broadleaved Trees, 8; Palm Trees, 8; Termites, 21

ANIMALS IN THE RAINFOREST

Different species of animals live at different levels in the rainforest. Birds and bats live in the topmost branches. Monkeys*, apes* and squirrels* live lower down and feed on the leaves, nuts, fruits and insects.

Monkeys, such as macaques, are smaller than apes and live in the treetops. The larger apes, such as orangutans, live among the lower branches.

The rainforest is also the home of many different species of wild cats, such as jaguars in South America, and tigers and leopard cats in Southeast Asia.

Clouded leopard cats climb trees and catch monkeys, small mammals, birds and reptiles. Their markings help to camouflage them among the shadows.

Animals that live on the forest floor are sturdily built so they can pass through the thick undergrowth.

Okapis live in rainforests in Africa. They are related to giraffes and their striped markings camouflage them in the undergrowth.

Peccaries (above) live in forests in South America and forage for roots.

Colugos, or flying lemurs, live in Southeast Asia and eat leaves and fruit. They climb trees with their claws and then glide between the branches.

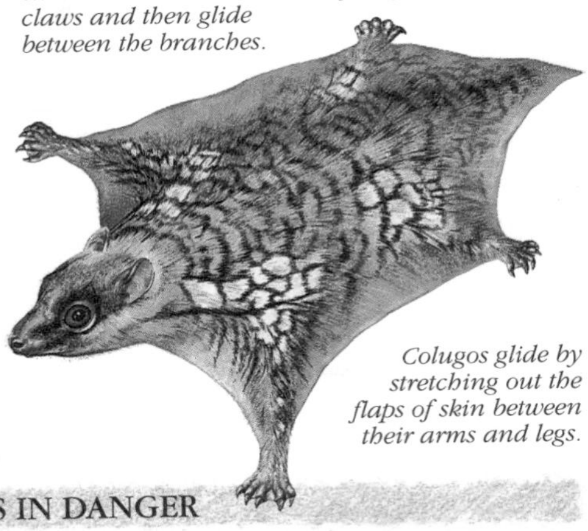

Colugos glide by stretching out the flaps of skin between their arms and legs.

RAINFOREST BIRDS

Over a quarter of all the different species of birds live in rainforests. Many of them have bright markings, perhaps to help them find each other in the thick foliage. Birds are important in the rainforest because they help to spread the plants' seeds. They eat fruits and the seeds are deposited in their droppings.

Quetzals from Central America eat small avocados and then bring the seeds back up from their stomachs and spit them out.

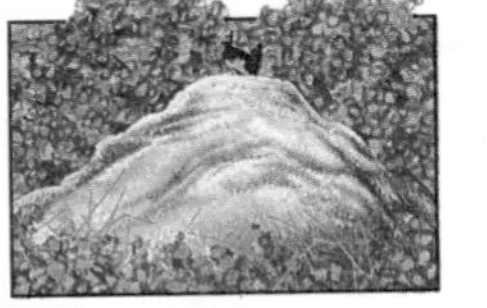

Megapode birds lay their eggs on the forest floor. They cover them with mounds of soil and leaves that keep the eggs warm.

The male bird tests the temperature of the mound with his beak. If it is too hot or cold, he takes away or adds some soil.

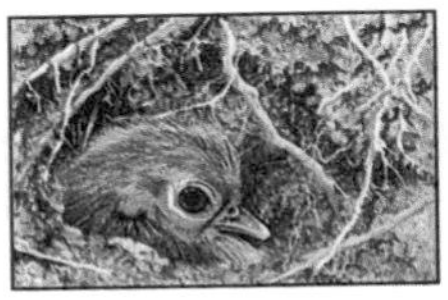

When the chicks hatch, they dig their way out of the mound and run off.

RAINFORESTS IN DANGER

Over half of all the world's rainforests have been cut down for their wood, and to clear land for farming and mining. The plants and animals that lived there have died out or are endangered.

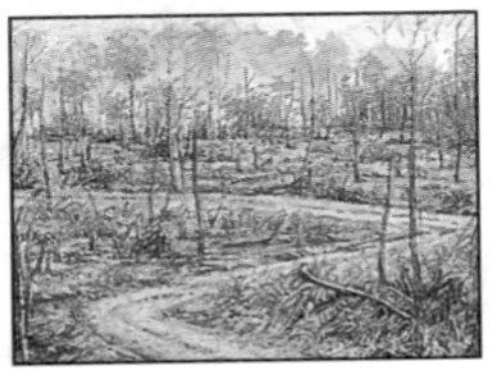

After the trees are cut down, the rain quickly washes the minerals out of the soil. Large areas of Amazonia, in South America, are now infertile.

Scientists believe that the destruction of the rainforest is also causing changes in the balance of gases in the atmosphere, and changes in the weather due to an increase in the greenhouse effect*.

Many rainforest plants have useful properties that will be lost if they become extinct. Rosy periwinkles are used to make a drug to treat a type of cancer called leukemia.

Hoatzins eat leaves that rot in their stomachs and smell like cow dung.

Capybaras are the largest species of rodent*. They live among the thick plants beside rivers and eat water plants.
Spoonbill flying
Scarlet ibises hunt small fish and insects by poking their long beaks into shallow, swampy water.
Giant water lily leaves
Young hoatzins have claws on their wings and can climb trees.
Amazon River dolphins are nearly blind. They find food and swim around using echo-location*, like bats.
Caimans are now rare because they were hunted for their skin.
Caimans, a species of alligator*, lie on the banks waiting for their prey.
Spoonbills catch fish with their wide beaks.

*Monkeys and Apes, 50; Greenhouse Effect, 69; Alligators, 31; Rodents, 58; Echo-location, 62

POLAR WILDLIFE

In winter, Arctic foxes have white coats to camouflage them.

In the polar areas at the very north and south of the world, the land and sea are frozen for most of the year, as temperatures rarely rise above freezing point. In winter, the sun never rises, so it is dark all day and night, and in summer, the sun never sets. Despite these conditions, many kinds of wildlife manage to survive.

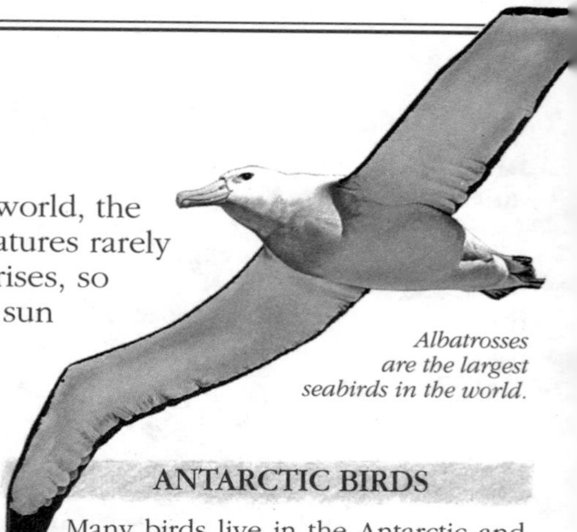

Albatrosses are the largest seabirds in the world.

THE ARCTIC AND ANTARCTIC

The area called the Arctic is bounded by an imaginary line called the Arctic Circle and the area called the Antarctic is bounded by an imaginary line called the Antarctic Circle.

Polar bears live on the ice and in the water in the Arctic.*

ALASKA
CANADA
Arctic Circle
ARCTIC OCEAN
North Pole
RUSSIAN FEDERATION
GREENLAND
SCANDINAVIA
ICELAND

The Arctic contains the Arctic Ocean and the lands bordering the ocean. Much of the sea is permanently frozen over with ice. The land around the sea is called the tundra.

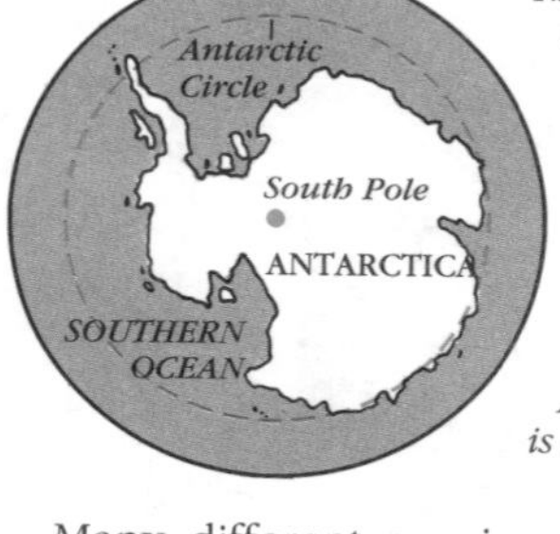

Antarctic Circle
South Pole
ANTARCTICA
SOUTHERN OCEAN

The Antarctic is made up of a continent called Antarctica, the Southern Ocean and some islands. Antarctica is colder than the land in the Arctic because it is closer to the pole.

Many different species of animals live on the tundra in the Arctic. No land mammals live permanently on Antarctica but seals go there to breed. There are also many insects, and seabirds, such as penguins, build their nests there.

Adélie penguins build nests of pebbles on Antarctica. Before mating, they do a courtship dance beside their nest. They stand face to face, stretch their necks upward and slowly flap their wings.

LIFE IN POLAR SEAS

In polar areas, there is more wildlife living in the sea than on the land. The seas are icy cold, but the temperature does not change as much as on the land, so it is easier for the animals to cope with. As well as fish, there are many different species of seals*, whales* and penguins. Many of the fish and whales feed on plankton*, or krill, which are small, shrimp-like creatures.

Huge numbers of krill live in the Southern Ocean. They are eaten by whales and other sea creatures.

Many polar fish have special adaptations that help them survive in polar seas. Ice fish have no red blood cells. In very cold water, blood can carry enough oxygen without red cells.

Ice fish

Antarctic cod have an antifreeze in their blood to stop it from freezing.

ANTARCTIC BIRDS

Many birds live in the Antarctic and fly over the Southern Ocean catching fish, squid and krill (see left). They only go onto the land to breed.

Snow petrels hover over the ice and dive between ice floes to catch krill.

Storm petrels flutter just above the surface with their legs hanging down. They look as if they are walking on the water.

Four different species of albatrosses breed on Antarctica. Thousands of birds nest together in large colonies. They make raised nests of mud and moss and each female lays a single egg inside. When the chicks hatch, they sit on top of the nests, waiting to be fed.

White-capped albatrosses make tall, tube-shaped nests.

JINS

Penguins are seabirds that cannot fly. They all live in the southern half of the world and seven species live in the Antarctic. They spend most of the time in the sea but come on land at breeding time. They lay their eggs in holes in the ground filled with pebbles, or on bare ground or ice.

Emperor penguin

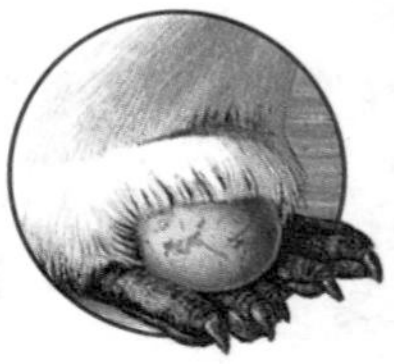

Emperor penguins keep their eggs warm under a special flap of skin.

Year after year, penguins return to the same breeding places, called rookeries, where they themselves were hatched.

Adult king penguin

Chick

Penguins have two layers of short, tightly-packed feathers to keep them warm, and a thick layer of blubber (fat) under their skin. Emperor penguins, the largest of the penguins, can survive temperatures as low as -20°C (4°F).

Penguins are very good swimmers and divers. They use their stiff, narrow wings as flippers and steer with their feet and tails. They catch fish, squid and krill to eat and can stay underwater for up to 18 minutes.

They come to the surface to breathe, and when in danger, leap back onto the ice. Although penguins look clumsy when they are walking, each year they travel long distances across the ice to reach their rookeries.

*Polar bears, 46

*Seals, 49; Whales, 48; Plankton, 82

Rough-legged buzzard

Arctic tern

Every year, Arctic terns travel from the Arctic to the Antarctic and back again. At the end of the Arctic summer, they fly to the Antarctic where summer is just beginning.

THE TUNDRA

The tundra is the land bordering the Arctic Ocean. During the summer, some of the ice melts and plants grow, insects hatch and small animals, such as lemmings, come out of their burrows. Caribou (reindeer), wolves and foxes, which spent the winter in the forests farther south, come to the tundra to feed.

In winter, many Arctic animals have white coats so they are less easily seen against the snow. In summer, their coats turn brown or grey.

Arctic fox in summer coat (for winter coat, see picture top of opposite page)

Stoat in summer coat

Each spring, hundreds of thousands of birds migrate to the Arctic to feed and breed there during the summer. In the autumn, they leave for warmer places farther south. A few birds, such as ptarmigans and snowy owls, live in the Arctic all year. In winter, their feathers are white to blend with the snow.

Snowy owl

Snowy owls live in the Arctic all through the year. This one is in its winter plumage.

Many different kinds of geese migrate to the Arctic in the spring.

White-fronted goose *Snow goose* *Brent goose* *Barnacle goose*

Arctic skua

Little auk

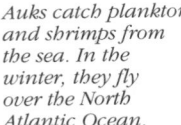

Auks catch plankton and shrimps from the sea. In the winter, they fly over the North Atlantic Ocean.

Red-legged kittiwake

Ptarmigans live in the Arctic all year. In the winter, they are white to blend with the snow. They dig plants out of the snow with their feet.

The plants on the tundra stay small to shelter from the cold winds. There are dwarf trees such as willows about 30cm (12in) tall, and mosses, lichens and many flowering plants.

Mosses

Lichens

Arctic poppy

Arctic azalea

Campanulas

In the spring, caribou in North America and reindeer in Scandinavia leave the forests where they spend the winter and travel over 1,000km (620 miles) to the tundra.

Caribou and reindeer dig with their antlers in the soft snow for mosses and lichens to eat.

LEMMINGS

Lemmings are small, plant-eating rodents. They live in burrows and have up to eight babies every eight weeks. When their numbers get very high, thousands of lemmings migrate to other areas to find food.

Norwegian lemming

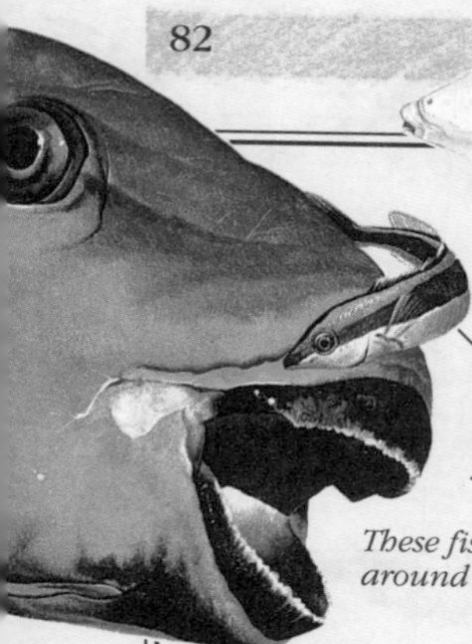

Trigger fish (above) and grouper (right)

Wrasse

Parrot fish

These fish live around coral reefs.

SEAS AND OCEANS

There are a number of different habitats under the sea, just as there are on land. There are deep ocean trenches, high mountains, shallow coastal waters and warm, sunlit coral reefs. Different types of sealife live in the different areas. Seawater is a rich mixture of minerals, such as salt, phosphates and nitrates, and microscopic plants and animals on which other sea creatures feed.

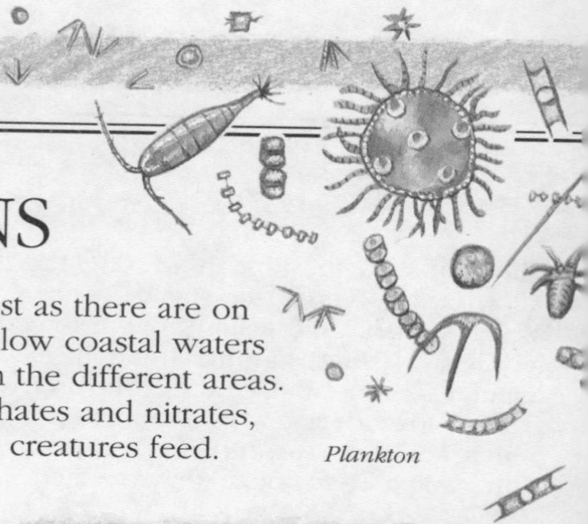

Plankton

WORLD SEAS AND OCEANS

Almost three-quarters of the surface of the Earth is covered by sea.

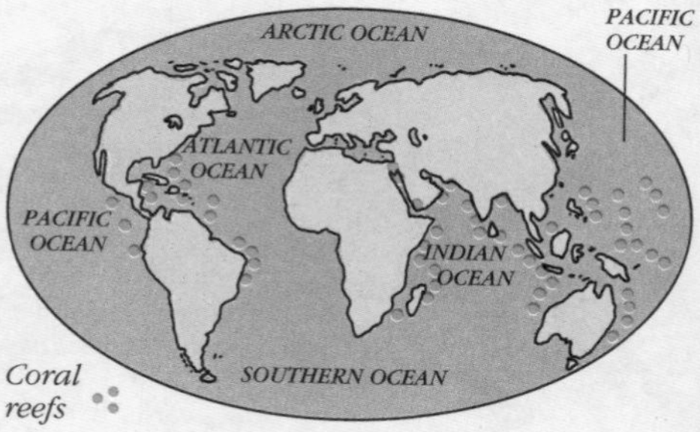
ARCTIC OCEAN
PACIFIC OCEAN
ATLANTIC OCEAN
PACIFIC OCEAN
INDIAN OCEAN
SOUTHERN OCEAN
Coral reefs

Map showing oceans and coral reefs

CORAL REEFS

A coral reef is a rock-like structure made of the skeletons of small animals called coral polyps. Corals live together in large colonies in shallow, tropical seas. A reef takes thousands of years to form. More fish and other types of sealife live around coral reefs than in any other part of the ocean, as shown in the picture below.

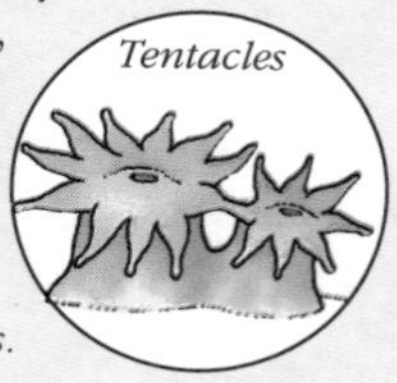
Tentacles

Coral polyps waft plankton into their mouths with their tentacles.

PLANKTON

This is the collective term for masses of microscopic organisms that float near the surface of the water. There are two types of plankton: phytoplankton and zooplankton. Phytoplankton is minute plant-like organisms called algae*, and zooplankton is microscopic animals.

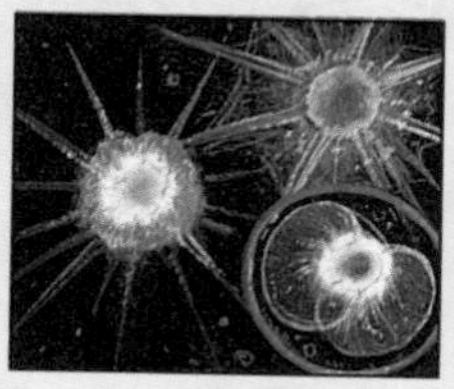

Phytoplankton consists mainly of microscopic algae called diatoms. There may be 50,000 in a single cup of sea water. They produce 70 percent of the oxygen in the air.

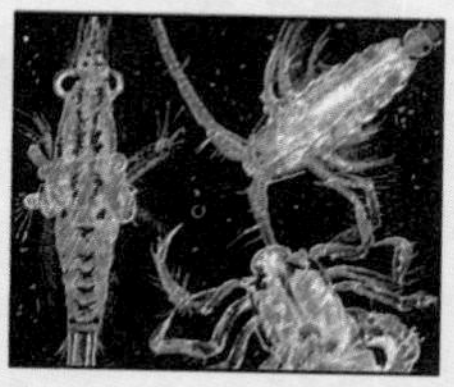

Zooplankton consists of tiny animals, and the larvae (young) of animals such as crabs, starfish and jellyfish. They feed on the phytoplankton and other zooplankton.

Most plankton is found in shallow waters and in the cool polar seas. Phytoplankton is found only near the surface of the water as the algae need the energy from sunlight to make their food by photosynthesis. Plankton is the main food of many of the creatures in the sea, from jellyfish to massive whale sharks and blue whales.

OCEAN FOOD WEB

Over 90 percent of all sea creatures are eaten by other sea animals, and all the life in the oceans is linked in a vast, complex food web*. Large animals, such as killer whales and leopard seals, eat fish, fish eat other fish or plankton and zooplankton eat phytoplankton (see left). Because so many microscopic plants and small animals are needed to feed the larger ones, there are always fewer large animals than small ones, as shown by this food pyramid diagram of life in the ocean.

Killer whale

Food pyramid diagram of ocean life

SEALIFE IN DANGER

Every year, 20 billion tonnes (22 billion tons) of pollution are dumped into the oceans. Much of this is chemicals that are very dangerous for sealife.

Dangerous waste is dumped on the seafloor, and factory waste and sewage are pumped into the sea.

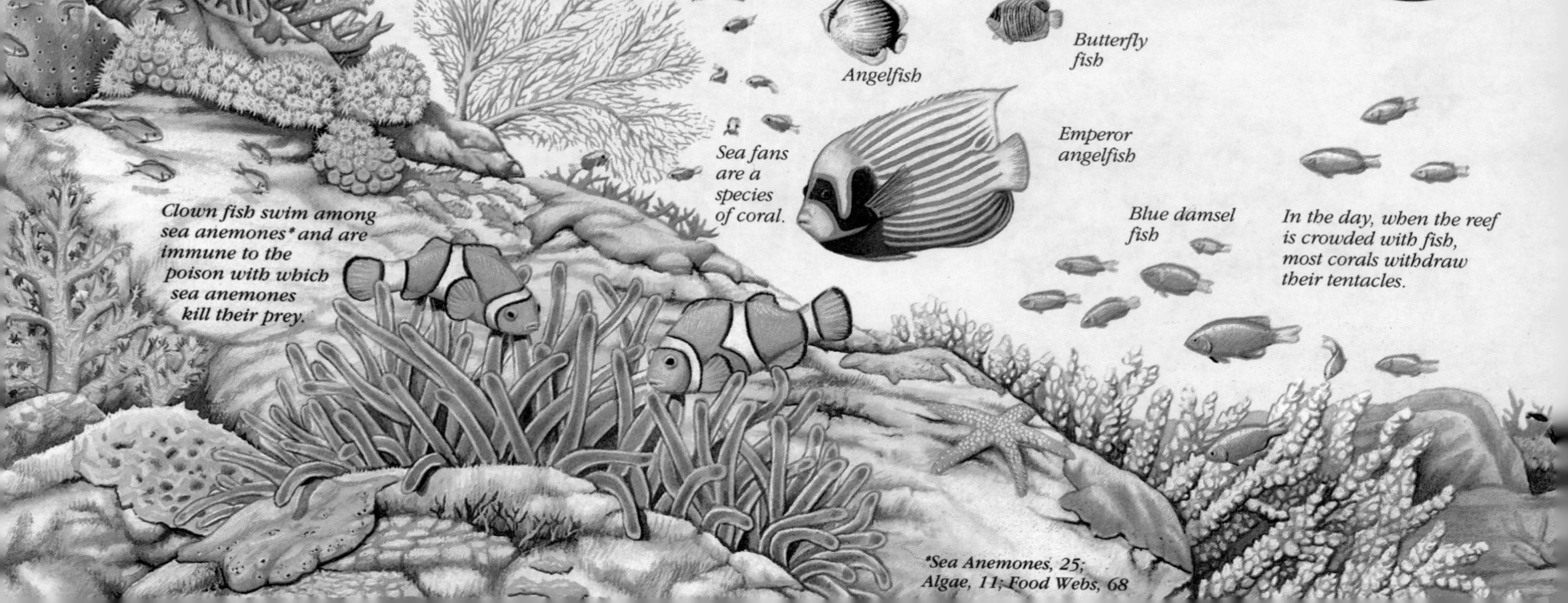
Angelfish
Butterfly fish
Emperor angelfish
Blue damsel fish

There are thousands of different species of corals that form different shapes, such as fine sea fans, "brain" shapes and massive boulders.

In the crowded waters of the reef, the fishes' bright markings help different species to recognize each other and find mates.

Sea fans are a species of coral.

Clown fish swim among sea anemones and are immune to the poison with which sea anemones kill their prey.*

In the day, when the reef is crowded with fish, most corals withdraw their tentacles.

*Sea Anemones, 25; Algae, 11; Food Webs, 68

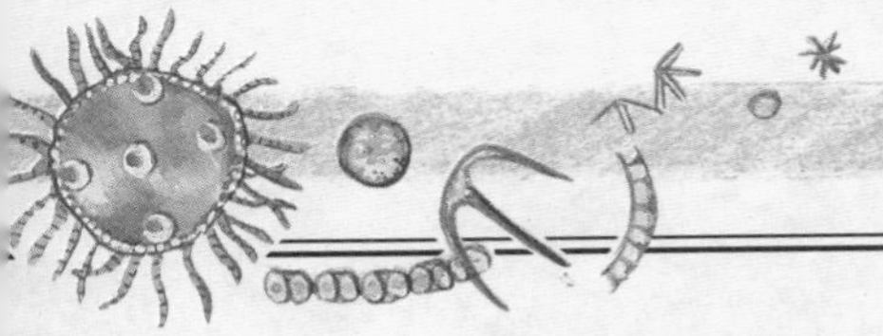

OCEAN WILDLIFE

Most of the life in the sea is found in the the top 200m (650ft) of water that is lit by the sun during the day. Some light filters down to about 1,000m (3,280ft), but below this, there is no light and no plants or algae can grow. Large sea creatures, such as octopuses and swordfish, feed on each other or on dead fish and plankton that sink from the surface. These pictures show some of the animals that live at different depths. They are not shown to scale.

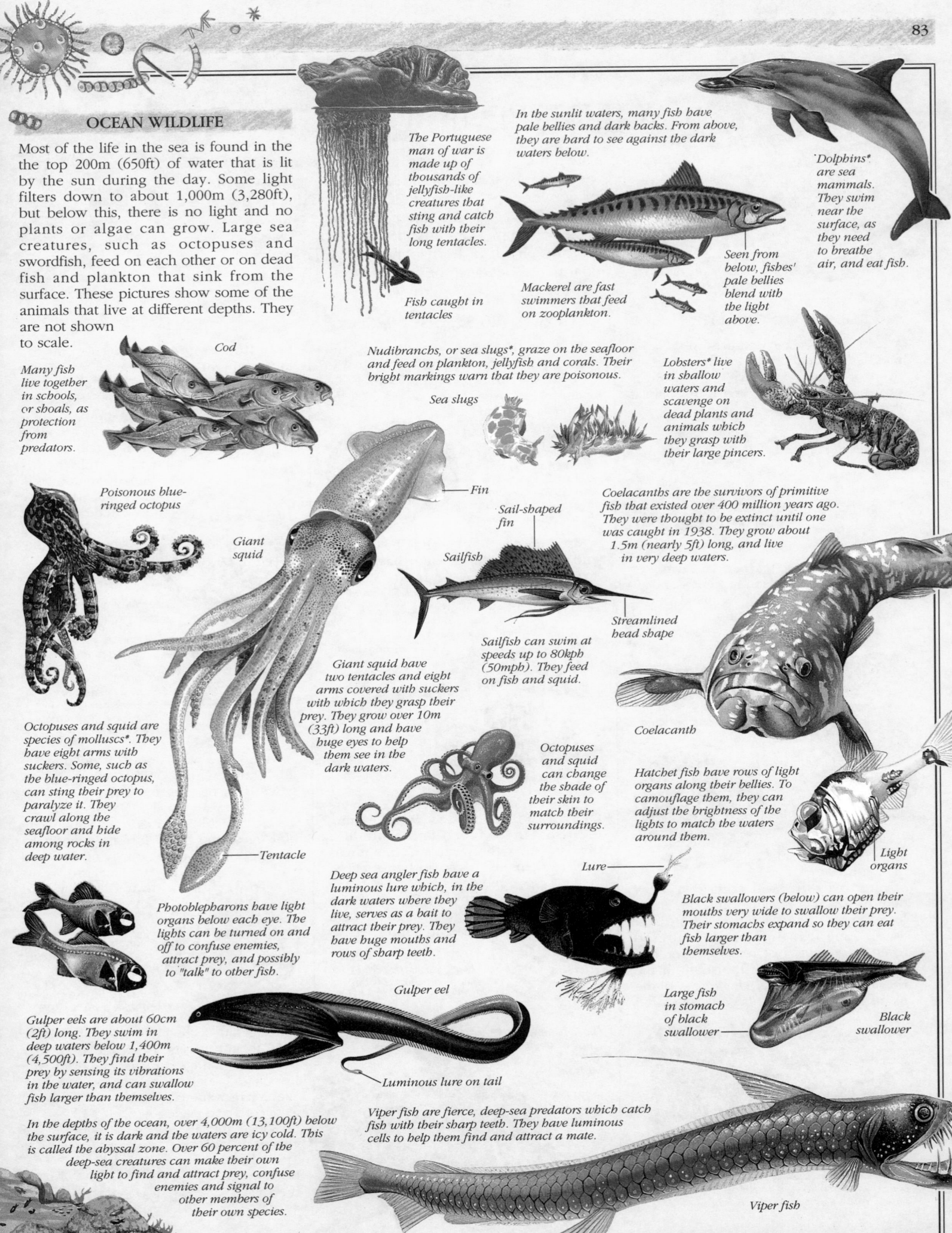

The Portuguese man of war is made up of thousands of jellyfish-like creatures that sting and catch fish with their long tentacles.

Fish caught in tentacles

In the sunlit waters, many fish have pale bellies and dark backs. From above, they are hard to see against the dark waters below.

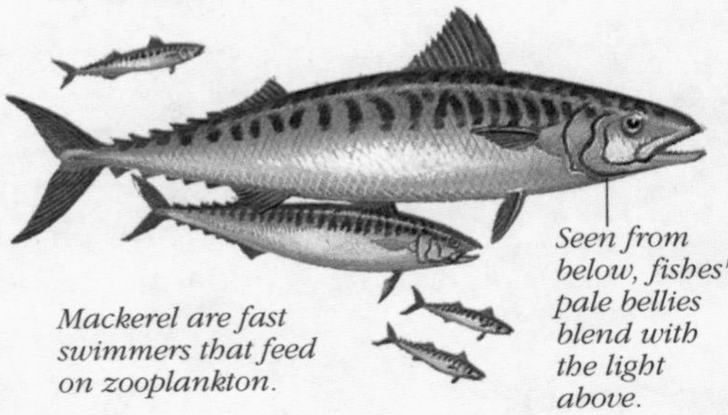

Mackerel are fast swimmers that feed on zooplankton.

Seen from below, fishes' pale bellies blend with the light above.

Dolphins are sea mammals. They swim near the surface, as they need to breathe air, and eat fish.*

Cod

Many fish live together in schools, or shoals, as protection from predators.

Nudibranchs, or sea slugs, graze on the seafloor and feed on plankton, jellyfish and corals. Their bright markings warn that they are poisonous.*

Sea slugs

Lobsters live in shallow waters and scavenge on dead plants and animals which they grasp with their large pincers.*

Poisonous blue-ringed octopus

Giant squid

Fin

Tentacle

Giant squid have two tentacles and eight arms covered with suckers with which they grasp their prey. They grow over 10m (33ft) long and have huge eyes to help them see in the dark waters.

Octopuses and squid are species of molluscs. They have eight arms with suckers. Some, such as the blue-ringed octopus, can sting their prey to paralyze it. They crawl along the seafloor and hide among rocks in deep water.*

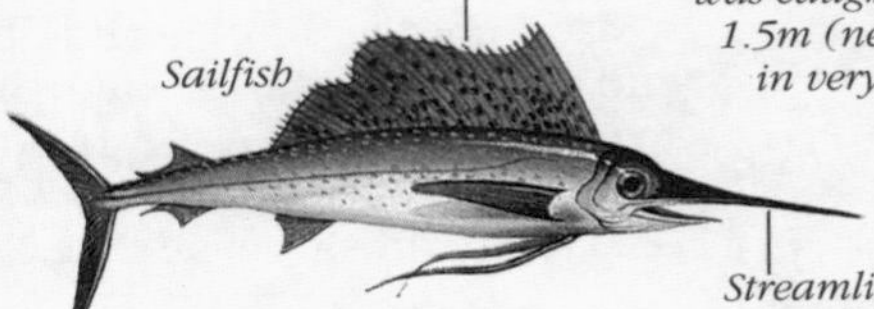

Sail-shaped fin

Sailfish

Streamlined head shape

Sailfish can swim at speeds up to 80kph (50mph). They feed on fish and squid.

Coelacanths are the survivors of primitive fish that existed over 400 million years ago. They were thought to be extinct until one was caught in 1938. They grow about 1.5m (nearly 5ft) long, and live in very deep waters.

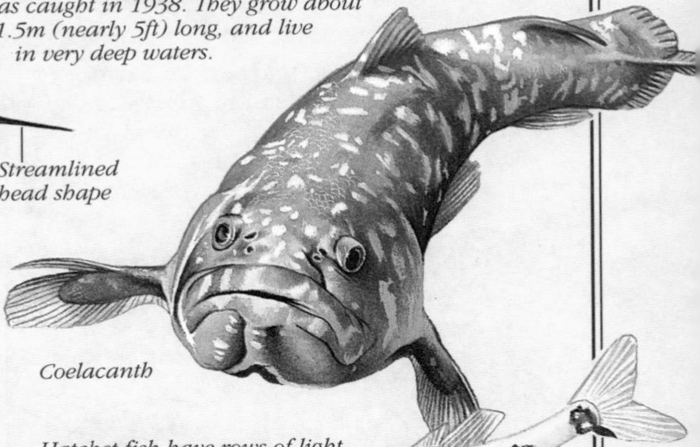

Coelacanth

Octopuses and squid can change the shade of their skin to match their surroundings.

Hatchet fish have rows of light organs along their bellies. To camouflage them, they can adjust the brightness of the lights to match the waters around them.

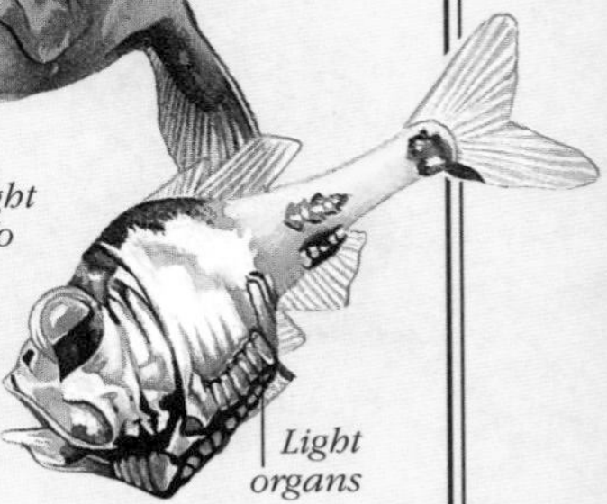

Light organs

Photoblepharons have light organs below each eye. The lights can be turned on and off to confuse enemies, attract prey, and possibly to "talk" to other fish.

Deep sea angler fish have a luminous lure which, in the dark waters where they live, serves as a bait to attract their prey. They have huge mouths and rows of sharp teeth.

Lure

Black swallowers (below) can open their mouths very wide to swallow their prey. Their stomachs expand so they can eat fish larger than themselves.

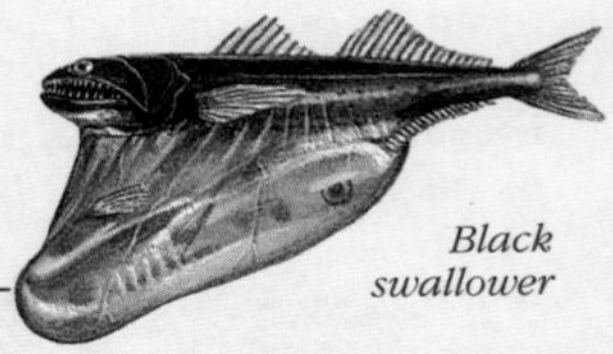

Large fish in stomach of black swallower

Black swallower

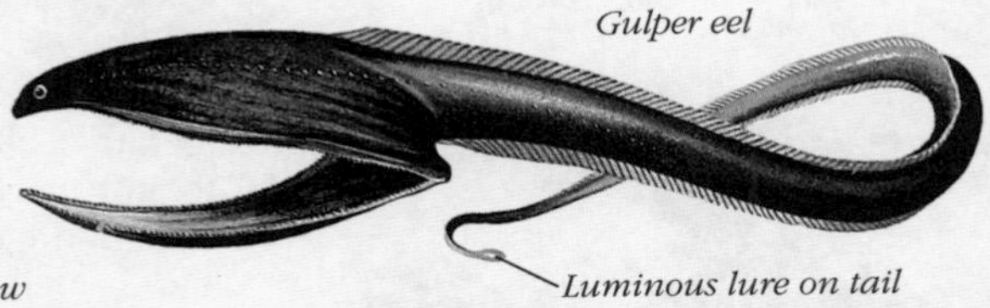

Gulper eel

Luminous lure on tail

Gulper eels are about 60cm (2ft) long. They swim in deep waters below 1,400m (4,500ft). They find their prey by sensing its vibrations in the water, and can swallow fish larger than themselves.

Viper fish are fierce, deep-sea predators which catch fish with their sharp teeth. They have luminous cells to help them find and attract a mate.

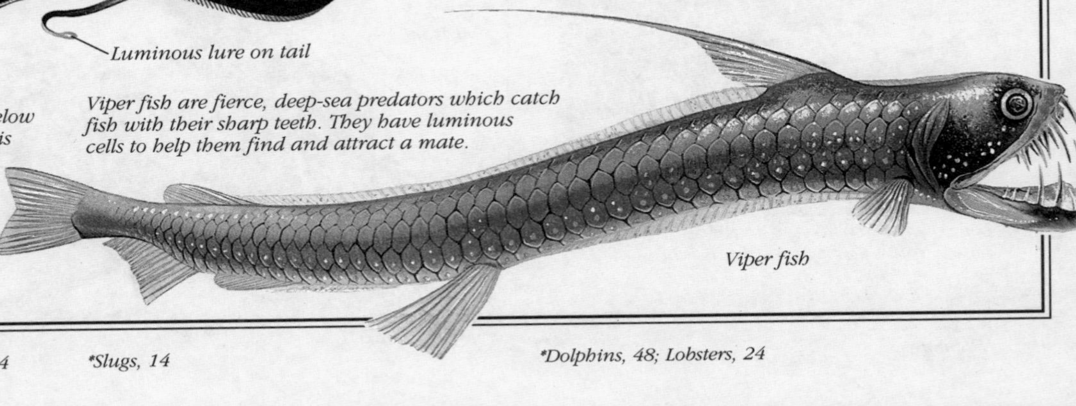

Viper fish

In the depths of the ocean, over 4,000m (13,100ft) below the surface, it is dark and the waters are icy cold. This is called the abyssal zone. Over 60 percent of the deep-sea creatures can make their own light to find and attract prey, confuse enemies and signal to other members of their own species.

*Molluscs, 24 *Slugs, 14 *Dolphins, 48; Lobsters, 24

WILDLIFE IN DANGER

Scientists believe that, over the next fifteen years, a million different species of plants and animals may become extinct, that is, they will no longer exist. The main threat to wildlife is the destruction of habitats - the places where the plants and animals live. Some species of animals are also in danger because they are hunted for their fur or horns, and many plants are endangered because they are collected.

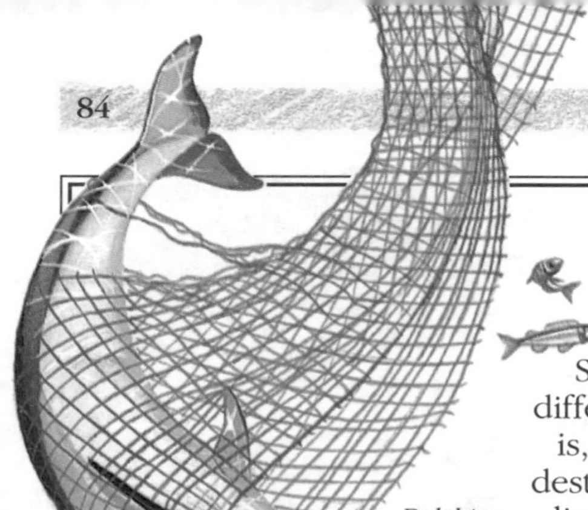

Dolphins die when they are caught in fishing nets.

Every year, two million seabirds are killed by litter on the beach and in the sea.

DESTROYING HABITATS

A habitat* is the environment in which a plant or animal lives. Each species of plant or animal is suited to living in its own particular habitat, and if this habitat is destroyed, it can no longer survive.

Golden lion tamarin monkeys are in danger of extinction because much of the rainforest where they live has been cut down.

Since they first learned to farm, people have been clearing forests and draining marshlands for farmland but, over the last 300 years, more habitats have been destroyed than ever before.

Forests are cut down to provide wood and land for fields and buildings.

Until recently, about six percent of the Earth's surface was covered with tropical rainforest. Now only half of this remains. In some areas, for example, the eastern coastal areas of South America, only small scattered reserves of rainforest remain. Over half of the wetland areas in the south of the USA have been destroyed, along with the plants and animals that lived there.

Mangrove forests, which grow in the muddy waters along the coasts of tropical countries, have been cleared for farms and timber, and many plants, animals, fish and shellfish have died.

THREATENED RIVERS AND SEAS

Wherever they live, water plants and animals are threatened by pollution caused by the dumping of waste chemicals in rivers and seas, and by the run-off of fertilizers from farmland.

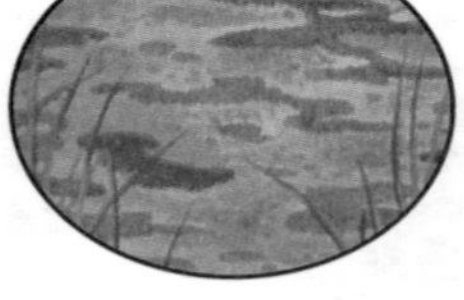

Fertilizers make water plants grow very fast and thick. The plants shut out the light and use up the oxygen that the water animals need.

Many species of fish and shellfish are endangered because they have been overfished to provide food. Modern fishing boats can catch up to 200 tonnes (220 tons) of fish at one time.

Modern fishing boats can use techniques such as echo-sounding to find exactly where the fish are before casting their nets.

When too many of a species of fish are taken from the waters at one time, the fish cannot breed and reproduce themselves. Other fish, and mammals such as dolphins, may also be caught in the nets by mistake. In the last 30 years, over five million dolphins were caught in tuna nets.

If fishing nets had bigger holes, young fish could escape and breed before they were caught.

Oil is the main cause of seabird deaths. Oiled birds may drown, die of cold or starve to death.

An oiled shag

POLLUTION

Pollution is the destruction of the environment with chemicals, and by garbage and litter. Chemicals from factories are pumped into the rivers and the sea, and fumes from burning fuels and vehicle exhausts pollute the air. Plants and animals cannot live in a seriously polluted environment. They may become sick and die, or not be able to breed and reproduce themselves.

Fumes and smoke are carried long distances by the wind, causing pollution far from the factories which produced them. Chemicals pumped into rivers and streams are carried in the water and pollute distant lakes and seas.

One of the worst forms of pollution is acid rain, which occurs when waste gases from burning fossil fuels (coal, oil and gas) mix with the water in the air and form acid rain. Acid rain kills plants and trees, and many forests in northern Europe and America are dying because of it. The rain also drains into rivers and kills fish.

Over half of the forests in Germany have been damaged by acid rain. The rain in Europe now contains 80 times more acid than it did in 1950.

Insecticides are poisonous chemicals used to kill insects. However, they also pollute the land and rivers and kill useful insects and small animals. When larger animals, such as falcons and eagles, eat poisoned animals, the chemicals build up in their bodies and they may die as well.

*Habitats, 68

THREATENED SPECIES

If there are fewer than 500 of a particular species of animal, that animal is in grave danger of becoming extinct. When a species is in danger, it may be declared a protected species so that it is illegal to hunt or collect it. Attempts may also be made to breed it in zoos and then reintroduce it to the wild, and animals may be fitted with radio transmitters so scientists can follow their movements.

Californian condors are reared in zoos and protected on reserves.

A third of all parrots are endangered, including hyacinth macaws.

Black-footed ferrets, which live on the prairie grasslands in North America, are almost extinct. The few surviving ferrets have been fitted with radio collars so scientists can keep track of them.

Birds of prey, such as eagles, have been hunted for sport and many have died after eating small animals poisoned by pesticides.

Golden eagle

At least a thousand species of birds are in danger of extinction. The main threat to birds is loss of habitats such as rainforests and wetlands. They are also endangered by pollution, hunting, competition with other species that have been introduced to their habitat by people, and capture for the pet trade.

Many species of whales are in danger because they are hunted for their meat and fat, and because of pollution.

Until 1981, millions of tortoises were transported from Africa to be sold as pets. Most died on the journey. Those that survived lived only about three years.

Some species of shellfish are in danger because their shells are collected for ornaments.

Kemp's ridley turtles have almost died out because so many have drowned in shrimp nets in the Gulf of Mexico.

Many species of frogs, such as red-eyed tree frogs, are endangered by the destruction of the rainforest.

African violets are now very rare in the wild because so many have been taken to be sold as houseplants.

It is now illegal to kill baby harp seals, but many older harp seals are still killed for their fur.

In Wales, Britain, seeds from the last two remaining tufted saxifrage plants were used to grow more plants. These were replanted in the wild to try to save the species from extinction.

The hunting of tigers was banned in 1970, and since then their numbers have more than doubled, but they are still an endangered species.

Tiger and cubs

Rhinos are endangered because they are killed for their horns. In parts of Africa, people are trying to protect rhinos by sawing off their horns so the hunters will leave them alone.

Rhinoceros with horn sawn off

Golden barrel cacti are now very rare in Mexico because of illegal collection.

NATURE CONSERVATION

Nature conservation is the management of the world's natural resources for the benefit of both the people and wildlife. There are now over five billion people in the world and this creates a huge demand for homes, food, fuel and raw materials. To preserve the forests, grasslands, seas and wild places of the world, areas have been set aside as nature reserves where plants and animals can live undisturbed.

Cheetahs usually hunt during the day, but some now hunt at night to avoid tourists in cars or vans.

Balloon rides over the savanna allow tourists to watch the wildlife.

SEE FOR YOURSELF

To find out more about the threats to wildlife, and about conservation projects, you could write to one of the organizations listed on page 96. These organizations have members in many countries and provide up-to-date information about endangered species.

You could also join, or start, a conservation group in your area to monitor changes in the local environment, such as new roads or building projects and pollution from industry. This is especially important in a city where wasteland and undeveloped sites are important havens for wildlife.

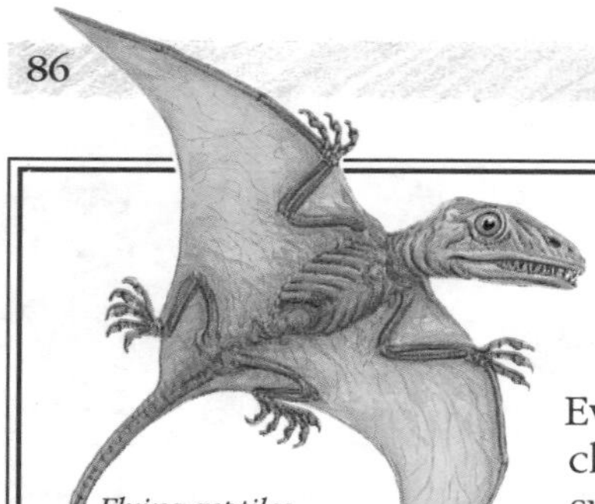

Flying reptiles, called pterosaurs, lived in the period from 195 to 70 million years ago.

Fossilized fern

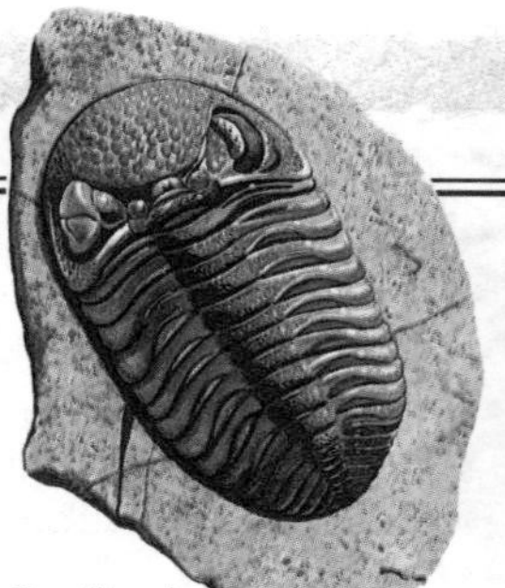

Fossilized trilobite, a species of arthropod that lived in the sea over 500 million years ago.*

EVOLUTION

Evolution is the process by which plant and animal species gradually change, over a very long period of time, and become more suited to survive in their surroundings. Most scientists now believe that all the plants and animals alive today have evolved from very simple life forms that existed over 3,000 million years ago. Remains of creatures that lived long ago have been found preserved as fossils in the rocks.

NATURAL SELECTION

In the nineteenth century, a British naturalist, Charles Darwin, put forward the theory of natural selection to explain how evolution takes place. According to Darwin's theory, individual plants or animals that have qualities that help them to survive in their environment, tend to live longer and pass on their useful qualities to their offspring.

Charles Darwin (1809-1882)

Fruit of the horse chestnut tree

The prickles on the fruits of horse chestnut trees discourage animals from eating them. Fruits with spiky prickles are more likely to survive and grow to become trees that also produce fruits with sharp prickles.

In this way, very gradually over a very long period of time, most of the members of a species (a group of plants or animals of the same type that can breed together), will have the useful qualities and be well suited to living in their environment.

A species of moths, called peppered moths, is an example of how species are still evolving. Originally, peppered moths had speckled wings but during the 19th century, trees became blackened by soot and the pale moths were eaten by birds.

During the 19th century, many trees became blackened by soot from factories.

Moths with light wings were spotted by birds, but those with darker wings survived.

Gradually, over the next hundred years, the number of moths with darker wings increased. But now there is less pollution from soot and the moths with pale wings are increasing.

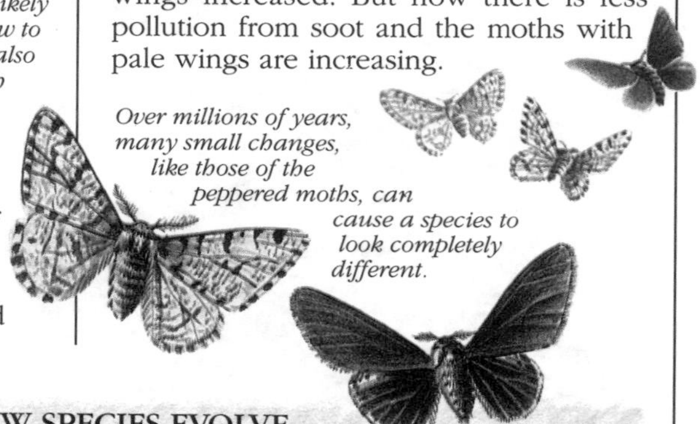

Over millions of years, many small changes, like those of the peppered moths, can cause a species to look completely different.

WHY SPECIES BECOME EXTINCT

A species dies out, or becomes extinct, when there are so few members of that species left that they cannot produce enough offspring to survive. Many species have existed for millions of years, and then died out, usually because their environment changed and they could not survive in the new conditions.

Dinosaurs may have become extinct because their environment changed and they could not adapt to the new surroundings or changes in climate.

More recently, many species of plants and animals have become extinct because people have destroyed their habitats, and due to hunting and pollution (see Wildlife in Danger*).

Dodos were flightless birds that lived on the island of Mauritius. They became extinct about 300 years ago, probably due to hunting.

HOW NEW SPECIES EVOLVE

There are millions of different species of plants and animals. The species can be organized in groups that share certain characteristics (see Classification of the Natural World*). For example, cows, horses, deer, giraffes and antelopes all have hoofs and belong to a group called ungulates*. All the species in a group are probably descended from a common ancestor.

As a young man, Darwin visited the Galapagos Islands. There he saw many small birds that he discovered were all finches.

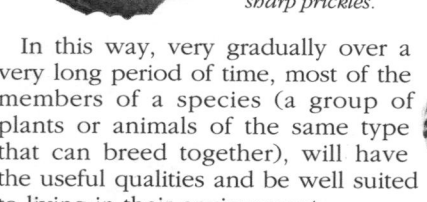

Hyraxes, which live in grasslands in Africa, are related to elephants and probably evolved from the same ancestor about 50 million years ago.

There are thirteen species of finches on the islands. Each has a different shaped beak, eats different food and lives in a different habitat. Scientists have discovered that these finches probably all evolved from one species that, long ago, flew over from South America. There were few birds on the islands, so the finches spread out and adapted to different habitats. They are now so different that they cannot breed with each other and form separate species.

Woodpecker finches use cactus spines to poke insects out of cracks in trees.

Warbler finches (left) use their pointed beaks to pick insects out of cracks.

Vegetarian tree finches eat fruits, buds and leaves.

FOSSILS

The surface of the Earth is made up of many layers of rock, each of which formed at a different time and may contain fossils of the plants and animals that lived then. When the rocks are worn away, the fossils may be discovered.

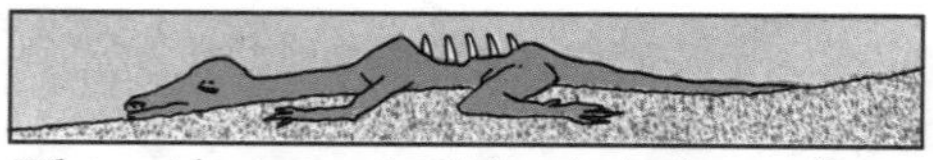

When a plant or animal dies, its body usually rots away, but if it is covered with mud or sand, the hard parts, such as the skeleton, may be preserved to become a fossil.

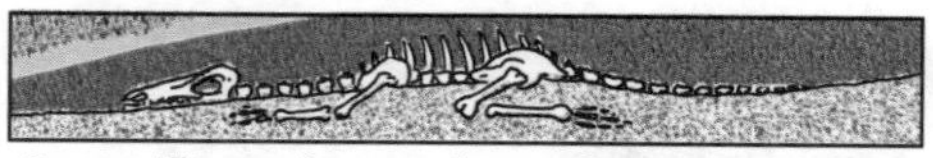

Over millions of years, the sand and mud build up to form deep layers. They become cemented together to form new rock with the shape of the plant or animal inside.

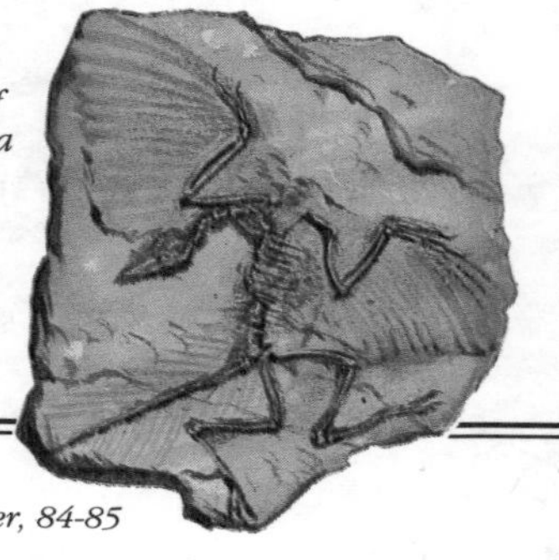

This is a fossil of Archaeopteryx, a prehistoric bird. Even the shapes of the feathers were preserved in the rocks.

*Classification of the Natural World, 88; Ungulates, 41

*Arthropods, 88; Wildlife in Danger, 84-85

THE STORY OF LIFE

These pictures show the ancestors of some of the main groups of plants and animals alive today, and the period of time when they lived.

Ammonites (above right) were molluscs related to squid and octopuses. They lived in the seas about 200 million years ago.

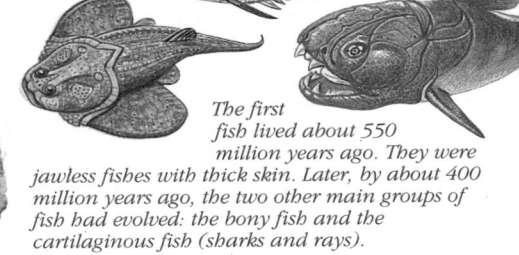

The first fish lived about 550 million years ago. They were jawless fishes with thick skin. Later, by about 400 million years ago, the two other main groups of fish had evolved: the bony fish and the cartilaginous fish (sharks and rays).

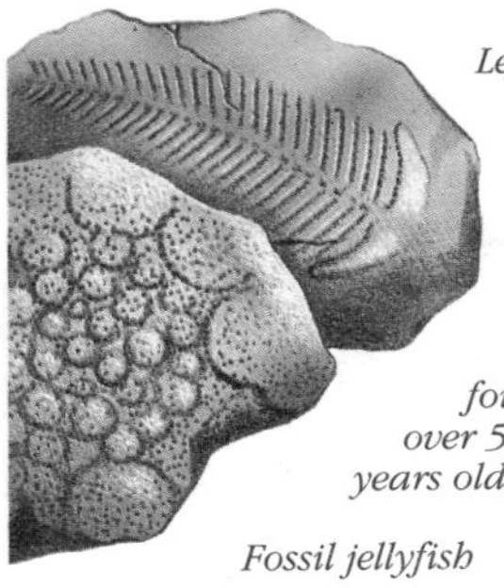

Left: Spriggina, a type of prehistoric worm

Fossil worms and jellyfish have been found in rocks over 570 million years old.

Fossil jellyfish

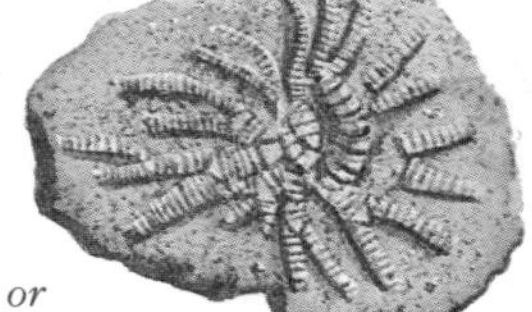

Fossil crinoids

Crinoids, or sea lilies, were early echinoderms, the group of animals to which sea urchins and starfish belong. They lived in the sea about 500 million years ago.

The first insects had no wings and lived about 410 million years ago. By about 300 million years ago, there were many different types of winged insects including Meganeura - a dragonfly as big as a kite.

Meganeura

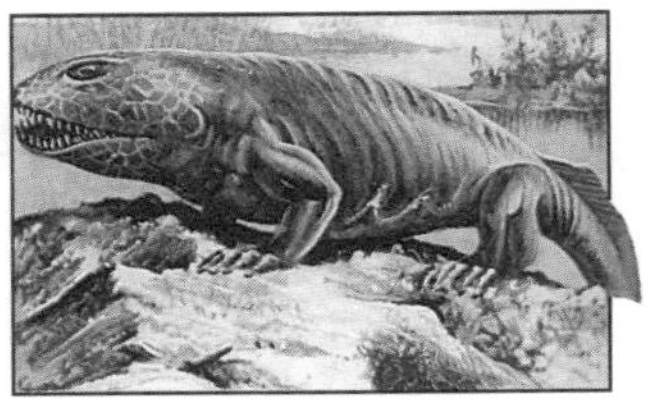

Amphibians (animals that spend part of their life cycle in water), evolved about 350 million years ago. Ichthyostega, one of the first amphibians, had air-breathing lungs and probably came onto land to feed on the many insects and other small creatures that lived then.

Ferns, horsetails and club mosses existed over 300 million years ago and grew as big as trees. Coal formed from the fossilized remains of these plants.

Seed fern Tree fern Horsetail Club moss

Flowering plants evolved about 165 million years ago. Fossilized pollen has been found in rocks 118 million years old. Magnolia was one of the first flowering plants.

Magnolia

Dimetrodon

The first reptiles lived about 280-230 million years ago. Dimetrodon had a sail of spines covered with skin. Reptiles are cold-blooded and Dimetrodon probably used the sail to help keep its body at the correct temperature.

Archaeopteryx

Birds are believed to have evolved from a small species of dinosaurs that lived about 150 million years ago. The first bird is called Archaeopteryx, which means "ancient wing". It had feathers like a bird, and teeth and a long bony tail like a reptile. The fossil was discovered in Germany in 1861.

The first mammals, such as Megazostrodon, were nocturnal, rat-like creatures that lived in the trees about 200 million years ago, at the same time as the dinosaurs.

Megazostrodon

Plesiadapis was an early primate, the group to which monkeys and apes belong.

The dinosaurs were the most advanced reptiles of all time. So far, over 800 different species have been discovered. They existed from about 200 million years ago until 65 million years ago, when they rapidly became extinct, probably because their environment changed and they could not survive in the new conditions.

Males fought for females with their huge antlers.

Herds of grazing animals evolved about 30-20 million years ago, when the climate became warmer and forests were replaced by grasslands.

Megaceros was a herbivore. It lived 30,000 years ago.

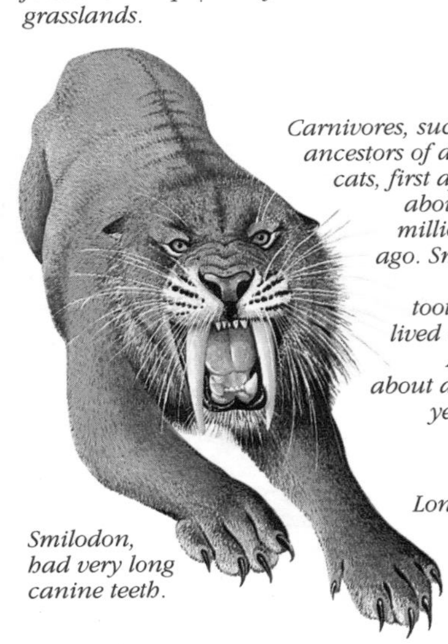

Carnivores, such as the ancestors of dogs and cats, first appeared about 65-55 million years ago. Smilodon, a sabre-toothed cat, lived in North America about a million years ago.

Long, sharp claws

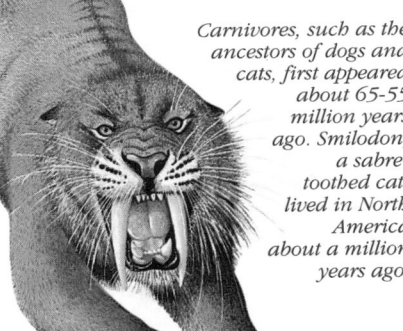

Smilodon, had very long canine teeth.

During the glacial period 19,000-10,000 years ago, a third of the Earth was covered with ice. Many of the mammals, such as this mammoth, became very large with thick, shaggy coats.

Teeth 18cm (7in) long

Tyrannosaurus rex was the largest carnivore that has ever lived. It was 5.5m (18ft) tall and 12m (39ft) long.

CLASSIFICATION OF THE NATURAL WORLD

All living things can be organized into groups. For example, dogs and cats belong to two different groups. But the groups also share certain characteristics, for example, dogs and cats are carnivores and they are also mammals. The way organisms fit into groups that can be sorted to form larger groups is called classification. The largest groups are called kingdoms.

THE ANIMAL KINGDOM

The animal kingdom contains all the living organisms that have more than one cell and which digest their food in a gut. It is divided into seven main groups, called phyla (singular: phylum).

Each phylum contains a number of groups called classes. The classes in the arthropod and chordate phyla are shown below. Classes are divided into orders, which are made up of families and the families are made up of genera (singular: genus). Each genus contains a number of species, which are the smallest groups. Members of a species are very similar and can breed together.

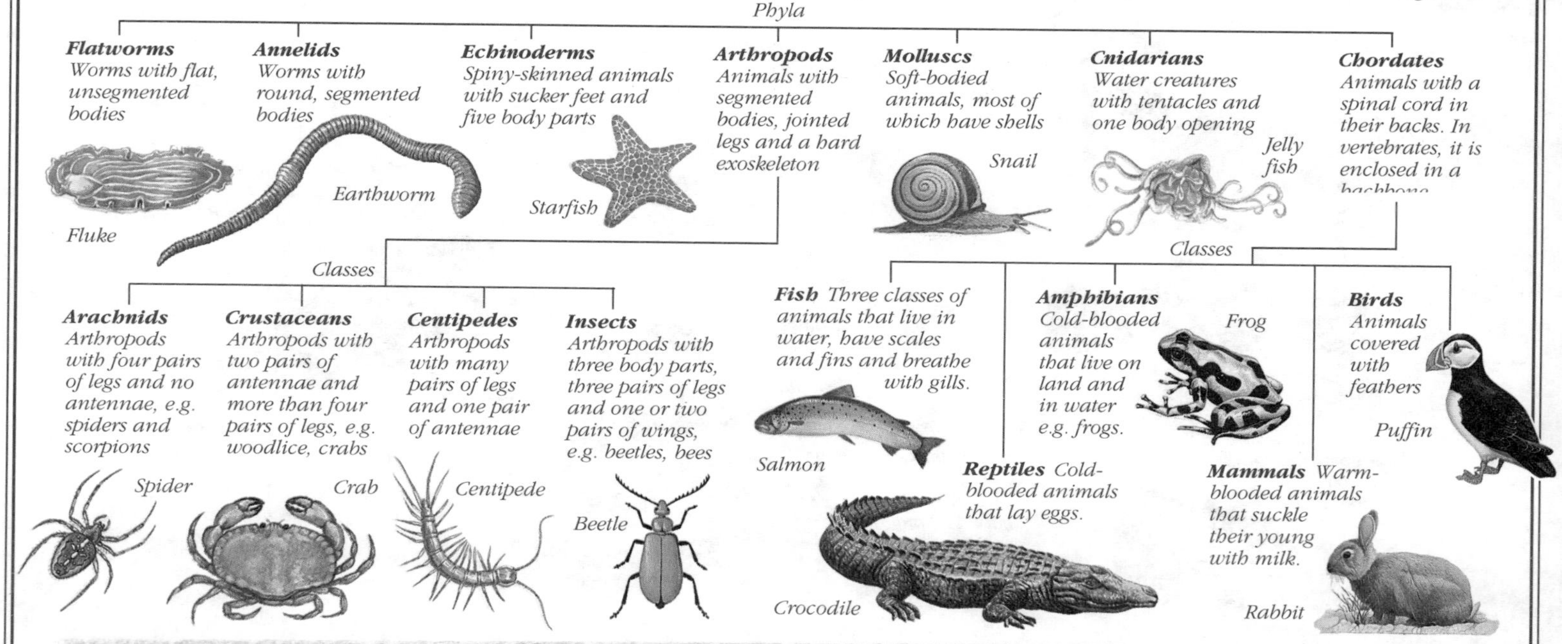

Phyla
Flatworms Worms with flat, unsegmented bodies
Fluke
Annelids Worms with round, segmented bodies
Earthworm
Echinoderms Spiny-skinned animals with sucker feet and five body parts
Starfish
Arthropods Animals with segmented bodies, jointed legs and a hard exoskeleton
Molluscs Soft-bodied animals, most of which have shells
Snail
Cnidarians Water creatures with tentacles and one body opening
Jelly fish
Chordates Animals with a spinal cord in their backs. In vertebrates, it is enclosed in a backbone
Classes
Arachnids Arthropods with four pairs of legs and no antennae, e.g. spiders and scorpions
Spider
Crustaceans Arthropods with two pairs of antennae and more than four pairs of legs, e.g. woodlice, crabs
Crab
Centipedes Arthropods with many pairs of legs and one pair of antennae
Centipede
Insects Arthropods with three body parts, three pairs of legs and one or two pairs of wings, e.g. beetles, bees
Beetle
Classes
Fish Three classes of animals that live in water, have scales and fins and breathe with gills.
Salmon
Amphibians Cold-blooded animals that live on land and in water e.g. frogs.
Frog
Birds Animals covered with feathers
Puffin
Reptiles Cold-blooded animals that lay eggs.
Crocodile
Mammals Warm-blooded animals that suckle their young with milk.
Rabbit

THE PLANT KINGDOM

The plant kingdom contains organisms of more than one cell that produce their food by photosynthesis. It is divided into four groups called divisions. The divisions are divided into classes that are divided into orders, and then families, genera and species as in the animal kingdom shown above.

Angiosperms, the division containing the flowering plants, is divided into two classes: monocotyledons and dicotyledons, as shown in the diagram.

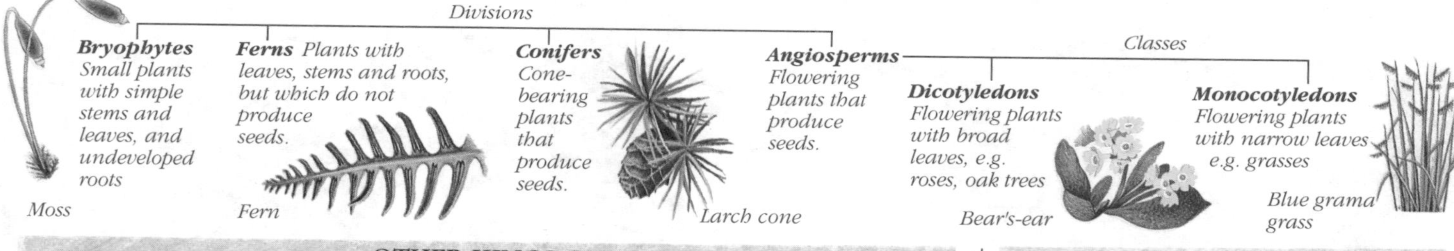

Divisions
Bryophytes Small plants with simple stems and leaves, and undeveloped roots
Moss
Ferns Plants with leaves, stems and roots, but which do not produce seeds.
Fern
Conifers Cone-bearing plants that produce seeds.
Larch cone
Angiosperms Flowering plants that produce seeds.
Classes
Dicotyledons Flowering plants with broad leaves, e.g. roses, oak trees
Bear's-ear
Monocotyledons Flowering plants with narrow leaves e.g. grasses
Blue grama grass

OTHER KINGDOMS

There are three other kingdoms apart from the plant and animal kingdoms. These are the fungi, protoctist and monera kingdoms.

Glittering ink cap

The fungi kingdom contains multicellular organisms that cannot photosynthesize and whose cell walls, unlike those of plants, do not contain the substance cellulose. For example, mushrooms, toadstools and yeast.

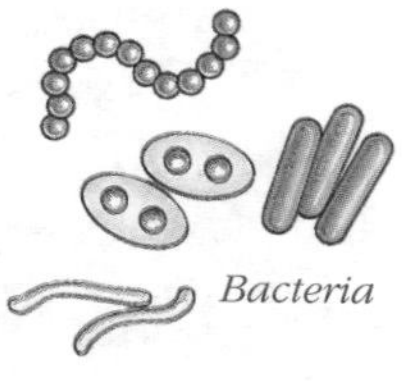

Bacteria

Bacteria are grouped in their own kingdom, called monera, but viruses are not included in any of the kingdoms in this classification system as they do not have a cell structure.

Protoctists are simple organisms, most of which are made up of only one cell with a nucleus. Amoebas and other protozoa belong to the kingdom of protoctists.

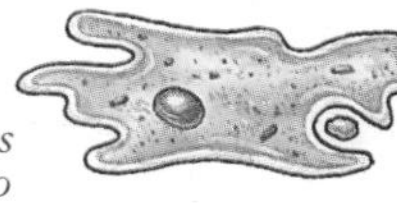

Amoeba

BIOLOGICAL NAMES

Biological names are in Latin so all biologists can use the same names. Each organism has two names. The first name is the name of its genus and the second is the name of its species. This is called the binomial system, and the names are written in *italics*. For example, most of the big cats belong to a genus called *Panthera*. The binomial name for tigers is *Panthera tigris*, leopards are *Panthera pardus* and jaguars are *Panthera onca*.

MAP OF THE WORLD

This map shows the places named in this book, and the main climate areas and their vegetation. The different climates and the plants that grow in each area are described at the bottom of the page. Each area has its own particular wildlife that is adapted to the conditions where it lives, for example, polar bears are adapted to living in the Arctic. An area with its plants and animals is called a biome*.

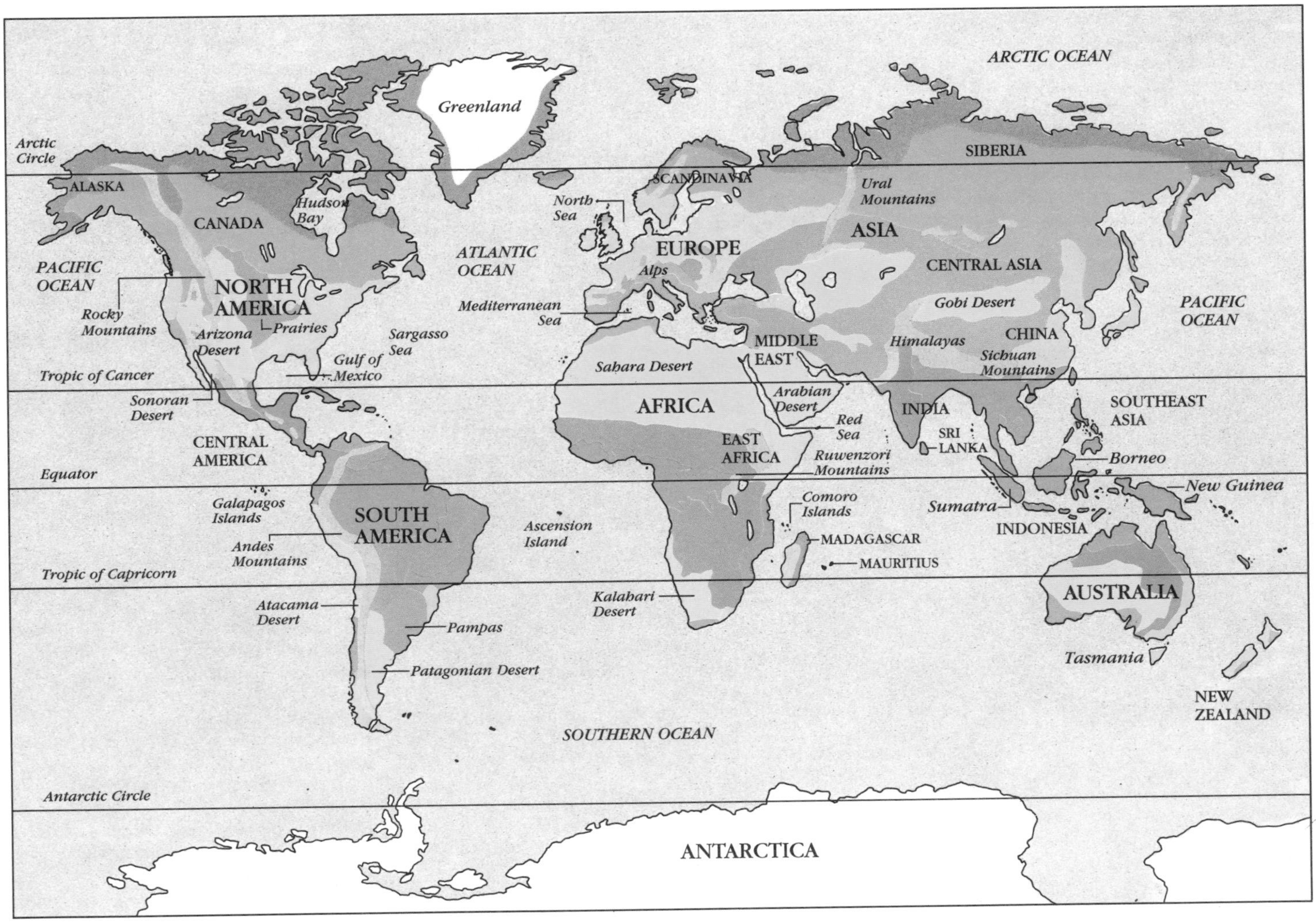
ARCTIC OCEAN
Greenland
Arctic Circle
SIBERIA
ALASKA
SCANDINAVIA
Ural Mountains
Hudson Bay
North Sea
CANADA
ASIA
EUROPE
ATLANTIC OCEAN
PACIFIC OCEAN
Alps
CENTRAL ASIA
NORTH AMERICA
Rocky Mountains
Prairies
Mediterranean Sea
Gobi Desert
PACIFIC OCEAN
Arizona Desert
Sargasso Sea
MIDDLE EAST
Himalayas
CHINA
Gulf of Mexico
Sichuan Mountains
Tropic of Cancer
Sahara Desert
Sonoran Desert
Arabian Desert
AFRICA
SOUTHEAST ASIA
INDIA
Red Sea
CENTRAL AMERICA
EAST AFRICA
SRI LANKA
Ruwenzori Mountains
Borneo
Equator
New Guinea
Galapagos Islands
Comoro Islands
Sumatra
SOUTH AMERICA
Ascension Island
INDONESIA
Andes Mountains
MADAGASCAR
MAURITIUS
Tropic of Capricorn
AUSTRALIA
Kalahari Desert
Atacama Desert
Pampas
Tasmania
Patagonian Desert
NEW ZEALAND
SOUTHERN OCEAN
Antarctic Circle
ANTARCTICA

Ice Areas near the North and South Poles, and at the tops of high mountains, that are permanently frozen and covered with ice and snow.

Polar bear

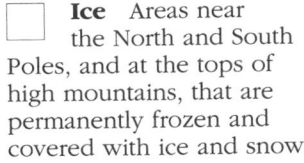

Tundra Arctic areas where the ice melts in the summer and small plants, and mosses and lichens grow.

Purple saxifrage

Mountains The vegetation near the bottom of the mountains is the same as the land around them. The zones of vegetation change as the air becomes cooler higher up the mountains.

Bighorn sheep

Coniferous forests Areas in northern Europe, Asia and America that have very cold winters and short summers and where vast coniferous forests of trees such as spruce, pine and fir grow.

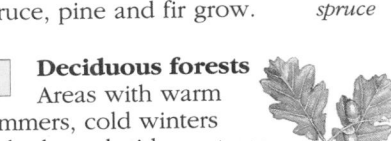

Norway spruce

Deciduous forests Areas with warm summers, cold winters and where deciduous trees such as oak and beech grow.

English oak

Temperate grasslands Open grassy plains in Central Asia and North America (the prairies) that have hot summers and cold winters.

Prairie dog

Maquis Areas around the Mediterranean Sea and in southern Australia that have warm, wet winters and hot summers. The main plants are small trees and shrubs.

Lavender

Deserts Areas with very low rainfall and very high temperatures.

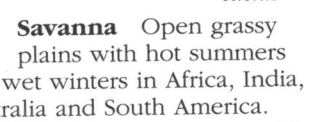

Barrel cactus

Savanna Open grassy plains with hot summers and wet winters in Africa, India, Australia and South America.

Tiger

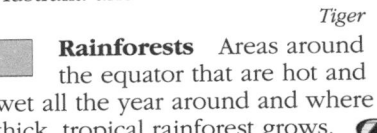

Rainforests Areas around the equator that are hot and wet all the year around and where thick, tropical rainforest grows.

Callicore butterfly

*Biomes, 68

GLOSSARY

The number at the end of an explanation shows the page on which you can find out more about that subject.

abdomen The stomach area of a mammal or, in insects, the rear part of the body (16).
algae Simple, plant-like organisms that grow in water (11).
amphibian An animal that lives in water when young and on land when adult (34).
antennae Thin projections on an insect's head with which it can feel or smell (16).
anther The tip of a stamen where pollen is produced in a flower (6).
arthropod A member of the phylum of animals that have segmented bodies, jointed legs and hard exoskeletons, e.g. a beetle (88).
asexual reproduction A method of reproduction that does not involve a male and female cell joining together (6).
atmosphere The layer of gases that surrounds the Earth.
bacteria Single-celled organisms that have no cell nucleus (11, 88).
baleen Fringes of tough skin in the mouths of baleen whales with which they filter food from seawater (48).
barb A backward-pointing spike such as the barb on a bee's stinger.
barbels Thin, tentacle-like sense organs around a fish's mouth (27).
barbule Part of a bird's feather (36).
binomial system The system of naming whereby each organism is identified by the name of its genus and its species (88).
biome An area of the world with a particular climate, and the plants and animals that live in that climate, e.g. a desert or rainforest (68).
bird of prey A bird that hunts and eats other animals (38).
blubber A thick layer of fat that helps to keep sea mammals warm (48).
boneless fish Alternative name for cartilaginous fish (26).
bony fish The group of fish whose skeletons are made of bone (26).
breeding grounds Areas to which certain animals return year after year to mate or give birth.
breeding season The time of year, usually early spring, when animals mate.
broadleaved trees Trees, such as oaks, that have wide, flat leaves (8).
browser An animal that feeds on shrubs and trees.
bulb A short, underground stem from which new plant shoots grow (6).
camouflage Body markings that make an animal difficult to see against its background.
canine teeth Sharp, pointed teeth for piercing and holding meat (42).
carapace The hard, protective shell of crustaceans such as crabs (24), or the upper part of a turtle's or tortoise's shell (30).
carbon cycle The movement of the element carbon between plants, animals and the atmosphere (69).
carnivore An animal that eats mainly meat. A member of the order to which meat-eating mammals belong (41).
carpel The female reproductive organ of a flower (6).
cartilage The tough, flexible substance of which our earlobes and noses are made.
cartilaginous fish The group of fish whose skeletons are made of cartilage, e.g. sharks and rays (28).
cell The basic unit of which all living things (except viruses) are made.
cellulose A substance found in the walls of plant cells.
cetacean A member of the order of sea mammals to which whales belong (41).
chiropteran A member of the order of mammals to which bats belong (62).
chlorophyll The green substance in plants that absorbs energy from the Sun to power the process of photosynthesis (4).
chloroplasts The tiny bodies in plant cells where food is made by photosynthesis (4).
chordate A member of the phylum of animals that have a spinal cord in their backs (88).
chrysalis Another term for pupa (18).
cilia Many tiny, hair-like structures by which simple animals move or waft food into their mouths (11).
class A group of orders in the classification system (88).
classification The system by which living things are arranged into groups that can be sorted into larger groups that share certain characteristics (88).
cocoon A layer of silky threads that protects a pupa, larva or eggs (18).
cold-blooded An animal, such as a fish or reptile, whose blood is about the same temperature as the water or air around it (29).
colony A group of plants or animals that live together, e.g. ants (21).
cone The structure in which seeds develop on coniferous trees (8).
conifer A tree that produces seeds protected by cones (8).
constrictor A snake that kills its prey by squeezing it until it suffocates (32).
corm The swollen base of a stem from which new shoots can grow (6).
cotyledons A new shoot's first leaves (7).
courtship display Ritual activities, such as dancing and singing, to attract a mate.
crustacean A member of the class of arthropods that have two pairs of antennae and more than four pairs of legs, e.g. a crab (88).
decapod A member of the order of crustaceans that have ten legs, e.g. a crab (24).
deciduous trees Trees that lose their leaves in the cold or dry season (9).
dentine The hard substance of which teeth and tusks are made.
digestion The process by which a living organism breaks down food into substances that can be easily absorbed by the body.
division A group of classes in the classification system of plants (88).
echinoderm A member of the phylum of animals that have spiny skin, five symmetrical body parts and sucker feet, e.g. a starfish (88).
echo-location The detection of objects or food by sending out sounds and sensing the echoes given off by the objects (62).
ecology The study of the ways in which living things and their environment are dependent on each other (68).
ecosystem An environment and all the things that live there (68).
edentate A member of the order to which toothless mammals belong (63).
embryo A developing animal before it is born (4) or hatches, or a developing plant in a seed before the seed begins to grow (7).
endangered species A species that is in danger of becoming extinct (85).
even-toed ungulate A hoofed mammal with an even number of toes, e.g. a deer (41).
evergreen trees Trees that do not lose their leaves in the cold or dry season (9).
evolution The way a species slowly changes, over a long period of time, and becomes better adapted to its environment (86).
exoskeleton A hard external skeleton, such as that of an insect (16).
family A group of genera in the classification system (88).
fertilization The joining of a male and female sex cell to form a zygote that will develop to become a new plant or animal.
filament The stalk of a stamen (6), or any thin, thread-like structure.
flagellum One of many very tiny, whip-like structures used by simple organisms to move around (11).
food chain The way the energy produced by plants passes to herbivores when they eat the plants, and then to carnivores when they eat the herbivores (68).
food web The many interlinked food chains in an environment (68).
fossil The shape of a plant or animal preserved in rock (86).
freshwater The water in rivers and lakes as opposed to the salty water of the sea (70).
fruit The structure that surrounds the seeds of a flowering plant (7).
fruiting body The part of a fungus that produces the spores from which new fungi grow (12).
fungus An organism, such as yeast or a mushroom, that digests living or dead matter and reproduces by producing spores (12).
gametes Male and female sex cells.
gastropod A member of the class of molluscs that have a muscular foot, e.g. a snail (15).
genus (plural: genera) A group of species in the classification system (88).
germination The stage when a seed begins to grow to become a plant (7).
gills The organs with which most fish absorb oxygen from water (26).
gizzard A sac in the digestive system of birds in which food is broken up by the squeezing of the muscles (36).
gland An organ that produces a substance such as scent or saliva.
global warming An increase in world temperatures believed to be caused by changes in the greenhouse effect (69).
glucose A type of sugar produced by plants during photosynthesis (5).
greenhouse effect The way that carbon dioxide, and other gases, stop heat from the Sun escaping from the Earth (69).
habitat The particular place where a plant or

animal lives (68).
herbivore Any animal that feeds on plants.
hibernate To pass the winter in a deep sleep with a slow heartbeat and rate of breathing.
host A plant or animal on which a parasite lives.
hybrid The young of parents that are two different breeds (65).
hypha A thin tube, many of which make up the body of a fungus (12).
incisor tooth A chisel-shaped tooth at the front of the mouth.
incomplete metamorphosis The way the young of insects, such as grasshoppers, gradually change to become adults and do not become pupae (16).
insectivore An animal that feeds mainly on insects (61).
invertebrate An animal without a backbone.
jawless fish The group of fish that have suckers instead of jaws, e.g. lampreys (26).
keratin The substance of which horns, fingernails and hair are made.
kingdom The highest level of grouping in the classification system (88).
lagomorph A member of the order to which hares, rabbits and pikas belong (60).
larva (plural: larvae) The young of animals, such as insects, that do not look like their parents.
lepidopteran A member of the order to which insects with scaly wings belong, e.g. a butterfly (18).
lignin The substance that strengthens the cell walls of plants.
mammal A warm-blooded vertebrate animal that gives birth to live young and suckles them with milk (40).
mandibles The biting mouth parts of insects (16).
marsupial A mammal that gives birth to tiny, unformed young that complete their development in a pouch on the mother's abdomen, e.g. a kangaroo (40, 66).
metamorphosis The change from tadpole to frog or toad (34), or from larva to adult insect (16).
migrate To move to a new habitat at certain seasons during the year in search of food or better living conditions (37, 74).
mineral salts Naturally occurring substances essential for the growth of all living things.
molar Large, flat teeth near the back of the mouth for grinding food.
mollusc A member of the phylum to which soft-bodied animals with shells belong, e.g. a snail (88).
monera The kingdom to which bacteria belong in the classification system (88).
monotreme A type of mammal that lays eggs (41, 66).
mucus A slimy protective fluid.
multicellular organism An organism made up of many cells.
nectar A sugary liquid made by flowers (6).
nitrogen cycle The movement of the element nitrogen between animals, plants, the soil and the atmosphere (69).
nocturnal Animals that feed and are active at night (40).
nucleus The control centre of a cell.
nutrient A mineral absorbed by a plant from the soil, or any nourishing substance.
nymph The young of insects, such as grasshoppers, that do not form pupae during their life cycle (16).
odd-toed ungulate A hoofed mammal with an uneven number of toes, e.g. a horse (41).
order A group of families in the classification system (88).
organism Any living thing.
osmosis The passage of water from a weaker solution to a stronger solution (5).
ovary The part of a flower, or female animal, that produces eggs (6).
parasite An organism that lives in or on another plant or animal and takes its food from it.
perching birds The group of birds that have three toes pointing forward and one pointing back and which can grip branches (39).
photosynthesis The process by which plants make their food (5).
phylum (plural: phyla) A group of classes in the classification system of animals (88).
phytoplankton Microscopic, plant-like organisms that float in water (82).
pinniped A member of the order to which seals, sea lions and walruses belong (41).
placental mammal Mammals whose young develop in the mother's uterus and are nourished by the mother's blood through an organ called the placenta (40).
plankton Microscopic organisms that float in water (82).
plumage A bird's feathers (36).
pollen Tiny grains containing male cells which are produced by the stamens of a flower (6).
pollination The process of transferring pollen from the stamens of one flower to the female parts of another flower by insects, birds, bats or the wind (6).
polyp A hollow, cylindrical body with a ring of tentacles, such as that of a coral (82) or a sea anemone (25).
predator An animal that kills and eats another animal for food.
prey An animal that is eaten by another animal.
primates The order to which monkeys, apes and people belong in the classification system (41, 50).
proboscis The tube-like mouth part of insects that suck plant sap or nectar (16).
protoctist A member of the kingdom of unicellular organisms, e.g. a protozoan (88).
protozoan (plural: protozoa) An animal-like organism made up of only one cell, e.g. an amoeba (11).
pupa (plural: pupae) The resting stage in an insect's life cycle when the larva changes to become an adult insect (16).
reproduction The process by which an animal or plant produces individuals similar to itself.
reptile Cold-blooded vertebrate animals that have scaly skin and lay eggs (29).
rhizoid Simple, root-like structures, such as those of mosses (10).
rhizome A horizontal, underground stem (6).
rodent A member of the order to which rats and mice belong (58).
ruminant An animal with a stomach with several chambers for digesting tough plant matter and which brings up its food to chew it a second time (54).
sap The solution of mineral salts and sugar that flows through a plant (4).
savanna Grasslands with scattered trees in the tropics (74).
scavenger An animal that feeds on dead animals, rather than killing its own prey.
scute Scales or plates of bone or keratin in the skin of animals such as snakes, crocodiles and armadillos.
seed dispersal The process of spreading seeds far from the parent plant so they have a better chance of growing (7).
segmented worms The group of worms whose bodies are made up of sections called segements, e.g. earthworms (14).
sexual reproduction Producing new individuals by the joining of a male and female cell (6).
social insects Insects, such as bees, that live together in large groups (20).
spawn The eggs of a fish or amphibian.
species A group of living things that are very similar and can breed together. The smallest groups in the classification system (88).
spore A reproductive body that develops into a new individual (10).
stamen The male reproductive organ of a flowering plant (6).
stigma The tip of a carpel - the female part of a flower on which pollen is deposited (6).
stoma (plural: stomata) The minute holes in the surface of a leaf through which water and gases pass in and out (4).
swim bladder A sac of gas in the body of a bony fish (26).
symbiosis Two different species of plants or animals that live together and benefit from each other (12).
tentacle A long, thin structure for feeding and grasping prey.
territory The area an animal lives in and defends as a source of food or nesting materials.
thorax The part of an insect's body to which its legs are attached (16).
threat display Activities to scare away another animal, usually of the same species, without actually fighting (38).
treeline The height on a mountain above which it is too cold for trees to grow (72).
tropics The area of the Earth between the imaginary lines called the Tropic of Cancer and the Tropic of Capricorn (89).
tropism The way a plant reacts to a stimulus such as light or water by growing towards it (5).
tuber A fleshy underground stem or root from which a new plant can grow (6).
tundra The land around the Arctic Circle where the ice melts in the summer and small plants grow (80).
ungulate A mammal that has hoofs, e.g. a horse (41).
unicellular organism An organism that consists of one cell.
uterus The organ in a female mammal's body where the developing baby grows (40).
vegetative reproduction A form of plant reproduction that does not involve male and female cells joining together (6).
vertebrate An animal with a backbone.
virus A living organism that has no cell structure (11).
warm-blooded An animal whose body is warmed by chemical reactions in its cells (40).
zygote The first cell of a new individual that results from the fusion of gametes.

INDEX

LIST OF ILLUSTRATORS

Graham Allen
David Ashby
Craig Austin
Graham Austin
Bob Bampton
Jeremy Banks
John Barber
David Baxter
Andrew Beckett
Joyce Bee
Stephen Bennett
Roland Berry
Andrzej Bielecki
Derick Bown
Isabel Bowring
Trevor Boyer
Wendy Bramall
John Brettoner
Paul Brooks
Peter Bull
Hilary Burn
Liz Butler
Terry Callcut
Martin Camm
Lynn Chadwick
Kuo Kang Chen
Peter Chesterton
Jeane Colville
Frankie Coventry
Patrick Cox
Christine Darter
Kevin Dean
Sarah DeAth
Peter Dennis
Richard Draper
Brin Edwards
Michelle Emblem
Sandra Fernandez
Denise Finney
Don Forrest
Sarah Fox-Davies
John Francis
Nigel Frey
Judy Friedlander
Sheila Galbraith
William Giles
Victoria Goaman
Jayne Goin
Peter Goodwin
Victoria Gordon
Rebecca Hardy
Alan Harris
Tim Hayward
Philip Hood
Chris Howell-Jones
Christine Howes
Carol Hughes
David Hurrell
Ian Jackson
Jacqueline Kearsley
Elaine Keenan
Roger Kent
Aziz Khan
Deborah King
Steven Kirk
Richard Lewington
Mick Loates
Rachel Lockwood
Chris Lyon
Kevin Maddison
Alan Male
Janos Marffy
Andy Martin
Josephine Martin
Nick May
David McGrail
Malcolm McGregor
Christina McInerney
Dee McLean
Annabel Milne
David More
Dee Morgan
Robert Morton
Patricia Mynott
David Nash
Susan Neale
Jan Nesbitt
Tricia Newell
Barbara Nicholson
David Nockels
Richard Orr
David Palmer
Patti Pearce
Justine Peek
Liz Pepperell
Julie Piper
Gillian Platt
Maurice Pledger
Cynthia Pow
David Quinn
Charles Raymond
Luis Rey
Phillip Richardson
Jim Robins
Andrew Robinson
Bernard Robinson
Eric Robson
Michael Roffe
Michelle Ross
Mike Saunders
Coral Sealey
Chris Shields
John Sibbick
Gwen Simpson
Gabrielle Smith
Guy Smith
Peter Stebbing
Ralph Stobart
Rod Sutterby
Alan Suttie
Treve Tamblin
Myke Taylor
George Thompson
Joan Thompson
Sam Thompson
Joyce Tuhill
Sally Voke
Ian Wallace
Sue Walliker
Peter Warner
David Watson
Phil Weare
David Webb
Sean Wilkinson
Adrian Williams
Roy Wiltshire
Ann Winterbotham
James Woods
David Wright
John Yates

ISBN 0-590-62172-6

12 11 10 9 8 7 6 5 4 3 2 1 6 7 8 9/9 0 1/0

Printed in the U.S.A. 08

First Scholastic printing, March 1996